TEACHING
PROSE

A Guide for Writing Instructors

TEACHING PROSE

A Guide for Writing Instructors

Fredric V. Bogel
CORNELL UNIVERSITY

Diane P. Freedman
UNIVERSITY OF WASHINGTON

Patricia Carden
CORNELL UNIVERSITY

Katherine K. Gottschalk
CORNELL UNIVERSITY

Gerard H. Cox
ITHACA, N.Y.

Keith Hjortshoj
CORNELL UNIVERSITY

Stuart Davis
CORNELL UNIVERSITY

Harry Edmund Shaw
CORNELL UNIVERSITY

EDITED BY

*Fredric V. Bogel and
Katherine K. Gottschalk*
JOHN S. KNIGHT WRITING PROGRAM
CORNELL UNIVERSITY

W · W · Norton & Company
NEW YORK   LONDON

Contents

3　CLASSROOM ACTIVITIES by Katherine K. Gottschalk

4　DESIGNING ESSAY ASSIGNMENTS by Gerard H. Cox

APPENDIX I   THE RAGGED INTERFACE: COMPUTERS AND THE TEACHING OF WRITING by Stuart Davis

Preface

This is a book for those new to the teaching of college writing: teaching assistants, novice instructors facing their first composition classes, experienced teachers in a wide range of fields who wish to combine instruction in writing with introductory or advanced study in their discipline—indeed, anyone who seeks to help students write competent English prose.

While there are probably few large notions on which the audience of *Teaching Prose* could be expected to agree, the practice of a large number of writing instructors, and the beliefs of at least most of this book's authors, might be reduced to something like the following set of principles:

1. Instruction in writing is best accomplished when writing is understood generously rather than narrowly: as a complex of intellectual, rhetorical, and experiential concerns rather than as a set of "composition skills" isolated from the rest of one's education and dominated by a dread of incorrectness.

2. We, and our students, should expect writing courses to be interesting, not just necessary or instrumental. Our students should study prose because it rewards serious attention and they should write it because we have helped them discover needs and purposes that writing answers.

3. Good writing and close reading go hand in hand. Patient, detailed attention to the texts one studies, and the development of analytic and interpretive subtlety in reading, foster the intellectual and verbal habits that make for effective writing.

4. Students profit from reading, and being asked to write in, a wide range of prose forms. Insofar as college writing instruction has a dominant rhetorical goal, however, it is to equip students to write thoughtful argumentative and analytic essays: essays that have a point (or that take a position) and argue that point cogently.

5. Argumentative essays ought to develop an original thesis, and students should know that originality is expected of them. We

cannot, of course, expect many factual discoveries (new planet, new subatomic particle), but we should expect a fresh interpretation of masterable texts and data, and we should encourage students to expect this of themselves. In practical terms, this means that, early on, students should learn to ask of their own and others' argumentative essays questions like the following: a. "What's the thesis?" b. "So what?" (That is, "Is this thesis non-trivial and non-obvious?")

6. Instruction in writing should attend to the earliest stages of the composing process (invention, finding something to say) and the latest (serious revision). In fact, the model "invention-writing-revision" is an artificially linear sequence since our efforts to write modify our original ideas and these modifications are both revisions themselves and the source of further revisions. Invention, writing, and revision are thus strands in a rope rather than boxcars on a train.

7. Good writing depends on awareness of style and rhetoric. Students should be taught to look *at* prose, as well as *through* it, and to analyze style, rhetoric, and other features of the linguistic surface. Exercises in stylistic analysis and imitation can be part of a writing course—in any field—from the very beginning.

8. As much as possible, students should be encouraged to view language as a generator as well as a transmitter of meaning, "the mother, not the maid, of thought," as Karl Kraus said. Moreover, if they are taught to view the fields in which they work—sociology or literary criticism or history—as not just a collection of facts but a perspective on the world, and a perspective that is as much linguistic as conceptual, their idea of the significance of writing will be correspondingly enlarged.

9. Students' writing improves most efficiently when individual classes and writing assignments build sequentially throughout the semester.

10. Grammar, usage, punctuation, and mechanics are most usefully taught in the context of specific writing assignments, revisions, and prose analyses rather than in isolation.

But even this mild list of compositional principles will provoke questions and counter-principles, some derived from individual ideas about writing instruction and some from the variety of approaches currently taken to the teaching of writing. Some courses and programs focus almost entirely on the writing, reading, and revision of student essays. Others add detailed work on the writing of student essays to introductory readings in a particular field. Still others seek to integrate composition and disciplinary study more fully—to consider writing as the construction of various perspectives on the world, and a given field (philosophy or anthropology or government) as one such perspective, the union of a certain conceptual framework with a certain set of stylistic and rhetorical conventions. Each approach has its particular character, advantages, and limitations. It is important for the beginning instructor to understand—early on—the kind of course he or she is teaching, since a good deal is determined by initial assumptions about the place of writing in a given course.

While this book is broadly applicable to many kinds of writing courses, it evolved out of a writing-across-the-curriculum program at Cornell University, and it therefore inevitably reveals particular interest in the connection of writing and subject matter, a connection of growing concern to writing programs at colleges and universities across the country. When, in 1982, at the recommendation of a Commission on Writing, Fredric Bogel accepted the directorship of the Writing Program and Katherine Gottschalk became associate director, one of the first charges they undertook was to provide guidance to the Program's staff, both faculty members and graduate students, staff who very well understood the facts and conceptual frameworks of their disciplines and were willing to share these with their students but who sometimes shied away from the actual teaching of writing. Out of that effort to encourage and inform, to help experienced faculty members discover more fully how writing can complement learning and be incorporated in the classroom, and to guide inexperienced graduate students facing a class for the first time and inquiring in disbelief about how to teach writing as well as anthropology or art, came *Teaching Prose.*

Eight teachers, all associated in one capacity or another with Cornell at the time of writing, agreed to take on a chapter to which they would bring special expertise. Because of the diversity of the Writing Program itself, in which courses range from ''Writing from Experience'' (which uses no texts other than the students' essays) and ''Forms of the Essay,'' to the many subject-matter courses such as ''Nineteenth-Century Russian Literary Masterpieces,'' and because of the varied teaching experiences of each writer, we knew that a diversity of approaches and experiences would, and should, be represented by these eight authors: that Patricia Carden, whose primary experience has been with Russian literature seminars, might see the teaching of writing rather differently from Fredric Bogel, who, as well as across-the-curriculum writing seminars, has taught "straight" composition courses and advanced comp. This diversity we were sure would be enriching for everyone, especially in its cross-fertilization on subjects concerning most writing teachers. The subject of revision, for example, of writing as process and product, appears and reappears as various of the eight writers find it a necessary part of their subject. In other words, while writing-across-the-curriculum courses form the dominant background of *Teaching Prose,* its writers address questions of interest to every teacher concerned with excellence of teaching and excellence of prose, whether our courses are English 101 or "The Politics of Science."

Teaching Prose begins in Chapter 1 with Keith Hjortshoj's intelligent, wry, and succinct overview of theories about writing and Fredric Bogel's innovative suggestions for courses integrating writing and subject matter. In Chapter 2 Patricia Carden offers practical suggestions for working out the design of a writing course and proposes seven sequences that integrate analysis of subject matter with writing assignments, locating occasions for writing in the discourse of the subject. Chapters 3, 4, and 5 address immediate concerns of every writing teacher: Katherine Gottschalk offers a relaxed discussion of various activities for the classroom including a lengthy list (written with Steven Youra, Cornell) of ways to elicit and guide revision and concluding with general advice for the new teacher; Gerard Cox shares his ideas about how to design essay assignments; Harry Shaw draws on many years of experience to explain a method of responding to (and grading) essays. With the reader's course established, in Chapter 6 Fredric Bogel offers a full and lucid survey of principles for understanding prose: how to explore the connections between style and meaning in what our students read, and in what they write. Readers may find the "how-to" portions of that chapter (Section III, "Tools of the Prose Trade: An Analytic Vocabulary" and Section IV, "Practical Prose Analysis") especially useful for classroom application to texts being read and written. Also useful will be Diane Freedman's presentation in Chapter 7 of sentence problems commonly appearing in student writing (with suggestions for exercises) and her review of the elements of grammar. Chapter 8, Keith Hjortshoj's "A Bibliographical Guide to the Profession" directs readers to intelligent choices of texts while providing cogent (and witty) discussions of issues underlying our choices of books. Section VIII, "Special Instruction for

Non-Native Speakers of English,'' for instance, analyzes the teaching situation we may encounter with non-native speakers. Computers are becoming a significant tool for some teachers of writing, and Stuart Davis's evaluative discussion in Appendix 1 may guide readers to thoughtful analysis of their appropriate uses, whether for guided revision of student essays or merely as spelling checkers. For courses whose chief subject is not writing, whether or not they are parts of writing programs, Katherine Gottschalk, in Appendix 2, proposes varieties of writing tasks that don't require grading but do encourage learning.

Without the encouragement of colleagues, friends, and family, this book certainly would not have appeared. At Cornell, Meyer Abrams, Scott Elledge, Mary Gilliland, Nancy Kaplan, Joe Martin, Beth Newman, and Beth Schwartz all provided encouragement and suggestions. Our reviewers provided invaluable advice: Kenneth Bruffee, Brooklyn College; Carol Hartzog, University of California at Los Angeles; Richard Marius, Harvard University; Linda Peterson, Yale University; David Roberts, University of Southern Mississippi; and Robert Siegle, Virginia Polytechnic Institute and State University. John Benedict of W. W. Norton prodded, encouraged, and remained flexible. And through four draft editions, Mark Hamblet, office manager of Cornell's John S. Knight Writing Program, used his rapport with the Macintosh to keep *Teaching Prose* beautiful and available for our staff.

Katherine K. Gottschalk
Fredric V. Bogel

TEACHING
PROSE
A Guide for Writing Instructors

1

Composition Theory and the Curriculum

FREDRIC V. BOGEL AND KEITH HJORTSHOJ

I. THE FIELD OF WRITING: AN AERIAL VIEW

This chapter aims to orient the instructor in two ways: by providing a very brief survey of the field of composition theory, and by suggesting a few ways in which the teaching of composition can enrich not just student prose but the undergraduate curriculum as well. It is our belief that the effects of writing instruction are—or ought to be—felt well beyond the central but limited activity of college essay writing, since writing instruction is both an invaluable part of the undergraduate curriculum and a unique means to comprehending that curriculum.

Among other kinds of transformation in the university and beyond, theories and methods of teaching writing have been in a state of flux over the past twenty years or so, and they remain in creative disarray. While E. B. White's old mentor, Professor Strunk at Cornell, now seems in many ways the epitome of the out-dated English teacher, sales of *The Elements of Style* suggest that things haven't changed nearly as much as the experimentalists of the sixties or the "new rhetoricians" of the seventies and eighties would like. But the English course based on rhetorical forms, grammar exercises, and weekly assignments that pass in silence from students to teacher and back again—as in a sad little factory that produces only seconds—is, if not a thing of the past, certainly in disgrace among many interesting and conflicting alternatives.

School of thought is not a reliable guide to quality, either in a writing text or in a writing class, but a brief survey of the major variations among theories and methods of teaching writing will give you a guide to some basic differences among the diverse approaches, courses, and programs in which you are collectively involved. Much of the improvement in one's teaching over the years results from an accumulation of lore too intricate to reduce to philosophical positions and methodology. Knowing where you stand, however, and being prepared to change your stance among these positions, will allow you to interpret and implement this lore more effectively.

A. *The Orthodox Approach and Traditional Rhetoric*

Most of you received this type of instruction at some point in your education, since it is firmly entrenched in the *Warriner's English Grammar and Composition Series* and other major textbooks used in primary, secondary, and college English programs. Fashionable rhetoricians now call this approach to teaching "current-traditional," because it has dominated writing instruction in American classrooms for more than a century. Although there have been serious challenges to this orthodoxy over the past twenty years, old and new versions of the traditional rhetoric are among the most popular textbooks on the market today.

At the foundation of the orthodox method, among all its variations, you will find an almost exclusive concern with writing as a finished product, and with the varieties of form, logic, and purpose—along with standards of "correctness"—that these finished products should represent. To the extent that the process of writing is relevant at all in this approach, ends determine means. In other words, the preconceived form and purpose of a particular type of essay determine the organizational strategy and procedures one should follow in order to produce this type of essay. Regardless of the subject, the source of the ideas, or the agonies involved in the actual process of writing, the finished product should be clear, concise, orderly, and correct, according to the rules and standards of good English. On the basis of these formal expectations, the teacher evaluates and corrects writing when it is finished; and through this trial and error students should gradually master the forms, standards, and procedures that govern rational uses of language and make the "content" of writing presentable, as the product of an educated mind.

This distinction between language and content rests upon positivist assumptions that many teachers would now reject in other circumstances but continue to employ when they teach writing. If the content of an essay is separable from the writing, then ideas, facts, and perceptions must first exist in some pre-linguistic or non-linguistic condition of the world or of the self. Language, therefore, is an insubstantial, ideally transparent vehicle for content. We first observe and reason, according to this approach, and then use language to record and convey our observations and ideas, which constitute the real substance of prose. Because the composition class attends primarily to the second half of this process—"the writing"—it is commonly viewed as a service or "skills" course, essential but insubstantial, like language itself. (In this case and in others, the theoretical foundations of the writing class tend to describe its position within the intellectual and political structure of the university as well.) The distinction between language and content has been such a fundamental premise in our education, and that of our students, that it is extremely difficult to avoid in a writing class. "Organize your thoughts next time *before* you write" we tell students. "Your ideas seem good, but the *writing* needs work." "I knew what I wanted to say," they reply, "but I just couldn't get it written down."

In the classroom and through the evaluation of finished writing, then, the composition teacher is responsible for impressing forms, standards, and procedures upon the minds and pens of students who presumably have ideas and information at their disposal, but would otherwise present this "content" in all sorts of irrational, erroneous, and distorted ways. To the extent that one can define the characteristics of good writing, therefore, one can also teach writing, according to established standards. Traditional rhetorics and composition classes attempt above all to provide definite, practical answers to the question, "What are the characteristics of good essays?"

Many junior high and high school English teachers attempt to answer this question in the simplest way imaginable, by condensing virtually all expository and argumentative writing into a single formula, such as the five-paragraph theme, that students can carry with them everywhere and always: a literary gizzard capable of grinding every type of material into a uniformly acceptable pulp. College rhetorics and composition classes along orthodox lines answer the question in more elaborate ways, through a classification of rhetorical forms and functions. At the broadest level of classification, then, an essay represents one of four modes of discourse: description, narration, exposition, and persuasion. (Rhetorics usually include argumentation as a subcategory of persuasion, though this order is often reversed.) With varying degrees of elaboration, traditional rhetorics subdivide these modes of discourse into more specific types, defined by their purposes and by the patterns of logic and organization they represent. Brooks and Warren's *Modern Rhetoric,* for example, distinguishes five "methods of exposition": comparison and contrast, illustration, classification, definition, and analysis. A mastery of exposition, therefore, implies increasing control over nuances of strategy and purpose, to the point at which one might be able to distinguish "lexical" from "stipulative" forms of definition.

In practice, of course, composition teachers define good writing in many different ways, with or without reference to a taxonomy of rhetorical forms. The central characteristic of the orthodox approach, in any case, is an almost exclusive concern with the qualities of finished writing, with little or no attention to the writing process or evaluation of work in progress.

B. Writing as a Process of Discovery, Expression, and Communication

The most radical challenges to traditional teaching methods emerged, just as one would expect, in the 1960s and early 1970s, in the midst of other challenges to the authority of institutions to dictate thought and behavior—for in the traditional writing class composition *is* taught, for better or worse, as a form of regulated thought and behavior, a matter of conformity to established standards for the use of language. In the atmosphere of this period, but with results that extended beyond it, writing teachers at every level of the educational system began to ask themselves serious questions about what they were doing and why: and some of them concluded they were doing everything wrong. The following passage from Ken Macrorie's *A Vulnerable Teacher* conveys the tone and some of the substance of this revelation:

For seventeen years I heard my students repeating badly to me what I had said to them and hundreds before them. I read their tired, hurriedly written papers conveying in academic dialect what they thought proper to give Teacher. One day in May in an Advanced Writing class I finally exploded. "I can't stand to read this junk any longer. Go back and write down as fast as you can whatever is in your mind— for fifteen minutes. Write so fast you can't think of punctuation or spelling or how you're going to say it. I would like for a change to read some truth that counts for you."

Since that day in 1964 I have turned my teaching around. Now in every course I begin by asking students to write anything that comes to their mind. Freed of the limitations and prohibitions common to academic writing assignments, they find unsuspected powers.

I then ask them to turn these powers upon the work for the course. (5–6)

Many other teachers in this period came to similar conclusions and adopted similar methods, described at greater length in the books by Peter Elbow and William Coles, Jr. Their pedagogical transformation shifted the emphasis of writing instruction from product to process, from ends to means, and from form to content: a total reversal of traditional priorities. To the extent that these teachers tried to define writing at all, they defined it as a process of discovery and as a means of communications with others: as the use of language as a way of coming to understandings. They began with the admission, then, that they and other writers they knew did not begin to compose by choosing a thesis statement and constructing an outline according to preconceived rhetorical designs. They recognized that writing is not, after all, a linear sequence of rational procedures for packaging ideas in language, according to prescribed forms. Instead, writers usually discover what they have to say, and what they can really believe, while they are writing, through a process of exploration and revision that is typically messy, recursive, and experimental—both illuminating and painful. "The authority I call upon in writing a book about writing," Peter Elbow announced in the preface to *Writing Without Teachers,* "is my own long-standing difficulty in writing."

This admission transforms both the writing class and the role of the writing instructor, who no longer teaches writing in the traditional sense, but helps students learn to use writing as a means of discovery and communication. The teacher becomes a facilitator for literary interaction, a fellow human and fellow writer, placed in charge by virtue of experience. The writing class, in turn, becomes a workshop or laboratory in which teachers and students experiment with language and ideas, individually and collectively, using freewriting, journals, and other methods for generating material, which is continually discussed, reformulated, and revised. Teachers and other students, as a genuine audience, respond to writing at every stage of this process, reserving concerns about "correctness" for the final stage of editing, when these concerns will no longer interfere with the real work of composition.

In recent years, and in the widespread belief that language skills have deteriorated, critics of this approach to teaching have accused its proponents of failing to teach the "basics" of writing: the standards of correctness and form, organization and logic, stressed in the traditional composition class. The most radical opponents of traditional teaching methods do maintain that concerns with form and correctness impose unnecessary constraints upon written expression, especially in early stages of the writing process. The lasting substance of their approach, however, is that they attempted to *redefine* the "basics" of writing. They observe, for example, that form and correctness are ultimately irrelevant if the writer has nothing of substance to say: no genuine reason for writing, no genuine voice, no genuine audience, and therefore no reason to *care* whether the writing is clear, orderly, and correct or not. Because this observation is undeniably valid, if difficult to implement, their emphases on the substance, context, and process of writing have outlasted radical opposition to educational institutions and to prescriptive methods of teaching.

Most of the teachers who viewed writing as a process of discovery were opposed on principle to "textbooks," and neither used them nor wrote them. Their emphases upon substance, context, and process, however, have been adopted as foundations of the "new rhetoric," and even the most traditional rhetorics now preface the description of rhetorical forms with perfunctory nods to "freewriting" and "prewriting" methods.

C. The New Rhetoric and the Composing Process

Institutionalized authority is back in vogue, and one small indication is that writing teachers have begun to call themselves "rhetoricians" once again, now with a new sense of enthusiasm, intellectual heritage, and academic status. Like the teachers who experimented with new approaches in the open classroom, these new rhetoricians reject most of the prescriptive methods used in the traditional composition course and view writing as a complex process of discovery and communication with a specific audience. While teachers such as Peter Elbow and Ken Macrorie viewed this emphasis on the writing process as a revolution in the classroom, however, others saw it as a revival and revision of classical rhetoric or—in light of modern philosophy, psychology, and linguistics—as the subject of a new field of scholarship and theory.

Modern rhetoricians disagree over the extent to which classical rhetoric coincides with and informs their profession, but there are some obvious areas of correlation. Unlike later rhetorical traditions, which codified modes of discourse as containers for ideas, classical rhetoric emphasized audience, the aims of discourse, and "invention," the process through which writers and speakers discover and develop topics for discourse. Classical rhetoricians considered this intellectual process an essential part of writing and speech, and thus attempted to answer some of the questions students ask most frequently, and which traditional instructors and textbooks most often fail to answer: "How do I find a good subject for my paper?" "How do I get started?" "Why am I writing this paper, and for whom?"

Teachers and scholars who view modern rhetoric as a classical revival have emphasized different elements of classical tradition and have elaborated these elements in different ways. Not all of them reject rhetorical modes and models, but James Kinneavy, for example, has reformulated these modes with emphasis on the aims of discourse in the process of communication. In *A Theory of Discourse,* Kinneavy represents this communication process as a triangle of "interrelationships of expressor, receptor, and language signs as referring to reality" (18). Other authors describe elaborate, formal techniques, both ancient and modern, for generating discourse. These invention strategies, or "heuristics," include Aristotle's *topoi,* or "topics" for discourse, Kenneth Burke's "dramatistic pentad" of questions used for examining and developing potential subjects, and the particle-wave-field approach derived from tagmemic analysis.

These classical revivalists tend to define writing as a rational, deliberative, strategic process—a way of performing effectively with language in particular situations. Other proponents of modern rhetoric define composition as a process of discovery, a way of knowing, and a use of creative imagination. While this definition of writing coincides with one that emerged inductively from experience and experiments in the classroom, it has since become the deductive premise of authors and scholars who have attempted to bring the theoretical and methodological foundations of writing instruction in line with modern developments in the study of language and cognition. Two of the most important implications of this intellectual, theoretical shift deserve emphasis: a new interest in the composing process, and the diffusion of writing instruction from the English composition class to the entire curriculum—a development to which we will return in the final section of this introduction.

Exclusive concern with the qualities of finished writing reinforces ignorance about the struggles writers face in the process of composition by defining this process as a private, solitary endeavor. Teachers who use this approach have always known, of course, that most of their students do not really follow linear, orderly, efficient procedures when they write, just as pastors know that the members of their flock do not really conduct their lives according to scripture. But as long as teachers can maintain their faith that good writing results, or at least *should* result, from routine construction skills, they can also maintain their prescriptive authority in ignorance of the messy and devious ways in which students actually produce their papers. Once the doctrine that good writing results from orderly, linear methods is challenged, as it has been in recent years, this prescriptive authority is challenged as well, and we are forced to admit that we know very little about the ways in which students and other writers think and behave when they compose. Attempts to teach writing as a process rely upon knowledge of this process, and in Chapter 8, "A Bibliographical Guide to the Profession," Section II, you will find references to books and articles based upon recent research in this field.

It is still difficult to apply most of this research and theory directly to teaching. And although authors of textbooks based upon modern rhetoric have attempted to convert theory to practice, their discussions of invention strategies and the composing process often remain abstract, mechanistic, or prescriptive—just the opposite of the approach to composition they advocate. Rhetoricians have also begun to use words such as "discovery," "creativity," "imagination," and "invention" as technical terms and abstract principles in a new academic jargon, intellectually detached from the actual contexts in which students write. In this spirit of professionalism, proponents of the new rhetoric often suggest that writing courses, like courses in biology or psychology, should be based upon current theory and research and should be taught, therefore, or at least designed, by scholars who are familiar with classical rhetoric and current literature in the field.

These scholars should be the first to recognize, however, that writing is not primarily an academic field, a body of theory and information, and that the best writing teachers are not necessarily those who have read the most about the history of rhetoric and the nature of the composing process. A teacher who is insensitive to language, to students, and to student writing will not be rescued by his grasp of tagmemics; and one who already encourages students to reexamine their ideas and use of the language in the process of writing will be more fashionable, perhaps, but no more effective if she calls her methods "heuristics."

Advocates of the new rhetoric have made substantial, positive contributions to classroom instruction. They have provided clear alternatives, first of all, to the popular but narrow and moralistic notion that teaching writing is akin to missionary work among the heathens—a task of establishing habits of virtue and stamping out corruption in primitive minds, at the periphery of academic life. To the extent that modern rhetoric becomes an independent academic discipline, however, it also threatens to undermine one of its most important premises: the recognition that writing, reading, and learning are directly related in every field of discourse and inquiry within the curriculum.

II. STYLE, RHETORIC, AND THE CURRICULUM

A. *Possible Relationships*

Most of the writing courses we teach are influenced by the character of the composition program in which we work, a program that, in turn, forms part of a larger undergraduate curriculum. This means that our pedagogical choices are limited. At times, we must teach courses that others have devised, perhaps Composition 100, the usual "straight comp" course offered to an entire freshman class. At other times, although we may have a hand in shaping an individual offering, we will be expected to offer courses of a certain kind (courses in Writing Across the Curriculum, say, or workshop courses); somewhat less frequently, we will devise our own writing courses. Occasionally, though, we may have the opportunity to devise courses that not only differ from but *work to transform* the curriculum of which they are a part. At such moments, we find ourselves not simply adding a writing component to the traditional curriculum but seeking to enrich the textual—the stylistic and rhetorical—character of that curriculum. This section of the introduction aims to suggest some possible ways to proceed if that opportunity arises.

The relation between prose style and rhetoric, on the one hand, and the undergraduate curriculum, on the other, can be conceived in many ways; we will consider only two here, formulated as questions. First, and more narrowly, *How can we supplement the existing curriculum so as to encourage better writing in our students?* The question has many answers. We can assign stylistically competent and interesting texts, whenever possible. We can encourage habits of close—rather than merely voluminous—reading. We can make prose analysis a significant part of writing courses and of non-writing courses. We can assign more essays (and, usually, shorter essays) and more revision of essays. We can offer more writing courses for juniors and seniors, perhaps focusing on topics within their major fields. And we can connect our students' work in close reading and stylistic analysis with their own efforts at writing. This last task can be accomplished by a variety of strategies, many of them suggested or explained elsewhere in this book.

But analysis of style requires attention not just to technical features like parataxis and prose rhythm, but also to some of the larger rhetorical coordinates of prose writing: subject matter, perspective or point of view, voice, relation to audience, and rhetorical purpose. In this view, writing is the construction of a certain perspective on the world, a perspective that determines both what we will look at and how we will see it. Since that formulation is also a loose definition of a discipline or field of study, it can serve to introduce our second question about style and the curriculum: *How can we encourage in our students a larger and more serious conception of writing, and what might be the effects of such a conception on the existing curriculum?* Notice that this question reverses the terms of the first one. There, we attempted to view style and rhetoric as parts of the traditional curriculum. Here, we are suggesting that much of the traditional curriculum can be conceived stylistically, rhetorically, textually. "The notion of a *conceptual* rhetoric," as Northrop Frye has said, " . . . suggests that nothing built out of words can transcend the nature and conditions of words, and that the nature and conditions of *ratio,* so far as *ratio* is verbal, are contained by *oratio*" (337). The change in perspective is significant and requires some spelling out, for it might make possible a fuller integration of writing with undergraduate study than we have as yet been able to devise.

Genuine integration of writing with disciplinary study requires, first, that we see each in relation to the other. Our students, that is, must be led to understand the conceptual implications of style and rhetoric, but they must also be led to understand the stylistic and rhetorical dimensions of conceptual investigation in a broad range of disciplines. It is one thing to teach them that a choice of style is a choice of meaning— that a string of short, paratactic sentences may be a way of enforcing a disjunctive and atomistic conception of what is being discussed. It is another to show that the conflicting views of the French Revolution put forth by historian A and historian B are not simply rival interpretations but different rhetorical structures: that each makes use of a particular metaphoric strategy, creates (through language) a different kind of interpretive voice, recounts events by means of a distinct pattern of narrative or "emplotment" that is itself interpretive, and so on. If the first sort of instruction reminds students that writing is a matter of meaning—of interpretation and understanding—and not of style alone, the second leads them to an even less familiar truth: that interpretation and understanding are themselves textual—and therefore stylistic and rhetorical—activities.

What can instructors do to make these truths part of our students' intellectual equipment? First, since students' preparatory education has in most cases encouraged them to subordinate the linguistic to the conceptual ("style" to "content," as they put it), writing instructors can engage them in a recovery of the linguistic dimension of their reading. Any approach, in any field, that pays close attention to reading, that looks at—and not just through—the verbal surface of the texts studied, will help students to write better. This, then, might be the first and most general aim of the writing classroom: a recalling of our students to language, to its visibility and hearability and manifold possibilities of structuring, and to its inseparability from the conceptual content that it both shapes and is shaped by.

Classroom attitudes, however, cannot do the job by themselves. To be effective, they must be given institutional shape and durability in integrative courses that will move beyond a simply additive relation between writing and subject matter. What forms might such courses take? The question is properly answered by those who do the devising and teaching, and it is of course answerable in many ways, most of them still unformulated. The four kinds of courses described below, both more and less traditional, are offered largely as first steps, as spurs to inventiveness and rigor in the integration of writing with disciplinary investigation.

B. Some Courses that Integrate Writing and Subject Matter

I. COURSES IN FIELDS OF DISCOURSE

These are introductions to particular disciplines, but introductions which assume that a "field" is as much a verbal and rhetorical as a conceptual space. "Discourse" here means a conceptual framework that is also a set of rhetorical strategies characterizing a field of knowledge or inquiry. From this perspective, "history" or "sociology" or "literary criticism" are names for certain kinds of writing, certain conventions of style and rhetoric. There is, naturally, no question of reducing these or other fields to "mere style" since we are not reducing style to "mere words" abstracted from the sense of those words. The point is to introduce students to a field by familiarizing them with its subject matter and basic concepts, but also with its principal linguistic conventions. (A version of such courses has been adopted by a number of American colleges and universities under the rubric "Writing Across the Curriculum.") Such an approach can help students to recognize the role of language in disciplinary investigation and thus in the formulation of questions and the constitution of various kinds of truth.

A history course taking this approach might be called "The Languages of History," "Writing the Past," or "History as Writing"; it might focus on various styles of historical knowing and writing and on the different conceptions of a particular event, period, figure, or problem that these styles yield. In their essays, students would be encouraged to pay close stylistic, and therefore intellectual, attention to the texts they read, and to be as conscious as possible of the linguistic strategies of their own analyses and arguments.

Such a course would not, as is sometimes supposed, provide an overly restricted introduction to the field in question, though it would certainly limit the number of pages a student could reasonably be asked to ingest in a single semester. Rather, it would sharpen the quality of the student's analytic attention while disclosing the inescapable and constitutive role of language in the field being studied.

2. COURSES IN MODES OF WRITING

Each of these courses focuses not on a particular field but on a particular kind of writing, and on the forms it takes across a variety of fields. One likely possibility is narrative, which plays a crucial role—and by no means the same role—in various forms of inquiry, analytic mastery, and explanation. Most obvious, and most thoroughly studied, in prose fiction, narrative is also an important mode of discourse in myths, history of many kinds (including histories of art and other cultural forms), biography, autobiography, psychoanalysis, case histories in a variety of social sciences, biblical interpretation, and journalism (not to mention the possibilities for micro- and macronarratives provided by recent physical accounts of the first few seconds after the Big Bang, and of the probable course of the universe to its Final Whimper).

A course in narrative as a mode of writing and a form of knowledge should probably indicate its emphasis in the title so as not to seem exclusively literary. Formulas like "Stories and Truth" or "Telling and Knowing," with appropriate subtitles ("Narration in Biography and Psychoanalysis," "The Function of Story in Historical Explanation"), would alert students both to the range of fields to be covered in a given course and to the expanded role that the idea of narrative could be expected to play.

During the semester, students would engage in a variety of activities. They might begin by studying literary narratives, or artfully selected pairs of prose narrative, one literary and one not, in order to establish a set of terms for describing narrative features and the range of significance of those features. They might then turn to the place of narrative in a few fields, supplementing their primary study with readings in selected secondary sources (in recent years, the analysis of narrative has played an increasingly significant role in a variety of fields). And narrative might occasionally be contrasted with non-narrative modes within a single field in order to bring out, by contrast, the particular way in which each mode constructs an object of study and seeks to render it intelligible.

Whatever the approach, or the particular topic, the general aims of such a course would be to increase understanding of the ways we use written and oral narrative to order, shape, and explain experience; to provide an enlarged context for particular studies (of prose fiction, or historical narrative, or psychological development) too often undertaken in relative isolation and comparative rhetorical innocence; and to place writing at or near the center of courses in a wide range of disciplines. And, of course, narrative is only one of several modes of writing suitable for such courses.

3. STRANGE LOOP COURSES

These are, simply, courses that circle back on themselves in some way, like a Möbius strip or similar structure (the phrase ''strange loop'' is borrowed from Douglas Hofstadter's *Gödel, Escher, Bach: An Eternal Golden Braid*). That is, they are courses in which students study and produce one kind of writing, but in which they also study—and produce—another kind of writing that takes the first kind as its subject. A course in narrative, for example, becomes a Strange Loop course if students write narrative in addition to writing about narrative. Such immersion in the sorts of text one is at other times studying and writing about should help students to read and write with greater precision, subtlety, and rhetorical sophistication. (Some of the primary texts for the course might be students' own writing, though the aim of a Strange Loop course is in no sense to avoid reading the prose of professional writers.)

In a course devised at the University of Pittsburgh and later adopted at UCLA, ''A Course in Autobiography: From Personal to Academic Writing,'' students wrote essays about significant recent changes in their lives and later produced a longer autobiographical essay. At the same time, they read a number of autobiographical works focusing on the years of adolescence, the thematic focus of the course. Then, while studying works exploring the concept of adolescence from psychologi-

cal, anthropological, and other perspectives, they began to write analytical essays about adolescence that took, as their primary materials,
the autobiographies they themselves had both read and written. Such a
course, in its secondary readings, supplies multidisciplinary perspectives on a significant theme, but it does much more than this. It builds
into the semester a progression from one kind of writing to another (in
this case, narrative to argumentative). It actively involves students in
two very different ways of writing about, and thus of imaginatively
apprehending, a significant topic. And it puts writing at the center of a
course that has a conceptual focus as well.

All that is required for such a course is an organizing theme with
significant primary literature in a mode that students can both read and
write about. A course in journalistic styles, for example, perhaps focusing on questions of ethics, factuality, and artifice in journalistic prose,
would meet this requirement, as would a course in biographical writing
that investigated different cultural models for representing the shape of
a human life. There are also various minor genres that bring together
themes of some range with modes of writing both imitable and analyz-
able. One of these, which might be called "The Outsider's Account,"
sets out to analyze familiar features of Western culture from an assumed
perspective (Eastern, Extraterrestrial, Anthropological) that leads readers to see their everyday lives with great freshness and, often, significant irony. Literary examples include the *Letters* ("Persian" and
"Chinese") of Montesquieu and Goldsmith, but the central impulse of
this genre extends beyond the traditionally literary to such writers as
Roland Barthes *(Mythologies)*, Lewis Thomas *(The Lives of a Cell)*,
and Thorstein Veblen *(The Theory of the Leisure Class)*, all of whom
treat everyday life as in some sense alien and therefore newly apprehen-
sible.

4. PERSPECTIVES COURSES

This final category of courses is related to the first group, "Fields of
Discourse," but it differs from that group in two significant ways. First,
each course investigates not one but several disciplines. Second, Perspectives courses work to introduce students to the very idea of disciplinary perspectives: to the fact of their existence and to the constraints
and liberties of intellectual vision that they inescapably carry with them.

In this sense, they are valuable introductions to university study as such, especially to the idea that disciplines are defined not simply by the objects they study but by the conceptual and verbal framework within which they study—or constitute—those objects. The *principal* aim of such courses, then, is not to introduce students to discipline A or B or C, but to help them discover what might be called, awkwardly enough, the "disciplinarity" of those fields: the identity of each as

> a relatively organized constellation of axioms, assumptions, beliefs, expectations, aspirations, attachments, obligations, preferences, evaluations, characteristically crystallized in a distinctive sub-language, conceptual structures and set of practices. That is to say, a way of "seeing the world" and acting within it as thus perceived. (Max Black 263)

Courses like these treat writing not as a set of compositional do's and don't's but as the verbal form of ways of knowing. They therefore represent choices in writing (stylistic, rhetorical, and so on) as, in part, choices of epistemological stance: decisions about what we will know and how. Such an introduction is intensely useful to college students, who are expected to master large quantities of "material" in a variety of fields but are offered little leisure, or incentive, to consider those fields as discursive spaces—constituted by certain kinds of conceptual and linguistic practice—that define just what shall count as proper "material," or as a fact, in any given discipline.

The usual argument for postponing such study—and it is often postponed indefinitely—is that it makes overly sophisticated demands on unsophisticated minds and that, even if students are capable of contemplating the frames of reference that define the character of the facts they are required to learn, they are too busy to do so. There are just too many facts to be learned.

One could offer many kinds of response to such an objection: that it underestimates the powers of students and of their instructors; that it unjustifiably treats "facts" as primitive rather than derived entities, thereby masking the role of institutional structures in creating various modes of the factual; that it depends on an educational model in which students are first shown how to do something and only later told what it is they are doing; that this sequence, only one of several very plausible possibilities, amounts to a curricular enshrinement of the way Aristotle's works came to be arranged (the *Physics* preceding the *Metaphys-*

ics); and others. From the point of view of a writing program, however, rather than a comprehensive effort to revise the nature of undergraduate offerings, the only necessary response is this: that students would profit in several ways if *some* of their courses, even some of their introductory courses, taught them what fields are, not just what is in them, and if those same courses also grounded the study of writing in the character of intellectual inquiry. (A fuller argument for perspectival education is made by Sidney Siskin in ''Education for Survival: the University in a Technological Society.'')

Whatever they might be called—''Writing about X,'' ''Perspectives on X,'' or something else entirely—courses in this category would share a basic but in no sense restrictive structure. Each would focus on a topic of relatively broad interest and multidisciplinary scope; each would assign good, accessible readings from several fields (two or three, at most four); each would study those readings not just as sources for ideas about the topic, but as ways of conceiving the topic and therefore *as ways of conceiving*—acts of articulation and understanding made possible by the disciplinary conventions in which they are produced. Students would necessarily be asked to pay close attention to the main conceptual and stylistic features of their readings. They would also be asked to do several kinds of writing, including close argumentative essays, other kinds of writing about the topic, and essays about particular ways of conceiving the topic (and thus about the particular perspectives of one or more disciplines). The topic of a Perspectives course need only be interesting to a variety of students and significant enough to have stimulated good writing in several fields, not all of them necessarily academic.

Thus, a course called ''Perspectives on Kinship'' would almost certainly investigate anthropological and sociological (not to say biological) views of kinship, but it might also explore the very different conceptions of the phenomenon of kinship provided by mythic narratives, by literature (Greek tragedy, for example, or nineteenth- and twentieth-century fiction), by psychoanalysis, or by historical studies of changing familial and social structures. Or one might offer a course called ''Perspectives on Health and Illness.'' Such a course would certainly treat medical definitions of health and illness, but it would also recognize that these concepts are far from exclusively medical. Even if we limit ourselves to physical health and illness (not always easy to do), these are defined and explored in a variety of ways, and by a variety of disciplines, and much could be learned from investigating the social definitions and symbolism, literary depiction, ethical import, and individual and cultural functions of the notions of health and illness. Here again, as in all Perspectives courses, the interest of the topic itself should not be allowed to displace a resolute concern with the fact of the topic's being multiply conceivable within the linguistic and conceptual frameworks of several fields, and with the different conventions of those fields.

There is little point in adding illustrations except to remark that topics may exist at various levels of specificity and concreteness. "Kinship" might be refocused as "Mother-daughter relations" or even as "Adolescence" (insofar as the latter itself is conceived as a familial phenomenon). Or adolescence itself might be investigated in a context larger than the familial: as a condition biologically and culturally defined; as a symbolic resource in various kinds of narrative literature and art (including film); as a liminal state central to a variety of social rituals derived from cultural definitions; and so on. Or still more abstract notions like those of rejection and stigmatization might be studied in a number of their concrete forms: from the biological mysteries of tissue rejection (and acceptance) to the patterns of ostracism and exclusion in animal and human societies, and to such verbal acts of casting out as cursing and flyting, legal disinheritance, excommunication rituals, exorcism, and literary satire in prose and verse.

Courses like these may seem to demand broad competence in their instructors and considerable sophistication in their students, and thus to be most appropriately offered to upper-level students by experienced professors. Students certainly need a much wider range of upper-level writing courses than is now available. But Perspectives courses also promise to provide a certain intensity of intellectual interest at the elementary level—the level of the basic, not the simplistic. This interest can lead students to an understanding of what is at stake in the activities of writing and learning even as it encourages more instructors to think of intellectual activity and instruction in writing as complementary, rather than mutually exclusive or merely parallel, forms of classroom activity.

There are unexplored places for style and rhetoric in the traditional curriculum, then, but there is also a place for much of that curriculum in the concepts of style and rhetoric, generously understood. If writing is the construction of one or another perspective on the world, a perspective as much rhetorical and stylistic as conceptual—a textual perspective—then many traditional and recent disciplines are themselves textual constructions. To teach our students this is to supply them with a map of the curricular terrain, not just soil samples, and it is to show them that writing cannot easily be detached from the intellectual investigation that is at the heart of university study. This project may require a bit more disciplinary self-consciousness, interdisciplinary awareness, and curricular rethinking than are sometimes exacted of us. But these efforts seem a small price to pay for a student body better informed about the very character of their studies and possessing a serious, rather than trivial, conception of writing.

WORKS CITED

Entries marked with an asterisk are described in Chapter 8, "A Bibliographical Guide to the Profession."

Black, Max. "Some Tasks for The Humanities." *Caveats and Critiques,* 254–67. Ithaca: Cornell Univ. Press, 1975.

*Brooks, Cleanth, and Robert Penn Warren. *Modern Rhetoric.* 4th ed. New York: Harcourt Brace Jovanovich, 1979.

*Coles, William, Jr. *The Plural I—The Teaching of Writing.* New York: Holt, Rinehart and Winston, 1978.

*Elbow, Peter. *Writing Without Teachers.* New York: Oxford Univ. Press, 1973.

Frye, Northrop. *Anatomy of Criticism: Four Essays.* Princeton: Princeton Univ. Press, 1957.

Hofstadter, Douglas. *Gödel, Escher, Bach: An Eternal Golden Braid.* New York: Basic Books, 1979.

Kinneavy, James L. *A Theory of Discourse: The Aims of Discourse.* 1971. New York: Norton, 1980.

Macrorie, Ken. *A Vulnerable Teacher.* Rochelle Park, N.J.: Hayden Book Co., 1974.

Siskin, Sidney. "Education for Survival: the University in a Technological Society." *Proceedings of the Philosophy of Education Society,* 153–63. Urbana, Ill.: Educational Theory, 1975.

*Strunk, William, and E. B. White. *The Elements of Style.* 3rd ed. New York: Macmillan, 1979.

Warriner, John E., ed. *English Grammar and Composition: Complete Course.* New York: Harcourt, Brace & World, 1973.

2

Designing a Course

PATRICIA CARDEN

I. INTRODUCTION: THE USES OF THE WRITTEN SYLLABUS

When I was an undergraduate I took several courses with a well-known poet and critic who never handed out a syllabus or even a reading list. During the week he could be seen browsing in a dusty corner of the library among volumes of Icelandic mythology or old psychology textbooks. He would turn up on our appointed Wednesdays with a choice morsel to read aloud to us and that text would become the occasion of the day's discussion. The very selection of what had peculiarly fascinated him, the vividness of his reading, his asides as he read, the way in which he drew us into his experience of the text—all this formed an epoch in my intellectual development. His syllabus was the daily lived experience of reading, ideas, and creation, generously shared with us as it unfolded for him.

This teacher's nonchalance required a boundless confidence—one justified, fortunately, by the results. It also required an understanding, shared by poet, department, and students, that his imaginative life was to be the substance of his teaching. Most of us labor under a different understanding. Our courses are offered within a departmental curriculum; they are often designed to engage a span of subject matter to a large degree defined for us. We have the opportunity for selection within that framework. The written syllabus gives us an opportunity to clarify our own purposes, to bring them into consonance with the departmental (and college) understanding of what we are to do, and to convey the finished plan succinctly and elegantly to our colleagues and students. A well-formulated syllabus will not simply tell the students what books to buy and read: it will anticipate the flavor of the course, it will adumbrate its central ideas, and it will establish a rhythm of work to hold the class together in common purpose.

While the suggestions that follow for planning a syllabus emerge from my experience with writing courses designed around a particular subject matter, teachers of other kinds of composition courses will find shared concerns in Section II, ''Practical Tasks,'' and may also find inspiration for reading and discussion among the syllabus sequences recommended in Section III. (Later chapters in this book focus less specifically on subject-matter courses.)

II. PRACTICAL TASKS

A. *Stocktaking*

When you begin to teach within a program, you need to find out what is expected of you: Are you going to be handed a complete syllabus and told to teach it? Will you have some choice in reading and writing assignments? Are you entirely responsible for selecting a set of readings and drawing up a schedule? If you are a graduate teaching assistant, lecturer, or first-time instructor, you may have a faculty supervisor. Faculty supervisors differ in style—some hold a tight rein on the design of the course, down to daily assignments; others think of themselves as resource people for their staffs. Either way, the faculty supervisor can give you the best word on what will be expected of you.

Talk to as many people as you can who know something about the program: graduate students and staff people who have taught in it before, students who have taken the courses. Ask to see the file of syllabi and assignments used in past years. If you are to be given considerable freedom to design your own version, make up a plan with alternatives and show it to your supervisor and any other people whom you've found helpful.

And don't underestimate your own resources, as a teacher of writing or of your subject. You already know, even in the first year of graduate school, far more about both than you can teach freshmen in one term. Rethink what you know to find opportunities for discussion and assignments. How can you teach a freshman—an inexperienced writer who is probably not at all informed in your field and has no intention of becoming a specialist in it—to write and think about that field? What writing topics and experiences will most interest and encourage a beginning student? How did teachers best help you with your essays? What kinds of writing do you do, and admire? What texts will provide opportunities to discuss approaches to writing in your field? What things did you read early in your exposure to your subject that turned you on to the intellectual excitement of what you are doing? What texts do you consider classics of your discipline? What ideas would most people in your field accept as fundamental to an inquiry in that field, and where have those ideas been best expressed or best illustrated? What are your own strengths within the discipline? What ideas and approaches of your own can you share with the students? How can these be made accessible and interesting to the beginning student? Even if you are given a syllabus and asked to teach it, you will be faced with many daily choices about how to conduct the course; you will find ample latitude for your own cast of mind and interests to shape it.

B. *Apportioning Class Time*

Before going on to the substance of the assignments, I'd like to begin with another side of course preparation, so habitual to long-time teachers that they may be hardly aware of it, and yet so mysterious and anxiety-provoking to the new teacher: Where do you start? What simple practical steps do you take to get a course together? Here's the situation: A number of compositional topics from punctuation to argument need to be explicitly addressed in the classroom; a number of tasks from framing a thesis to revising need to be demonstrated and practiced; a subject matter must be done justice to. And all this must occur within the framework of a course where each element bears upon the others.

You might begin simply by listing each class hour that you have at your disposal with the day of the week on which it occurs (Mon., Sept. 5; Wed., Sept. 7; etc.). The day of the week will be important in articulating the assignments. Don't forget to exclude official holidays and breaks when instruction is suspended. The chart will make it easier to juggle the multiple superimpositions of composition tasks, writing assignments, reading assignments, library work, and thematic units that compose the texture of most writing courses. It's also chastening to see how very limited is the time at your disposal.

When you apportion class time, the writing work has to come first. The course will have more coherence and will give the students an enhanced sense of the uses of writing if the composition instruction is not rigidly set apart from the discussion of the reading. A well-taught course will address the development of writing skills in every class meeting: by shaping the discussion of the materials to show the students how their own ideas can be made into the stuff of good essays; by looking at the texture of writing in the reading; by developing the habits of thinking that lead to well-constructed arguments; by helping the students define their responses precisely and express them clearly and vividly. Nevertheless, in blocking out a syllabus you must set time aside for composition work or it will inevitably be crowded out in the day-to-day rush to "cover the material." Practically, that means you can't fill every slot on the syllabus with reading assignments. You need a leisurely pace of reading to accommodate the work in writing.

You can ensure adequate leisure to address questions of rhetoric and composition by setting aside a block of time at the start, perhaps a third of the class meetings. Some time will be needed for addressing fundamental topics (how to punctuate complex sentences, how to frame a question for argument). A substantial chunk should be devoted to going over samples of the students' own writing, from sentences and paragraphs to whole papers. The composition work need not (probably should not) be confined to one day a week. When you are talking mechanics, it may be wisest to take up a few conventions of punctuation at a time to avoid confusing and boring the students. Ten minutes at the beginning of each class may suffice to present the rules and practice them briefly. Some topics (finding strategies to begin papers, working on revising) will require whole periods. After I've read a set of papers, I usually spend a third to a half of the following class talking about one or two of the most prevalent patterns of weakness and revising examples from the papers.

It's important, too, to set aside time for a second kind of compositional work: using the reading materials themselves to illustrate and practice the current compositional topics in the course. There's no reason why this practice can't be part of the class's intellectual exploration of the course materials, but the link to the students' own writing needs to be made explicit. Try to preserve tautness in the conduct of the course so that opportunities for discussing writing as a task are constantly taken advantage of. I like to keep some of the classes freer, not so relentlessly centered on composition tasks. The students' exercise of their minds in the examination of ideas can't but shape their writing. The requisite tautness can be maintained by keeping in the foreground the shape ideas take as writing. Chapter 6, ''Understanding Prose,'' suggests many ways to engage students' attention in the very shape and texture of the material they are studying. Ideally, the work in reading and writing will merge into one fluent discourse.

When you assign papers and what length you ask for will depend upon the larger articulation of the course units, but it helps in shaping those larger units to decide tentatively how many papers of various lengths you plan to assign and to block them in on your calendar. You will need to have the students writing every week. We might assume that about thirty pages of writing during a semester is a reasonable amount to aim for in the syllabus. To divide the thirty pages into three ten-page papers would not allow the practice students need to work through a variety of compositional problems. Papers of 1 to 2 pages can be alternated with papers of 4 to 5 pages. A colleague suggested to me that at least one paper should be 7 to 8 pages to more nearly approximate the work that students do in other courses. Indeed, when I assigned a longer paper I found that the students enjoyed the more ambitious assignment; it tested their powers of organization and argument as the shorter papers had not. Remember, too, that it's fairer to vary the days of weeks when the assignments are due. Freshmen often have labs on a regular schedule, so a staggered schedule of assignments will avoid burdening a few students harshly. And it's patently unfair to call for a paper every Monday, putting a lien on the students' every weekend.

No doubt you have in mind a number of items you want the students to read. When selecting readings you need to pay attention to the fit of the materials to the work in writing. You will want to include certain texts to flesh out the profile of your topic, but usually you can choose among a number of readings, selecting to illustrate a point, for example, a clever strategy of argument. A course will be more intellectually substantial if it concentrates on major instances of writing in the discipline. Most students have not read widely and in the short four years at their disposal for a liberal education they can ill afford to spend a whole course with the trivial. You might begin by asking: What are the classics of my subject? Are there essays or books where a major thinker has formulated fundamental ideas in a powerful way? You don't always have to choose the most civilized, graceful, and urbane style to illustrate good writing; a major thinker's very knottiness and complexity of expression is worthy of analysis. It's a tonic to students who may be achieving lucidity by reducing what they have to say to simple terms to see that wrestling with a complicated idea can involve some loss of clarity.

When you have in mind what readings you mean to assign, try them out on your chart for fit. Usually you will find that you have more pages of reading than you can easily accommodate in the course. A hundred pages of reading a week is about the maximum that students can handle and still attend to their writing, but it is wise not to keep the reading assignments at the maximum pace week after week. When a longer paper is due, the students may stagger under the weight of a full reading assignment. They can do it, of course; but if you are talking about the process of composing, asking the students to take their papers through several drafts, calling upon them to revise the finished product, then you had better leave a reasonable amount of time for those tasks.

Finally, a plea that you shape your course plan humanely. Freshmen find the first round of college mid-semester exams hard to handle. You don't need to stop your course for that period, or even to cease giving writing assignments, but it is wise to take the stress into account. After polling the class during the last week in September to find out when examinations cluster, I restructure the assignments to shorter readings, shorter papers, more in-class writing—whatever will take pressure off the students. I discuss the problem with the students, tell them I have taken the exams into account when setting up the assignments, and call upon them to keep up their work in good faith during this trying period.

The same principle can be applied to the course as a whole: keep a realistic relationship between means and ends. A student said to her adviser about an instructor's scrutiny of her papers. "Why, she looks at every word!" If you want your students to consider every word when they write their papers, I'm afraid you have to look at every word when you read them. If you want your students to read every word you have assigned, a good share of those words must come into play in one way or another in the class's work.

C. Ordering Textbooks

I first realized how badly the novice needs a little collegial assistance when one of my TAs, after speaking with tremendous enthusiasm about her choice of reading and why she had elected one thing over the other—a stimulating intellectual discussion, a thoroughly professional discussion—asked timidly how one orders books. Lord knows there is enough mystery in teaching without puzzling over how to get books for your students.

If you are lucky, there will be an anthology or two of selected readings that will perfectly suit your topic and the strategy you have worked out for the course. Many courses in the humanities depend on a selection of inexpensive paperback editions, often supplemented by photocopied or mimeographed handouts (but check to see how many handouts the department can afford—and also if they are legal [see Section IX, "Copyright Laws Concerning Reproduction of Published Material" in Chapter 8]). You may assign reading on a reserve shelf at the library, but the inaccessibility of the texts during class time makes it difficult to do the kind of close analysis a writing class calls for. If you depend on a reserve shelf for the bulk of your reading, you should reproduce some passages for use in the classroom.

You can find out what books are available by scanning the advertisements in current editions of the professional journals in your field, talking to colleagues, and examining recent syllabi. When you have your list together, check current availability in *Books in Print* (or *Paperback Books in Print*) at the library or bookstore. Even so, you will likely be notified after you order that some items are out of stock at the publisher. Be prepared to substitute alternatives. Some campus bookstores send order forms for courses each term to faculty members who have ordered before. Book ordering is often taken care of by the faculty supervisor, sometimes after consultation with section instructors.

III. DEVISING SEQUENCES

Now that we've gone through the course as a set of practical tasks, let's go back and look at it again, from the more interesting (and demanding) vantage of its substance. You may ask, how much formal articulation does a course really need? I wouldn't go so far as to say that the unexamined composition course is not worth teaching. An experienced teacher can teach effectively with little overt structure, nothing more perhaps than a list of books and a set of intuitions about what she wants to accomplish. Conversely, beginners often err by relying too much on formal structure and are bound so firmly to their plan that the course loses all flexibility and spontaneity. Courses need a little air and opportunity. But there's no denying that much of the fun in teaching comes in the working out of combinations. Well-defined units give punctuation to the work in a course; putting things together engages your own intellectual energies, particularly when you are teaching the same materials for a third or fourth time and beginning to go a bit stale. The search for new forms of articulation in the materials keeps the instructor and the class alive and attentive.

At its most successful the articulation of materials can create new intellectual opportunities, become more than the sum of the parts. I don't want to promise too much. How students learn remains a mystery even to the most experienced teachers. We can never be sure just what we have taught: information? skills? an attitude towards the subject matter? a deepening of their own sense of engagement with ideas? a feeling of control over their lives? Students, evaluating courses, will attest to having learned any or all of these things, but whether they have or not is difficult to discover. Our goals have to be modest in their specifics. In the short term we mostly judge the success of mimicry: Have we been able to get our students to reproduce without too much stiffness and self-consciousness the forms and styles that we ourselves practice or would like to practice? There's nothing dishonorable about mimicry—artisans have always learned their craft by sitting next to a practitioner—as long as we understand the process and use it flexibly. Writing is so complicated, there are so many things going on at once, that putting together all the skills can perhaps only be achieved finally by imitation.

Nevertheless, you may find recent work in cognitive psychology and discourse analysis suggestive of tasks that can be undertaken with profit in the classroom. Both these fields approach the problem of teaching writing by breaking the task down into a number of discrete stages, each of which can be addressed in turn. The linearity of presentation is a fiction, but a useful one that lets a teacher show students the kinds of processes skilled writers engage in, including the free play of the mind upon the subject. You can follow this research in professional journals like *College Composition and Communication* and *College English*. The authors of some textbooks have assumed that natural sequencing in writing means beginning with the sentence, working up to the paragraph, and finally addressing the essay as a whole. Recent work in discourse suggests rather a series of cognitive stages common to structure at every level, from sentences and paragraphs to larger units of discourse. No definitive analysis of writing has been achieved thus far; we still work with sequences suggested by logic and experience.

The pursuit of a subject in coordination with instruction in composition means devising assignments where the many dimensions of the course are brought simultaneously into play. When you begin thinking about how to do this, it is helpful once again to proceed analytically by jotting down the items in each category of work that you want to cover in the course. An experienced teacher can hold these in the memory, but making a list does help you to see if you have included everything you mean to; a list keeps the range of possibilities before you as you move back and forth between the topic and writing instruction.

Following our rule that the writing comes first, I'll begin with composition topics. You can get help from many sources—this book, the training sessions that most writing programs provide for their instructors, the faculty supervisor, other instructors, textbooks. In fact, if you are a novice teacher of writing, you could do worse than simply follow a good textbook. That's one way of covering the ground and ensuring that your students are introduced to the fundamentals. When choosing a textbook, look for one that centers on the process of writing, on argumentative strategies, and on the ways in which sentences serve different rhetorical strategies, rather than one centered on prescriptive grammar and the conventions of presentation (consult ''A Bibliographical Guide to the Profession,'' Section III, for analytical descriptions). Many people find that in the current fluid state of research no textbook satisfies all their prerequisites. If you reach this conclusion you will need to put together your own plan of instruction, drawing on many sources.

I offer here a list of composition topics followed by a list of tasks. It is not meant to be prescriptive; many kinds of lists may be drawn up. My list illustrates how to go about working out a set of priorities for instruction with an accompanying set of tasks. Whatever your list of topics, you should take care that your students are given the opportunity to discuss and practice writing at a variety of levels in the process, from finding topics to making arguments, from sentences to essays.

A list of compositional topics:

1. Mechanics:
   Passive constructions.
   Over use of forms of "to be."
   Vague pronoun references and agreement of pronouns with antecedents.
   Vaguely related modifiers ("dangling" and otherwise).
   Failure of parallelism.
   Forms of subordination in the sentence.
   Semantic mismatches between subject and predicate in the sentence.
   Unidiomatic expressions.
   Consistency/sequence of tenses.
   Use of commas and semicolons to punctuate compound and complex sentences.
   Punctuation with quotations.
   (See Chapter 7 for an extended analysis and discussion of "Common Sentence Problems in Beginners' Writing.")

2. Finding an idea to write about. (I will say more about this presently.)

3. Strategies for beginning a paper, for taking up new sub-topics in mid-stream, and for concluding.

4. The paragraph as a unit of discourse with a variety of strategies for achieving coherence.

5. Developing an argument through several stages.

6. Syntax: eliminating wordiness, formulaic language, and excessive use of passives and nominalized forms. Use of a variety of rhetorical devices to achieve coherence and stylistic effectiveness.

7. Revising at each level from the sentence to the structure of the argument.

A list of tasks:

1. Work in class on sentences from the students' papers with characteristic mechanical problems, followed by an assignment in which students are asked to edit a paper for mechanical errors.

2. Analysis and reworking of sample paragraphs from the students' papers followed by an assignment in which the students are asked to rework the paragraphs in their last papers.

3. Discussion of the reading materials to examine strategies of organization and style.

4. Discussion of the reading materials to discover cruxes and frame questions worthy of argument.

5. Practice in the use of a number of rhetorical devices and stylistic strategies.

All these topics and tasks need to be taken up not once, but repeatedly, and reinforced throughout the term by comments on papers, in-class analysis and practice, and the students' own revisions of their work.

After you have constructed a list of composition topics and tasks, make a second list based on an analysis of your subject matter and reading assignments. You can include fundamental terms and concepts the students will need in order to talk and write about the subject, key intellectual cruxes, and characteristic modes of argumentation, analysis, and presentation. The composition list and the subject list can be matched back and forth against each other to find opportunities for units and particular assignments integrating the two aspects of the course work.

In the remainder of the chapter I will suggest ways to integrate analysis of the subject matter with writing assignments. My emphasis will be on finding occasions for writing in the discourse of your subject. A number of other chapters in this book suggest classroom procedures and assignments that serve the same end; what I have to say here simply extends the list of possibilities.

SEQUENCE I. IN-CLASS WRITING TO PROBE A SUBJECT

The first sequence I propose is designed to use informal in-class writing to probe a subject matter. It has the virtue of allowing the student to begin at a level where the stakes are not high. The in-class writing will be used to extend the student's thinking in the context of the class discussion and it will not be graded. The sequence concludes with a short paper which can be commented on and graded by the teacher. I am indebted for general principles to an article by C. H. Knoblauch and Lil Brannon, "Writing as Learning Through the Curriculum." The strategies they propose work particularly well when you are defining the fundamental terms central to discourse in a subject, and they can be employed very early in the term.

The unit begins with class discussion of a term or concept. You might use the reading assignment as your point of departure or you might elicit discussion by your own comments and questions. For example, in a course in political science you might want students to think about how to define power. In a popular writing course at Cornell the discussion begins by investigating distinctions among a set of related terms: fantasy, nonsense, dream, and wonder. As these examples show, you are not searching for a dictionary definition but for an understanding of the complexities inherent in a powerful concept. After twenty minutes or so of discussion, you might ask the students to write for five minutes, exploring potential meanings and distinctions in meaning for the term under consideration. Several students can be asked to read their comments aloud for class discussion. The discussion should center on the adequacies of the definition: does it include the core of the meaning; does it extend the meaning far enough; does it account for the principal ambiguities in the term? Students can be asked to annotate their own definitions as the discussion goes along and rewrite them in the evening for inclusion in their notebooks.

The work in defining a concept can be followed up in a subsequent class by asking students to apply the concept to the day's reading assignment. Students begin by writing for ten minutes in response to a question: What are the rules of logic that govern Alice's fantasy world? What disadvantages do you see in recent laboratory experiments to study power? The question should be one that invites a range of responses, rather than a "correct" answer. Students know from an earlier discussion what questions can be raised about "power" or "fantasy"; the class is ready to be used as an audience for its own writing. Ask the students to exchange papers and write for another ten minutes in response to a classmate's ideas. You can then turn the discussion to the day's topic, inviting the students to share the ideas they have formulated in their writing. The annotated papers can be included in the notebooks.

This sequence of activities has helped the class create a field of discourse about the topic under discussion. They should have some insight into a key term, a notion of the contexts in which it is used, and a sense of how to manipulate it when discussing an example. Their knowledge can be deployed in a short paper to be handed in for the teacher's scrutiny. This is a logical point in the sequence for individual conferences, which generally work best when centered on a specific task. Ask each student to turn in two short paragraphs, each of which describes a question or problem that has occurred to her during the discussion.

In conference you might range rather freely over the subject, exploring the student's understanding of the concept and her range of responses to it. (She may have better ideas than she happened to get down in her two paragraphs, but the paragraphs will have been useful in getting her to start thinking.) You can conclude the conference by helping the student choose a specific topic for exploration in the paper.

SEQUENCE 2. IMITATING STRATEGIES OF PERSUASION

Reading materials can also serve the writing assignments as objects of imitation. Of course, students cannot be taught to write well, as was once thought, simply by exposing them to good writing: while good writers may be developed by much reading over many years, it is unlikely that a student can improve her writing by osmosis in the two terms at her disposal in most composition programs. Nevertheless, we can look to a more sophisticated variant of the method, one developed by the poet Kenneth Koch in his work with children. Koch succeeded in getting children to write fresh and interesting poems by having them imitate certain salient structural features of poetic language. For example, he might ask his class to write a series of lines using the syntactic formula, "I used to . . . , but now . . ." (13). Koch's success appears to stem from his isolation of fundamental features of poetic discourse. He didn't simply read a poem to the children and say, "Now write a poem." He showed them something about the poem that they could use to create another poem.

You may doubt that Koch's method can be made applicable to disciplines outside the arts. Yet every discipline has its characteristic structures of discourse and with a little attentiveness to key texts you can easily discover some of them. These structures are generally expressive of cognitive modes characteristic of the discipline. For example, in fields of investigation where scholars think of themselves as dealing with the facts of reality, central texts tend to cut across the grain of received ideas in the field. Scientific writing is rich in forms of discourse designed to disarm a preconceived notion and create room for a new understanding, or paradigm. James Gibson, who was for many years the ornament of Cornell's psychology department, made use of such a radical tactic in his book, *The Senses Considered as Perceptual Systems:*

> The face of the earth consists of wrinkled surfaces of rock and soil along with smooth surfaces of water. The liquid surface is everywhere exactly perpendicular to the line of gravity; the solid surface is on the average perpendicular to it.
>
> The curvature of these surfaces is so small that it approaches the zero curvature of a plane. The size of the planet, in other words, is so vast in comparison to the size of any animal that for ordinary purposes the substratum is flat. The ancient men who assumed that the world was flat were thus not mistaken in this observation either; they were only limited in their conception of the size of the world. The measurement of this substratum conformed to the plane geometry of Euclid, and its geography was, and still is, excellently represented by a plane map.
>
> The environment of a terrestrial animal, then, during the millions of years of evolutionary history, had certain simple invariants. They were the earth "below," the air "above," and the "waters under the earth." The ground was level and rigid, a surface of support. The air was unresistant—a space for locomotion, open to the daily cycles of warmth and light from the sky, penetrating everywhere among the furniture of the earth. The air was always and everywhere a medium for breathing, the occasional bearer of odors and sounds, and transparent to the shapes of things by day. (8)

Gibson's work in perceptual psychology departed radically from earlier studies of vision, which had been dominated by a branch of physics, optics. In earlier experiments subjects would be seated in a darkened room (to eliminate distracting and irrelevant sense impressions) and asked to follow a moving pinpoint of light. Gibson rejected this model of the controlled laboratory experiment. He argued for an "ecological" study of the senses where vision would be examined in the context of everyday experience, in an environment bathed in ambient light. The striking passage above asserts a view of the world derived from sensory experience. To shock his readers from their preconceived "scientific" bias, Gibson opposes the formulas of a lost "mythical" consciousness to modern scientific knowledge. And because he wants to affirm the dignity of our direct perception of reality and to assert its claim on science's attention, he echoes the most dignified and solemn style available in English, that of the King James version of the Bible.

Courses in history, psychology, political science, sociology, or any of the sciences lend themselves to a unit on similar strategies of persuasion. It should be easy to find a sequence of texts that mark turning points in the thinking of a discipline and illustrate how authors went about persuading a recalcitrant audience. Each passage could be used as a springboard to a writing assignment. A class discussion of Gibson's passage could be followed up by this assignment: Ask students to identify an old wives' tale or piece of traditional wisdom generally regarded as outdated or untrue, then to look at the belief from a new point of view—what kind of truth did it embody for those who believed it? What new possibilities does it suggest to people of our time? Ask them to write a page in the manner of Gibson, asserting the truth of the proposition from a different perspective.

Passages that employ a range of rhetorical strategies to counter conventional wisdom can be examined in turn and their strategies practiced in short assignments. The sequence can both teach students an important fact about the nature of scientific thought and help them learn the fundamental structures of argumentative discourse as they are practiced in the discipline.

SEQUENCE 3. FINDING TOPICS AND ASSEMBLING EVIDENCE (INVENTION)

The two sequences I have proposed leave a fair amount of room for the students' individual responses, but their general direction is prescribed by the teacher. They are essentially instruments for teaching what the instructor has in mind. Much investigation of how students learn to write suggests that they improve most rapidly when they have an investment in what they are writing about. In the preceding sequences the motivation (not a trivial one) lies in the student's desire to master the key concepts of the course. But you will want to move quickly to assignments which ask students to find their own terms of engagement with the materials by identifying key concepts and cruxes for themselves.

Assignments of this sort bring us squarely into the realm of composition theory called "pre-writing" or "invention." (For a fuller discussion, see Chapter 1, "The Field of Writing: An Aerial View.") The advocates of pre-writing have tended to see writing as an instrument for discovering what we want to say and have proposed that the first step is to write. The advocates of "invention" (the term is Aristotle's) have stressed logical procedures for discovering a topic to write about. They have proposed a number of procedures or "heuristics" for finding out what there is to say about a given subject. The heuristics have been derived from formal logic, from more contemporary explorations of argumentation in philosophy and linguistics, or from the "dramatistic" method developed by Kenneth Burke for critics to use in the analysis of texts and cultural situations. (See Chapter 4, "Sequence 2. Following Traditional Rhetorical Divisions," for a full discussion with examples of how Burke's five questions may be used for student writing.) Richard Larson has laid out a rather complete set of questions in his article, "Discovery Through Questioning: A Plan for Teaching Rhetorical Invention."

Pre-writing and invention can be combined to effect in classroom teaching. The exercises I have described above partake of some of the characteristics of pre-writing since the student first actively engages each topic in a piece of informal writing. Ten to fifteen years ago, many teachers of composition thought that having students keep journals would automatically provide them with ideas to write about. Teachers who have employed the device seem to have reached the conclusion (judging from articles reporting their experience) that the journal simply pushes the problem of invention back to an earlier stage. Students must be taught to keep a journal good enough to serve as a source of ideas. Instructors must actively intervene to suggest strategies for reading and annotating the materials, to encourage students to write down all their questions and ideas freely, and to check the journals and comment on their possibilities.

Still, the journal's usefulness is well attested to by the many thinkers and writers who have employed it. Undoubtedly, the proper keeping of a journal engages a student more actively with the materials of a course and makes it more likely that she will find something worth saying when it comes time to write a paper. The journal forms a bridge between writing done to increase the student's own understanding of the topic and writing done to convey ideas to others. You might encourage your students to think of their course notebooks as journals in which they record their exploration of the topic in a variety of modes. Class notes might alternate with in-class writing exercises like those described above, with notes on the reading, and with brief commentaries embodying the student's own responses and ideas. When a student raises a promising question in class, you could suggest that she begin to follow it through in her journal. She might observe, for example, that writers' definitions of power seem to depend on what social class they come from or what social class they take as the focal point of their definitions. The student might be asked from time to time to read to the class from her journal entries for that day's reading. She might write several short papers exploring how individual authors' social biases influence their theories. The work could conclude with a more ambitious paper on how class bias influences definitions of power.

At the same time that you are encouraging students to record their full range of responses, you can be teaching them to broaden their responses by employing a series of systematic questions. You might use questions derived from Larson or from Jacqueline Berke's *Twenty Questions for the Writer*. Or you might devise a series particular to your subject. Ask yourself, what kinds of questions do people in my field characteristically ask? How do these questions define the subject matter of the field? In courses in Russian literature we have found that students tended to confine their observations to a few tried and true formulas, often too general to engage the particular story on its own terms. I devised the following heuristic for our teaching assistants to use with an eye toward getting students to attend to other dimensions of the text:

1. List the principal characters with four or five words or phrases used by the author to describe each one.

2. List the key events in the story and where they take place. Note four or five key words or phrases used by the author to describe each place.

3. List three significant actions in the story. What motivations lead to each?

4. Who tells each segment of the story? Does the narrator change from part to part? Are some narrators characters in the stories?

How does each narrator influence the story he tells?

5. List all events in the story in the order of their telling. Relist them in the order in which they are supposed to occur in chronological time. What differences do you see in the two sequences? How can you account for them?

6. List as many examples as you can of each of the following: Things that seem to be repetitions in one way or another. Things that seem to be opposites in one way or another.

7. Note five striking figures of speech and where they occur.

8. Write down three words that characterize this author's style for you (avoiding widely applicable generalities like "vivid" and "good").

Students are given copies of the heuristic early in the course. On any given day the instructor may ask them to attend to one or two of the items when reading the assignment, but the presence of a range of questions in the background of the discussion tends to sharpen students' responses, even if those questions are not the central focus of inquiry. The list can subsequently be employed as a device for finding topics to write about or for assembling evidence in a number of dimensions to make any argument about the text.

SEQUENCE 4. FINDING CRUXES

Finding a crux for argument is a way both to engage the subject of discussion in searching analysis and to explore possibilities for writing. The best argumentative papers are not just expressions of a position; they seek to unravel, solve, resolve, and interpret. An argument that contains nothing problematic is not a genuine argument. When teaching students to search out promising occasions for argument, it is worthwhile to point them to what seems difficult, opaque, uncertain, or inexplicably powerful in the materials. In a course on "Science as Literature" students may be asked why Galileo, whose theories undermined Church dogma, was a passionate believer in and defender of the Catholic Church. Here is just the kind of crux whose analysis leads to a deeper understanding of the subject (in this case, how scientific thought proceeds) and provides an occasion for an argumentative paper.

You might spend a week or more helping the students to conceive the material as a chain of cruxes for argument. You could begin by asking them as they read the next day's assignment to jot down notes about anything in the text that strikes them as unusual or difficult to account for. In class you can simply go around the table asking each student what he observed. Observations will usually group themselves into two or three key responses to the text. Write each on the blackboard, keeping the initial formulation concrete and close to the students' language.

You can anticipate that certain kinds of disparities will be disorienting for students—disagreement among authorities, for example. Students may say, "Weber said power is x, but Memmi says it is y." Such disparities provide an excellent point of departure for analysis of any thinker's position. Explore the ramifications by asking a series of questions: Why can't thinkers agree on a definition of power? What does that show about the nature of power? About the nature of definition? Students are also often puzzled by attitudes and actions that go contrary to ethical norms: "All the princes who try to rescue Sleeping Beauty are killed, but it doesn't seem to matter." You could ask, Is this the only example of detachment we find in fairytales? Where else does it occur? Do fairytales obey our ethical norms? What rules govern behavior in fairytales? You can anticipate many of the questions your students will raise and devise strategies for developing them as potential arguments. Some syllabi build in the central cruxes and alert students to them in advance. At least when you are teaching how to find a crux, it is better to let the students come with their own responses. This unit (and to my mind the entire course) should give students confidence that they can find the central issues in a subject, even if they aren't sure yet how to resolve them.

Even when the central issues are not entirely clear to students, there are devices they can employ to discover them. Kenneth Burke likes the "representative anecdote," a short narrative in which the salient features of a situation are summed up. A compelling example of the representative anecdote occurs in the physicist Freeman Dyson's memoirs. Dyson was puzzled that in the 1940s Oppenheimer had supported the development of tactical nuclear weapons. When he asked Oppenheimer whether he regretted his stand, Oppenheimer replied, "No. But to understand what I did then, you would have to see the air force war plan as it existed in 1951. That was the goddamnedest thing I ever saw. Anything, even the war plans we have now, is better than that." Dyson concluded that "The 1951 war plan was, in short, a mindless obliteration of Soviet cities'' (137). This short narrative embodies the central cruxes in the nuclear disarmament debate: the pressures of policy-making, the uses of power, and individual ethical choice.

Not every text will yield a representative anecdote (although a surprising number do), but other features of the text can be equally revealing. Encourage students to look for the telling detail, telling repetition, telling rhetorical device or structural principle that reveals a writer's preoccupations or the peculiarities of his thought. The Russian Formalist critic Boris Eikhenbaum revolutionized the way we read Gogol by asserting that the important words in "The Overcoat" are the particles (equivalent to English expressions like "uh-huh," "kind-of," etc.) rather than the adjectives of pathos that had moved social critics of the nineteenth century. The psychoanalytic tradition has focused on inadvertent mistakes, puns, wordplay, lapses, as the most telling parts of discourse. In public discourse "he doth protest too much" provides a clue to the speaker's real stand: bombast often accompanies uncertainty or bad faith. There are many examples of such linguistic bad faith in Martin and Ohmann's textbook, *The Logic and Rhetoric of Exposition.*

SEQUENCE 5. LEARNING HOW TO CONSTRUCT AN ARGUMENT

As you analyze telling anecdotes and details, you are teaching students how to develop an argument by asking leading questions. After a few sessions of informal practice, you may want to introduce your students to some of the formal principles of coherent argument. Two books that suggest distinctions in strategies of argument and their proper use are the Martin and Ohmann book just referred to and John Wilson's *Thinking with Concepts.* Wilson makes clear to what a striking degree argument rests on definition of terms. For teaching students how to construct and test arguments, I like the procedures worked out by Stephen Toulmin in *The Uses of Argument* and summarized in a simplified form for students in *Writing in the Arts and Sciences* by Elaine Maimon, et al. Toulmin's model of argument consists of three elements: a ground, a claim, and a warrant. The ground is the evidence or information from which a conclusion is drawn. The claim is the conclusion drawn. Usually students have no difficulty understanding that they must provide evidence or examples to substantiate their claims. Yet their arguments seem thin. Often the inadequacy of an argument can be attributed to its failure to establish a warrant, that is, a general principle underlying the inference.

Every field of discourse has its own warrants—the definitions, principles, modes of procedure, rules or laws upon which all inferences depend: "Power is defined in terms of domination and subordination." "Rhymed words at the ends of lines are particularly stressed." "The narrator and the author are not the same." Some warrants are part of the shared wisdom or lore of the general community: "Fools rush in where angels fear to tread." Presumably you have been teaching your students the warrants of your discipline—its primary definitions, concepts, assumptions—as you go along.

When they practice constructing arguments, they should make explicit what warrant underlies their inferences. Here are examples of how to find a warrant, using materials from freshman courses:

> 1. Claim: Though Hamlet's failure to avenge his father's death may make us think him a coward, he is not one.
> Ground: He behaves in many situations in such a way as to defy his opponents and achieve the upper hand. (examples)
> Warrant: We do not call a man a coward who is capable of commanding the situation as Hamlet does. (The warrant is a commonly accepted understanding of what constitutes cowardice.)
> 2. Claim: Though Monet's late paintings often appear to the observer to be washes of color, they are not abstract.
> Ground: If we examine the paintings closely, we can detect the forms of flowers, leaves, and moving water.
> Warrant: Abstract painting eschews all representation. (The warrant is a definition fundamental to defining modern art.)

When teaching the students to find the warrant of their arguments, you are teaching them the need for integrity in argument: the willingness to recognize and stand behind their basic assumptions.

Finally, teaching argument is no automatic solution; it can trivialize the task of writing and render it an empty exercise for students. Students can be taught to find cruxes, phrase their topics as questions, adopt the rhetorical modes of argumentation in their presentation—and still write intellectually feckless papers. We need to teach them, along with discovery, analysis, and rhetoric, a concept like Yury Tynianov's "dominant." Tynianov sought in every discourse the fundamental organizing principle to which everything else in the discourse subordinated itself. The "dominant" is primarily conceptual—it is the idea of a discourse phrased at its most general level, but it manifests itself in the style and structure of the discourse. By analyzing the particular features of a given text we can formulate its primary concept. Of course, any given formulation is always open to argument, but the attempt to isolate a text's central idea teaches students to look for what is most significant, to attempt to comprehend the discourse as a whole, and to avoid an easy and trivial approach to the material.

SEQUENCE 6. CREATING AN INTELLECTUAL CONTEXT FOR A TOPIC

Richard Larson and others who employed heuristics for invention soon ran into a problem. However many questions students used to examine a subject, they could only come up with answers that were already in their heads. They couldn't get outside the limit that circumscribed their own understanding of the topic. In the learning situation heuristics have to be combined with an expansion of the base of knowledge if the student is to use writing as a vehicle of intellectual exploration. In courses that have a subject matter to be explored, we assume that reading assignments and class discussion provide new information and ideas which students can manipulate in writing assignments. Often, though, students lack the contexts that would allow them to arrive at non-trivial interpretations.

When devising units for your course, you should give some thought to what context the student needs to think incisively about that unit's work. You can build in opportunities for students to get the information that they need for themselves. Library research assignments can be structured around key pieces of information. (One traditional assignment in the Russian literature course asks students to investigate the term "nihilism.") Individual members of the class can be asked to give informal reports providing background needed for the day's discussion. You can also structure the reading assignments so that each central text is framed by other readings that give the student a context for thought.

In the freshman writing course in Russian literature we devised two assignments that work particularly well. When we assigned Dostoevsky's "White Nights," a story that makes explicit reference to Rossini's opera, ''The Barber of Seville,'' we arranged to put a recording of the opera with its libretto on reserve at the Music Library. Students were asked to write short papers commenting on the relationship between Rossini's opera and the story. (One student's essay won a prize as the best freshman paper that term.) A more ambitious unit called for recreating the assumptions of a bygone cultural era. For many years we have assigned Pushkin's short story ''The Shot.'' Students like it because it is vivid, fastpaced, and full of action. We had always had difficulty in the discussion, however, because the story concerns dueling and involves a point of honor—a concept foreign to our students. Far from understanding that the hero Silvio turns out to be a very paragon of honor, the students always condemned him as an egotist. I decided that students lacked two important pieces of the context. First, in our egalitarian social ethic, a man who asserts his superiority is condemned. As an antidote to this presumption we asked the students to read the excerpt from Aristotle's *Nichomachean Ethics* on the ''magnanimous man,'' which says that the best man is that one who knows his own deserts and neither claims too much nor too little. Many phrases in Aristotle's essay resonate with situations in Pushkin's story and force students to reconsider their interpretation of Silvio's character.

The second thing the students badly needed to know about was Byron. Pushkin's story is a meditation on the Byronic hero as the figure evolved in literature and society in the 1820s. Silvio dies in the Greek revolution; the parallel with Bryon's celebrated end cements the reading of his character as essentially noble. But the students had no idea how to ''read'' Silvio's death. Some said that it was foolish, others that it was exhibitionist. To give them a sense of the social and ethical context Pushkin takes for granted, we had them read two essays, one a straightforward account of Byron's participation in the Greek revolution, the other Bertrand Russell's brilliant (and biased) account of the meaning of Byron's life and career. These essays provided not only information the students needed to follow Pushkin's story but additional occasions for discussing how authors take positions and make their arguments. The discussion of the many ways in which individual self-assertion might be viewed opened the students' eyes to the possibility that Pushkin does not judge Silvio as they do.

SEQUENCE 7. CREATING A COMMUNITY OF DISCOURSE

You may have noticed that the sequences I have proposed begin in the classroom and lead through stages to a student's independent and isolated work on a paper. I believe that this is the right pedagogical vector. We often talk about writing for an audience, yet what do we mean? Writing for a composition course is inevitably an exercise and the obvious audience is the teacher. A class can be the audience for its own writing, but only if its members have an understanding of themselves as a community of discourse. You cannot dominate the discussion yourself and then expect the students to write for each other.

Discussions can originate as a rule in the students' own observations (though they need not end there). You can begin by asking an initial question and then simply going around the table, asking each student for a response. This removes the class from the question-answer format with its emphasis on "correctness." I try (when I can remember to do so in the heat of teaching) to ask initiatory questions that invite a broad range of responses. My favorite (the students tease me about it) is, "What struck you in the reading?" There's a place for the simple-minded question in teaching; it opens up a field for exploration without specifying something that the teacher "wants." You can use specific questions to follow up a student's response, sharpen the inquiry, and develop a topic once initiated. (Sometimes it's fun to begin with a silly or trick question to remind the class that play, invention, and surprise are part of intellectual life.)

On days when students have papers due, you can have a lively class with no more complicated a device than asking each student to describe her argument. If members of the class are working on similar or related topics, their accounts will begin to loop in and out of each other, one taking up where another leaves off until they achieve a rich texture of discourse. Best of all, the students will see themselves sustaining a serious discussion and will realize that they form an intellectual community which, taken together, can arrive at more than the sum of its parts. These occasions provide special opportunities for weaker students, who may get pushed aside in the Nature-red-in-tooth-and-claw atmosphere of the daily discussion, but who will have found in work on a paper that they have something to say.

You will discover from time to time that certain students are "hot" on a topic. Encourage them. Give them more time in class. Ask them to make informal reports. Draw them out with questions. Get them to answer questions from other students. It's all the more important to remember to do this with students who have been less active in the class or who seem to lack confidence in their own opinions. Students can sometimes make a point better than the instructor. The class expects the instructor to perform intellectual feats of derring-do, but they doubt that they themselves can. Once, when I had been trying with little success to get students to pay more attention to patterns of detail, one student suddenly caught on to the significance of occult references in Pushkin's *Queen of Spades*. The class was electrified when he read them a draft of his paper. His experience of wonder (in his own powers and in Pushkin's) caught them; they became convinced that they could grapple with Pushkin successfully. Get the student to make an informal presentation before the paper is due. Sketching out his ideas in some detail in an informal report or reading a draft of his paper will allow him to use the class as an audience in earnest. The class response will show him what issues still remain to be addressed, what further information or examples are needed, and where explanations must be fleshed out. When you see several students working on papers that move in the same direction, you can organize a class session around their topics. When we were discussing *Crime and Punishment* in my seminar, two students became interested in the character of Svidrigailov. One identified an interpretive crux: Given that Svidrigailov is an evil and dissolute man, why does the reader feel some sympathy for him? The second student was studying Utilitarianism in his ethics course. He thought that Svidrigailov was the spokesman for certain Utilitarian doctrines. (His was a shrewd guess; the notebooks for the novel show that Dostoevsky did mean to rebut Utilitarian doctrines.) We spent a class session on the character of Svidrigailov, first listening to the two reports and then discussing them. The student who had felt Dostoevsky's ambivalence toward the character steered the other away from a too ideological reading; in turn he helped her to see how the conflict in Svidrigailov's character reaches down into the novel's ideological substratum.

You might assign the class a question for investigation that will call upon their combined resources. In a writing course on "Science as Literature" students may be asked "to take an imaginative leap backward by examining how the absence of some technology we take for granted would change our lives." Students will select a variety of technologies, depending on their interests, but they will arrive at some of the same issues. The question is ideal for generating a class discussion where each person has something particular of her own to say and yet can participate in the whole.

Students too often think of the life of the mind as remote, divorced from their interests, a process that they are not qualified to participate in. Writing, as part of the package, is also set aside for "doing homework." The sequences recommended here have as their aim overcoming the students' alienation from what is, after all, a major part of their lives during their time in college.

WORKS CITED

Entries marked with an asterisk are described in Chapter 8, "A Bibliographical Guide to the Profession."

Berke, Jacqueline. *Twenty Questions for the Writer: A Rhetoric with Readings.* 2nd ed. New York: Harcourt Brace Jovanovich, 1976.

Dyson, Freeman. *Weapons and Hope.* New York: Harper and Row, 1984.

Gibson, James. *The Senses Considered as Perceptual Systems.* Boston: Houghton Mifflin, 1966.

Knoblauch, C. H., and Lil Brannon. "Writing as Learning Through the Curriculum." *College English* 45 (September 1983): 465–74.

Koch, Kenneth. *Wishes, Lies, and Dreams: Teaching Children to Write Poetry.* New York: Vintage Books, 1971.

Larson, Richard. "Discovery Through Questioning: A Plan for Teaching Rhetorical Invention." *College English* 30 (November 1968): 126–34.

*Maimon, Elaine, et al. *Writing in the Arts and Sciences.* Cambridge, Mass.: Winthrop, 1981.

Martin, Harold C., and Richard M. Ohmann. *The Logic and Rhetoric of Exposition.* Rev. ed. New York: Holt, Rinehart and Winston, 1963.

Toulmin, Stephen. *The Uses of Argument.* Cambridge: University Press, 1958.

Wilson, John. *Thinking with Concepts.* Cambridge: University Press, 1963.

3

Classroom Activities

KATHERINE K. GOTTSCHALK

I. TEACHING WRITING IN THE CLASSROOM

No matter how carefully we have planned a syllabus for the semester or the year, day to day in-class activities can present a challenge, whether the course we are teaching is "Expository Prose" or "Art History." How can we implement our goals? What can we do in the classroom *today* with that chapter from our grammar handbook or with that reading assignment? And, of course, teachers of subject matter courses sometimes feel uncomfortable about including discussions of writing in the classroom. Doubting they can successfully do so, they find it simpler to work on short stories or Sibelius and leave the writing instruction to comments on essays and conferences. Even the writing workshop in a composition course can turn into group therapy rather than group writing sessions. There are, however, two important points to remember: 1) Teaching writing need not mean leaving behind sonnet form or Zen or South American politics: we can teach students about our disciplines or themselves by teaching them to write. 2) No matter what subject matter we are using to teach writing, the subject of writing demands classroom time.

A. *Using Course Readings to Teach Writing*

Probably the best way to ensure a person's writing abilities is to arrange that she be born into a reading, writing family. In fact many freshmen arrive at college having read little other than TV captions, magazine picture captions, newspaper headlines, and lead paragraphs. When they read for our classes, they read first sentences of paragraphs without being able to find an essay's thesis or purpose, its governing arguments, its evidence. Take a look sometime at what students underline. Too often they underline either minor points or everything indiscriminately: the pages glow with fluorescent colors, but their minds don't. So we start where we can with our eighteen-year-old freshmen, and we know that to write well students must read. They need to absorb sentence patterns and writing structures for their own conscious or unconscious later use. Teaching students to read well, to be able to analyze what they have read, can move them toward becoming good writers themselves. Furthermore, if our students are writing about what they read, they will certainly write better as they understand the text better.

It's important, then, to use readings in a course, whether from readers or from subject-related materials, not just as sources of information or inspiration, but as texts for teaching students to read closely and as written texts instructive to students as writers. Some students may need to begin at very basic points: for example, can they find transitional sentences, words, and paragraphs in the texts they are studying—and can they find them in their own essays? We can ask students to pinpoint, in class, and out loud, a writer's transitional devices between sections of an essay, and follow work on this particular point or similar ones by having students underline all the transitional words, sentences, and paragraphs in their own or their neighbor's essay (presumably due that period). Obviously, a study of transitional devices in a particular essay can be supplemented on that or a following day by our own favorite handouts on the topic and perhaps by some exercises. This particular topic leads naturally to the question of organization—for instance what the essay's parts are and why they come in the order they do. By the time such study of an essay is completed, students will see how important a writer's transitional devices are if his work is to be understood correctly, and they will see why it is important for them to take similar care with their own work. They will also now be excellently prepared to discuss the writer's argument and ideas, because they will be working with a common, clear reading of the essay, and not, as is too often the case, with a hazy memory of a few of the more striking ideas, or with a completely mistaken notion of what the essay is trying to achieve. If you have a class which needs this kind of work, you will have saved yourself considerable teaching time when you come to direct discussion of ideas and argument.

With many classes it's profitable to look closely at a writer's style. Students may examine style to see what it teaches them about the writer and her ideas—and then consider that principle as they look at their own writing or that of their classmates. They can try to imitate in a sentence, paragraph, or an entire essay the style of Hemingway or of Macaulay. When, and if, you spend time on imitation or on improving style, students can work at home on their own models, or they can take fifteen minutes of class time to do so. These models can then be shared in small groups or can be written on the board where everyone can see and discuss them. (See Chapter 6, ''Understanding Prose,'' for a fuller discussion of this subject.)

Obviously, there's much more we can do with texts as writing examples besides looking at their structure or style. For example, students can also determine what role a writer has chosen for herself (an older, established chemist?), or what role she has assigned her audience (ignorant, lay housewife anxious about pesticides?). How have her choices affected content, organization, diction, syntax? Each teacher, then, needs to determine how to discuss a text as writing in accordance with the needs of the class and the nature of the text. (See Chapter 2, ''Designing a Course,'' Sequence 2, for suggestions on analyzing a text when teaching students to imitate strategies of persuasion.)

With any approach to a text it's a good idea to keep in mind that we are teaching a method. Just as we want our students to learn how to write and revise on their own, so we want them to read well independently. If we don't make them aware of method, they will look only for answers to our questions about a particular text and will be lost when they come to the next one. Some teachers like to distribute study questions with each reading assignment, guilding students to the kinds of issues they ought to address and anticipating trouble spots (easier to do the second time we teach a course, when we ourselves are more familiar with the teaching of a text). Gradually students are encouraged to locate the trouble spots and to come up with questions on their own. It's a good idea to ask students to bring these questions to class—in writing, of course. (For detailed suggestions about ways to encourage students to incorporate writing into their studying, see Appendix 2, Section IV ''Writing as Part of Studying.'')

With the idea firmly in mind that texts can provide either inspiration or warning to our students as they themselves write, we can constantly draw on assigned reading for analogies to our students' writing work. Choose and use texts purposefully, then, balancing the needs of your students as writers with the particular needs of your subject. If possible your students should read some books and articles worth looking at as models for writing. Consider the purposes you have for your texts as you choose and teach them. Will your students read works written only by scholars for scholarly journals? In a poetry course perhaps students can read not just poems but also some critical essays to serve as models for their own work. A science class in a writing-across-the-curriculum program may read newspaper releases and articles in popular magazines as well as textbooks and scholarly essays. Having our students study works written for varying purposes and audiences can enrich their reading abilities and move them toward better conscious control of their own writing. As students learn to read well, to understand what they have read, they will also learn to write well.

Let me illustrate what I have been saying by explaining how I sometimes teach the first six paragraphs of a chapter by Jacob Bronowski. Here are the paragraphs (numbered, for convenience):

1. What is the insight with which the scientist tries to see into nature? Can it indeed be called either imaginative or creative? To the literary man the question may seem merely silly. He has been taught that science is a large collection of facts; and if this is true, then the only seeing which scientists need to do is, he supposes, seeing the facts. He pictures them, the colorless professionals of science, going off to work in the morning into the universe in a neutral, unexposed state. They then expose themselves like a photographic plate. And then in the darkroom or laboratory they develop the image, so that suddenly and startlingly it appears, printed in capital letters, as a new formula for atomic energy.

2. Men who have read Balzac and Zola are not deceived by the claims of these writers that they do no more than record the facts. The readers of Christopher Isherwood do not take him literally when he writes "I am a camera." Yet the same readers solemnly carry with them from their schooldays this foolish picture of the scientist fixing by some mechanical process the facts of nature. I have had of all people a historian tell me that science is a collection of facts, and his voice had not even the ironic rasp of one filing cabinet reproving another.

3. It seems impossible that this historian had ever studied the

beginnings of a scientific discovery. The Scientific Revolution can be held to begin in the year 1543 when there was brought to Copernicus, perhaps on his deathbed, the first printed copy of the book he had finished about a dozen years earlier. The thesis of this book is that the earth moves around the sun. When did Copernicus go out and record this fact with his camera? What appearance in nature prompted his outrageous guess? And in what odd sense is this guess to be called neutral record of fact?

4. Less than a hundred years after Copernicus, Kepler published (between 1609 and 1619) the three laws which describe the paths of the planets. The work of Newton and with it most of our mechanics spring from these laws. They have a solid, matter-of-fact sound. For example, Kepler says that if one squares the year of a planet, one gets a number which is proportional to the cube of its average distance from the sun. Does anyone think that such a law is found by taking enough readings and then squaring and cubing everything in sight? If he does, then, as a scientist, he is doomed to a wasted life; he has as little prospect of making a scientific discovery as an electronic brain has.

5. It was not this way that Copernicus and Kepler thought, or that scientists think today. Copernicus found that the orbits of the planets would look simpler if they were looked at from the sun and not from the earth. But he did not in the first place find this by routine calculation. His first step was a leap of imagination—to lift himself from the earth, and put himself wildly, speculatively into the sun. "The earth conceives from the sun" he wrote; and "the sun rules the family of stars." We catch in his mind an image, the gesture of the virile man standing in the sun, with arms outstretched, overlooking the planets. Perhaps Copernicus took the picture from the drawings of the youth with outstretched arms which the Renaissance teachers put into their books on the proportions of the body. Perhaps he had seen Leonardo's drawings of his loved pupil Salai. I do not know. To me, the gesture of Copernicus, the shining youth looking outward from the sun, is still vivid in a drawing which William Blake in 1780 based on all these: the drawing which is usually called *Glad Day*.

6. Kepler's mind, we know, was filled with just such fanciful analogies; and we know what they were. Kepler wanted to relate the speeds of the planets to the musical intervals. He tried to fit the five regular solids into their orbits. None of these likenesses worked, and they have been forgotten; yet they have been and they remain the stepping stones of every creative mind. Kepler felt for his laws by way of metaphors, he searched mystically for likenesses with what he knew

in every strange corner of nature. And when among these guesses he hit upon his laws, he did not think of their numbers as the balancing of a cosmic bank account, but as a revelation of the unity in all nature. To us, the analogies by which Kepler listened for the movement of the planets in the music of the spheres are farfetched. Yet are they more so than the wild leap by which Rutherford and Bohr in our own century found a model for the atom in, of all places, the planetary system?

What can be done with such a text in a writing course? In a writing-across-the-curriculum program the perspective will certainly differ depending on the discipline: a History of Art course may be interested in the connection between art and science, in the influence of Blake and of the Renaissance image of man; a History of Science class will be concerned with the nature of scientific reasoning. A sociologist may look at group interactions and social values, a psychologist at the nature of creativity and imagination.

But in the context of writing, before getting to the ideas and perspective especially concerning us, we can start by seeing how well our students use the book the selection appears in and how well they can read the passage. The Bronowski selection appears in *The Norton Reader,* so did the students look up the thumbnail biography of Bronowski? When did he live? Is he still alive? Did they watch his TV series, *The Ascent of Man?* Where did the selection come from? Was it an article or part of a book? When was *Science and Human Values* published and for what audience? What does the title suggest about the selection they are reading? Freshmen often have no idea that what they are reading fits into a cultural or historical context. For them a text may have no reality outside the classroom, so we can try to make them put what they read into a real world of ideas and events of which they are part. (They will have to do the same thing with their own prose.)

Knowing that many freshmen are poor or inexperienced readers, I help them learn to read effectively by examining how Bronowski's six paragraphs act as an introduction to the selection. The first paragraph, they can discover, poses questions which announce the subject but not the thesis. The first answer to the posed problem (how does the scientist see into nature?) is wrong; it is the one normally given by the literary man, Bronowski's reader: for this reader, science and literature are of two worlds, one fact gathering, one creative, and it is the scientist who gathers facts—he cannot be creative. In paragraph two, still writing for his literary audience, Bronowski continues to work with the world of literature in order to answer his question: why should what is patently false in one discipline (that writers can be mere fact-gatherers) be true in another, science? Paragraphs three and four narrow in on scientists: did Copernicus (paragraph three), did Kepler (paragraph four), simply gather facts? Paragraphs five (Copernicus) and six (Kepler) answer those questions and define the scientist's method, paragraph five showing that Copernicus imagined, that he found a new perspective from which to view his world; paragraph six that Kepler too imagined, finding like-nesses where none had been imagined before in order to see into nature. The last sentence of paragraph six and of the introduction leads outward into the rest of the essay by analogy to modern scientists, Rutherford and Bohr, to continue the application of the thesis: scientists gain insight into nature through analogy-making, perspective-shifting imagination.

The introduction, then, both announces the thesis and traps its audi-ence into interest and acquiescence. Students can observe that Bron-owski works first with a negative definition, because it is the one more familiar to the audience he has chosen and so the one he must fight. Only after spending four paragraphs questioning the prevalent notion of science as fact gathering does he assert his own opposite and more unusual point of view. Students will notice that, in consideration of his audi-ence, Bronowski chooses two excellent examples to make his point: almost everyone reads about astronomy, and almost everyone is famil-iar with the work and significance of Copernicus and Kepler. But the examples also support Bronowski's proposed theory that everyone, including scientists, learns by imagination. These two figures connect elegantly with modern science, since Rutherford and Bohr used the planetary system as their imaginative analogy for the atomic model. Using our own imaginations as readers, we may wonder for what the atomic model will in turn be a model. Finally, students may notice that in a wide range of references from past to present Bronowski calls up artists, historians, and scientists specifically because he is trying to break down the false dichotomy between science and literature, the false dichotomy with which his introduction begins.

By now students will have noticed that Bronowski does a nice job of writing, and that while their own introductions will have to be shorter, they can profitably imitate him. So point out some other characteristics of his writing. For instance, he uses extensive metaphor and analogy— what we like to call concrete writing. In paragraph one the photographic plate, an image drawn from the sciences, is also a funny one, designedly so, because Bronowski intends to laugh the science-as-fact-collecting view into disgrace: any proper reader will be ashamed to associate herself with it. In the second paragraph, two filing cabinets have a chat, again the false notion of historians and scientists as fact-filing containers; paragraph three conjures up Copernicus with a camera, another silly perspective. Paragraph four imagines Kepler squaring and cubing everything in sight and compares certain readers with electronic brains: neither can make a scientific discovery.

Why, in the first four paragraphs, so many images, so many occasions on which we are asked to see? I don't let my students answer that question with the facile reply that concrete writing is lively and appeals to the reader. The answer is more serious and more important. Bronowski wants to show that the nature of reasoning itself is imaginative. Copernicus and Kepler saw in new ways by using their imaginations, not by gathering data. Bronowski asks us to see, to discard a false, ridiculous vision and accept a truer one, to discover the real nature of a scientist's insight. And Bronowski himself is reasoning with his imagination: He *sees* what Copernicus and Kepler could not have done, he *sees* what they did do, he *imagines* how Copernicus must have imaged the planetary system, and then draws up his own vision, Blake's *Glad Day*. Finally, using Kepler's method, Bronowski makes an analogy between Kepler and two modern scientists, Rutherford and Bohr.

Students may observe, then, that to understand how someone writes may also be to understand what the writer thinks; a good writing style is part of the thought of the writer. With Bronowski we see that metaphors invest his writing because he deeply believes in the metaphoric nature of the universe, in its ultimate harmony: atoms are like solar systems. There are links everywhere he looks. And we see metaphor embedded in his argument because Bronowski believes metaphor is embedded in the process of discovery. Man identifies his imaginative constructs with the outside world. His writing, matter, takes the pattern of his mind, because the pattern of mind and matter is one.

It's probably not worth looking at the structure of an essay unless we conscientiously connect it with a writer's ultimate purposes, his meaning. And style is worth examining only if we find its connection with meaning. If we make this clear as we work with texts, students will absorb the point for their own work: how they write should at every point reflect the audience, the writer's voice, the nature and development of the argument, the nature of the subject.

Occasionally we can take just one paragraph of an essay and give it a thorough going over. In paragraph five, for example, I have my students locate the topic sentence, discuss its transitional function and the abrupt, assertive tone of the negative statement, a relief after all the hypothetical, foolish imaginings. Students can profitably examine sentence length and rhythms ("I do not know") and the transitions between sentences ("His first step," "Perhaps"). They can examine sentence structures, which from study will become available to them: "We catch in his mind an image, the gesture of the virile man standing in the sun, with arms outstretched, overlooking the planets." This sentence beautifully exemplifies how to build a sentence with modifiers; more important, the extension of modifiers with its own shape creates the picture of the virile man extending his vision over the planets. Students can also note the use of viewpoint: it is "we" who catch in Copernicus's mind an image, but it was not "we" who pictured scientists as photographic plates. Bronowski the discoverer emerges with "I" and "to me" when he learns about Copernicus by imagining how he imagined. Finally, if your students know few verbs other than "to be," "to have," and "to use," pick out verbs: found, find, to lift, to put, catch, took, see—all verbs matching the discovery of Copernicus and Bronowski.

At some time during the study of a text students can connect its ideas with their study of writing. Bronowski, for example, sees a false dichotomy between fact gathering and conceptualizing, pointing out that we need both, with the test of what we learn being the real world. Perhaps we can observe a similar false dichotomy between research papers and creative papers. Only at their very worst are research papers just collections of facts, and creative papers not founded in emotional or physical reality don't amount to much either. Perhaps now could be a good time to try using metaphors to explore reality: have students come up with one or two good ones and see what can be learned from them. Can students use what Bronowski says about the nature of discovery when they must write papers or think about the many ideas in the course?

Finally, as teachers we can ask ourselves if we create a false dichotomy by teaching writing as "fact" and teaching music, or psychology, or whatever, as "art." Have we forgotten the embeddedness of one in the other? What joyful leaps and wild speculation can we bring to our own works as teachers? What productive metaphoric links can we forge between anthropology or history or literary criticism and the writing of English prose?

B. Using Student Essays in Class to Teach Writing

We need not, and indeed should not, confine our study of writers to the professionals on our syllabi. We can use the essays our students write. Admittedly, some teachers profess to find using their students' essays embarrassing to themselves and to their students. This embarrassment, however, is often generated by a teacher's own attitude. If a teacher says, "I know hearing other students discuss your essay will make you very uncomfortable and it makes me nervous, too, but we really have to do this," he will have nervous, uncomfortable, resentful students.

If, however, we take as a matter of course that we all need criticism and suggestions because revising is a fundamental operation in writing, that no one learns to sing without taking lessons and giving recitals, our students will generally follow us with the same matter-of-fact attitude. As Frank O'Hare pointed out (at a seminar on "Current Theories of Teaching Composition," Purdue, 1983), we should think of our classes as workshops—art classes in which, of course, everyone works together and shares ideas. We can also remind our students that all writing is for an audience—and that classmates are the first and most helpful audience for what they have written. Through their writing, students can join in intellectual discourse. No real writing goes unread, uncriticized. Naturally, we can make essays anonymous when we want to, but given a good classroom atmosphere students often prefer knowing who the writer is so they can adjust and direct their comments accordingly—they become the real audience of a real writer, and the discussion improves. When not anonymous, the student who wrote the paper has an unambiguous position in the conversation and can openly participate.

It's possible, of course, to find commendable features in the least promising paper. There's always something. Or we can praise with faint damnation: "This student has provided the perfect example of what you're all doing wrong right now, and I'm very grateful to her." (This kind of jocular bluntness works for some teachers but not all—know yourself). We can also point out that the student who gets her essay discussed in class learns the most and will be able to do the best job of revision.

Why do we want to use student essays in class? Because they show students that others like themselves have trouble; they teach students how to revise writing most like their own (as opposed to professional essays, which students can find discouraging); they teach students what to look for, how to look for it, and what to do once they have located it. Student essays can also be used to emphasize issues of writing currently under discussion in class, from semicolon usage to argumentation. And student essays can help students learn how to write on a certain subject matter within a discipline: they can criticize their fellow student's apprehension or misapprehension of a topic or the relationship of function to form.

Once the decision has been made to use student essays in class, choose them with care. Some teachers, following alphabetical order, have students ditto up their own essays and bring them in for discussion, but when essays aren't preselected, you can end up without the needed examples: you'll be working at random. It's probably better to choose for yourself from the latest batch of essays. Just be sure that over the course of the semester everyone has at least one of his or her essays discussed. I mention this because often one or two students consistently come up with the best or worst examples, and it's tempting just to keep using their work. You'll automatically eliminate essays too long to discuss during one class period, but you may pick two or three very short essays or parts of essays that work well together.

Practical considerations about reproducing these essays: If your department will pay for photocopying, photocopy. Black- or white-out the student's name and private comments, or type up a clean copy—if you type fast. (If your students are working on word processors, they can easily provide clean copies.) Typed copies should be doublespaced with wide margins. Our students don't react to crowded, hard-to-read materials any better than we do. Don't worry about typos: correct them and use them as good examples of how to proofread final copies. Do remember to number the paragraphs and lines—numbers eliminate a lot of searching time in class. When dittoing, don't be careless; make sure the copies look good. Learn to use the ditto machine, and, if it's available, the thermofax (which creates instant dittos). The whole thermofax-dittoing process can be faster than photocopying, and, contrary to popular opinion, you *can* keep your hands perfectly clean through the whole procedure.

Be careful about giving students copies of these essays to take home and read in preparation for the next class: half the students, knowing that reading the material will not count toward their final grade and knowing that their "real" homework must get done, may not read the essays and/or bring them back to the next class. Then you still have to read the essays out loud, and in addition students will have to peer over each other's shoulders. If you choose short models, you can read them in class, and get on with the discussion. If the essays are long and students must take them home, try giving an assignment related to the essays which the students must complete and submit for credit so that they'll come back to class prepared.

It's sometimes a good idea to discuss the essays *after* a general discussion of the essay topic and of how students might have written successfully on it. Just as we grade essays better after deciding what a "best" effort might include, our students evaluate model essays better and more efficiently when they begin with some common notion about the topic. For example, if students wrote about the functions of art museums, discuss those functions first, so that the class will recognize good definitions, bad or good arguments, poor evidence, good examples, and so on, when they do get to the model essays. Such prediscussion means that when you turn to the student essays you won't be diverted into discussing what the criteria for an art museum should be while you're supposed to be considering how someone wrote on the subject.

When you turn to the essay, begin by reading it aloud or having a student read it aloud. Of course, everyone can read it silently, but many people feel nervous and rushed if they have to read while feeling that others may be watching them or reading faster than they are. In addition, as Walter Ong has observed, when people read silently, they stop being a group and turn into isolated individuals (11). You'll be working hard to create a discussion group, and may find it hard to recover from that splintering effect. Before reading the essay, give the students suggestions about what to watch for, and then follow up the reading with a discussion of those points. You can also read the essay aloud and discuss it sentence by sentence, but this method tends to be less focussed, and you have to keep summarizing what is going on and noting digressions.

Some good subjects to cover in discussion of student essays are:

The thesis
The beginning and ending
Paragraphs—main idea, development, transitions, order
Rhetorical mode—classification, comparison and contrast, series,
    analysis, description, argument by example, definition
Argument and evidence
Style
Mechanics: usage, punctuation, grammar, use of quotations

Obviously, we rarely, if ever, cover all of these areas thoroughly. As students should check their own essays for all of them, however, it doesn't hurt to have a class habitually check a model essay for most of these areas before settling down to your major concern. In fact, you'll find it hard to stop students from commenting on the mechanics of an essay, and they should indeed learn the importance of proofreading. As Richard Lanham says,

> Spelling mistakes, typos, mistakes in idiom, unfashionable usages, all these characterize you as a writer controlled by language rather than controlling it. You present yourself as still in rompers. It is not a question of being *clear*. These revelations of self don't usually obscure ideas: they obscure you. Worse, they reveal you. They reveal that you have not paid attention to your own writing and invite the reader to respond in kind. They model the history of your mind. (81–82)

So let students have their initial success at criticism by finding the spelling errors, the commas outside the quotation marks. Then get on to more important issues. At least once, however, you could look at a student essay exclusively for its mechanics and follow up the exercise by having the class proofread each other's essays on the day the final copies are due. (Have the proofreader sign his name. Then you get to comment to him on his work.)

If the thesis is your writing topic, you may want to use more than one essay, so that you can compare theses; some teachers regularly type up a whole sheet of thesis statements from a batch of essays as they grade them and use those for discussion. Having students write on the same assignment proves useful here, because they can compare thesis statements more easily. At the same time they can see how professional writers go about making their thesis statements.

When studying the beginnings and endings of essays, students can examine which are most clear and helpful; they can note whether the conclusion follows from the introduction, whether the body of the essay really follows from the first paragraph, whether the conclusion is rich in thought or purely mechanical. Help them discover that a good introduction usually clearly introduces a problem or subject and possibly the approach the writer will take in her article. Help students discover that even a ten-page essay may not need a formal summary of the argument or a formal restatement of the thesis. Especially awful, they should learn, is a word-for-word repetition of the thesis statement that appeared in the first paragraph. You may want your students to summarize and to repeat the thesis; if so they should learn to do so with fresh enthusiasm and wording. No audience thrives on boredom. What makes a conclusion boring or interesting? Are there fresh, concluding ideas, an expansion outward of thought? Is there a final anecdote? What makes an introduction good? Does an essay begin with an example? a question? a quotation? Note good and bad features; turn the students to the professional writing they have been studying to see what published writers actually do.

When studying paragraphing and organization, try selecting two essays on the same topic that use very different methods of organization: have the students figure out the outline for each of these (probably by finding the topic of each paragraph), put the outline on the blackboard, and then discuss the relative merits and disadvantages of the two modes—why did classification work where comparison did not? Have students underline transitions and topic sentences, and note sections of evidence. Was the evidence convincing? See if they can locate digressions or redundant material. Take the time once or twice to type up each paragraph of an essay on a separate page; then have the students see if they can put them back together in the original order, and, if not, why not. If they could, what helped them to do so?

When concentrating on style in a model essay, students can learn or review methods for editing style that they should also use on their own essays. For instance, have them try the paramedic method Richard Lanham describes in *Revising Prose:* direct your students to circle every "is" or "are" (or "was" or "were") and all prepositions. Pick the sentence with the most prepositions and "is" verbs and revise it (the class can do this together or in small groups). Joseph Williams also has a good editing checklist (107–108). For instance, he suggests underlining the endings of sentences—does every sentence end with "the most significant new information"?—and counting the length of the sentences. Again, you can turn to one of the syllabus readings for supplementary examples while you are working on the student essays. You may even provide some bad examples from the syllabus, as well as good ones.

A good way to reinforce the notion that sentences can be revised, and often need to be, is to take five minutes of a class period in which students are submitting finished essays and have them choose one sentence for revision. Take a quick trip around the room, as you can spot these sentences faster than they can, although they should be learning to do so. Have each student revise that sentence, with your help or a neighbor's if necessary. The results can be impressive. However, constant demonstrations to students that even their most finished essay is still unfinished can wear down morale, so don't overwork this particular exercise. After all, revision is most constructive before the student has completed his final copy.

C. Using Class Time to Prepare for Writing, to Write, and to Revise

So far we have been considering work that can be done with finished essays, but class time can also usefully be spent in which students prepare to write, write, and revise.

Inexperienced writers often do not write well unless they really care about a problem and want to write about it. Furthermore, if a specific problem hasn't been assigned, many students don't know how to find one to write about, just as many students don't know how to go about exploring a problem, how to develop and then organize their ideas about it. It's a little unfair to grade and criticize a finished product without ever having taught the student how to create it. Obviously, helping our classes learn to discover problems they care about and to work through them for the essays they must write also helps them learn to think and care about the non-writing subjects of courses.

Another reason to use class time preparing for writing and actually writing is that students shouldn't think of writing as purely product. An essay is like a tree: It starts as a seed and grows slowly; it has to be pruned and shaped once it has reached a certain size; it's a vigorous organism that the student has created and that remains alive for him.

We should help our students see writing as growth. If we look at essays only when they are finished products, it's too easy to view them as wounded or disabled bodies whose injuries will have to be patched up into something only resembling health. But as writers we know that what we write grows and continues growing, that it needs some weeding, some heavy pruning, some light shaping; we also know that we ourselves grow with the growth of what we write. We can use class time, then, to help our students discover that writing is a process and that writing is a way of learning.

While planning ways to help students find and explore problems, keep in mind that we don't all use the same ways of thinking, which means we may want to suggest a variety of exploratory methods. Some students think linearly, logically, in parts and sequences (left-hemisphere thinkers); others think spatially, holistically, in images, metaphorically and by analogy (right-hemisphere thinkers). (If this is news to you, read Ross Winterowd's "Brain, Rhetoric, and Style." Winterowd defines appositional [RH] and propositional [LH] thinkers and the implications for teaching composition.) Try to avoid encouraging and rewarding only the students who most resemble you and who take to your preferred methods, especially since writers can benefit by taking advantage of both kinds of thinking. Also, as you consider how to approach problem-finding and exploration in your classroom, occasionally recall this grim bit of news: researchers in at least one study have found that parents know how to encourage creativity in their children but *do not want to*. Make sure you are not that kind of parent, or teacher.

What can we do to teach our students how to discover and explore a subject? Obviously, in an interdisciplinary or subject-centered writing program, we can teach our students the methods of inquiry characteristic of our disciplines. How does a critic analyze "The Love Song of J. Alfred Prufrock"? How does an historian investigate World War II? What questions do they ask? What problems do they write about, what evidence do they look for, what arguments do they develop? After discussing a problem in an anthropology course, pause a minute at the end of the discussion to review the methods you followed, the kinds of questions asked, the evidence and arguments needed. In other words, help students become conscious of the methods of your discipline, not just of useful answers for the exam or the "right" position for the paper. (See "Devising Sequences" in Chapter 2 for advice about developing this kind of work.) You can then draw analogies between the problem finding and solving you do in normal classroom discussion and analysis of course readings and what your students should be doing on their own. You may very well work through a subject on which the students will write, teaching them how to find and refine theses and giving them suggestions for avenues of exploration. Students can also break into small groups to brainstorm and then share their ideas. At times you may help a class continue the exploration of a problem by actually beginning to write an essay on the blackboard. Let students see you and their peers struggling to find ideas, organize them, and express them. Group writing can work surprisingly well—don't be afraid of trying it occasionally.

If, while brainstorming, students come up with lots of words and fragments relating to a subject, those can go on to the blackboard for examination, to see what categories they might fit into and how those categories can fit together. In other words, a discussion of rhetorical modes can often arise as a natural consequence of analyzing how we think about things—for example, comparison and contrast as a possible method of organization compared with classification, or definition by example. Sometimes you can bring in a list of relevant terms for a topic and have the students try to work them into several possible categories that suggest a thesis.

The ways in which writers can find and explore problems has become a popular topic in articles and textbooks. *Four Worlds of Writing* puts to work the tagmemic method, having a student move through three steps: she first views the situation or problem statically—she describes it; she next views it dynamically—she looks for changes; finally she takes a relative view of the situation or problem—she looks for its field; and as part of this last process she compares it, she looks for analogies and metaphors. In "Paradigms and Problems: Needed Research in Rhetorical Invention" Richard Young describes three other major heuristic procedures: Aristotle's classical topics, which help the writer develop an argument; Gordon Rohman's prewriting method, which "requires that the student keep a journal, practice principles derived from religious meditation, and employ analogy as the primary instrument for probing experience" (38); and Kenneth Burke's dramatistic method, "a pentad of heuristic probes—act, scene, agent, agency, and purpose—for analyzing human motives and motifs in human experience, which, broadly construed, include virtually everything we think and do" (37). The pentad, when "brought to bear on nonlinguistic events . . . serves a function similar to the heuristic frequently used by journalists, the familiar Who? What? When? Where? How? and Why?" (37). (See Chapter 4, "Sequence 2. Following Traditional Rhetorical Divisions," for a description of the pentad at work when students write.) Janice Lauer, in a 1980 survey, found the tagmemic model to be most popular with college teachers, followed by Burke's Pentad and Rohman's pre-writing techniques. "Other procedures mentioned [by those surveyed] included brainstorming, freewriting, Pepper's four root metaphors. Kinneavy's aims and modes, Larson's questions, Gordon's synectics, The Toulmin model, Crosby and Estes' questions, D'Angelo's topics, semantic mapping, cubing, looping, clustering, and Flower and Hayes' problem solving strategies" (136). In other words, if you want them, many formal techniques are available for helping students find and explore topics. (See Chapter 8, "A Bibliographical Guide to the Profession"; Chapter 2, "Designing a Course," Sequence 3, describes work with pre-writing and invention.)

In-class writing itself encourages the exploration of a topic, as it may force a student's writing and thinking machine into operation. The Bard College Institute for Writing and Thinking demonstrates this in its workshops. There, one participant reports, workshop writers may, for instance, listen to a poem read aloud four times; then without looking at the poem they jot down five or six images that come to mind; pick three of the images in some "natural" order and list them; write for five minutes on the first image and its relation to the poem; write for five minutes on the second image; write for five minutes on the third image; write for seven minutes on what common themes their discussions of the three images revealed; and write for about ten minutes on one or more assertions about the poem to which the focused free writing led them. The sections often resolve themselves into an essay: writing (appositional writing at that) becomes learning. The plan can be adapted to many subject matters. When I've tried this method myself (although not using responses to images in a poem), I've found that students are especially pleased with how much they easily think of when they *have* to write. Moreover, they learn that writing can be a way of learning. A good follow-up procedure to the writing is to have students exchange papers with each other and then discuss in groups the ideas beginning to develop.

However you prefer, then, from time to time do some prewriting work in the classroom. It's not time off from World War II or from "real" writing. Your students may cover less material on World War II or on the proper use of the comma, but they'll have learned they can and should think about World War II, and that they need those commas. It's time well spent.

An occasional class period may be devoted to having students write an entire essay to be submitted at the end of the hour. Besides providing practice, the procedure ensures that students get advice about what to do in a situation they'll face constantly for the next four years. Further-more, by looking at their in-class writing, we learn more about our students' writing habits. Some students, for example, write better in class than they do at home, perhaps because they have acquired weird theories about what good writing (revising) looks like, theories they escape only when speed makes unconscious learning take over. So we can reteach them. Other students write impossibly slowly in class and simply need practice and suggestions about how to hurry. At least once students can write an in-class essay they think must be turned in at the end of the hour—but then they actually have to take it home to revise and submit at the next class period. Some students thus learn they can get through a rough draft faster than they thought they could. They also are forced into a rough draft that must be revised (insist that the in-class version be submitted with the final copy).

In-class peer review of rough drafts is a system recommended by many writing teachers to sharpen students' critical and writing faculties. For example, Frank O'Hare (at the Purdue seminar) reported that his students submit rough drafts of their essays to two or more readers for criticism. Each reader enters his comments on a separate sheet of paper, each comment being coded by number to the student's rough draft. Each reader uses a different numbering system (letters or numbers) or a different colored pen. The readers of an essay do not get to see what criticisms other readers made, and the students do not get to argue the criticisms, although they may ask for clarifications. The teacher receives these criticisms with the student's final copy after he has used, at his discretion, the criticism he received; the teacher grades the essay and also the readers for the quality of their criticism. The student may be praised or criticized for his use of the advice he received. Students who bring no rough draft on peer review day receive a zero that counts toward their final grade. Otherwise the whole system can break down.

Many teachers who use peer review find that, as might be expected, students don't help each other very much at the beginning of the semes-ter. After all, they're inexperienced writers, and even more inexperienced teachers. But as we also know, teaching a subject can be the best way of learning it, and if we supply our students with well-planned guidelines, handouts, for instance, that list the questions they should ask and answer as they evaluate each other's work, students have a better chance of learning the principles (whatever they are) that we are trying to teach them about writing than they would simply by writing and rewriting their own essays. It's easier to see someone else's strengths and weaknesses than our own.

Again, peer review time is not time badly spent away from the other material of a course. Students learn to judge critically the ideas of their peers, as these ideas appear not just fleetingly in classroom discussions but in writing, where, for whatever they are worth, they remain fixed and easily arguable. Being critical of what they read is a practice most students desperately need to learn. In addition, students discover that it's not just the teacher who is fussy or who stubbornly won't understand or appreciate their essays. Peer review drives home the point that when we write we have only words with which to persuade—no hand waving, no understood leaps of agreement—and that all writing really has an audience. The more seriously a student takes her writing, the more seriously she will take her ideas and her subject.

In the following list, Steven Youra (Director of the Writing Program in Cornell's Engineering College) and I have summarized some methods for encouraging students to revise rough drafts (or to produce them), and to revise what they have considered to be "final" copy. The list suggests work that can occur in or out of class, although almost all of it should receive in-class attention; and of course these suggestions can and should be tailored to the particular needs of a course. Most are designed to inspire students who have limited notions about what revising means, who start with the idea that rewriting means changing a few words, or perhaps (at most) adding a paragraph somewhere.

ELICITING AND GUIDING REVISION

SOME PREPARATORY EXERCISES

STUDYING ROUGH DRAFTS

Help students to study rough drafts of professionals and of their fellow students, naming goals and identifying strategies to achieve those goals.

Revise or rewrite an entire (short) student essay with your students. This is invaluable work to undertake in the classroom. The job can be accomplished at the blackboard, but it's made immeasurably easier and more effective if you use a projector connected to a wordprocessor. (If you have access to a classroom so equipped, Appendix I on "Computers and the Teaching of Writing," Section III, offers excellent general advice about teaching and sharing the revision process and specific advice about in-class use of projectors for revision work of many kinds.)

[Beginning writers often work with a limited array of possibilities. These activities introduce them to new options.]

STYLE STUDY

Ask students to imitate and parody individual sentences drawn from professional writing; discuss the strategies used in the original sentences, and attempt to develop vocabulary for such discussions.

[This work may make strategies (parallelism, for example) more accessible to students at conscious and unconscious levels.]

Pick samples of sentences from student essays to discuss in class. (a) Work with students to rewrite the sentences. (b) Have students write imitations of the rewritten, improved sentences, if the example demonstrates a useful principle. (c) Have students completely rewrite—paraphrase—the new "correct" sentence.

[In other words, move students past locating error to producing correct and effective sentences themselves; help them look beyond one "correct" choice to various possibilities, based on subject, audience, persona. Of course, paragraphs work as well as sentences for this exercise.]

Ask students to rewrite a paragraph or essay using an extended metaphor.

[This work stimulates new thinking and demonstrates relationships between formulation of language and formulation of concepts.]

DUPLICATION EXERCISE—STYLE & STRUCTURE

Students read a paragraph closely and then try to write down an exact copy of the paragraph without looking at it; they then check to see how close they got to the original version.

[Students may notice how their own voice differs from that of the original, and they may notice what stylistic choices were unfamiliar or

uncomfortable. They can also check the accuracy of their reading; good discussion can arise from comparisons of a student's choices with those of the author.]

SCRAMBLING EXERCISE

Have students type out the sentences of a short essay or of a paragraph individually and out of order. Can they rearrange them? Do some sentences repeat each other? Do the transitions help the student locate the correct order? Are the sentences all of the same structure or length? Should some be combined?

[By decontextualizing each sentence, this scrambling process can help students re-see both the phrasing of individual sentences and larger aspects of the essay.]

WORKING WITH ROUGH DRAFTS

QUESTIONING THE THESIS

Have students list objections to the thesis of a classmate's essay (with or without reading the entire essay). Then they may write rebuttals and / or talk about the criticisms with each other. Further work on the essay follows.

[Students too often simplify their ideas, letting theses (habitually, theses with three supporting points) dominate their thinking about an essay. Any exercise such as this that can help interest them in fruitful ambiguity, and in complexity, and that can make the audience real, will be beneficial.]

ENRICHING THE ARGUMENT

After students read only the first paragraph of a classmate's essay, they describe two or three points they expect the essay to develop.

After they select one or two paragraphs from a classmate's essay, students expand, modify, or rewrite by adding examples / evidence.

Further investigation: Between drafts, students research contexts, such as an author's biography; other work by the same writer; other versions of the same subject; the social / historical climate in which their subject first appeared; and so on.

[These suggestions are designed to stimulate new thinking, rather than mere tinkering with existing ideas.]

RETHINKING THE ARGUMENT OR THESIS

Ask students to select from their rough drafts one or two paragraphs they consider to be the most important. Then have them throw out everything else and begin again. Or students may make these choices for each other—or make the choice yourself for each student.

[Sometimes "best ideas" occur in the last paragraph or somewhere else along the way. But often students get committed to the three-point thesis they announced in the first paragraph. It's hard to learn to throw out that first paragraph or that thesis and to refocus an entire essay— and then refocus again. This exercise can teach students to do this stressful, but fundamental, rewriting.]

Ask students to throw out the two weakest paragraphs of a draft and then rewrite or revise as necessary. Again, students may make these choices for each other.

[The shape of the essay may change when students are forced to reconsider their aims, their arguments. As above, this exercise forces students to generate new ideas, to look with fresh eyes at their argument or thesis. The changes may not elicit improvements, but they may inspire new thinking. And students may learn what more experienced writers know: that while it's hard to throw out big chunks of material, it's often necessary. More important, revision often means not just changing diction for ornamental purposes but examining ideas and how they are connected. Both exercises may also work with a "finished" essay: even good writing can be better.]

ORGANIZATION EXERCISES

Have students extract the gist of each paragraph. Do the "gists" form a coherent paragraph summarizing the essay the writer envisioned? Then encourage manipulation and examination of the gists to elicit a new format for the essay. Students rewrite the essay on the basis of this new summary. In preparation for this assignment students can practice extracting gists from essays or any written materials being studied for the class to see how they form summaries of the essay. Or have students write extracts.

[This exercise forces students to re-examine the rationales for the organizations they have chosen, and to experiment with conscious possibilities rather than relying on instinctive "flow."]

After students have completed an essay, ask them to compose two alternative versions of the introductory or concluding paragraphs, any one of which could be the "right" choice.

[To overcome the notion that any essay has a single "right" approach; to wean students from over-reliance on habitual strategies.]

Students write their essay's thesis on a separate sheet of paper. Then they should actually hold that thesis next to each paragraph in their essays to see how the paragraph contributes to the thesis.

[Though less effective with long essays, this exercise encourages students to make explicit how the parts relate to the whole.]

READING ALOUD

Require students to read their own rough drafts aloud before writing the final version; have students read each other's drafts to each other.

[Reading out loud often clarifies problems of phrasing or diction. It doesn't do as much for problems of thesis or logic.]

WRITING ABOUT REWRITING

When students revise essays, require them also to submit a paragraph or two in which they describe the goals of their revisions and the strategies they used to achieve those goals.

[A consciousness-raising exercise.]

ESSAY ASSIGNMENTS THAT TEACH NEW STRATEGIES

IMITATION EXERCISE

Students write an imitation of an exemplary essay, using their own subject matter but mimicking structure and / or style of the professional example.

[By asking students to rewrite another's polished work, this exercise may raise awareness of their own voices and introduce discussion of conventions within the discipline.]

SHIFTING EXERCISE

Ask students to rewrite an entire essay (or rewrite a paragraph from a reading or another student's text)—

using a new organizational strategy,

addressing a new audience,

assuming a different voice (for example, assuming you still have the same point of view, imagine that a member of the opposition is your roommate / colleague / teacher / boss)

arguing the other side (and then perhaps combining the two essays, granting points to the opposition).

[This exercise again can help force students to move beyond unconscious choice and deliberately examine new possibilities, to explore the organizing principles suggested by their subject rather than imposing a predetermined or habitual style or structure, e.g., chronology.]

COLLABORATIVE ESSAYS

Have students write essays together. Students report informally to the reassembled class; or they write reports on the collaborative process; or they submit the individual rough drafts with which each began the collaboration; or they write together and then go off to complete the process on their own; and so on.

[Students can learn how to rewrite from each other; they provide alternative organizations, facts, theories, theses, stylistic choices, and so on; they practice the close reading process crucial to rewriting.]

Divide the class into groups of four or five students. Give each group a copy of the same two-page essay to revise. Instruct groups to spend the class hour rewriting together (one student in each group should act as secretary). At the end of class, collect the results; duplicate these and, in the following class session, students can discuss the differences in strategy and outcome.

[This work will demonstrate how an essay can be revised in a variety of ways (more or less successfully). Students who have argued for various choices may care more about which ones are better.]

———

As students become more advanced, they can exchange "finished" essays in order to revise them, in class or at home. (Students find this job easier and more enjoyable if they have written their essays on word-processors.) Grade each student on the revised essay she submits—which was, of course, originally her neighbor's work. This exercise is fun and has amazingly good results. It's also an important exercise: in their future jobs these students may have to take responsibility for what someone else wrote.

Remember that you are teaching students to revise and that you are probably bucking their long held superstition that writing is muse-inspired, that once a sentence has been written down it is sacred. The more revising exercises you engage in and the more interesting you and your students find them, the more their writing will improve.

D. Using Class Time for Grammar and Other Exercises

Correcting essays usually informs us about how much work students need on mechanics, grammar, and other editing concerns. If a handbook has been assigned, we can hope our students will use it. As the handbook may not be clear, inclusive, or convincing enough by itself, however, we may need to spend class time going over certain topics.

A good way to choose classroom topics is to collect sample sentences or chunks (groups of sentences) from students' essays as you grade them. Perhaps you'll notice that half the class doesn't know how to use semicolons or that many students have trouble with fragments. Keep a ditto sheet in your typewriter as you grade (or use your word processor's resources), and every time you hit a sentence good for class analysis, type it down. Students take a real interest in sentences hot from their essays; they know the problems are real. Some teachers recommend working on problem areas only with the students actually having the problems, as you might possibly teach mistakes to students who wouldn't otherwise have thought of the wrong or less preferred way of doing something. If you see this as a problem, take the group needing help off to one part of the room, and get the other students into another interesting project—perhaps a discussion they must lead once you've finished with your group.

Generally, however, close attention to sentences helps everyone. Students enjoy beginning a class period by revising a sentence or a chunk written on the board or distributed on dittos. With a chunk you can get into structural and stylistic questions: are the lengths and rhythms of the sentences suitable for the subject? should the ideas be subordinated? combined in longer sentences? should the main clause begin or end a sentence? are the transitions between sentences adequate? You can also spend five minutes having students imitate a particularly striking sentence from one of the reading assignments for the day and then compare their efforts on the board. Or take a long sentence from one of the day's readings, break it down into unit sentences of three or four words, and have the students see if they can recombine it back into its original shape. (Notice that students will be prepared for a discussion of style when they get to the day's reading.) Or share with the class a fine piece of writing one of the students achieved and figure out why it works so well. Let your imagination and the needs of the class guide you. Students can learn a great deal in five or ten minutes of concentrated attention to writing, and you will have the pleasure of seeing that close attention reflected in their own writing.

You may decide to supplement your sheet of student sentences needing work with exercise sheets that you make up and with assignments in a handbook (handbooks usually include exercises: see Chapter 8, "A Bibliographical Guide to the Profession"; see also exercises and suggestions for exercises in Chapter 7, "Improving Sentences"). Other teachers are one of the richest sources of inspiration: if you talk regularly with colleagues, you get fresh ideas for solving problems, and you can share good exercises with each other.

Most students pay scant attention to corrections made on their exercises, and in any case we often have too little time to grade them carefully. But grades aren't the point: the goal of exercises is improvement. Therefore, when exercises have been assigned, whether on the semicolon, quotation marks, sentence coordination, or whatever, it's often most efficient, and most effective, to have the class correct them. (Students learn more if they correct their own work, not a classmate's.) Go around the table or call on people so that everyone must give answers and get their misunderstandings cleared up. When students have created new sentences, these probably ought to go up on the board for visual examination.

Students often find it more stimulating and informative to do the exercises in class rather than at home, and better yet in small groups. They then put some of their exercises on the board and discuss interesting solutions or peculiar misunderstandings. When handbook reading has been assigned, five minutes at the beginning of class can be spent having students do a bit of writing or a short set of exercises to show what they have learned. Check these at home or on the spot, or have students check each other's.

Sometimes I turn these five minute checks into spot quizzes that I do grade. As I point out, my students expect to memorize math formulas and French vocabulary, and they can expect to memorize some basic vocabulary and rules for my class, too. Why should I repeat all semester that a comma goes inside a quotation mark or that the active voice is usually preferable to the passive? Students can memorize our dearest principles: "Don't dangle participles!" (By the way, the vocabulary problem is serious—students may not know what a participle is, let alone how to avoid dangling one. Locate the level at which your students are working. Fortunately, these educational lacunae often come to light during hands-on work in class.)

Be warned that most students will resent, and rightly so, whole classes devoted to grammar or mechanics. They know, and indeed should know, that these are editing matters, to be cleaned up during the writing process or in editing sessions. Class time should be spent on them only when a problem becomes intrusive enough for the group as a whole to justify that time. But insist that your students recognize their responsibility to these editing concerns. Faulty agreement between a pronoun and its antecedent is no more acceptable than $1 + 1 = 3$ in a genetics problem. A biology professor does not expect to find adding mistakes, and he will penalize his students for them: students know they have to check the mechanics of the genetics problem carefully. Similarly, our writing students should learn to proofread their essays so that the reader can keep her attention where it belongs. They must learn to blame themselves if their teachers turn into editors rather than readers of their essays.

So, use class time as you must to teach your students the mechanics they need in order to edit. Assign exercises enough so that they will know what to watch for and what to do once they've spotted it. Students with severe problems not manageable in class should come in for private conferences with you and possibly should do some individual assignments. Your college's writing workshop may be able to provide additional remedial assistance.

How can we teach organization? transitions? argument? Rather than here offering many specific solutions for each kind of problem, I have suggested that we use the experiences students can have in the classroom with course readings, with essays other students have written, with their own ideas, and with the variety of exercises we can provide. No one method works for everyone, or for anyone all the time. Many methods work and many are needed because people learn differently, and in fact learn best when they have learned in a variety of ways, from their hands to their head, as Thoreau says. You can never rest on one solution: you won't want to, and the classroom situation won't allow you to.

II. SUGGESTIONS FOR THE NEW WRITING TEACHER

A. *In the Classroom*

ENSURING A GOOD CLASSROOM ENVIRONMENT

Before teaching anyone anything, we have to make sure our students stay awake—and at almost any time of day they may feel like going to sleep. It's 8:00 a.m. and they went to bed at 3:00 a.m., or it's 1:00 p.m. and they've just had lunch, or it's 12 noon and they've been going to classes steadily since 8:00 a.m. Our students may be so intensely interested in our subjects and find us so fascinating that staying awake will never be a problem for them. But don't count on it. Here are some tips.

Make sure your room is well lit. Teachers often neglect to pull up the shades or turn on the lights, or both, and unwittingly create a soothing atmosphere perfect for falling asleep. Be equally sure to open up windows if the room is overheated, as it often will be. It's better to have a student hopping up and down adjusting a window that lets in too much cold air than to have everyone undistracted but somnolent.

Try keeping everyone moving, physically, including yourself. Many teachers, of whom you may discover yourself to be one, come alive when they get on their feet, and sometimes your students do, too. On a sleepy day think up reasons to get your students to the blackboard where they can be actively involved. While you are leading a discussion, walk around the classroom. Students who have to keep track of your whereabouts are more alert. Try to use the blackboard at least once in every class period. It's amazing how seriously students take anything written on the blackboard: they immediately pay close attention, and whatever you have written down they copy into their notes.

On the other hand, if you turn your back on your students and take work at the blackboard as an excuse to look no one in the eyes, your students will feel free to close theirs. Eye contact, with every student, not just the favored few, is a major way of making each student feel important. How you direct your eyes and position your body can tell students a great deal (even if unconsciously, both for you and them) about whom you like, whom you don't, who you think is a good student, on whom you have given up. Do you always face one group? One student? Do you look at the same person every time after you've asked a question? Are you afraid your lesson plan is no good, and do you therefore look at no one?

When you talk, notice whether everyone can hear you easily and whether you have an interesting voice. We've all had professors who spoke in monotones but so eloquently that the monotone didn't matter. If you're convinced you're that eloquent, go ahead with the monotone. (Get a friend to sit in on your class sometime. Often we hear ourselves as more—or less—lively or persuasive than we actually are.) On the other hand, don't confuse a loud and lively voice, and great jokes, with good teaching. Your ultimate success as a teacher and your own satisfaction with yourself depend on how completely you and your students engage with texts and problems. The goodwill you win with funny stories is nothing compared to that which students feel after they have written a really fine sentence or deeply concerned themselves with the problems of *Othello*. The energy of commitment, yours and theirs, will serve the entire class best.

Another way to keep a flagging class alert and involved is to vary the pace and type of activity. If you always follow exactly the same pattern, you and your students may find yourselves getting bored. Even for one class hour it can pay to plan a variety of activities or at least have them in mind in case you find your one planned activity going badly. For example, you can both discuss an essay and do some writing exercises; and when you discuss an essay, you don't always have to ask the same questions about it. Discuss style, discuss structure, discuss content or argument; ask the students to come up with questions; get their personal reactions to the essay. If you must repeatedly concern yourselves with the same issues, find new formats for addressing them.

About those 8:00 a.m. classes. Attendance can be a problem, but good attendance is important. Sympathize with your students about the agonies of getting up so early, but take roll ostentatiously if attendance starts dropping. Occasionally give a quiz during the first five or ten minutes and count it toward the final grade. Lock the door at five past. (I've never actually done this, but I know someone who does—it takes a special type!) Give dirty looks, if you can do so effectively without undermining class spirit. Some classes solve the problem of getting up early by gradually beginning later and later, with the teacher arriving as late as the class. Don't let this happen. Occasionally, if everyone is really tired, take a collection and buy coffee. Or improve morale by bringing in a dozen doughnuts to share—people think better once they've had some food. In some classes students take turns bringing in food so that everyone looks forward to croissants with their conversation. I used to feel guilty about this kind of catering to my students, but Cornell's Marvin Glock, professor emeritus of educational psychology, points out that people can get on to higher level, cooperative work only when their basic needs have been satisfied. At 8:oo a.m., coffee and doughnuts may be a basic and insistent need.

LEADING A DISCUSSION

Much of our classroom success—how well our students stay alert and learning—depends on how we lead discussions. (Composition classes at their best are discussion classes; no suggestions for lecturing appear in this chapter.) A well-led discussion is usually a well-planned one, and most of us can't plan a discussion successfully while we're on our feet leading it. It pays to have a head start if you're new at the business or have never taught the materials before. Planning a discussion can be very much like organizing an essay: You have to decide which problems you want to consider, which ones aren't important, what your goals are, and what organization you prefer. Since you are leading a discussion, however, you won't be able to type out the text for the day; you'll want a series of canny questions to ask.

But do not depend on your native wit to inspire you with these questions as you face the class. Inspiration may not arrive, especially at first, and you'll find yourself asking. "Well, what do you think about this?" Your students may not have thought, and their own spur-of-the-moment inspirations may not be worth much more than your question. Have your goal in mind or your areas of interest and develop a whole series of questions to elicit the kinds of discussion you want. For example, if your topic is structure, ask how many parts the essay has and what the transitions are between the parts; if you are studying introductions, ask why the text begins with a certain statement. If you want a general discussion, you may ask "What is really at stake in *Bleak House?*" but if you are feeling more specific about the answer you want, ask "In what ways is personal freedom central to *Bleak House?*" or even, "*Bleak House* is filled with threats to personal freedom. What are some of these, and what—if anything—do they have in common?" You can always jumble up the order of the questions you have planned, create new questions, and scrap any number of the old, if the class and you begin some inspired exploration, some genuine thinking through of a problem. Be especially careful to avoid having students guess the "right answer" you want. When this starts happening, it means either that your questions are too specific and "yes" or "no" oriented or that you are not responsive to answers that don't correspond exactly with what you had in mind. You'll notice at once when this situation arises. Once you notice, change it.

It pays, then, to prepare material well, to decide what students ought to learn and to keep those purposes in mind throughout the class. We're far less apt to lead discussions successfully when we have fuzzy goals and ill- or unprepared methods for achieving them.

In discussions, *call on people*. If some students are too shy to talk, try having them read aloud. (Don't always appropriate for yourself the fun of reading aloud, by the way. Students often enjoy that easy way of participating, and later they'll feel comfortable talking. Occasionally you may even have students prepare selections to read at the next meeting. You can also use this system as an easy way of finding out which students have reading handicaps.) Most students, even if they don't respond well the first time they are called on, will try to redeem themselves later in the class period, and so you have a new participating person. *Don't* wait until half way through the semester to start calling on people. That's too late. If you've told students that class participation counts and if you call on them all regularly from the start, they'll resign themselves to paying attention and participating and you'll all have a better time.

A tempting situation we all labor to avoid is conversing only with the two most fascinating people in class. The other students won't be as fascinated. This situation easily arises, however, if a class includes some strong, talkative personalities, and if we haven't the courage to call on the more timid souls. Students will seldom let us know just how much they dislike being cut out of class discussion or not being helped to enter it, but they will be resentful nevertheless. We may think everyone is happy with the status quo, but we learn differently when our course evaluations turn up acid comments about students who dominated the class and our inability to control the situation.

Personalities should not, in any case, dominate discussions. The joy of a good discussion is the submission of personality to the exploration of a topic, so help everyone become part of that exploration. In your role as discussion leader encourage students to respond to each other, rather than always to each other through you as mediator; politely turn aside or put off until later contributions or questions which are inappropriate; respond honestly to poor contributions—but find something good in them when you can—and always, always, listen to what each student says: respond with more than a glance of despair or a ''hmm,'' and try to weave each student's remarks into the total shape of what the class is creating.

USING SMALL GROUPS

In discussion classes it's not necessary to work with the entire group all the time. From time to time a class can work in groups of three or four people. Small groups are advantageous in that students have to talk, work out ideas with each other, and then share their ideas and argue about them with the other small groups. All groups can have the same project to work on, or topic to discuss, or each may have different problems.

Students working in smaller groups sometimes have to be bullied into taking proper advantage of the situation. Tell them to move their chairs so that they can see each other (students are very shy about moving chairs—they're afraid to make noise and to leave their chosen spot at the table). Then after a few minutes insist on noise; whispering students won't get much done, but at first students refuse to believe it's OK to talk out loud all at once. Leave the room for five minutes so that everyone can get relaxed and unselfconscious. But then circulate and find out if each group is really accomplishing what it ought to. (Don't get stuck on one group's problems.) Set a time limit and mean it. And get feedback from each group. If you run out of time in one class period, make sure that in the next you hear from the small groups that didn't report before. If you don't, the activity may not be taken seriously next time. Furthermore, if a group worked hard, it deserves your attention. If each group has to write its results on the blackboard, you get hard evidence of what work was done, better work done, and good material for discussion.

What projects work well in small groups? If you have culled sentences needing revision from student essays, have each group work on revising one or two and then put the results on the board. If each group works on the same sentences, you can compare and argue over the results. If you've given the groups a student essay to criticize, have one group comment on its organization, one on its grammar and mechanics, one on its argument. Or have students break into groups to work on one of your discussion topics—they're apt to argue for their own ideas when you reconvene. Have small groups work out possible new paper assignments or decide what the group should discuss, and then in both cases you can talk about essay topics, about theses, about how they ought to be reading and thinking as they prepare themselves for your class discussions. You'll come up with plenty of ideas for using small groups on your own, once you get used to them, and if you like them.

LETTING STUDENTS TEACH

If you haven't taught before, you'll soon discover, as everyone does, that one of the best ways to learn anything is to teach it. What you teach you rarely forget. Take advantage of this wisdom by encouraging students themselves to be the teachers. Students can effectively lead discussions, present reports, teach the use of quotation marks, or anything else your imagination suggests will be helpful. Many students become more active, committed participants in a class once they have taught it. (See Sequence 7, "Creating a Community of Discourse," in Chapter 2.) You may also discover what students don't know that you thought they did. For example, I once thought my students, if warned in advance, were well prepared to read aloud and explain Browning's dramatic monologues. But when they actually read aloud I discovered that they still could not assess the speaker's personality and follow the unfolding of the dramatic situation. Other students, hearing "My Last Duchess" read aloud badly by a peer, were able to analyze what had gone wrong and learn how to think about the poem. Had I read aloud myself and led the discussion of the poem, I'd never have discovered these fundamental problems.

If you do have students teach, be sure everyone gets a chance, however brief, in front of the classroom. Give students adequate time to prepare, and let them know the work counts toward their grade. You, yourself, must prepare for the class as if you were going to teach it as usual. If you don't, you'll judge less well the quality of what the student teacher does, and you won't be able to leap in and save the class should the student do a poor job.

B. Working with Individual Students

KEEPING RECORDS

A registrar's class list does not itself tell you everything you may want to know about your students, so in the first class you might have them turn in answers to a few questions about themselves: find out for whom English is a second language, who knows three languages, who plans to be a novelist, who hopes to build bridges and never touch a pen again. You may learn something helpful by inquiring about what they hope to get out of the course or what they consider to be their major writing problems. In answering these questions, students will try to please you, so solicit honesty. Certain things you may learn in conferences, if you remember to ask about them and can do so tactfully, but you may not have conferences with some students until well into the semester, and this kind of information can be important earlier.

Students, by the way, rarely resent your efforts to get to know them. Writing courses are often the only small discussion classes freshmen take, and you may be the only teacher to know a student personally. The freshman year is a traumatic one, and many students will appreciate your attention. Even if they don't appreciate it, their parents will if you're the only faculty member close enough to a student to notice when he gets into trouble. (Find out what student services your school provides and keep a list of them handy.)

There are many "best ways" to keep records on your students. I myself prefer a looseleaf notebook with a separate page for each student. At the top of the page I list the student's name, her major, her year, her native language and other languages she knows, and anything else worth remembering. I leave space at the top of the page to enter two or three lines about every conference, describing what we had to say and what the student will probably expect me to remember. On this page I also record the grade for each of the student's essays, its subject, the gist of what I said to the student, and what I said to myself privately. Such a sheet is invaluable for a number of reasons: when I look it over before grading each new essay, I remember to take into account the fact that the student just spent two weeks having flu, or that while the organization of this essay may be poor, at last Jean successfully worked out a good thesis. The record sheet is obviously a time saver when it comes to conferences, because I can spot at a glance the major problems we ought to discuss and can remember the personal details that may help make the student more comfortable—the professor knows and remembers her. Good records also help when it's time to write recommendations.

Detailed records come in handy for emergencies, such as a student's challenging your grade or the help you have given her. If you have recorded the fact that you called in a student for conferences three times but that she never came in, you can point this out when once again she produces an essay with the same problems the earlier ones had. You can remind her that she was told to work on certain exercises. In the cases of a student who fails because he didn't attend classes or turn in work you will have an accurate record, should he complain to other authorities, of just when you told the student he was failing and what procedure for recovery he was supposed to follow (but didn't). Having a visible record that you did the best you could will, moreover, keep you from worrying unduly or feeling guilty about how you handled the student.

Some instructors save all the papers their students hand in. Looking over all previous papers before you grade the next has obvious advantages, and you won't have to worry about remembering what you said to each student. The disadvantage is for the student: she doesn't have access to her work and your comments when she begins her next writing. And you have to keep track of or carry around all those essays.

If you keep your students' essays, you should save them for at least a semester after the course is over. You should certainly keep a record of their grades for at least that long, if not permanently. Get your grades in to the college registrar or your department on time, and, if you go away for vacation immediately after getting them in, let the department secretary know where you can be reached in case of unforeseen complications.

CONFERRING WITH STUDENTS

My first advice is to not use up all your time—which is undoubtedly scarce anyway—with the kind of conference whose major function is to prove you are the student's friend or relieve the guilt you feel about not correcting essays impeccably or teaching brilliantly. Your time will be better spent planning your next class or thinking about how to write comments.

If you like spending extra hours with your students and have time to do so, fine. You don't need to. My own experience and the advice of excellent writing teachers have convinced me that we can do much if not most of our teaching in the classroom and in our comments on the essays. So use the conferences to supplement classroom work and paper grading, not to take their place because you dread teaching writing in the classroom or can't make yourself clear in your comments.

How many conferences should you have and what should you do in them? Have as many as a student reasonably needs—and this varies from none to ninety, although two a semester seems like the bare minimum to most teachers—and as many as you have time and sanity for. As I've indicated above, students appreciate a show of personal concern for their work, and their lives; the freshman year is a rough one. In addition, writing is a terribly exposing process. Your students will often be afraid. They need reassurance that error is a normal and necessary part of every writer's process, that they are having growing pains and that you are helping them grow—that they are not just wounding themselves each week for you to practice applying bandages.

Of course you can and should use the conference to address individual problems that don't belong in a class. If a student seems stuck, examine a first draft together to locate the root of the problem and help the student succeed with his next essay. Look over a group of the student's essays to locate and analyze strengths and weaknesses. Discuss the topic of a forthcoming paper so that the student can develop and explore ideas. Give a private lesson on uses of the semicolon. Some of my best conferences (although not my shortest ones) take place when a student brings an essay on disk into my office, where I have a Macintosh. We then actively go over her draft: I can insert comments that record the gist of our conversation; under my guidance she can write and revise, gaining confidence in her abilities through concrete results. And then she goes away with a project that looks promising, not with the vaguely recalled conversation and illegible marginal notes that occasionally seemed to be the only remaining traces of collaboration for the students in my "pre-Mac" days. The writing-together conference especially helps students for whom the essay seems to be an alien medium of expression and who need to observe and imitate ways to think through a question, gather evidence, introduce a topic, or connect paragraphs.

An alternative or supplement to the one-to-one conference can be conferences with groups of three or four students. Students come to these meetings prepared to comment on rough drafts of papers, copies of which they have shared with each other in preparation. There are obvious advantages to group conferences: you can see more students more often; students participate more freely and comment more openly and helpfully in the intimate setting; and students prepare unusually carefully for a "class" this small. The exchange of ideas is often excellent, especially if you use your role as moderator with tact.

Prepare for conferences: cherish both your time and your student's. Look over your records and know what you'll need to do. Make sure the student knows, too: it's annoying when a student turns up for a conference but has failed to bring in the essay you planned to go over with him—or when, worse yet, you left his essays at home. If you have trouble saying goodbye at the end of a conference, go to your department office for your mail or to the restroom. The student will disengage himself on your way there.

WORKING WITH DIFFICULT STUDENTS

If you were simply lecturing, your only worries, aside from preparing the lectures, would be the occasional flea-chewing dog or snoring, hungover student. When leading a discussion, however, you must not only plan that more complicated event but be ready for the problem students whom discussions stir up. For example, one talkative student may try to dominate a discussion if you haven't thought about how to draw out the other less-assertive members of the class. Or, even if you are good at drawing out those quieter students, one student may still insist on dominating and interrupting. What do you do then? I try two solutions: the first is to smile at the interrupting student while saying, with upraised hand, "Not now, I need to hear from James"—and I persist in not letting the student speak when I really want to hear from

James. If this method doesn't take, I catch the student outside of class and, after expressing great admiration for her enthusiasm and ideas, ask her to help me get those other students into the discussion by being careful to give them a chance. This usually takes care of the situation. Another kind of problem student is the one who uses the class period to talk to his girl friend or the other guy on the football team. My solution here is simple. Whenever whispered conversations start, I stop conducting the class. I don't say a word until I have the attention—or at least the silence—of everyone.

Which leads us to another kind of problem student, the sleeper. He stays up late every night and sleeps late every morning, in class. This one I call into a conference where I express concern for his well-being and suggest he get a good breakfast and a big cup of coffee before starting the day. Then I pester him a bit in class, perhaps asking a question as he's about to drop off. Another solution is just to let such students sleep on, but in a small class, one slow snore alters the atmosphere.

And finally there is the student who isn't appearing for your class but should be. Don't let absence after absence accumulate without taking action. Most colleges require class attendance, and for good reason: a large part of the learning in a writing course takes place in class. Students must appear there in order to learn. You may want to announce your own policy about class attendance and how it will affect grades. When a student attends erratically or not at all, send him a note or call him up; give him formal notice of the effect on his work and on his course grade. See if the student is having a problem that someone—a dean or advisor—ought to know about.

Most of these suggestions about how to handle difficult students simply involve bothering to think a problem through and then doing something about it: you'll find your own solutions without much trouble. You have had a lot more experience than your students, and you also have a lot more authority. In any case, usually students who create problems are fairly naive. You'll probably end up liking most of your students a great deal, and they will like you. Occasionally, of course, students won't like you: don't let that damage your ego, as the reasons for such dislike often have little to do with your teaching or personality (you represent the establishment; they can't stand red hair) and anyway, no one can be liked by everyone. Some students will like you too much; work that problem out for yourself. Do be careful about partying with your students. Many staff enjoy bringing students into their homes, and that's a great thing to do, but freshmen are often underage: don't serve them liquor or drugs. You represent your institution, and you'll be breaking the law.

MANAGING STUDENTS AND THEIR ESSAYS

Much of the work in writing classes consists of turning in and getting back essays. If students don't turn in their essays at all or turn them in late, keep track of that fact. Remind them from time to time of what they have and haven't done and of the effect on their work and grade. If you wish, set up and announce a policy on late papers at the beginning of the course. Then stick to it. Try to avoid letting students turn in late work at all. (For further advice on late work see Chapter 5, "Responding to Student Essays.")

A further problem with essays may be plagiarism. Some students, if not taught about the proper use of sources, may commit inadvertent plagiarism, so make sure you've done your part to teach the rules and provide practice in methods for note-taking and the direct and indirect use of sources in a student's own written work. If a student of yours submits a deliberately plagiarized essay, check on your college's plagiarism policy rather than simply failing the essay or failing the student in your course. Many colleges consider it important that faculty members report cases of plagiarism so that appropriate action may be taken when students plagiarize repeatedly.

Few of the problems discussed will arise in a given semester. In most cases, your teaching will be a combination of hard work and intense pleasure, and you will go into the next semester wondering if your new students can possibly be as terrific as the ones to whom you just said goodbye.

WORKS CITED

Entries marked with an asterisk are described in Chapter 8, "A Bibliographical Guide to the Profession."

Bronowski, Jacob. *Science and Human Values*. New York: Harper and Row, 1965. Selection reprinted as "The Nature of Scientific Reasoning" in *The Norton Reader: An Anthology of Expository Prose*. 6th ed. Edited by Arthur M. Eastman. 951–54. New York: Norton, 1984.

*Lanham, Richard. *Revising Prose*. New York: Scribner's, 1979.

Lauer, Janice M., Gene Montague, Andrea Lunsford, and Janet Emig. *Four Worlds of Writing*. New York: Harper and Row, 1981.

Lauer, Janice M. "Issues in Rhetorical Invention." *Classical Studies and Modern Discourse*. Edited by Robert Connors, Lisa Ede, and Andrea Lunsford. 127–39. Carbondale, Ill.: Southern Illinois Univ. Press, 1983.

Ong, Walter, S. J. "The Writer's Audience Is Always a Fiction." *PMLA* 90 (1975): 9–21.

*Williams, Joseph M. *Style: Ten Lessons in Clarity and Grace*. 2nd ed. Glenview, Ill.: Scott, Foresman, 1985.

Winterowd, Ross. "Brain, Rhetoric, and Style." *The Territory of Language: Linguistics, Stylistics, and the Teaching of Composition*. Edited by Donald McQuade. 34–64. Carbondale, Ill.: Southern Illinois Univ. Press, 1986.

Young, Richard E. "Paradigms and Problems: Needed Research in Rhetorical Invention." *Research on Composing: Points of Departure*. Edited by Charles Cooper and Lee Odell. 29–47. Urbana, Ill.: NCTE, 1978.

4

Designing Essay Assignments

GERARD H. COX

I. INTRODUCTION: MISSED OPPORTUNITIES

Imagine the following scenario: Your writing class begins in one hour. Life has been hectic recently, and you haven't had the time to sit down and plan a writing assignment before now. So, feeling guilty, you hastily type one up, make the rest of your preparations, and go off to class. Near the end of the period you write the assignment on the board and ask if there are any questions. To your relief, there aren't. You dismiss the class and hurry off to your next tasks.

When the papers come in, some days later, they are a disappointing bunch. Some are inadequately focused; some merely review secondary materials instead of venturing an interpretation; others discuss their way around the topic but do not attempt to argue a single large point (a "thesis"). And the students' uncertainty about the assignment does stylistic as well as intellectual damage to their essays: vagueness, wordiness, passive constructions, needless summaries, arch self-consciousness, uncertain or spurious transitions. Reading such essays is disheartening. You begin to wonder what sort of enchantment has turned the lively students you know from class into a bunch of timid, vacuous drudges.

Virtually every teacher of writing has enacted a comparable scenario. Our concern here is less to denounce pedagogic dereliction than to point out missed opportunities. First, the instructor has neglected to recall that assignments elicit responses, and that before giving an assignment it is important to decide what responses are desirable. Second, the instructor has made no effort to integrate writing into the learning process, or into the syllabus of the course as a whole. Third, giving such an assignment at the close of the class period, when discussion is least likely, makes it especially hard for your class to grasp its purpose. In all probability your students will approach the essay as a chore rather than as an intellectual enterprise. They will not be satisfied with what they turn in, and if they are not you can be sure that you will not be satisfied either. For all intents and purposes, writing has become divorced from the learning that takes place in the course.

There is, of course, a better way than this to give assignments. This better way consists simply of regarding assignments not as individual, isolated topics to be invented as necessity requires but as a coherent sequence designed to elicit responses appropriate for your course and, ideally, to build upon these responses. Each assignment should have a specific focus; each should have a clear purpose; but more important still, each should connect with the assignments preceding and following it. This chapter begins by offering some axioms useful to keep in mind when you design course-specific assignments. Three ways to generate coherent sets of assignments follow, with examples of each. Finally, this chapter treats some possible applications of these three approaches to specific subject matters. While the chapter focuses on across-the-curriculum writing courses, the axioms and suggestions for approaches to designing assignments apply equally well to composition courses.

II. FIVE AXIOMS ABOUT ASSIGNMENTS

Whatever your subject matter, however you structure your syllabus, no matter what your goals for writing assignments, you may find the following axioms useful when designing your assignments.

AXIOM I. ANTICIPATE AND PLAN RESPONSES

Assignments elicit responses. The better you can anticipate your students' responses to an assignment, the better, in general, their papers will be. Try to make the purpose of your assignments transparently clear by providing as specific and as meaningful a focus as possible. Your own rhetorical mode is important: If your assignment is declarative, for example, most students will be content to paraphrase your statement and give it back to you. If you ask questions, on the other hand, you are encouraging students to think for themselves—and in trying to come up with answers they are halfway to formulating their thesis and finding a way to structure their essay.

As a guide to thoughtfully structured essay assignments, Harry Shaw (author of Chapter 5) developed the following series of questions for beginning teachers to consider while designing assignments:

  1. *Does a topic give a command or ask a question?*
Many topics that give a command suggest a thesis that echoes the command; thus,

> "Write a paragraph explaining why it was important for Konrad Lorenz to observe the shrews in captivity"

will be likely to produce:

> "It was important for Lorenz . . . "

Sometimes asking questions can produce the same result. Is there a significant difference between the above command and its conversion into the following question?

> "Why was it important for Lorenz to observe the shrews in captivity?"

  2. *Does the topic suggest a mode of organization to the student?*
One of the following suggests an organization; the other does not:

> "How does Lewis Thomas feel about 'visible death'? Does his attitude change between the beginning and the end of his essay?"

> "Do Thomas's attitudes toward and assumptions about death differ from those of religion? (You may talk about religion in general or you may choose a particular religion.)"

  3. *Does a topic suggest a procedure for the student to follow in attempting to deal with it?*
One of the following suggests a procedure; the other does not:

"Henry Thoreau uses 'life,' 'alive,' and 'living' a number of times in 'Observation.' What does he think being alive means?''

"What does being alive mean to Thoreau?''

Similarly, one of the following suggests a procedure; the other does not:

"Why does Eisely entitle his essay "The Brown Wasps" and not "The Field Mice"?

"Why does Eiseley entitle his essay "The Brown Wasps"?

4. *Does the topic demand a thesis of the student?*
One of the following demands a thesis; the other does not:

"Niko Tinbergen views the wasps as both personal acquaintances and as objects of study. Does he choose one view over the other?''

"Offer an interpretation of the following page from a businessman's diary."

5. *What kind of thesis statement does the topic suggest? Does it imply that the student should arrive at a thesis by*
a. echoing the wording of the topic itself?
   One of the following suggests a thesis that echoes the question:

"Niko Tinbergen views the wasps as both personal acquaintances and as objects of study. Does he choose one view over the other?''

"What one aspect of Lorenz's personality comes through most clearly in "The Taming of the Shrews?" (The student can echo this one, but the results will sound mechanical.)

b. answering a question the topic poses?
   The Lorenz example under "a" would fit here.

c. defining further or redefining certain key terms introduced in the topic?

For an example, see question 3 above concerning Thoreau's use of "alive"; other examples are topics which ask why something was "important" or which of two essays was "more useful," without providing explicit definitions of "important" or "useful."

[The questions thus far have been intended to be primarily descriptive. The next two are more polemical.]

6. *Is the question asked in such a way that procedure and organization tend to overwhelm thesis?*

Thus: Is Nate Shaw a realist or an idealist? Define both terms, and explain what evidence you used to make your judgment.

7. *Does the question demand that the student choose between one of two implied theses, or even between one of two subjects?*

Thus: Does Hoffer feel differently about the "undesirables" than he does about the pioneers? Do you? Why?

[Two final questions:]

8. *Are certain kinds of questions better suited to your course than others?*

9. *Is it possible that a certain sequence of kinds of question would best serve the needs of your students?*

AXIOM 2. START AT THEIR LEVEL

You have to begin at the beginning. That is, you may need to accommodate what you have planned to assign to your students' level of writing. You can find out how well they write by the time-honored diagnostic method of having them write something right away, either in class on the first day or out of class for the second meeting. You can also determine their conception of revision by having them do both, treating the in-class piece as the first draft and revising it before the next class when both drafts have to be handed in together.

It is good to remember that freshmen are not experienced or mature thinkers, and that you will need to match your assignments, to some extent, to the intellectual level you infer from their first few essays. William Perry, in a study of Harvard students ("Cognitive and Ethical Growth: The Making of Meaning"), reports that most undergraduates start out as dualists: they believe that right answers and wrong answers are always securely distinguishable, on "objective" grounds; that one's chief intellectual duty is to seek the former and shun the latter; and that education is a process in which know-nothings (students) acquire bits of true knowledge from experts (professors). Students move only grad-

ually to a recognition that truth is partial and relative, that while it may
be "objective" it is never context-free, and that such recognitions are
perfectly compatible with commitment to one kind of truth rather than
another.

If you expect your students already to be sophisticated thinkers (they're
smart, after all), to be able to think through a problem from many angles
and with a knowledge of investigative methods in several disciplines,
you will be unpleasantly surprised when you read their essays. Gauge
your assignments, then, to your students' present level, even as you use
those assignments as challenges to more sophisticated forms of thought.
For example, you may want students to start their writing with a précis
of a difficult article or book or with the answer to a fairly straightforward question about a text, listing functions or characteristics; as
they come to terms with the vocabulary and questions typical of your
course, they may compare what two writers have to say about one problem or how they define one term. A research paper involving large-
scale classification and analysis may come at the end of the semester as
the culmination of a series of such shorter projects. (See Malcolm Kiniry and Ellen Strenski for their discussion of this kind of sequencing
approach.) In other words, you can help students become more sophisticated thinkers in your subject by using linked essay assignments that
build connections between readings and gradually develop the concepts
of a course.

AXIOM 3. RELATE ASSIGNMENTS TO THE COURSE EXPERIENCE

You have to give assignments that your students can relate to their
own experience, and you have to make those relations clear to them.
This is less a plea for sixties-style relevance than an appeal to treat
students as you would be treated. Students are incredibly accommodat-
ing if you explain the relation of this particular assignment to what they
have done before and what you hope they will learn by doing it. Instead
of writing a brief assignment on the board during the closing minutes
of the class, have the assignment written out in as full and as specific
detail as possible. This of course means that you must have spent some
time yourself formulating the assignment; it would be even better to
have tried to write it yourself before you make the class do so. When
you hand it out, be sure to allow enough time to discuss it fully, allowing and encouraging questions. This can be an appropriate moment to

discuss ways to generate ideas, and, at least initially, you can go on to discuss with the class how a writer makes choices among things to say and what in turn these choices entail. And you can point out that this process of invention and selection is also one they can follow for in-class writing and for examinations.

AXIOM 4. PLAN ASSIGNMENTS THAT CAN BE REVISED

Your assignments should stand up under the pressure of revision. That is, the assignment ideally should be of sufficient interest that its possibilities will still be worth exploring in another assignment. Learning how to write better is typically a matter of becoming more skilled at revising. Other things being equal, the more you can emphasize writing as discovery by building into your syllabus occasions for thorough revision, the more rapidly your students will progress. When considering a given sequence, be sure to give some careful thought to the ways it lends itself to revision. "Teaching writing" typically means "requiring rewriting," for, generally speaking, most students improve only when they are required to rewrite their essays. For revision to be helpful, however, you need to move them beyond what they believe revision involves: correcting misspellings and incorporating whatever nit-picking comments the teacher has made in the margins. (For suggestions on how to make useful comments, see Chapter 5, "Responding to Student Essays." See also Chapter 3, Section I.C, for a list of ways to elicit revision.)

One way to enlarge student understanding of the process of revision is to spend some time early in the term discussing what revision means: "a re-seeing." You can profitably point out that writing is frequently a process of learning what one has to say, and, in consequence, a first draft (which all too often in student writing doubles as the last draft) is more often a record of false starts and abandoned ideas than a coherent essay. As the root suggests, however, "revision" offers the opportunity to look again at the essay and make it coherent. Students should "review" such time-honored devices as seeing whether the first paragraph is not just an occasion for the written equivalent of throat-clearing and thus can be deleted, seeing whether the idea expressed in the last paragraph would not make a better opening than an ending paragraph, seeing if the essay follows a line of argument, and so on. (By-the-bye, some students have real problems trying to figure out what their thesis is, yet they often feel quite comfortable sketching out a working hypothesis which they then can test in the subsequent paragraphs. Depending on how they end up, they can then either adopt their hypothesis as their thesis or suitably modify it. Such experimentation can provide useful, in-class writing exercises.)

How—and when—to grade revisions can be a vexing problem. If you do not grade the first, supposedly finished version, some students will interpret the lack of a grade to indicate unimportance and thus will not exert themselves. If, on the other hand, you grade the first, "finished," draft and then require revision, it seems altogether appropriate to grade that as well, for otherwise the student may well believe that you are not in earnest about the importance of revision. One difficulty with grading revisions is that the revision may not be materially improved—but the student will typically feel that the effort alone of redoing it should raise the grade by at least one increment. With this kind of presumed grade inflation, it does not take long to reach a level at which you feel uncomfortable.

Depending on your sense of the class, you might want to give the first, supposedly "finished," draft a tentative grade and then have a reworked version of that assignment be due so many days later, when you will award a permanent grade. When the assignment is good enough, and, perhaps more important, when the student remains engaged by the challenge, a given essay can be reworked and regraded still another time.

You can also design a sequence of assignments so that the student must turn in, say, three thoroughly revised essays that will be graded yet again and will constitute the major percentage of the grade for the course. I've had most success with this procedure when I've specified due dates for each of the thoroughly revised essays and then scheduled conferences a week or so ahead of the due date, at which time each student had to bring in a draft that had been reworked at least once from the last version I'd seen. In the conference, you quickly read the draft and suggest some further revision. Ideally, the readings for the course will also play a part in helping the students reconceive and refocus what they have previously written. The closer you can make these relations between reading, writing, and rewriting, the better.

AXIOM 5.   PUT STUDENTS ON THEIR OWN

In giving assignments, you must try to develop a feel for times when you should step back and let the students go out on their own. Some—perhaps even most—of your students may want to come up with their own writing topics. If they can do this, and if they can develop their topics in a length appropriate to those topics, there is much to be gained from giving them their head.

Typically, however, freshman-level writers do not know how to find good, and appropriate, questions to ask in what is as yet *your* subject, not *theirs*. On their own, therefore, they may try to treat love and death in two pages, or three if you're lucky. Such students will in all probability learn faster through a sequence of structured assignments. By directing their responses, these assignments encourage students to develop and demonstrate a reasonable opinion about a suitable question. The better your assignments, therefore, the sooner your students will begin to write clearly and well.

III. THREE APPROACHES
TO DESIGNING ASSIGNMENTS

At least three kinds of assignments can be distinguished, according to the varying relations among subject, writer, and audience. The first kind of assignment emphasizes the structures of the essay being written about this subject; the second kind emphasizes the writer's relation to this subject; and the third emphasizes the relation of the writer's audience to this subject. We shall treat each of these in turn.

A. *Emphasizing the Essay's Structure*

Into this category fall two sequences of assignments that are concerned with the essay as an exercise in form, taking form in the conventional sense of the shape and structure of something. The rationale for this approach is that freshmen are often unclear about what "a paper" consists of. Not only do they frequently not know what "a paper" is, they do not know what it is for. By emphasizing how to develop a structure, you can help your students come to grips with the topic on which they must write. To generate a thesis statement, for example, they must have some understanding both of the subject and of their own attitude toward that subject. In these terms, an essay assignment is itself a primary means of encouraging your students to develop informed opinions that they can demonstrate and, if need be, defend in coherent and straightforward prose.

The first sequence of assignments emphasizes a progression from smaller to larger units; the second emphasizes the traditional divisions of rhetoric.

SEQUENCE I. PROGRESSING FROM SMALLER TO LARGER UNITS

Students often imagine prose to be an outpouring of expression at once spontaneous and rational. In consequence, they see no connection between what they read for the course and what they themselves write. One way to make these connections clearer to them is to construct a sequence of assignments that progresses from smaller units of meaning to larger units.

The initial assignments could focus on generating a thesis. Your students could take a list of assorted subjects and turn them into topic sentences by stating what about the topic is interesting and then why it is interesting. After they can write a topic sentence, you can move to ways to construct an opening paragraph. Looking closely at the openings of the texts you are reading can be useful here, especially if you can contrast paragraphs that state their thesis in the opening sentence to ones that reserve it to the last sentence of the first paragraph, and those in turn to paragraphs that keep their thesis implicit rather than explicit. From opening paragraphs you can go on to discuss how one idea can control the beginning, middle, and ending of essays and how to make the necessary transitions from one paragraph to another. Even such exercises as having the class highlight transitional phrases or make lists of them can help them become more aware of ways to order their own essays. It can of course be objected that such a set of assignments results in writing that is less formal than formulaic, but you can always let students experiment with looser structures later in the term.

While "straight" writing courses easily use this approach, freshman courses built around a selection of readings can benefit equally from it, especially during the first few weeks they are in session. The following series of assignments was developed for a particular writing course in order to introduce incoming students to the not entirely self-explanatory business of reading and writing about a literary text.

First assignment, due 8/31: Read Bellow's short novel *Seize the Day* and bring in a list of at least 5 things about the book that strike you as odd, problematic, provocative, effective, or otherwise worth discussing.

Second assignment, due 9/2: Select from your list or from subjects brought up during class discussion one aspect of the novel that you think might be interesting to explore in an essay. Read *Seize the Day* again, this time isolating and copying (on file cards) at least ten passages that bear on your topic. Bring the note cards to class with you.

Third assignment, due 9/5: Write a statement of your thesis using the form, "In this essay I shall argue that . . . " This thesis statement will not appear in your essay; its purpose is to help you clarify what it is that you'll be writing about.

Here are some examples of the form your thesis statement could take [the examples you give to your class need not be so elaborately phrased, but it is gratifying to see how often students will rise to such a rhetorical occasion]:

> "In this essay I shall argue that Bellow's protagonist Tommy Wilhelm is in part responsible for his own failures and in part a victim of an uncaring society, and that Bellow is careful not to locate the blame too exactly because the tension between individual and social responsibility is one of his most important themes."

> "In this essay I shall argue that Bellow uses images of flight and of vertical structures that lead the eye upward to suggest a transcendent dimension of experience that seduces and yet eludes the major characters of *Seize the Day.*"

> "In this essay I shall argue that the conclusion of *Seize the Day* promises no salvation for the protagonist, whose retreat into tears is more a regression to childhood than a mystic embracing of the grief inherent in the human condition." [Detailed examples are particularly helpful if you are requiring a kind of writing—like a thesis statement—that many students have not encountered before.]

Fourth assignment, due 9/7: Bring to class (1) an outline of your essay, and (2) a draft of the closing paragraph, in which your argument effectively comes to a conclusion.

Fifth assignment, due 9/9: Bring to class a typewritten finished draft of your essay. [Teacher comments on draft over the weekend, returns it on 9/12.]

Sixth assignment, due 9/14: Hand in finished paper.

Depending on your students and your views about the recursive nature of writing, you may want to require more than one rough draft, and you may want to request these drafts before rather than after outlines. It's a good idea, however, to require students to outline their essays at some point during the series of assignments.

SEQUENCE 2. FOLLOWING TRADITIONAL RHETORICAL DIVISIONS

Another way to emphasize writing as formal construction is to work out a series of assignments deriving from the first three divisions of the art of rhetoric: invention; *dispositio,* or arrangement; *elocutio,* or style. You could began with *invention* in its Renaissance sense of "finding a subject" (a sense still current in the word "inventory"), and give your class a number of exercises that teach them how to discover what they didn't realize they knew as well as, perhaps, some things they didn't know. Kenneth Burke's generating device of the pentad might be useful here, as it is a strategy for viewing a topic from a variety of essential perspectives. Burke formulated the pentad when he attempted to answer the question, "What is involved, when we say what people are doing and why they are doing it?" As Burke describes his scheme in *A Grammar of Motives,* you think about something as if it were a drama and then ask interrelated questions focusing on Act (what took place, in thought or deed), Scene (where or when it was done), Agent (what person or what kind of person did it), Agency (how he did it), and Purpose (why he did it). This scheme is especially helpful to those students who characterize themselves as never having any ideas to write about.

Obviously this "pentad" works well in the context of a literary narrative, and it has the advantage of suggesting permutations and combinations that go beyond the answers derived from the reportorial questions of "who-what-where-when and why." Students will feel comfortable answering "what happened?" with a synopsis of plot and "who or what did it?'' with observations about characters or forces of one kind or another within the story, but a few of them may discover on their own that ''what happened?'' might inquire about the writing of a story and that ''who?'' might well refer to the writer: it is in the context of such genuinely critical questions that ''how?'' and ''why?'' become most interesting.

The pentad can also be used to ''unpack'' lyrics. As you would imagine, the pentad is readily adaptable to poems that in one way or another may be termed ''dramatic'': Wyatt's ''They Flee From Me,'' or Herbert's ''Love (III),'' or Edwin Arlington Robinson's ''How Annandale Went Out.'' This last is short enough—and, at least initially, baffling enough—to be an excellent example for demonstrating in class how to use the pentad.

HOW ANNANDALE WENT OUT

> ''They called it Annandale—and I was there
> To flourish, to find words, and to attend:
> Liar, physician, hypocrite, and friend,
> I watched him; and the sight was not so fair
> As one or two that I have seen elsewhere:
> An apparatus not for me to mend—
> A wreck, with hell between him and the end,
> Remained of Annandale; and I was there.
>
> ''I knew the ruin as I knew the man;
> So put the two together, if you can,
> Remembering the worst you know of me.
> Now view yourself as I was, on the spot—
> With a slight kind of engine. Do you see?
> Like this . . . You wouldn't hang me? I thought not.''

On a first (and perhaps even on a second or a third) reading, the situation dramatized in this poem will remain an enigma to students: unfamiliar with unravelling a dramatic monologue, they will not readily hear the physician explaining the death to which he helped a suffering patient. ''Wreck'' and, especially, ''engine'' will suggest to many that Annandale is a racecar (although I once had a student argue passionately that Annandale was a sinking battleship); and when you point out that Annandale is a ''him'' as well as an ''it'' they frequently will accommodate this evidence by making Annandale the dying driver of the racecar. So much for an open-ended discussion.

Fortunately, by offering a strategy that allows us to ask questions about what the speaker is doing and why he is doing it, the pentad can open up other interpretations. What Act is being described? What took place, in thought or deed? To what and to whom does "Do you see?" refer? Are there any other examples of looking or seeing in the poem? What about watching? Is what is being watched the original action, or a reenactment? What does "Like this" suggest? Given the associative quality of class discussion, Act will soon give way to Scene (where or when it was done). How specified is the place? Why does the speaker describe it only as "there"? Is the there-ness important? (Good students will discover that the first and last lines of the octave end with "and I was there.") What does the speaker mean by being "on the spot"? Does "on the spot" refer to Scene, or something more? The latter suggests Agent (what person or kind of person did it). Here the class can discover more of the significance of "Liar, physician, hypocrite, and friend"—including, perhaps, a revision of the dangling-modifier reading that makes all these words refer to "him" instead of "I." They may then go on to the implications of negative understatement: "I watched him; and the sight was not so fair / As one or two that I have seen elsewhere." Given the initial obscurity of "a slight kind of engine," Agency (how he did it) may still be an open question. If you need to, you can ask what small mechanical contrivances a physician is likely to have. The answer will probably lead to the last element of the pentad, Purpose. If the situation of Annandale—"An apparatus not for me to mend— / A wreck, with hell between him and the end"—has not already been fully understood, you can ask why the poem uses both masculine and neuter pronouns for Annandale. Why is the impersonal important for the speaker's Purpose? What does it have to do with a hanging matter? What, finally, is being encapsulated by the phrasing of the title, "How Annandale Went Out"?

Useful as the pentad is for generating a more comprehensive understanding of a dramatic lyric, it is perhaps even more useful for generating topics for an essay on the poem. In this case, you can encourage your students to ask the same questions about the poem as they have asked about the events narrated within the poem. What kind of poem is it? Formally? In terms of what it is doing? Why does it have this form and not some other form? What is the rhyme scheme, and how does this rhyme scheme contribute to the process of revelation? What rhymes are especially emphatic? What effects do they produce? Why does the poem divide into an octave and a sestet? What happens in the turn from one to the other? Why is the mode of narration that of a dramatic monologue rather than, say, that of an external, third-person narration? Who is the audience for this narration? What does the poem achieve by positing an internal audience for the first-person speaker? What is our relation as the poem's audience to the speaker's audience in the poem? Why have a revelatory process at all? What effect is produced by the amalgamation of clues, the invitations to decode, as for example in the shift of pronouns from "it" to "him"? To what degree do we view ourselves as the speaker was, "on the spot"? What difference does it make if we see from another's point of view? Obviously, these questions can be extended. Perhaps the ultimate question—the meta-meta-critical question—might be which of these questions (certainly there may be more than one) can be followed up in a focused, interesting essay?

The pentad is equally useful in generating ideas about non-literary topics. For example, let us assume that you are teaching a sociology course, "Social Change," and that you want your students to write about the advisability or feasibility of legalizing marijuana. Your students can use the "who?" of Burke's pentad to ask a number of questions that open up promising lines of development: who wants marijuana legalized? who doesn't? who cares about the issue? who benefits now? who would benefit? Or let us assume that you want your students taking an Africana Studies course, "Infancy, Family, and the Community," to write about their relationship to their grandparents. The student who focuses on her grandmother can find in "who?" the questions that can help her to define that relationship: who is she, really? who am I to her? what did I represent to her when I was born and was named after her? what does she represent to me now? and so on.

As William Irmscher demonstrates in *The Holt Guide to English*, the pentad can also be used to generate a surprising number of things to say about a painting, in this case Edward Hopper's *Nighthawks* (34–44). These examples are especially telling because *Nighthawks* seems so straightforward in its realism that students often have difficulty in going beyond a one-sentence declaration of liking it or not. By following Irmscher, however, you can demonstrate to your students that they can invent any number of things to develop in an essay.

You could follow invention with some equivalent of *dispositio*, the arrangement or disposition of the parts of the whole. To use the legalization of marijuana as an example again, you could have them write a

documentary account of this controversy that is to be included in a time
capsule. Because the audience of this essay will not be familiar with
this topic, the essay virtually has to begin with an introduction of a
particular kind. By the same token, the arguments for and against marijuana may well fall into categories or divisions; each of these divisions
has to be explained, the evidence pro and con evaluated, and a conclusion reached.

Another, more extended treatment of *dispositio* can involve the traditional forms of rhetorical assignments: comparison and contrast; cause
and effect; definition; analysis; and process. Comparison involves one
of the most basic modes of thought, for much of what we learn involves
comparing things for their similarities and contrasting things for their
differences. For a ''compare and contrast'' essay, you can have your
students show likenesses and differences between two (or more, but
usually only two) subjects: persons, places, things, ideas, or actions.
You will get better essays if you emphasize that they need to do more
than merely assemble and present information about the topic: they should
instead compare and contrast for a purpose. Typically, this purpose can
take one of several forms: a) to explain an unfamiliar phenomenon by
showing its similarities to a familiar phenomenon, despite its apparent
differences; b) to demonstrate the superiority of one thing over another—
X is more interesting, or more useful, or better than Y. Here is one such
assignment:

> T. S. Eliot has observed, ''The progress of the artist is a continual
> self-sacrifice, a continual extinction of personality.'' How well does
> Eliot's statement hold for the last paragraphs of the second and the
> third chapters of *A Portrait of the Artist as a Young Man?* Compare
> and contrast the degree of self-sacrifice in these two episodes, making
> sure that you cover two points: a) what, if anything, does Stephen
> Dedalus sacrifice himself for? and b) what progress, if any, does he
> make towards becoming an artist? Finally, compare and contrast what
> you say about b) to the status Stephen has achieved at the end of the
> novel. Is Eliot's observation pertinent here, or is Joyce working from
> a different conception of the artist? If so, what is that conception?

Here is a ''compare and contrast'' assignment on a social-science
topic:

> In ''The Culture of Poverty,'' Oscar Lewis has offered a specific
> conceptual model of poverty as a subculture of Western society. Lewis

argues that the culture of poverty has its own structure and rationale: "it provides human beings with a design for living, with a ready-made set of solutions for human problems, and so serves a significant adaptive function." In *Blaming the Victim,* however, William Ryan argues that the work of social scientists like Oscar Lewis is flawed by an ideological error: "they identify the culture of poverty and lower class culture and the presumed life styles of the poor as themselves causes of continued poverty!" Poverty, Ryan contends, is best understood not as a result of the unfortunate characteristics of the poor but as a lack of money.

Compare and contrast the ways Lewis and Ryan arrive at their definitions of "poverty." How comparable are their basic assumptions? Do both use the same kinds of evidence? Why, or why not? Does either writer express anything other than a calm, reasonable, "objective" attitude to this topic? If so, why, do you suppose? Finally, which of these two views do you find more persuasive, and why?

Cause and effect need little glossing. It sometimes can be stimulating, however, to let your students decide whether they are to write about a given subject in terms of "cause and effect" or in terms of "effect and cause." "Cause and effect" tends to emphasize the why of things, "effect and cause," the how. Either version is a good way to teach your students how best to use evidence. Here is an example in which the quality of the response depends almost entirely on the nature and consequence of the evidence:

In *A Vindication of the Rights of Woman,* Many Wollstonecraft declares, "It is vain to expect virtue from women till they are in some degree independent of men; nay, it is vain to expect the strength of natural affection which would make them good wives and mothers. Whilst they are absolutely dependent on their husbands they will be cunning, mean, and selfish, and the men who can be gratified by the fawning fondness of spaniel-like affection have not much delicacy, for love is not to be bought, in any sense of the words; its silken wings are instantly shrivelled up when anything beside a return in kind is sought." Test the validity of this view by reference to two recent American films. [This kind of assignment is also readily adaptable to sociological accounts of marriage in this country and in others, to differing philosophic accounts of marriage, to views of marriage in recent feminist theory, and so on.]

"Definition" as a rhetorical mode extends well beyond what the dictionary says a given term means: it includes what its functions are, what its purposes are, and what it is like or unlike. An assignment involving definition can be an excellent means of bringing hidden assumptions to the surface. Here, especially, explanations and examples both clarify and make definitions more complete—and hence more persuasive. The following assignment has students define terms in order to relate what they study to what they perceive in the world around them:

> Marx declares in *The Communist Manifesto* that the fall of the bourgeoisie and the rise of the proletariat "are equally inevitable." If Marx came back from the grave to visit today's America, would he see here a refutation or a vindication of his beliefs? Be sure in your essay to define carefully how Marx uses the terms "proletariat" and "bourgeoisie." Of course, either vindication or refutation can be partial rather than complete, but remember that in this case also you must define your terms.

"Analysis" of course involves division and classification. Analysis breaks something complex into smaller, simpler elements and then systematically discusses how these elements form the whole. Process analysis distinguishes and explains a sequence of steps or actions, like those in baking bread. Classification is a kind of analysis that systematically groups things into categories based on shared characteristics or traits: apples, for example, can be divided into the Lord Derby group (smooth, sour, green apples), the Granny Smith group (sweet, green apples), the Worcester Pearmain group (red-skinned apples), the Blenheim and Cox's Orange Pippin group, and so on. A more complex kind of writing assignment involves moving beyond one kind of classification to set up comparable ones, as in the following:

> In *The Social Contract,* Rousseau declares, "The oldest form of society—and the only natural one—is the family." Do you think this analysis is adequate? Are there any other forms of society evident to you? What are they? Would you call them "natural," or not? Why? And is the family "natural"? Why?

All of these forms—comparison and contrast, cause and effect, definition, and analysis—are the rhetorical equivalents of investigative and argumentative procedures. That is, "analysis" is a search for meaning and significance rather than an acceptance of appearances; "analysis of process" is nothing other than investigation of change and persistence in time (or diachronic analysis); "comparison and contrast" is a placing of things in various relations. In other words, ways to write are directly and intimately related to ways to learn

After invention and *dispositio* you can treat *elocutio,* or style. Broadly conceived, style is the verbal form of the writer's attitude toward experience. More narrowly considered, style can be usefully treated as the management of verbal devices such as repetition or parallelism. Freshmen typically have only a vague sense of parallelism, so an assignment that calls attention to this figure in, say, the opening of Bacon's essay "Of Studies"—"Studies serve for delight, for ornament, and for ability" (an order of increasing importance that is reinforced by the increasing syllabic numbers: de-light; or-na-ment; a-bil-i-ty)—can easily lead to a consideration of argument itself: what kinds of writing employ parallelism? what are its functions? You could then juxtapose to Bacon's "Of Studies" a passage by Montaigne, a writer who was at some pains to avoid parallelism.

Given that Montaigne and Bacon were writing at roughly the same time, why would Montaigne want to declare, "I am prone to begin without a plan; the first remark brings on the second" (*Essays,* I, 40)? Which style seems more impersonal, which more personal? You could then give an assignment that has the class write on a topic first as Bacon would and then as Montaigne would. (For a fuller discussion of style, see Chapter 6, "Understanding Prose.")

This last assignment of course emphasizes imitation, one of the most important principles of rhetoric. Your assignments can make further use of imitation by having the class imitate writers with a distinctive personal voice: Margaret Atwood, say, or Hunter Thompson, or Woody Allen, or Fran Lebowitz. Such assignments also serve a larger purpose, for they force students to hear what they read, and the sooner you can get them to hear what they read the sooner they will start attending to the rhythms of their own prose (see the discussion of rhetorical situation and of prose rhythm in Chapter 6).

B. *Emphasizing the Writer*

Another set of possible assignments involves your students' personal experiences. The rationale for this approach is that although freshman students may not command large stores of learning, they do have a fairly wide range of experience to draw on. By giving assignments that enable them to write about what they are most familiar with, you can motivate them to write better. If the most important knowledge is self-knowledge, moreover, then writing becomes a means to know oneself. For example, you could ask your class to isolate one time when they learned something in a formal setting. They then could describe why that learning occurred, and go on to speculate about why that particular set of conditions doesn't occur more often. In the next assignment, you could ask them to describe an occasion when they learned something in an informal setting. How did this experience take place? What difference did it make to them? How would they compare it with the formal learning they described in the first assignment? In the third assignment you could ask your class to reflect on the process they experienced when they wrote their essays for the first two assignments. Did they realize immediately what they wanted to say? How did they proceed to discover their subject? Were there any changes that occurred as they wrote about them? Did the act of writing itself generate new possibilities? What did they do—or not do—about these possibilities, and why?

Inexperienced writers will often have an interesting idea—and one that may be at odds with their thesis—virtually buried about two-thirds of the way through their essay. If this is the case, you can have them start with that idea in the next assignment and follow its implications. In this way, the class begins to see that writing can be a process of discovering meaning, and that rewriting in turn can become a process of exploiting that meaning. And they begin to see their own experience as a source of material for reflection, interpretation, and prose investigation.

With only a slight change in focus, you can give assignments that emphasize their own reader-responses. Such assignments can be particularly helpful for teaching your students how to read well independently. The constant, recurring assignment is to have your students write their personal, subjective reactions to a short work each time they read it, perhaps by keeping a journal. Besides forcing students to reread texts (a procedure that few initially may think necessary), this assignment also has the advantage of helping students "invent" paper topics, for they rapidly compile a record of different ways of experiencing the same text. By focusing on why these changes occur, your students can begin writing about the process of learning itself, a process that is rarely linear, infrequently progressive, but always engaging.

C. *Emphasizing an Audience*

A third approach focuses not on the writer so much as on her or his audience. Student writers often have little sense of audience, for nearly all of their required writing has been for their instructor (hence that dogged questioning from students about what it is you "really" want). When you have them write for a different audience, however, their work can improve dramatically. The relatively recent theory of situational writing embodies this assumption (see Gene H. Krupa, *Situational Writing*). As the term implies, the student is asked to imagine that she or he is in a specified situation. Each student in a government writing course, "Politics and the Environment," for example, might imagine that she is a taxpayer writing a letter to her congresswoman on the proposed increase in taxes to eliminate acid rain. Whether she is for or against the increase, she must marshal her arguments in logical order and back them up with whatever evidence is appropriate. This kind of situation can be easily adapted to what Charles Schuster has termed situational sequencing: asking the writer to enter a series of situations, each of which involves a reshaping or reconceiving of the original subject. In assignment 2, the student is asked to assume she is now the congresswoman who wants to respond to the original letter. In assignment 3, the student could be the President of the Audubon Society trying to rally support for a bill in Congress, and so on.

Such a sequence can help the freshman writer learn more about invention as a means to writing and about writing as a means to invention. It can also teach a great deal about audience and rhetorical situation. Even more important, assignments like these can demonstrate the importance of revision, both in its customary sense and in its root meaning of reseeing. All too often even the most intelligent students conceive of revision as a process merely of correcting spelling and eliminating typographic errors. Assignments based on the principle of situational sequencing quickly involve the student writer in a process of writing and rewriting according to differing rhetorical constraints of audience, form, intention, and voice.

IV. USING THESE THREE APPROACHES WITH SPECIFIC SUBJECT MATTERS

All of the preceding assignments can be adapted for use with the subject matter of a given writing course, but "content-oriented" essays do present certain problems of their own. For instance, it is often tempting to regard the subject matter as a sufficient explanation of what is required, and to make an assignment like "Write a paper on the problem of the observer in ethological studies." The trouble with this sort of topic is that although it would be adequate on an essay test, where the student is required to exhibit mastery of a given body of information that is not on the desk in front of her, it encourages only paraphrase if it is offered as an out-of-class writing assignment.

Assignments, we recall, elicit responses, so the teacher should first consider what responses are desirable. In this situation, the instructor needs to define the purpose of the assignment in terms of the student's grasp of the material. If the instructor is not clear about what she wants the essay to do, her students will write grudging and perfunctory essays, and she in turn will have little basis for grading the finished papers. If the instructor is new to teaching writing, perhaps participating in a writing-across-the-curriculum program for the first time, this experience may well cause her to feel that such activities are the legitimate province only of "writing teachers," and that her own training and interests are completely at odds with the writing aspect of the course. As in our opening scenario, writing has become divorced from learning.

The following are some things that this instructor might decide she wants this particular essay assignment to do.

A. *Have the Student Apply a Theoretical Construct to a Concrete Experience*

There is an old saw which asserts that a student has not grasped a theory until she can apply it to an immediate, ''hands-on'' experience. In the case of any ''problem of the observer,'' for example, the student hasn't really understood the implications of this problem if she hasn't realized that she might very well be the observer in question. The following assignment, drawing on Mary Midgely's *Beast and Man: The Roots of Human Nature,* ideally will provoke this realization.

> *''Assignment 3:* The Problem of the Observer''
> Midgley maintains that although we may be inclined to dismiss the possibility of knowing anything about another's mental states, in fact we do have certain common sense grounds for claiming knowledge of other people's, and even other animals', motives and purposes. She points out that while we tend to assume an absolute distinction between description and interpretation, in practice our descriptions always contain an element of interpretation, and we feel fairly confident about making these interpretations: even though they contain the inevitable element of projection, we can argue that such projection is warranted because it is based on a recognition of shared characteristics.
>
> Is Midgley going too far in making this claim? In order to evaluate her position, set up a situation in which you observe for half an hour or more the behavior of one individual human or other animal, preferably when the animal is interacting with others of her or his species. You might pick an unobtrusive table in a dining hall or a centrally located patch of grass for your observations, or you could pay a visit to some group of pets or settle down to look at crows, or jays, or joggers. The important thing is to remain uninvolved in the behavior you are observing, insofar as this is possible. Take detailed notes on the behavior of the animal you have selected for study.
>
> Then write an essay that reports on your experience. The essay should consist of three parts:
> 1. a summary (perhaps two or three paragraphs) of your observation and the behavior you observed;
> 2. an analysis of this summary, in which you isolate those elements of your observation that seem to be interpretation rather than description (this may prove to be difficult; if so, the difficulty is part of the problem, and thus should be written about);
> 3. a closing reflection (anywhere from 2–5 paragraphs) on what this experience has shown you about Midgely's claims. In this sec-

tion, obviously the most important, you will be using particular elements of the first two sections to make informed generalizations. One of the things you'll find you have to generalize about is whether, and when, such generalization is warranted. The complete essay will be anywhere from 4–8 pages.

B. Have the Student Learn by Teaching

A second purpose for a writing assignment could be to help the student pull together a body of knowledge by asking her to explain it to a younger or otherwise less-informed audience. The rationale here is that you never learn anything so well as when you have to teach it. (See "Letting Students Teach" in Chapter 3 for application to classroom activities.) The student who is given a chance to teach something, even in a hypothetical situation, will often forget some of the insecurities inherent in the student role, where the student is required to offer explanations to a teacher who already understands all too well.

> *"Assignment 3:* The Problem of the Observer"
> Your favorite high school teacher is so impressed with the work you've been doing in your college class that he or she has asked you to contribute an article on "The Problem of the Observer" to a new magazine about animals and their behavior, which will be distributed to all high school students in your state. As you have only recently graduated, you're in a position to know what interests high school students, what they can understand, and what approach will avoid the pitfalls of being over their heads or condescending. Because the magazine has already allocated space for your article, you will have to keep your piece between 750 and 1,000 words, or between three and one-half and four typewritten, double-spaced pages.

C. Help the Student Evaluate a Position by Comparison and Contrast

Yet another purpose for a writing assignment could be to help the student evaluate a position by comparing and contrasting it to a somewhat different position. This kind of assignment also forces a student to read intelligently and thoroughly, and for that reason may motivate a certain number of students in the class to stop being lazy or uncritical readers and to start coming to terms with the material.

"Assignment 3: The Problem of the Observer"

Although Midgley maintains that we do in fact "observe" such mental phenomena as motives and purposes in our normal interactions and that we have legitimate grounds for saying that we know something about these mental phenomena in others, many ethologists take a somewhat different position. The attached article by Bloggs makes some very different assumptions and implicitly draws conclusions from these assumptions that make ethology a different kind of discipline than Midgely makes it.

Read Blogg's study and then write an essay comparing and contrasting its major points with at least two of the relevant arguments Midgely has advanced in Chapters 1–4. Your essay should include:

    1. a summary of the positions you will address;

    2. your reasons for choosing these positions for special consideration;

    3. a summary of how both Bloggs and Midgley arrive at the positions they do;

    4. an evaluation of the assumptions and the reasoning from these assumptions that each author engages in;

    5. an overall evaluation of the two positions and a reflection on what implications your own evaluation has for ethological study.

A variation on the essay evaluating an opinion involves creating an "authority" to contest, as in this initial assignment from a Women's Studies writing class:

"Assignment 1: The Significance and Value of Women's Studies"

"As an educated person, I of course have nothing against women per se. In fact, it's because I am sympathetic to their situation that I think the whole idea of women's studies is misguided. Certainly women got a rotten deal in that they were kept from participating in virtually all the great social and cultural movements that constitute our tradition. It is because they have not been allowed to participate in these movements, however, that their experience and perspective are inherently trivial and uninteresting. Surely we have more important concerns to occupy us in a major university."

Write an essay that analyzes the statement above. In this essay you should not simply agree or disagree with the speaker; you must examine what assumptions he or she is making and the logic by which he or she reaches conclusions. Here are some strategies you might want to (but need not) use:

1. argument by analogy: if the speaker's logic were applied to some academic discipline other than Women's Studies, would it lead to conclusions that the speaker might find dubious? Present an argument based on some particular analogy.

2. challenging definitions: is the speaker presuming that certain words or phrases in this statement have specific meanings, meanings that are either a) too limited or b) in error? Examine the way he or she is using key words and demonstrate how certain of these words are being misleadingly used.

3. reasoning in a circle: is the speaker really starting out from the place he or she wants to end up? That is, does this argument presume at the outset what it wants to prove? Identify the questionable assumption and show how the speaker has used it to arrive at this objection to the whole enterprise of Women's Studies.

It is probably simplest to place this quotation at the beginning of your paper and to follow it with your analysis.

A final word of caution, and advice: no matter how hard you work on your writing assignments, be prepared to cope with the apparent lack of progress of a significant portion of your class. It may be heartening to remember that even under optimal conditions of learning, only 70 percent of your class, on the average, will respond to your methods of teaching writing. Another method will have the same results, on the average, but the 70 percent who learn this time will not necessarily be the same ones who made up the original group. In other words, the success rate remains relatively constant, but the population of the two groups changes. By being alert to this phenomenon, you can tailor alternative assignments for the 30 percent or so who aren't responding to your particular method. It often helps to ask the students in conference why they are having problems and what they would like to do about them. After years of internalizing teachers' comments, students are sometimes more clear-sighted about their writing problems than you may be, and asking them what they would suggest to remedy the problem may bring about a change in their behavior. Given their insight, and your own careful planning, your writing assignments can give students excellent opportunities to write thoughtfully, and well.

WORKS CITED

Entries marked with an asterisk are described in Chapter 8, "A Bibliographical Guide to the Profession."

Burke, Kenneth. *A Grammar of Motives.* New York: Prentice-Hall, 1945.

*Irmscher, William. *The Holt Guide to English.* 3rd ed. New York: Holt, Rinehart and Winston, 1981.

Kiniry, Malcolm, and Ellen Strenski. "Sequencing Expository Writing: A Recursive Approach." *CCC* 36 (May 1985): 191–202.

Krupa, Gene H. *Situational Writing.* Belmont, Cal.: Wadsworth, 1982.

Midgley, Mary. *Beast and Man: The Roots of Human Nature.* Ithaca, N.Y.: Cornell Univ. Press, 1978.

Perry, William, Jr. "Cognitive and Ethical Growth: The Making of Meaning." *The Modern American College: Responding to the New Realities of Diverse Students.* Edited by Arthur W. Chickering. 76–116. San Francisco: Jossey-Bass, 1981.

Robinson, Edward Arlington. "How Annendale Went Out." *Collected Poems.* New York: Macmillan, 1948.

Schuster, Charles. "Situational Sequencing." *The Writing Instructor* 3 (Summer 1984): 177–84.

5

Responding to Student Essays

HARRY EDMUND SHAW

I. INTRODUCTION: HOW TO COMMENT?

Commenting on student essays is the central activity in the teaching of writing. This very centrality, however, implies that there should be as many styles of commenting on papers as there are styles of organizing and teaching courses. The problem of how to comment on papers, in other words, quickly collapses into the problem of how to design and teach writing courses. Producing a comprehensive account of useful responses to papers is therefore a quixotic task, and I shall avoid it. Instead, first by means of direct discussion and then by means of a specific example, I'll raise a number of central issues. In taking simple stands on complex problems, with the hope of illuminating what's at stake but without aspiring to final adjudication, I'm guided by Bacon's dictum that truth emerges more readily from error than from confusion—or, as a celebrated teacher of Cornell composition classes put it, "If you don't know how to pronounce a word, say it loud!"[1]

Much of my discussion will describe a style of commentary that aspires to affect students as they write future assignments—and indeed, as they write in the life that's rumored to exist after graduation. My focus will rest on comments combining a general precept about writing with a specific application to the paper at hand: the hope is that students who are shown precepts in action will become better readers, and thus better revisers, of their own prose. But another lasting effect commentary can achieve deserves to be mentioned at the outset.

Students are unlikely to pay attention to their prose if they think it doesn't matter. We can encourage them to respect their own writing by responding with comments that tell them, implicitly and explicitly, that what they say and how they say it matter a great deal. If our commentary shows that we care about their writing, generally and in detail, they will be more likely to care about it. If we listen to their voices with respect, so may they. What a respectful hearing involves will doubtless vary from field to field. In my own field, English literature, a respectful hearing needn't mean pretending that every student insight in a paper is wonderful, or assuming that students have a right to ignore the text, or to make unsupported generalizations, or to sound less intelligent than they are. A respectful hearing does mean, among other things, that students have a right to their experience of the text. If they react to something, we should honor the existence of that reaction. We may question the terms in which they couch their reaction, or the ways they generalize from it, but if the reaction responds to a specific part of a text, we should try to help them make something of it.

What cultivating an attitude of respect for student voices in other disciplines might mean I'm not in a position to say. I will venture to say that students are likely to transfer from one paper to the next, and into their future careers, the sense that someone is listening to them who supposes—even demands—that they be clear, coherent, and interesting. In time and with luck, the "someone" who listens to a paper's voice and makes demands upon it will become the student herself.

In the latter part of this chapter, I shall give an account of one way to comment on one kind of paper, the paper that makes a point about something, that states a thesis and defends it. I'd be distressed if my suggestions were taken as normative for all papers, in all courses, though I hope they'll prove useful, suitably adjusted, in a reasonably wide range of teaching situations. If there's one thing of which I'm sure, it's that writing courses should be coherent packages, not random collections.[2] In the end, the only way to know how to comment on papers is to decide what you want your course to accomplish: effective comments are those that further your larger aims.

Much of my discussion is based upon a general conception of the purpose that marks on a student paper should serve, and I might as well make that conception clear at the outset. I believe that commenting on a student paper shouldn't mean editing it for the student, or creating a record of what's wrong with it, or justifying its grade, or commenting on its conceptual material alone (which in practice generally means commenting not on the paper at hand but on one's best guess at what the author was "trying to say" or might be persuaded to say at some future date). Nor should comments be short-hand notes about problems a teacher intends to explain in a conference and is therefore excused from explaining on the paper itself. Indeed, comments should offer suggestions that in the short run will lead the student to write the next paper more effectively, and in the long run will promote linguistic habits likely to lead to good writing in general.

Here, in no particular order, are a number of things that follow from this notion about paper comments:

• Comments should be accurate enough to guide the student's writing in the future, not so acerbic that they inhibit writing altogether. (The worst comments are those that accuse the student of a failing without defining it precisely enough to suggest how to avoid it in the future—comments like "awkward" and "vague." The theologians tell us that despair results from conviction of sin without hope of amendment.)

• Comments on local stylistic matters are of great importance, since they are likely to influence the mental habits involved in writing the individual sentences of which an essay is composed.

• Selectiveness in commentary is necessary, since no one can learn all aspects of a practice at once. It's best to stress a limited number of central concepts, defined flexibly enough so that they can be used to diagnose and suggest possible cures for a wide variety of writing ills.

My discussion has already taken a number of stands, some of them unfashionable. It seems useful to make these issues and their implications explicit.

II. SOME ISSUES IN TEACHING WRITING AND COMMENTING ON PAPERS

A. *Writing: Product or Process?*

A watchword of much recent composition theory is "process": teachers are warned against concentrating on papers as products and invited to engage with papers as part of the writing process. (See Chapter 1, "Composition Theory and the Curriculum," for a fuller and more nuanced analysis of trends in composition theory and practice.) An absolute distinction between writing as product and writing as process would probably be impossible to sustain with any rigor: those who try to erect such a distinction tend to do so by turning the position of which they disapprove into a straw man or caricature (a practice I shall myself undoubtedly fall into at some points). But the distinction between process and product, made less rigidly, is hardly trivial. If we focus on papers as products, we are likely to make different choices in commenting on papers, and indeed in constructing a writing course, than we will if we focus on the "writing process."

Teachers interested in the writing process may turn their classes into writing workshops in which commentary on papers is designed to spark an ongoing process of revision. In at least one influential model, this workshop atmosphere follows from the belief that students already know how to express themselves, that writing is based on an innate competence for expression. This belief is sometimes, though by no means always, accompanied by the more dubious conviction that the proper subject matter for writing should always arise from students themselves, with teachers providing at most external stimuli. Given such assumptions and procedures, good paper comments will be those that challenge students to move their thinking and writing ever onward: they will be heavily oriented toward content, questioning and probing student perceptions in the hope of enabling students to express their own rich potential. Questions of grammatical form and correctness will tend to be relegated to the realm of "copy-editing," mere polishing which attempts to give static form to a practice constantly in motion.

An interest in student papers as products is likely to lead in a different direction. Writing will tend to be considered a skill to be learned, not the expression of an innate competence that need only be elicited. As with other skills—skiing, playing the piano, driving a car—certain procedures, reducible at least in principle to precepts, will lead to success. It's therefore up to the teacher, who knows those procedures and precepts, to pass them on to the student. (To place the teacher in this role is to deal in a relatively benign way with the inescapable fact that teachers have power over students.) Inherited linguistic forms and structures, and even conventional standards of grammatical correctness, become not external or artificial "constraints" but potential enablements, just as the various combinations of finger, hand, and arm movement which produce different qualities of sound from the piano are anything but artificial or unnecessary "constraints" for those who wish to master that instrument.[3] Instead, the possibilities of form and grammar on the one hand, and thinking on the other, merge: to teach a student how to employ parallel structure (or even to use semicolons) is to teach a technique useful in certain situations, but more than that, a possible way of organizing experience and thus, ultimately, a possible way of seeing the world.

Of course, a certain kind of attention to essays as products can become an exercise in stultifying triviality, a matter of pouncing on lapses from a mindlessly narrow sense of correctness: writing "correctly" can become an end in itself, without reference to the allegiances and purposes of the writer, or to the nature of the writer's audience, or to the significance of the issues which the writer is addressing. As Keith Hjortshoj suggests in Chapter 1, the "process" theorists have been so persuasive in pointing out the limitations of such an approach that they've effected a dramatic and valuable shift in vision for anyone who thinks about writing: my own version of a product-oriented view of writing is, partly as a result of this shift, significantly different from the "orthodox" approach.

But a focus on the products of writing need not be myopic. We actually know little about the writing process (or should it be processes?), but we know a good deal about what words on a page can do. And in many situations, what is ultimately valuable to the writer and certainly to those around the writer is, not writing in process, but writing produced. To be sure, commenting on writing as a product requires tact, to avoid discouraging students whose best products may be far from exemplary, whether viewed (unhelpfully) from the vantage point of a presumed universal standard of correctness, or even from the vantage point of the writer's own purposes.

Attempts to prove that a single vision of writing is correct, proper, in accordance with the true nature of writing and learning, are not yet supported by enough hard evidence to be persuasive, and one can't help wondering if adducing such evidence is possible, even in principle. In the end, it may be better to ask what sort of writing and thinking one wants to encourage, what sort of students one has—and what sort of teacher, and person, one is oneself. Good teaching results from a fruitful meshing of the teacher's interests and abilities with those of his or her students, by way of methods that can bring out the strengths of both. To suppose that any one methodology is intrinsically so fruitful that it could replace this subtle interaction is to engage in wishful thinking or in needless despair ("If only I could find the one true method!").

B. Revision: End or Means?

One of the more important implications of the process / product controversy involves revision. At the extreme, a process-oriented course may view all writing as part of a process of revision; a product-oriented course will view revision as more means than end. The practical implications here are significant. Assignments for papers that will undergo continual and radical revision are likely to be looser than those for papers that are meant to be finished. Appropriate responses will also differ. Process-oriented teachers are likely to provide comments that seek to be supportive and open-ended. There is, however, a danger that such commentary may also be over-immediate: the question in the back of the instructor's mind may simply be, "How can I help this student to make *this paper* richer and more interesting as it evolves?" Product-oriented teachers, at their most flexible, may instead emphasize the attainment of skills that will lead to more successful products in the future, by asking themselves, "How can I show the student how to turn this sentence or paragraph into a finished expression of thought, in a way that will be 'portable,' helping the student to acquire habits that will lead to excellent products in the future?" Here the aims, and to some extent the methods, of the two allegiances may in fact begin to meet, for the product-oriented teacher is in fact interested in a certain kind of process too, a process in which the student internalizes useful writing practices ever more completely by producing a series of finished essays, thereby attaining an ever-expanding repertoire of possible modes of expression.

The virtues of teaching students to revise effectively are obvious enough. Everyone who writes knows that good writing results from good revision. Less obvious are certain problems that may arise from asking students to revise entire papers. Many students find it difficult to rethink a topic once they have written a response to it: they're mired in their first attempt. In such a situation, moving on to another, perhaps more congenial topic may be effective (and humane). Further, as I suggest below, many of the benefits associated with large-scale revising may also result from asking the student to produce revised versions of specific phrases or sentences.

A course which sees the essence of writing as a process of revision seems well suited to produce willing revisers, able to cut loose from earlier versions of their work in their search for something better. A product-oriented course may achieve something of the same effect by asking for local revisions of every paper, and by encouraging students to revise substantially those papers which seem least in need of revision. Revising stronger papers will probably be easier and more obviously successful for students, and revision may come to be seem what it ought to be, a process of enrichment and growth.

C. Two Rhetorical Contexts for Comments: Essays and Writing Classes

Theories of composition emphasizing process have proven fruitful in stressing the rhetorical situation in which writing always exists. This stress is neither the invention nor the sole property of such theories, but it is particularly well developed in them. Any intelligent view of writing must take into account the writer's purposes, the nature of his or her audience, and the kind of authorial voice or presence he or she wishes to create. These matters can drop out of sight if one's view of the products of writing is too narrow.[4] A particularly useful form of commentary on student papers relates a given problem or strength to the writer's purposes, the voice the writer has assumed, or the nature of the writer's audience. Among their many virtues, such comments remind the student that there is no such thing as a single good (or plain) style: styles are good for given purposes and given audiences.

Comments on papers are always framed by other contexts: in particular, their meaning and effect are influenced by the design of a course and by what goes on in the classroom.[5] Teachers who have clearly defined in the classroom the intended audience for an essay need not redefine it in full when they comment on a paper. Teachers who concentrate on one kind of essay for a semester need not always make explicit reference to the purposes of the essays their students write. No style of paper commentary will be effective that is not consciously adjusted to instruction in the classroom and in conferences.

D. *Rules and Precepts Underlying Comments*

One issue which should certainly be dealt with in the classroom is the nature of the precepts about writing that underlie your comments (or appear in them). In class you can make clear that precepts are (over-) compact approximations designed to reveal potential problem areas and suggest solutions, not rules to be blindly followed. We all know that the only reasonable answer to the question, "Should I avoid the passive?" is "Yes, when the passive is inappropriate." It's also clear why some teachers—unwisely, in my view—proscribe the passive entirely. At best, this proscription is a form of compulsory overcompensation (explicitly presented as such to the student), an attempt to bend the stick too far back in the hope that it will straighten out when released. At worst, it reflects a belief that there is something intrinsically (and perhaps morally) "bad" about the passive. Such beliefs should not be propagated, explicitly or tacitly, in responding to papers.

Intelligent discussion of the nature of (not "rules" but) precepts can help prevent them from seeming to be the rubrics of a ritual taken on faith. Students employ rules of thumb all the time in their daily lives, and there's no reason why they can't be brought to see their place in writing. Indeed, grasping the nature of precepts can itself be part of a liberal education. Wittgenstein points out that the space between stations on a subway map, and the direction in which the lines on the map seem to indicate the trains proceed, may have little correspondence to physical reality: you wouldn't be wise to use a subway map to find your way above ground. But the very simplifications such maps employ make them useful for their intended purpose, which is to help passengers decide where trains go and when to get on and off them. These things are a parable with implications for what we mean by "truth."

A special case in which careful explanation in class can enlighten students about the nature of linguistic (and social) reality involves the question of grammatical competence in its narrowest sense. Instead of blustering about sentence fragments, one can explain that for any dramatic stylistic device to be effective, it must seem both unexpected and (retrospectively) intended. And one can add that those who use sentence fragments indiscriminately, no matter how intelligent they may be, tend to destroy their intellectual credibility among educated teachers. If one then goes on to explore the political and social implications of this fact, so much the better, for such implications are themselves part of the context of writing.

Classroom context can alter the meaning of comments which, taken by themselves, would be misguided. Still, I'd be inclined to say on a paper "Avoid inappropriate passives" or "Is this passive necessary?", not simply "Avoid the passive." And I'd try not to fall into the trap of supposing that the much more important matters of audience and purpose can be left entirely to class discussion. Or to put it more positively: I'd take advantage of chances to reinforce explicitly the student's sense of the importance of purpose, audience, and self-presentation.

III. ONE METHOD OF COMMENTARY

I'll spend the remainder of this chapter discussing a product-oriented method of commenting on one sort of paper, the paper that explains something, that states and discusses a thesis. I've chosen to place my focus here for a number of reasons. I suppose that many, perhaps most, student papers are thesis papers. I believe that teachers may find it easier to produce comments designed to spur a student's thinking than comments designed to specify the ways in which problems in style and even grammar merge with problems in thought. Examples of the latter kind of commentary, more obviously useful to those who concentrate on the products of writing, may prove useful for even the most resolutely process-oriented teacher.

It seems appropriate to say a few words about the course from which the approach outlined below evolved, if only to emphasize that any effective style of commenting on papers must take into account the design of a course and what transpires in the classroom. Three peculiarities of the course are particularly relevant. First, it asked students to respond carefully to intellectual prose of a certain complexity. The assumption was that the best thoughts of others could interest students; indeed, the course assumed that one purpose of an education is precisely to give students access to other minds. A distinction is sometimes made between student-centered and teacher-centered writing. The course I taught aspired to center neither on teachers nor on students, but on *texts*—texts produced by published authors, by students, and by the instructor in the form of commentary on student papers. A second peculiarity, associated with the close attention I asked students to give the texts they read, was that the course tended to ask students to write on questions, not topics. Finally, the course asked for relatively short pieces of writing, so that both the students and I could pay minute attention to their sentences. The influence of these peculiarities on the style of responding to papers presented below will be obvious, as will the necessity of adapting this style to make it useful for other courses with other purposes.

A. *Making Local Comments*

SELECTIVITY

Writing effective local comments depends upon sizing up a paper through a quick initial reading, to determine its major strengths and weaknesses. Instead of extending the time required to comment on papers, an initial diagnostic reading should save time by promoting purposefulness and selectivity once commenting begins. My own selection of what to comment on is based upon a general mental list of problems that (at any given point in the semester) cannot be allowed to pass unchallenged, plus a sense that evolves as I read the paper of the two or three things this particular student most needs to hear at this particular moment.

KEYS

Many teachers distribute keys, informing students that "awk" means "awkward," "frag" means "sentence fragment," and so on. Keys can save a certain amount of time, and some teachers swear by them, but they can easily promote the sort of commentary that simply records a paper's weaknesses, in terms that would be obvious to another teacher but that may mean little to the student. It's easy to slap down an "awk" next to a sentence that offends one (for reasons one hasn't quite determined) and then move on to the next "awk" or "vague." What will this kind of commentary teach students?

Even using abbreviations to identify problems that are limited, local, and well defined may have drawbacks. How much longer does it take to write a brief, common-language explanation of a problem than to write the abbreviation of a grammatical term? (If space on the student paper is a problem, that problem can be elegantly solved by employing the "number system" explained below.) A short list of abbreviations for simple problems a teacher will explain fully in class may have some utility: such a list can act as a précis for one aspect of a writing course. But it seems important to question the use of long lists of abbreviations and the style of commentary they can encourage.

B. *Candidates for Comments: Organizational Problems (Transitions and Theses)*

Problems in the organization and structure of an essay are natural candidates for end comments. But it can also be useful to comment on such problems as they occur in a paper—to note a weak thesis, or a missing transition, or a muddled formulation that leads to an incoherent structure later on. Such matters are vital; they are also complex enough to demand clear explanation. Announcing that a transition is weak or missing (via the abbreviation "trans") will help only those students who already have a firm grasp of what it is to make a transition and therefore have erred through inattention, not ignorance. For most students, a sentence or two addressing the problem as it exists in the paper at hand will be considerably more effective, especially if it is reinforced by class discussions of problems with transitions, using examples from student papers.

A great many organizational problems, including many weak or missing transitions, can be treated as problems arising from a paper's thesis. Particularly during the first weeks of a semester, I try to make my first comment on every paper a comment, positive or negative, on its thesis. Sometimes more drastic measures are necessary. After receiving from a student three or four papers that lack structure and coherence, one might write an end comment like the following:

When I read over this paper, I see a number of ideas, many of them potentially useful and interesting, some of them misleading. I see, in other words, the raw material for a paper. What I don't see is a coherent organizational principle that molds this material into a whole and points it firmly in the direction of answering a question. And this is largely a result, I think, of your not making yourself put down at the very beginning of the paper (probably as the result of one or more previous drafts of the paper) a clear, sharp thesis that answers the question in a sentence. Such a statement would guide the reader. It would suggest to you as a writer how to organize your ideas. It would also stand as a point of reference against which you could test your ideas to see how well they serve your purposes.

This comment suggests the characteristics of a good thesis: it provides an organizational principle for an essay, it guides both reader and writer, it serves as a touchstone for ideas, and it belongs early in a paper. (How early depends on many things, among them the level of sophistication of the paper's organization and the kind of audience to which it is directed. Students who are having trouble with theses and organization, however, often profit from stating a thesis early and prominently.)

One sign of a good thesis is that it contains grammatical subordination. Grammatical subordination implies the existence in the thesis of at least two ideas with a determinate logical relationship to one another, often one of cause and effect. Such a construction, in other words, contains the germ of an explanation. Asking students to title their essays can also help them to produce better theses.

Attending to theses can provide a concrete way of dealing with a great variety of weaknesses in student papers. A useful tactic is to view theses in the light of the student's purpose in writing the paper. Incoherent papers often result when students write without a specific purpose in mind; their lack of purpose implies that their thesis is inadequate or that at some point they abandoned it. In your commentary, say so. For example, ''Your thesis needs to be accurately focussed. It answers the question, 'How, according to Weisstein, have psychologists limited human potential?' instead of 'How have psychologists limited the discovery of human potential?' But the latter is in fact the question she's interested in, and it's the one I asked you to think about.'' If you can relate problems in a thesis to the topic you set or the question you asked, students can see them more clearly.

''Answer the question'' comments also allow you to deal with essays that appear to be mere summaries. It's probably best not to write simply "Interpret, don't summarize," since all summary includes some measure of interpretation. Instead, you can write, "This is a useful summary, but it doesn't address the question . . ." and so on. If you haven't asked the student to respond to a direct question, you may want to uncover the question to which the essay in fact implicitly or explicitly responds, and then to suggest ways in which the student might have come up with a more interesting question.

Students may rely on long quotations, often with unfortunate results. A comment can remind them that they need to explain to the reader the meaning of quotations: "What exactly does this mean? Why is it important to the author? Show the reader its point and relevance." Encourage students to paraphrase if they must rehearse an author's arguments: paraphrasing well usually requires them to understand a passage. Suggest that they quote not entire sentences, but only the most important phrases or the key words. And remind them that their primary task is to produce their own argument, not to reproduce someone else's.

Another way of handling problems of incoherence, irrelevance, or purposeless summary is to invoke the audience to whom the essay should be addressed. (This of course implies that you and the writer have concretely defined the audience for whom each essay is intended—a matter of critical importance.) Needless summary means needless for a certain audience, incomplete explanation means incomplete for a certain audience, and so on. The more your comments remind students that they are writing for other people (or at the very least for their reading selves, not their writing selves), the better. Training them to focus on an audience helps to break their stultifying circle in which writing becomes simply the recording of signs which have meaning to the writer and the writer only, and only at the moment of writing.

Some of your students may have been taught to use Sheridan Baker's celebrated "inverted funnel," in which the thesis sentence comes at the end of the first paragraph, preceded by more general material designed to catch the reader's attention (a procedure that would appear to assume that theses are inherently uninteresting). The "inverted funnel" has its uses, but also its abuses. Especially toward the beginning of the semester, you may save your students from writing, and yourself from reading, a great deal of empty verbiage by making them state their theses early.

Even if students begin with a workable thesis, problems may still arise. Stylistic lapses often signal these problems, as the discussion of local corrections later in this chapter will try to show. Problems may also arise from a failure to make logical connections clear and explicit. For example, in an essay that intends to show how Kepler used his imagination in arriving at his celebrated laws, the statement that Kepler theorized the existence of elliptical orbits needs further elaboration and might prompt a comment like the following: "Fair enough, but what part did imagination play in this theorizing?" The student here knows on some level the answer to the question this comment asks; with encouragement, he or she will bring that knowledge to the level of conscious explanation.

Sometimes an analytical essay with a strong thesis and explicit logical connections will seem nonetheless lacking in argument. Often the reason is that its narrative mode of organization defeats its analytical or argumentative purposes. A narrative mode of organization is attractive to student writers for a number of reasons, some of them good ones, but it can easily weaken their arguments, and it can lead to prolixity and irrelevance.

The clearest sign of a narrative mode of organization is the presence of narrative verbs (and adverbs): "FitzGerald begins by . . . She then . . . She concludes by . . ." A sentence informing you that the author about whom a student is writing "begins by" or "continues to" or "finishes by" doing or saying something often calls for this kind of comment: "Your verb here suggests that (1) you're following X's organization, not your own; and (2) you're telling a story, not providing evidence for a thesis of your own." If this writer later brings up an issue extraneous to his or her topic, you will probably want to comment not only on the issue's irrelevance, but also on how the narrative organization led to its inclusion. Students may be surprised to learn that different kinds of organization have embedded within them powerful constraints, that the logic of a certain mode of organization can covertly replace their own logic and thus defeat their purposes in writing an essay.

Topic sentences often have the same importance for paragraphs that theses have for essays. The habit of writing topic sentences may help students achieve greater clarity and unity in their writing, particularly in essays which aim to explain complex matters. Attempts to produce topic sentences can clarify thought—or reveal the lack of a substantial idea. And when students do produce a topic sentence, it is a reasonably simple task for them to gauge its relevance to their thesis. As with theses, however, it's important to stress that writing a good topic sentence doesn't necessarily or even usually precede writing the rest of the paragraph. Often a writer arrives at an adequate thesis or topic sentence by a process of discovery involving a series of approximations made through a series of revisions.

A simple and generally reliable technique students can use to determine whether they've constructed an orderly argument is first to find the topic sentences of their paragraphs and then to read them through in order. To be sure, this technique will fail for certain kinds of discourse, organized to be less explicit in argument: even there, however, it may help to remind the writer of gaps in explicit argumentative design that need to be bridged by other means.

It's worth noting that justified doubts have been cast on the usefulness of topic sentences: the argument is usually made by showing that certain kinds of writing by competent writers in fact do not rely on topic sentences. Whatever one feels about the examples and methods involved in making such claims, they suggest an important point—the dubious value of all-purpose generalizations about writing, especially if such generalizations are made into before-the-fact prescriptive models which students are to follow in producing essays. The present chapter is concerned with *responding* to essays. Its claim is not that we should tell all students to produce topic sentences all of the time. Instead, when we receive an essay that seems ill-organized and also lacks topic sentences, we can recommend the use of them as a possible cure.

C. More Candidates for Comments: Problems with Individual Sentences

Aspects of an essay we're likely to perceive as involving fuzzy thinking or poor organization may often be more concretely and helpfully located in style or grammar. Here, for example, is a comment responding to a student essay on the philosophy of history: ''Your use of unnecessary passives allows you to avoid deciding exactly what you mean by 'history' here: do you mean 'what happened in the past' or 'writings about the past'?'' This comment asks the student to do something specific (specify agency by avoiding inappropriate passives) instead of something general and, to many students, both insulting and daunting (think more clearly). One of the sentences to which the above comment responded read as follows: "History is usually determined by an author's interpretation, reflecting past and present." Had the writer used the active voice—"the author determines history"—he would probably have realized that something was wrong with his argument, or at the very least with his verb.

Whenever you can, then, write comments that locate conceptual problems in stylistic habits with specific remedies. Merely telling students that they are being vague or awkward has little utility. Explaining the particular intellectual mistake that has created vagueness or awkwardness is better but still not ideal, since your explanation may be local and non-transferable. It's more promising to comment on the local problem in a way that encourages linguistic habits likely to lead to clearer thinking.

Commenting on the sentences of a student essay is a complex task which, like recognizing a face or riding a bicycle, is easier to perform than to describe. Happily, two considerations spring to mind, suggesting that an attempt to offer advice on all possible aspects of the process is unnecessary—that the same problem can be approached in a variety of ways, and that since students are more likely to learn how to apply a small number of precepts than a large number, it's better to stretch those precepts than to multiply categories endlessly. I offer below a brief list of major areas on which students and teachers can profitably concentrate. You will obviously wish to modify and supplement this list, to meet the needs of your students and the requirements of the particular kind or kinds of writing you wish them to master.

VERBS (AND THE PASSIVE)

When a sentence appears to have gone wrong, look first at the verb or verbs it contains. Does each verb really mean precisely what it should? Does it represent an action, or simply assert a state of being? If it's in the passive voice, does it need to be? Students who learn to question every verb they employ are well on their way to becoming clear and effective writers, for posing and answering such questions will involve them in a continuing process of fruitful revision.

Two common verb problems involve the verb "to be" and the passive voice. Both the verb "to be" and the passive have their uses, but both may be more abused than appropriately used by inexperienced writers.

The verb "to be" can hardly be dispensed with entirely, but it needs to be used with discretion. The problem is that it doesn't do anything: it simply asserts a state of existence. Vigorous, clear writing demands sentences in which agents perform actions. The verb "to be" too often gives rise to a construction Joseph Williams has aptly called the nominalization, which turns what ought to be a verb into a noun coupled with a less specific and forceful verb, often a form of "to be." Thus: "We need to know more" becomes "There is a need for more information," or "We decided what to do" becomes "We made a determination on the proper course of action to be followed." (Williams, 9–19, gives an illuminating discussion of nominalizations; on this and other points, he has much to teach those of us who correct student papers.)

Unnecessary passives, like weak verbs, vitiate prose. Because the passive can obscure agency, it encourages students to skirt important issues. When they turn passive voices into active, they may clarify their ideas by supplying missing links. Here is one example of how changing from the passive to the active voice can promote clarity:

1. Original version with passives:

"Facts become historical when it is determined, according to how society is presently affected by them, whether the facts should be noted as historically significant."

2. Intermediate version, with passives turned into actives or otherwise removed:

"Facts become historical when a historian determines whether or not to treat them as historically significant: historians base this decision on how the facts affect society at present."

3. Final version, prompted by the clarity that using the active lends to the issue the student wishes to discuss (and with "historians," finally, as the agents throughout):

"Historians transform mere facts about the past into historical facts by choosing to include them in their narratives. Why do they dignify some facts in this way, but neglect others? They promote 'mere facts' to the status of 'historical facts' because of their relevance to present-day concerns."

The active voice has many virtues. It's vigorous. It promotes conciseness. It presents action directly (Strunk and White 18–19). It takes less time and effort to read (Hirsch 93). Finally, by helping to make the subjects of sentences consistent, it aids coherence. (I'll have more to say about consistent sentence subjects in a moment; Williams, 21–23, is illuminating on this point with respect to active versus passive voice.)

Focusing on verbs yields several benefits. For you, it provides a starting point: by attending to a paper's verbs you can pinpoint many of its problems. For students, it provides something to concentrate on, a place to begin to revise: they can focus on the central category of verb problems more easily than on several smaller categories.

SENTENCE SUBJECTS

If verbs are the first place to look in a sentence gone wrong, the grammatical subject of the sentence is the second. Avoiding unnecessary passives, as we've already seen, will help to avoid one kind of objectionable subject, the subject that doesn't do anything, that isn't an agent. A second problem arises when a subject doesn't match its verb: this is sometimes called a "statement error" or "faulty predication" (terms which in my experience convey little to students). Thus in the sentence "Her goals tend toward living up to the legends of the past," the subject and verb almost certainly don't match: "her goals" aren't likely to *tend toward* anything, they *are* something.

We've already touched briefly on a third problem with sentence subjects. In general, paragraphs are clearer and easier to follow if the grammatical subjects of their sentences occur in an appropriate and predictable pattern (or "sequence"). In the "Talk of the Town" section of *The New Yorker,* for instance, the same grammatical subject and its cognates often serve for an entire paragraph. Some students seem to go out of their way to find an unrelated subject for each new sentence; they may lapse into an unnecessary passive simply to avoid repeating a sentence subject. Such students need to learn better ways to achieve sentence variety. A subject and its cognates should continue to be employed until their usefulness is exhausted, probably because the writer has shifted to a slightly different aspect of his or her topic. When you come upon a student paragraph that seems jumbled or fuzzy but find it hard to determine why, pause a moment to consider the sequence of sentence subjects it contains.

Exploring fully the problem of the sequence of sentence subjects would necessitate analyzing several long paragraphs. I offer instead a more modest example, drawn from a student discussion of Kafka's *The Metamorphosis,* a story in which the hero awakens one morning to find himself transformed into a beetle:

> Gregor awakes to a new awareness of his existence. He awakes to inexpressible feeling of alienation from the world around him, a world to which he had adapted himself to the point of self-oblivion. His complete inner loneliness, the inaccessibility of his real self in contrast to the world around him and to his ordinary self-consciousness, are given expression in his new shape. The hard shell of a beetle represents his defense against the emptiness of his life.

The first two sentences here employ the same basic subject, using first a proper name and then a cognate (here, a pronoun). The third sentence shifts subjects, and the fourth shifts again. Schematically, we might represent this pattern with the notation "a, a, b, c." But what if we change the third sentence from the passive to the active? We then get:

> Gregor awakens to a new awareness of his existence. He awakes to an inexpressible feeling of alienation from the world around him, a world to which he had adapted himself to the point of self-oblivion. His new shape expresses his complete inner loneliness, the inaccessibility of his real self in contrast to the world around him and to his ordinary self-consciousness. The hard shell of a beetle represents his defense against the emptiness of his life.

Schematically, this becomes "a, a, b, b." This revision makes the sentences clearer and easier to read, partly because keeping to the same sentence subject tends to make a writer adhere to the principle of introducing new material at the end of a sentence and using the opening of the sentence to prepare for such new material.

In this example, the added efficiency in expression comes at the expense of some rhetorical drama. The original version forces the reader to wait an unusually long time for the verb in sentence three: the writer has constructed what is known as a "periodic sentence." Accordingly, one might argue that this is a moment when the writer ought to break the rule concerning continuity of sentence subjects. But such a rhetorical maneuver will itself be most effective if, in the sentences surrounding the passage, the writer has kept to the rule, if the sentence subjects in the paragraph as a whole exhibit a clarity and orderliness which throw this rhetorical moment into relief.

NEEDLESS WORDS

Needless words should always be avoided, because wordiness obscures meaning. But there's a difference between taking the time to buttress an assertion with several apt examples or to explain a complex idea thoroughly, using a number of different formulations, and wasting the reader's time with repetitiveness or redundancy. Students may think you're being contradictory in telling them to use more words at one point in their paper, but fewer at another: it's important to explain both in class and in your paper comments why your request is anything but contradictory.

A common kind of wordiness involves the use of what I call the "doublet," a pair of words or phrases where one word is needed. Sometimes one of the words expresses the writer's meaning and the other is simply unnecessary. More often, neither is right: the student writes down a word, subliminally realizes that it won't quite do the job, and then produces another, hoping to edge the first word into the conceptual space it won't quite fill. Usually (not "almost invariably"), what's needed is a third word to replace both the others.

Often when students use pairs of words, they betray uncertainty or misunderstanding. They may also be registering in an overcompressed form an insight that is worth pursuing, as in this sentence on Gothic cathedrals: "These were perfectly functional, but at the same time displayed great beauty and artistic value." Students who distinguish between "great beauty" and "artistic value" in this context may simply be wasting words; they may also have something further to say on the subject that deserves eliciting. Urge them to think further by asking, "How are these different? Are they different? Are you interested in saying something further about aspects of Gothic style that are artistically valuable but *aren't* beautiful? Are such aspects functional? Students who, encouraged by your paper comments, develop the habit of examining their paired words will probably produce less wordy essays: they may also learn to take fuller advantage of half-formed insights.

Clichés and prefabricated phrases (for example, saying that a combination of factual information and conceptual insight is what knowledge "is all about"—which, by the way, relies on a weak verb) can lead to more than wordiness: they can inhibit thought. Rephrasing usually makes the meaning clearer to writer and reader.[6]

CONNECTORS

Connectors are, broadly speaking, any words that make connections. They include not only "moreover," "furthermore," "also," and the like, but also "and" and prepositions. Many student writers employ subordinating conjunctions as connectors less often than they should, and coordinating conjunctions more often. The coordinating conjunction "and" has many legitimate uses, but too often it allows a writer simply to place side by side two parts of a sentence that require a stronger connection. In the sentence

> "X believes that students should not just memorize facts and that facts depend on frames of reference,"

the student should be urged to begin revising by replacing "and that" with the subordinating conjunction "because." Similarly, a word like "moreover" will work well when a series of things is being listed, but it may also enable a writer to slide from one issue to another without making a strong connection. Prepositions also can keep connections from being clear: "X praises what he provocatively calls 'bull' while [should be 'by'] discussing facts and interpretation." In commenting on such problems, it's helpful to repeat a key word or phrase (here "connection" or "logical connection") to ensure that students become aware of the underlying issue.

PARALLELISM

I've mentioned the usefulness of working with a relatively small number of concepts in commenting on papers, to avoid convincing students that even the names of their writing problems are beyond counting, much less surmounting: awe at the grammatical sublime can freeze the mind. One concept that will cover a multitude of stylistic and conceptual sins is parallelism. In its simplest form, the injunction to put parallel ideas into parallel grammatical form makes for a precise and elegant style (or "makes for precision and elegance in writing," but not "makes for precision and an elegant style"). Any good style manual will provide a discussion of this kind of parallelism: see, for instance, Chapter 7, "Improving Sentences."

The notion of parallelism can also be extended to locate faults in basic sentence structure like the following:

> He enjoys the power he has over people and that he can choose to use it or not.

It would be possible simply to label what has gone wrong here: one could talk of a shift of sentence structure or resort to the useless "awk." But telling the student to make the sentence elements that follow the verb parallel provides a task to perform and suggests something to attempt in writing future papers, instead of a giving a mere diagnosis. (Here as in the case of "doublets," one hopes that, in the process of trying to create parallelism, students will come to recognize those moments when they need to produce a completely new formulation instead of trying to salvage the old one.) Student success in creating parallel structures will, of course, depend in part on your having spent time in class explaining parallelism and revising some examples of faulty parallelism, preferably taken from their papers—a task that's relatively painless, since unravelling problems in parallelism can be intricate enough to have a certain entertainment value.

MY TWO ARBITRARY PROHIBITIONS—AND YOURS

In my responses to papers, I tend to proscribe the use of the "lonely this" (that is, "this" instead of "this person," "this idea," and so on) as well as the use of parentheses. These are artificial prohibitions, since both can be useful tools in writing. But in the world of my experience as a teacher, as opposed to the world of theory, I've found that students usually go astray with both: students use the lonely "this" when they haven't bothered to decide exactly what they're referring to, and they use parentheses to shoehorn words into sentences without making logical connections.

Prohibitions that are practically useful though theoretically exceptionable have a certain utility because of their very arbitrariness, so long as you make that arbitrariness a subject of discussion with your students, and so long as they involve relatively minor aspects of style. Such prohibitions provide a reminder that the style you're promoting is one kind of style, not style itself, and that expository writing is more a bag of tricks to get a job done than a state of grace. They promote distance on writing as writing. And they are specific and concrete, giving students trouble spots to look for as they learn to become their own editors.

D. Planning Comments

RUNNING COMMENTARY

Much of my discussion is based on the assumption that local comments are where the job of teaching writing gets done. But dense local commentary, and even local commentary that is appropriately selective, can have dangers. These dangers are perhaps most acute in comments on a paper's content, but they can extend to comments on style as well. Running commentary is at best a helpful and productive dialogue between teacher and student; it can easily become a less productive form of discourse. The dialogue can become a monologue, recording in various shades of irony or pity one's exasperation with the paper at hand; it can also become a form of competition, in which the teacher demonstrates how much more intelligent, erudite, and verbally gifted he or she is than the student. Reducing the student to a dramatically vivid sense of his lack of wisdom may be an important end in some celebrated dialogues; commentary on student papers should have a less corrosive character.

END COMMENTS

A good strategy in an end comment is to mention the paper's main strengths and to tell the writer the two or three most important things he or she needs to do to improve in the future. You needn't justify your grade in your final comment, though it doesn't hurt to give a general sense of what enhanced or detracted from the paper's quality.

It is probably unwise to connect praise and criticism with "but" or "although": your praise may seem perfunctory, a matter of giving something with one hand only to take it back with the other.

Some teachers find the end comment a particularly appropriate place to deal with a paper's content and argument. A focused response of several lines to the argument of a paper lets your student know you've read an essay with care, treating it as an argument rather than an exercise, and it avoids the problems of competitive running commentary.

REWRITING FOR STUDENTS

Rewriting phrases or sentences for students comes as something of a last resort, based on the judgment that another kind of comment would be too complicated to be worth the trouble for you or your student. In most instances, mere rewriting for students is unnecessary. You can, if necessary, spell out problems like ambiguity ("this is ambiguous: do you mean 'x' or 'y'?" or dangling participles ("be careful: you're saying that you were in a dilapidated condition; you mean to say this about the house you're describing"). Rewriting can be appropriate, however, when it illuminates a problem. Students who have a poor ear for diction, for example, sometimes need to see an alternative phrasing. In the following sentence from an essay on Machiavelli, you could replace "cheap" with "stingy": "The prince should budget, but not overtax or be too cheap with his money."

In other situations, you may think that seeing a suggested revision will itself help a student understand the underlying problem; in these cases you're hoping that your revision will serve as a model that will linger in the mind. Sometimes you can rewrite simply to give students (usually good ones) an idea of other possibilities. Thus in the sentence, "Even the constancy of history, once prevalent in schoolbooks, has disappeared" you could mark "constancy of history" as "unclear," and add, "Do you mean 'uniformity among textbooks' or something more than that?" But rewriting can become addictive, transforming commentary into mere editing. Students need to learn how to make their own revisions, and they shouldn't be led to think that you're primarily interested in remolding them in your own (peculiar) stylistic image. Whenever you can, try to show them how they might have recognized a problem themselves.

When you can't easily define an error, never resort to a bare "awkward.'' If you find direct, rigorous explanation difficult, an *ad hominem* appeal may serve, as with the slip of diction in this sentence from an essay on Machiavelli: ''If a prince's people disapprove of his actions, they will dispose of him.'' A useful comment might read, '' 'Dispose of' is awkward—sounds like paper towels.'' If all else fails, giving a concrete sense of what's gone wrong by rewriting a phrase for a student is likely to be more helpful than simply putting an ''awk'' or ''vague'' next to it.

THE ''NUMBER SYSTEM'': COMMENTS THAT ELICIT RESPONSE

The simplest way to ensure that students will understand and respond to your commentary is to ask them to re-write the phrases and sentences you've singled out, and hand their revised versions back to you for checking. Such checking will consume a certain amount of your time, but it can help prevent the energy you spent commenting on the paper in the first place from being wasted. In some courses, rewriting entire papers is the norm. In most, a less rigorous approach may serve.

If you make your comments by writing numbers on the student paper, keyed to comments you write on a separate sheet of paper, your students can respond on yet another sheet, also keyed to the numbers you've given your comments. I call this, for want of a better term, the ''number system.'' The number system has a number of advantages. It makes it easier for students to revise individual phrases and sentences you've commented on, and for you to check their revisions: with assiduous students, this can develop into a genuine dialogue, in which the student can tell you which of your comments he can't understand or doesn't wish to accept, and you can reply. It makes for legibility, since you needn't squeeze your comments onto whatever space is left on the student paper. It saves you from having to write anything but numbers on smeary erasable bond. If you have scanned the paper in advance, it facilitates grouping comments: a single number can refer to a multitude of, say, verb problems or unnecessary passives, providing a clear reminder of repeated errors, and thus of *patterns* of error.

The number system is particularly useful for teachers who prefer to write on a word processor, as I myself do. Besides speeding and making more legible the job of responding to papers, using a word processor and the "number system" allows you to make individual comments as you go along, but then to regroup them by category. A word processor also allows you to write your end comment last but to place it at the top of your sheet. Students appreciate this visual sign that what matters most is your over-all assessment of their work, and it's easier to achieve a positive, supportive tone in an extended end comment than it is in the necessarily briefer, more telegraphic local comments.

Comments made by the number system may involve only a few words, not complete sentences. A useful exercise late in the semester is simply to underline and number problems, asking students to name them as well as to revise them.

No matter what system of correcting you use, the moment when you return student papers in class has a certain immediacy. You can take advantage of your students' focused interest in your reaction to their papers by having them begin to respond to your comments at once. Wander around the classroom helping each student decipher your handwriting (if you don't correct with typewriter or word processor); explain what a weak passive is and how to rewrite the sentence in which one appears. Especially at the beginning of the semester, when you and your writing vocabulary are unfamiliar to your students, in-class correcting can be invaluable.

COMMENTS ON PAPERS THAT WILL BE COMPLETELY REVISED

Though it's always unwise to blanket student papers with corrections and suggestions, overwhelming commentary is particularly counter-productive with papers you expect students to revise from top to bottom. Major revision depends upon a writer's willingness to discard sentences and even paragraphs, to move things around, to abandon the old and try something new. There's little point in asking students to concentrate on improving sentences that might better disappear to make way for new material and new thinking.[7] Local corrections for papers that will be entirely revised should probably be light; the emphasis should fall on marginal and end comments that suggest concrete steps to take in revising, challenging the student to rethink ideas.

Does this mean that in commenting on such papers, it's best to ignore individual sentences? Not quite. Certain sentences, after all, guide the progress of an entire essay: the thesis, topic sentences, transitions. It's often possible and desirable to anchor one's suggestions for complete revision in a discussion of how a thesis might be strengthened or a transition negotiated. We can comment on the key sentences in an essay and still avoid inadvertently encouraging students to fixate on the sentences they have written, in the order in which they've written them.

E. Considering Your Students' Needs, and Your Own

CONFERENCES

Conferences can play an important role in the teaching of writing, but it is unwise to skimp on paper comments with the tacit assumption that you'll take care of everything in conference. You probably lack the time to teach writing to your class on a tutorial basis; you can, however, teach a great deal through written commentary. For a more extended discussion of conferences see "Working with Individual Students" in Chapter 3.

MORALE AND TONE

Writers are easily discouraged. No matter how helpful your commentary on a paper may be, a student may find the growth it requests threatening or at least unwelcome. There is no easy solution to this problem, particularly when you're dealing with weak papers. Empty praise is likely to sound empty, especially if it's intended to counterbalance substantive indications of a need for improvement. Misleading praise is worse than nothing.

An accurate diagnosis of problems seems to me imperative as I comment on papers. I hope that a friendly and supportive manner in class and in conferences will counterbalance the austerity of much of my commentary. Perhaps it does. But time spent looking for and acknowledging aspects of a paper that deserve praise is never wasted. It is particularly effective to praise a student in a way designed to transform haphazard, intuitive moments of verbal felicity into consciously possessed skills. You can praise a student for using parallel structure effectively by writing a comment that tells the student why parallelism is effective in this place and for this purpose. Or you can praise an insight and at the same time suggest how it ties in with other insights in the paper, even if the student hasn't made the connections explicit.

You should always praise a paper's strengths in your end comment; you can sometimes do so elsewhere as well, even in places where promise is accompanied by problems. Here, for example, is the first sentence of an essay on history: "Historians process facts to determine whether or not they are pertinent to their historical views, just as one sifts sand to find the finest grains." Here's a possible response: "I'm glad to see that you're using your imagination to come up with this simile. It doesn't quite work, however, because you don't give us a clear connection between the grains of sand and pertinent historical facts: smallness and pertinence aren't adequately analogous." In general, it's a mistake to attempt to lighten the tone of your comments by making jokes at the expense of the student writer: flights of fancy about sifters or trips to the sea-shore wouldn't help much here, even if you managed to make them amusing. Even well-intentioned humor can seem snide and super-cilious to people struggling with their prose.

PROMPTNESS

No matter how well you comment on papers, your commentary needs to be prompt for students to benefit fully from it. Ideally, this means returning papers during the class meeting after they are handed in. At the very least, it means ensuring that students have the benefit of your response to each paper before they must write another. (Splitting a class into halves that write papers on different topics and hand them in on different days will help you to return papers promptly.) Be prompt; your class will appreciate it, and the success of your course demands it.

HOW LONG, O LORD, HOW LONG?

Commenting on papers takes time, but it need not take an eternity. Speed comes in part with experience, as you discover which problems are most important to you and how to handle them. It can also be pro-moted by a thoughtful strategy of selection, based on the quick initial reading of each paper I've already recommended. I help maintain my own sanity by splitting my class into halves so that I never comment on essays from more than half the class. I find that my commentary deteriorates in speed and quality after that point, the topic having lost its bloom.

Commenting on papers, like many other tasks, will expand to fill as much time as you allow. There's no point in swamping students with more comments than they can reasonably be expected to take in at a sitting. Time yourself if necessary: force yourself to keep near an appropriate time limit. The concentrated, pointed attention necessary to respond to papers in a reasonable length of time is likely to produce comments that promote learning.

Teachers with large classes, or with several composition classes to teach simultaneously, may have to consider special, perhaps drastic methods to keep the task of responding to papers from becoming an impossible burden. It would seem reasonable to comment on only a portion of student work fully, and simply to look over the rest with little or no commentary, if the alternative is to respond to all the student work in a rushed and haphazard manner.

MECHANICS: LATENESS AND FORMAT

It's important to set policy about certain matters with yourself and your students from the beginning of the semester. Late papers should be severely discouraged. They place an added burden on you, and they tend to short-circuit the circle of writing and response on which the success of any writing course depends. Some teachers allow each student one or two late papers for the semester; others refuse to look at late papers at all. Pick a rule and stick to it, except in cases of genuine hardship.

It makes sense to ask your students to hand in their work in a physical form you find congenial. If you want typing, require it. If you assign papers too frequently to demand typing or you believe that typing discourages last-minute revisions, demand legibility, which can be promoted by writing on every other line. If you like wide margins, ask for them.

It's useful to require students to keep their work in a folder, which you may or may not wish to see every time they hand in a paper but will definitely want to see when they come in for conferences, and at the end of the semester. You may also find it useful to keep your own record of each student's work, perhaps in the form of a page devoted to brief comments on each student's essays.

F. Checklist and Sample Commentary

A SUMMARY CHECKLIST FOR COMMENTARY

Aims: 1. To improve the student's linguistic habits.
2. To improve the student's next paper as much as possible.

1. A Useful Context for Paper-Commenting:
Whenever possible, make paper commentary part of a process of *directed revision.* Try to:
- have students respond, in writing, to your comments
- assign substantive revisions regularly
- plan revisions with the student after you return the original essay
- respond to the revised version (comment on it, discuss it if possible) so as to acknowledge its achievements
- revise a paper in class, collectively, from time to time.

2. Significant Writing Problems:
- The thesis
- Verb problems (especially over-reliance on forms of "to be," and on passive constructions)
- Paragraph unity and development (this means also looking closely at transitions between sentences and between paragraphs)
- Subjects of sentences (and of sequences of sentences)
- Needless words
- Parallelism

3. Procedures for Commenting:

a. Read through the paper quickly.

b. Comment on it (by whatever system).
   - Mark significant errors.
   - Make sure students understand your comments:
   - write clearly

- use prose rther. thn. abbrvs.
- discuss widespread or especially complicated errors in class
- don't rely on conferences to clarify comments and corrections

c. Write an end (or summary) comment that:
- addresses the writer and his or her thesis as though both were real and counted for something, even beyond the boundaries of your course
- focuses on the 2 or 3 things that—at this time, and for this student—would most improve the next essay
- adopts an encouraging and forward-looking tone, as much as is consistent with honesty. Think of yourself as recommending improvements rather than offering a bill of indictment.

d. In marginal and end comments, make specific technical recommendations wherever possible, connecting questions of meaning with questions of style and rhetoric. This will give your students concrete, specific things *to do*.

e. Keep a record of your comments on each student.

What You Can Do in a Comment:

1. Place a problem in a useful category.
2. Show how a problem can be dealt with. As a last resort, rewrite.
3. Show how a problem can be recognized next time.
4. Refer to a fuller discussion in a style manual, but only if you have reason to believe the student will consult the manual. (One reason would be that the student will have to produce a revision.)
5. Relate a problem to the writer's purpose, or to a difficulty it's likely to cause a reader.
6. Never write just "awkward."

A PAPER AND SAMPLE COMMENTARY

The page that follows transcribes a brief student paper, written early in the semester, and one possible way of commenting on it. The paper took as its text an essay by Frances FitzGerald comparing current American history textbooks with those of the 1950s. The student was asked to respond to the question, "What is FitzGerald's attitude toward the new textbooks?" The audience for the paper was, by the announced convention of the course, the members of the composition class (including, but not limited to, the instructor): that is, a group of intelligent people who had read the essay but might not have understood it fully. The paper grasps FitzGerald's basic attitude toward both newer and older textbooks, though it misses her reservations about the newer ones and fails to take advantage of the full richness of her discussion.

The commenter here has chosen to group his comments and to be selective, ignoring certain problems in favor of others. He passes over or simply revises a number of obvious problems, such as vague diction ("most history texts were *similar*" [to what?]) and a tendency toward wordiness in certain sentences ("They served as *a source of* propaganda to the American child *growing up in the fifties*"). The focus lies instead on thesis, verbs, and the sequence of sentence subjects. Apparently the commenter believes that, at this particular moment, the student most needs to improve in these matters and shouldn't be distracted from them by a host of other, less important problems. There's a marked attempt to locate problems of thought in problems of style, but the commenter hasn't neglected content. Apparently considering the paper a relatively successful effort from this student, and one which contains the germs of insights the student might profitably develop, the commenter suggests (but does not require) that it be a "revision paper," one of a specified number of papers the student must completely rewrite during the semester.

Two further points. In comment 2a, the commenter has chosen not to raise the question of how to use the verb's "comprise." The assumption here is that the specific problem will disappear when the student tries to apply the general precept of avoiding unnecessary passives. Finally, in a number of comments, the commenter uses abstract terms for key concepts ("agency," for instance), but pauses to give a common-language equivalent, supposing that it's too early in the semester for the student to have a concrete grasp of these terms and their practical consequences.

Student Essay

In "Rewriting American History," Frances FitzGerald states that recent history textbooks offer a more realistic view of history than their ~~1950's~~ predecessors. In the 1950's, most history texts were similar. They were comprised of a series of chronological statements that seldom revealed American's bad points. They served as a source of propaganda to the American child growing up in the fifties. The books displayed America's glory and left little room to question it. The new texts, on the other hand, provide a full spectrum of information about America's historical past. The student, unlike those in the fifties, is asked to draw his own conclusions about historical events. He receives widespread cultural information which he applies to various questions concerning American history. Memorization is no longer stressed. Instead, students are asked to consult various points of view about a topic and conclude "why" events occured. FitzGerald believes that this approach to history offers a better view of history. The historian interprets; why not the student? *good question*

Commentary:

The most interesting sentence here, Karen, is your last, where I think you come closest to saying what you want to say about why FitzGerald seems to prefer the newer textbooks. It would have been good to incorporate the insight of this sentence into the way you formulated your thesis, so that in your opening sentence you'd have used a word of praise other than ''realistic'' (see #1 below).

In general, your insights in this paper seem headed in a useful direction, but they need to be more developed, and the paper could easily be longer. This means that you might want to make this one of your revision papers. If you do, you should look over

F's essay again with an eye to catching any reservations she has about the new textbooks. And you might also want to ask yourself how one set of textbooks could represent American history more accurately than another, if all history simply reflects the beliefs of the person who writes it. (F's discussion implies some interesting things about this problem.)

Some local comments:

1. It's important to pay close attention to the precise terms in which you formulate your thesis. The key word you use here to describe your subject, FitzGerald's view of the recent textbooks, is "realistic" (1a). Is "realism" really at the center of her interest in the textbooks? The rest of your essay begins to suggest that other issues may be more important to her, and your thesis should be worded to reflect this. Similarly, at 1b, is it really "information" that the student gains from the new texts, but not from the old? And in your last sentence, you talk about a "better" view of history but don't really define what's better about it.

2. Are these passives necessary? Or do they unnecessarily obscure *agency*—do they hide who's doing what to whom?

3. In both these cases you need to give a more extended account of *causality*, of why things are happening and who's making them happen. Note that in 3b your use of "and" simply associates the two ideas in the sentence, instead of suggesting the logical relationship between them. Do you mean "The books spent so much time praising America's glory that they left little room to question it?"

4. At 4a, you shift from talking about textbooks to talking about "the student." But since what you're interested in discussing is how different kinds of textbooks *do* something to students, it would probably be better to keep textbooks, here the *new* textbooks, as the sentence subjects and thus the agents, the things that are doing something in the sentences. Try revising these sentences in this way, and I think you'll see an improvement; among other things, you'll be able to get rid of some of the passives I've questioned (2b—2d).

IV. GRADING

I find that my interest in grades decreases as the years go by: I'd rather spend my energy on the task of writing helpful responses to student papers. But students tend to care about grades, and assigning grades can have pedagogic value. The problem of grading student papers in a writing course is probably best approached by asking the question, "What style of grading is most likely to help students learn how to write?" When the question is asked in this way, one thing becomes clear: giving high grades to a student whose writing doesn't deserve them is counterproductive, since they will imply that the student has little to learn.

Two kinds of papers present particularly difficult problems for the grader in writing courses: papers in which content seems much better than form (or vice-versa) and linguistically weak papers by students whose first language is not English. In both cases, the following rule can help put things in perspective, though it probably won't remove all doubts and questions: *never give a paper in a writing course a grade higher than its writing deserves*. It's always tempting to give a thoughtful but badly expressed paper a high grade, but this temptation ought to be resisted. You're not doing bright students a favor by giving them grades that suggest, erroneously, that they already command the stylistic resources their thinking requires. This is likely to be just what their teachers have been tacitly telling them all along, or they'd be better writers. Students can generally learn to write as well as they think; your job is to encourage them to do just that.

Papers that are technically competent but vapid in thought raise a different problem. One way to deal with such papers, as I've already suggested, is to point out the inadequate complexity of their theses, but what about grading them? Clearly enough, such papers will never get A's, but is it really fair to give them a higher grade than one gives a thoughtful but grammatically and stylistically incompetent paper? The answer seems to me a qualified "maybe." I'm convinced that intelligent but incompetent papers should be marked down; if this involves giving them lower grades than competent but vapid papers, so be it. In the end, one hopes that the more thoughtful student's writing will improve so that he or she will overtake the less thoughtful—one hopes this, but one shouldn't take responsibility for making it happen through an unrealistic adjustment of grades.

In theory, my discussion should already have covered a special category of papers that seem less accomplished in language than in thought:

papers written by students whose first language is not English, and who have not yet mastered English. In practice, I find these cases difficult to deal with as a grader, perhaps because I assume (often wrongly) that the necessary linguistic improvement will be relatively hard to come by. But again, it seems ultimately counterproductive to give such a student an unrealistic sense of his or her abilities as a writer. (Fur further comment, see Chapter 8, Section VIII, "Special Instruction for Non-Native Speakers of English.")

In my initial reading of a paper, I try to form a reasonably fixed estimate of the grade it deserves. I do this before turning my energy to detailed commentary, so that my sense of the paper's quality will be based on my impression of it as a reader, instead of being skewed by the problems (or exhilarations) it gives me as a writer of comments. Laying out schematically a process that is more or less intuitive, I'd say that in grading "thesis" papers of the kind I've been discussing, I ask myself the following set of questions:

1. Does the paper have a thesis?
2. Does the thesis address itself to an appropriate question or topic?
3. Is the paper free from long stretches of quotations and summaries that exist only for their own sakes and remain unanalyzed?
4. Can the writer produce complete sentences?
5. Is the paper free from basic grammatical errors?

If the answer to any of these questions is "no," I give the paper some kind of C. If the answer to most of the questions is "no," its grade will be even lower.

For papers which have emerged unscathed thus far, I add the following questions:

6. How thoughtful is the paper? Does it show real originality?
7. How adequate is the thesis? Does it respond to its question or topic in a full and interesting way? Does it have an appropriate degree of complexity?
8. How well organized is the paper? Does it stick to the point? Does every paragraph contain a clear topic sentence? If not, is another kind of organizing principle at work? Are the transitions well made? Does it have a real conclusion, not simply a stopping place?

9. Is the style efficient, not wordy or unclear?

10. Does the writing betray any special elegance?

11. Above all, can I hear a lively, intelligent, interesting human voice speaking to me (or to another audience, if that's what the writer intends) as I read the paper?

Depending on my answers to such questions, I give the paper some kind of A or some kind of B.

The criteria different teachers use in grading, and their relative weighting of those criteria, will of course differ. (For a useful, and more extensive, discussion of grading criteria, see Irmscher, Chapter 13.) The ones I have given here may be of limited use to other teachers. However that may be, it seems important for all teachers to become as self-conscious as possible about the criteria they in fact employ when they grade. Further, there's no point in keeping this information secret from students. The set of "Characteristics" listed below provides an example of one way to convey to students a sense of what's important in one kind of writing course. I think it's a good idea to distribute some such description, appropriate to the kind of course you're teaching, to your students—and to read it through before you grade each set of papers.

Characteristics:

A Detailed understanding of the text; sound organization; few or no mechanical mistakes; clear, unambiguous sentences, perhaps with a touch of elegance—in the best A papers, a lively and intelligent voice seems to speak; it has something interesting to say, says it clearly and gracefully to an appropriate audience, and supports if fully.

B Clear thesis, organization, and continuity; probably some minor mechanical errors but no major ones; slightly awkward style at times; ideas that are reasonable and are anchored in the text—thought has obviously gone into the paper; it is solid but not striking; the writer has a definite point to make and makes it an organized and competent way, and to a definite audience; as the Bowery bum said of his bottle of Thunderbird wine, it's "good but not great."

C A weak, fuzzy thesis and perhaps illogical arguments to support it; a certain amount of confusion about what the text at hand actually says; many minor mechanical errors and perhaps some major ones (such as incomplete sentences); examples given for their own sake or to demonstrate that the writer has read the text, not to prove a point; organization rambles or disappears; words are misused; diction is inconsistent; proofreading is weak; the intended audience is unclear—there are some ideas here, but the writer needs help and work to make them clear to another reader.

D Thesis missing; major mechanical problems; poor organization; serious misreadings of the text; stretches in which the writer simply gives a narrative account of the essay for no apparent purpose; the paper is much shorter than the assigned length—the writer doesn't really have a point to make and has serious problems in writing and reading at an appropriate level.

F The paper is plagiarized in part or as a whole, or it shows general weaknesses even graver than those of a D paper.

In multi-sectioned courses, course leaders often help to set standards and check for uniformity of grading from section to section. Beyond that, it's always helpful to discuss these matters with other teachers, comparing notes and student papers.

Finally, here is a list of ideas about grading which you may find helpful:

1. Try not to inflate your grades. Your comments will be more incisive (and helpful) if you force yourself to make honest distinctions between good and not-so-good work.

2. Don't give everyone a B. Unless considerable teaching experience suggests otherwise, assume that your students represent something approaching a normal distribution of A's, B's, and C's.

3. Don't allow grades to swamp commentary. Writing comments primarily intended to justify a grade and writing comments primarily intended to teach students how to write are different occupations. Prefer the latter.

4. At the beginning of the semester, a check-plus, check, check-minus grading system may be good for everyone's morale. Some teachers use this system throughout the semester or simply refuse to grade papers at all. It's possible to convey a sense of student achievement by making comments on papers and inviting students to come in for a conference periodically to gain a more precise sense of how they're doing.

Indeed, some teachers consider it pedagogically useful to discuss in detail with their classes general criteria for grading student papers, but leave the specific application of those criteria to the students themselves (at least until the end of the semester). Tactics like these make me uneasy, but many teachers I respect swear by them. If you decide not to put grades on papers, be prepared for resistance, at least initially: students generally like to know where they stand.

5. If you ask students to make local responses to your comments (perhaps by using the "number system" I described above), the check-plus, check, check-minus system provides a useful method of grading those responses.

6. Students may encounter the plateau or quantum-leap phenomenon, in which they receive the same grade for an extended period, because as they improve in one area they regress in another. This lack of movement can be discouraging. Explain its cause and predict its ultimate passing.

7. Don't mistake a wish to be loved for generosity. Remember how frustrating and counter-productive it is to have students who are writing at a C-level and getting a C in your class announce with justifiable anger that in a similar writing course taught by someone else they received a B + .

8. Weight the final grade toward performance at the end of the semester. Writing teachers should be more interested in where students have arrived than in how they got there. By the same token, begin the semester by grading on the low side. Experience suggests that as teachers we tend to exaggerate the improvement of our students anyway: if you begin by giving high grades, you may find yourself boxed into a corner at the end of the semester.

9. Some benefit of the doubt is due to those who have been assiduous in making revisions, contributing to class discussions, and the like. But grades in a writing course should reflect a student's writing.

10. Make sure that your students understand how you are grading.

11. Don't agonize over your grades.

NOTES

1. My discussion in this chapter draws on a handbook Evan Radcliffe and I wrote for use in English 136, a freshman composition course taught in the College of Arts and Sciences at Cornell University; in general, I'm indebted to the staff of that course (and especially to Scott Elledge, Katherine Gottschalk, Mike Twomey, and Kim Noling) for many of the ideas here presented. My discussion of writing as process is heavily indebted to C. L. Knoblauch and Lil Brannon's *Rhetorical Traditions and the Teaching of Writing.*

2. Whether it's possible or even desirable to tie the package rigorously into a given epistemology is another question. Connections will surely exist, but I doubt that a given epistemology has a univalent set of consequences at the pragmatic level on which writing and the correction of writing take place.

3. One might object to the analogy between learning to write and learning to play an instrument by suggesting that in playing a piece on the piano, one is "merely" producing an interpretation but that in writing, one is producing something new and original. But recent speculations concerning intertextuality and the de-centering of the subject, even if not followed to their wildest extremes, weaken such objections. These speculations suggest that in using language we are constantly working and re-working a repertoire of possible thoughts and expressions already put into place by the society that surrounds us. We give this repertoire new inflections, or we discover new potentialities in it. How different is this from interpreting a piece of music by performing it? To put the point another way: one weakness of much otherwise useful composition theory is its tendency to romanticize and mystify what it assumes to be a radical, and radically valuable, subjectivity in the writer. Bad writing then becomes "alienated" writing. George Lukác's distinction between (negative) "alienation" and (positive and dialectically inescapable) "objectification" might offer a valuable corrective here.

4. In my own teaching and thinking about writing, questions of voice tend to collapse into questions of purpose and audience: one creates a certain kind of voice to affect a given audience in a given way. But for those who teach different kinds of writing courses, considerations of voice or "ethos" might well take a more central place. For a discussion of ethos, see Chapter 6.

5. For a perceptive discussion of how failing to take into account the classroom context can vitiate research into styles of paper-correcting, see Knoblauch and Brannon, "Teacher Commentary on Student Writing: The State of tne Art," 1–4.

6. George Orwell's "Politics and the English Language" discusses this issue at length. For a good discussion of wordiness, its forms and its cures, see Joseph Williams, *Style,* Lesson 4.

7. In "Responding to Student Writing," Nancy Sommers warns against

"interlinear comments [that] encourage the student to see the text as a fixed piece, frozen in time, that just needs some editing" (151). For a presentation of some of the research from which this warning derives, see her "Revision Strategies of Student Writers and Experienced Adult Writers."

WORKS CITED

Entries marked with an asterisk are described in Chapter 8, "A Bibliographical Guide to the Profession."

Baker, Sheridan. *The Practical Stylist.* 5th ed. New York: Harper and Row, 1981.

FitzGerald, Frances. *America Revised.* Boston: Little, Brown and Company, 1979. Selection reprinted as "Rewriting American History" in *The Norton Reader: An Anthology of Expository Prose.* 6th ed. Edited by Arthur M. Eastman. 775–81. New York: Norton, 1984.

Hirsch, E. D. Jr. *The Philosophy of Composition.* Chicago: Univ. of Chicago Press, 1977.

*Irmscher, William F. *Teaching Expository Writing.* New York: Holt, Rinehart and Winston, 1979.

*Knoblauch, C. L. and Lil Brannon. *Rhetorical Traditions and the Teaching of Writing.* Montclair, N.J.: Boynton/Cook, 1984.

———. "Teacher Commentary on Student Writing: The State of the Art." *Freshman English News* 10 (Fall 1981): 1–4.

Sommers, Nancy. "Responding to Student Writing." *College Composition and Communication* 33 (1982): 148–56.

———. "Revision Strategies of Student Writers and Experienced Adult Writers." *CCC* 31 (1980): 378–87.

*Strunk, William, and E. B. White. *The Elements of Style.* 3rd ed. New York: Macmillan, 1979.

*Williams, Joseph M. *Style: Ten Lessons in Clarity and Grace.* 2nd ed. Glenview, Ill.: Scott, Foresman, 1985.

6

Understanding Prose

FREDRIC V. BOGEL

I. WHY ANALYZE STYLE?

A. *Style and Meaning*

People who wonder why we should analyze prose style are usually no enemies to stylistic analysis as such; they are skeptical only about its relevance to the principal kinds of intellectual activity engaged in at colleges and universities. Prose analysis, of course, has played a traditional role in the teaching of composition and of literature, where close attention to style promises to help students acquire certain skills, or to appreciate certain aspects of literary art. Thus most teachers in those fields that use written texts but are not considered "literary"—fields like anthropology, government, history, philosophy or psychology—consider close stylistic analysis a proper part of courses in composition or literature. When asked whether they themselves devote much class time to prose analysis, however, they answer that they do not, for they believe that their own fields (anthropology, government, etc.) are focused neither on the acquisition of skills, as composition is frequently thought to be, nor on the aesthetic appreciation of texts, as literary criticism is sometimes thought to be, but on something else: the understanding of content, or the mastery of material, or the acquisition of knowledge—in short, on meaning.

This focus on meaning is rarely wide enough to include stylistic analysis. Yet what suffers most from a reading insufficiently attentive to style is precisely the meaning of a text. The argument of this chapter, then, is that stylistic and rhetorical analysis—apart from its utilitarian or aesthetic benefits to students of composition and literature—is essential to the study of virtually all texts because it is our most powerful tool for revealing the full range of meaning that written prose commands.

The truth of these assertions may not be immediately obvious. If the analysis of style is so important to the understanding of meaning, how have so many of us survived for so long without undertaking it? Or, to ask the question in another way, can something so familiar and useful as the distinction between what is said (meaning) and how it is said (style) really be a false distinction? The answer to this second question, I think, is not that the distinction is false but that it is easier to make in theory than in practice. And the answer to the first question is that in our practice we perform much more in the way of stylistic analysis than we are aware of performing. We simply make the leap from style to meaning so rapidly and smoothly that we are often unaware of the former at all. We are able to make this leap with such ease precisely because style and meaning—"How it's said" and "What is said"—are not, in fact and in practice, very separable at all, though they are theoretically distinguishable. Cardinal Newman, in the nineteenth century, said that thought and expression were the convex and the concave of a single curve; much of our reading practice—if not our theorizing about style— seems tacitly to endorse such an image.

The separation of what is said from how it is said, then, is an artificial one. Much of the time, it's simply impossible to grasp all of "what" is said without paying attention to "how" it is said, and sometimes the most important "what" *is* the "how." Consider the following exchange:

> Q: "Do you consider the acquisition of effective habits of speech a
> goal to which members of your social stratum can legitimately aspire?"
> A: "Nothin' to it."

It would be a mistake to say simply that A responds in the affirmative; the real "content" or meaning of his message lies precisely in the terse, confident challenge that it poses to Q's snobbish notions of correctness, and this meaning is a matter of style.

Here is another example, Julius Caesar reporting a victory to the Roman senate:

> Veni, vidi, vici.

"I came, I saw, I conquered." Even this translation requires attention to its linguistic surface, to the patterns of structure, sound, and stress that make the message far more than the simple reporting of a victory. Consider the levels of organization that give this utterance its full meaning.

First, there is parallel structure, the verbs arranged in the neat equivalence of a triple past tense. This parallelism is reinforced by *alliteration* (the repetition of initial sounds—here the "w" sound of the Latin "v"), and even by rhythmic patterning, since all three words are disyllables, and all are stressed in the same trochaic way:

$$\text{V\'eni, v\'idi, v\'ici.}$$

Moreover, the lack of grammatical subordination *(parataxis)* further underlines the independence and thus equivalence of the three verbs, as does the absence of conjunctions *(asyndeton)*. All of these features impose a powerful equivalence on the elements of this utterance. Multiple modes of structuring conspire to give each term the same weight. "Veni, vidi, vici." Boom, boom, boom. (See Richard Lanham's analysis of this text in *Analyzing Prose,* 33.)

So much for formal patterning. The semantic pattern, however, tells a very different story, and a story that gains much of its force and clarity by contrast with the patterns we have been observing. For the meaning of the words suggests a pattern of development rather than of pure repetition, and of climactic development at that. First, the commonplace statements of arrival and observation ("I came, I saw"); then the momentous declaration of victory: "I conquered." The pattern of progressive triple repetition familiar from myth, folk-tale, and literature— three attempts, the third successful and the first two necessary to make the third third—governs the semantic shape of Caesar's laconic sentence.

What is interesting, though, is that the sentence seems so *un*climactic. If it is read aloud with heavy emphasis on the final element, it doesn't sound climactic but over-emphatic, as though the reader were insisting on an emphasis that the utterance itself suppresses or masks. That is exactly what happens. All those instances of rhetorical patterning (parallel structure, alliteration, and so on) that imposed equivalence on the three terms work against the pattern of semantic climax and almost completely subdue it—not quite, but almost. And the point about these different kinds of structuring is that they are not simply stylistic or rhetorical features of the utterance but the heart of its meaning. For a rough paraphrase of "Veni, vidi, vici," if it is to be at all accurate, must catch the way in which Caesar treats progression as mere series, the climactic as just more of the same, and conquest as commonplace—all in a day's work.

This meaning, the meaning of the utterance as a whole, is at least as much a matter of "how" as "what." Or rather, *what* this utterance means will forever escape us unless we investigate *how* it means, though perhaps not at such length as I have resorted to in order to demonstrate the point. Whether we conduct a conscious, full-scale stylistic and rhetorical analysis, then, or take in stylistic significance rapidly and unreflectively, as we often do, the simple truth is that an adequate understanding of meaning depends on an informed attention to style. It is not an exaggeration to say that the reader who persistently refuses to see the stylistic and rhetorical dimensions of a text lest they distract him from the meaning is an incompetent reader. And not because he is failing to acquire "composition skills," or because he is insufficiently responsive to the "aesthetic dimension" of the text (whatever that is). He simply misses too much of the meaning.

B. Intended Meaning and Textuality

What underlies our students' belief that style gets in the way of meaning, and that "reading for meaning" and "reading for style" are competing activities, the former essentially serious and the latter suspiciously frivolous? Many things, I suspect. An ancient identification of rhetoric with the ornamental, reinforced by a traditional American distrust of ornament. A refusal, as Richard A. Lanham has eloquently argued, to see the plain style as one among many rather than the norm to which all prose should aspire. A powerful Western system of values ("logocentrism," Jacques Derrida has called it) that distinguishes immaterial entities like souls and concepts from material ones like bodies and language, and implies not only that these two realms are clearly separable but also that the former is superior to the latter.

And, related to these, a model of communication that is so economical, agreeable, and commonsensical that it is almost too bad it is incorrect. According to his model, I first formulate an idea or meaning or concept; then, intending to communicate it to someone else, I wrap my meaning in linguistic form (speech or writing). The hearer or reader does just the reverse, inferring from the utterance the idea or meaning that I intended to communicate. Thus at both ends of this communication, the meaning itself appears, and it is only in the middle stage— when the idea must pass into language and out again—that words are required at all. Communication here is *ideally* a perfect oneness of sending and receiving minds; this oneness is interrupted by an effort of coding and decoding, however, that is understood to be merely a concession to our fallen state or human imperfection. Like an immaterial freight train, the concept enters the dark tunnel of linguistic mediation only to re-emerge, unchanged, from the other end.

Given this model of communication, there is not much incentive to study style. Language, here, has only a loose and temporary alliance with thought. It serves as a disguise behind which lurk an intention to communicate and a recoverable non-linguistic concept. Once we have inferred the concept, intuited the intended meaning, we can discard the language. Detailed attention to style, it follows, is an idle and misdirected activity, much like the close analysis of envelopes or the patient tasting of peanut shells—a confusion of the external with the internal, the accidental with the essential.

What must be rejected, however, is the model itself, not the study of style. Based on a metaphor that equates meaning with a thing contained and language with its container, this model assumes that a (non-linguistic) concept can be housed in—yet not altered by—a verbal formulation. It assumes, that is, that a language is not a system for the generation of meaning but a kind of haberdashery for the clothing of pre-existent concepts. Once the speaker or writer outfits the concept, all the hearer or reader need do is undress it and contemplate the naked meaning.

If that were the case, however, the same meaning would be "clothed" in different outfits without being unrecognizable or unrecoverable. Indeed, those "outfits" need bear no significant or appropriate relation to the meaning. The same person, for example, is easily recognizable not only in a range of outfits, both conventional (suit; bathing trunks; overalls) and unconventional (suit jackets with bathing trunks; tutu plus combat boots), but "packaged" in a wide variety of items or substances not regarded as clothing at all: crepe paper, a cardboard carton with holes for limbs and head; a layer of whitewash.

The relation between concepts and language, however, does not work this way. I can't wrap the concept of an asteroid in the words "tea" or "nevertheless" or "Burckhardt" and expect you to recognize it. And if I were to stipulate, "By the word 'Burckhardt' I mean the concept 'asteroid,' " I still would not attain my goal of housing the concept of an asteroid in the linguistic shell of the name "Burckhardt." For when you then heard "Burckhardt" you would replace it not just with the concept "asteroid" but with the word "asteroid" as well. It would take a long time indeed for the concept we now designate as "asteroid" to be designated by—to become wedded to—the word "Burckhardt," and by the time it had done so, we would find it as difficult to drive a wedge between them as we now find it to drive one between the idea of an asteroid and the word "asteroid." For at that hypothetical point in the future, those smallish objects whirling through space would *be* Burckhardts.

Instead of being a matter of packaging, then, the relation between ideas and language, style and meaning, is one of great intimacy; if it were not, translation from one language to another would entail nothing more than re-wrapping. And it is a matter of many kinds of intimacy as well, more than can be suggested by the simple example—based on one or two nouns—that I have relied on here. Perhaps all that we can offer as a general rule is that meaning and textuality, the conceptual order and the order of discourse, are always significantly related. To consider either alone, therefore, is to consider only the concave of the curve, or only the convex. We may, at times, wish to do just that, but we should remember that the curve itself knows no separation of convex from concave.

Indeed, a particularly fertile effort of recent thought in a variety of fields has been to disclose the effects of discourse on meaning, and not just the reverse. This effort has resulted in a new awareness of what might be called the constructedness of our ideas of fact, evidence, knowledge, meaning, and truth itself. Instead of a world existing "out there," replete with meanings we seek first to discover and then to communicate in a language aspiring to the neutral, the unrhetorical, the transparent, we have a very different picture: a multiplicity of perspectives each capable of permitting only certain sorts of fact or formulation or truth to exist within it. In this view, truth is always mediated or constructed, and what mediates it is a conceptual scheme that is also a structure of linguistic conventions, a rhetoric, a verbal solution that permits certain kinds of crystal to grow while inhibiting the formation of others. As the philosopher Nelson Goodman puts it:

> If I ask about the world, you can offer to tell me how it is under one or more frames of reference: but if I insist that you tell me how it is apart from all frames, what can you say? We are confined to ways of describing whatever is described. Our universe, so to speak, consists of these ways rather than of a world or worlds. (3)

Goodman situates this point of view in a historical movement "from unique truth and a world fixed and found to a diversity of right and even conflicting versions or worlds in the making" (3). This kind of diversity is different from the more traditional sort produced by viewing a particular object from a variety of perspectives, as Newman imagines us viewing the "large system of complex fact" of "all that exists." The human mind, says Newman,

> cannot take in this whole vast fact at a single glance, or gain possession of it at once. . . . [A]s we deal with some huge structure of many parts and sides, the mind goes round about it, noting down, first one thing, then another, as it best may, and viewing it under different aspects, by way of making progress toward mastering the whole. So by degrees and by circuitous advance does it rise aloft and subject itself to a knowledge of that universe into which it has been born. (53)

However difficult the universe may be to know, it is still "one," for Newman, and it is a totality of "facts and their relations" existing independent of human efforts to investigate it. The various branches of knowledge, then (and note the old oaken unity implied by that metaphor of "branches"), would be various verbal and conceptual languages illuminating the universe, or some smaller object of study, from a multiplicity of perspectives.

Let a twentieth-century skeptic contemplate that "totality," however, and she will immediately want to revise this picture, questioning the intrinsic meaningfulness of the universe, its oneness, and the ultimate compatibility of the various perspectives from which Newman imagines us coming to know it.

All of this might be clearer if we scale down the terms a bit and turn from talk about the universe to talk about a paperweight, or something that may be a paperweight. Imagine yourself entering my study and noticing an object—X for short—resting on top of a pile of papers.

Moments after you enter, I seize the object,, hurl it out an open window, and snarl, "Missed him." I bring the object in from outside and put it back on the papers. You now see that it is a fairly smooth stone, perhaps water-polished granite, on which a simple design has been painted. The question is, "What *is* the object X?" One sort of answer is that it is a stone, first, foremost, and essentially, though a stone that may function as a paperweight, a missile, an art object, a souvenir of the Oregon coast, or an exhibit in an elementary philosophical discussion. This answer presumes an essential identity, on the one hand, and numerous—perhaps innumerable—functions or subsidiary identities on the other, as the following diagram suggests:

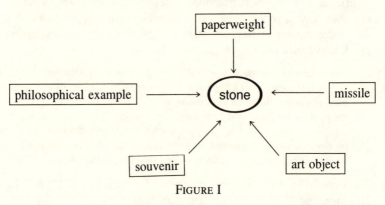

FIGURE I

The modern skeptic to whom I alluded a few sentences ago, however, would draw a very different diagram, something like the following:

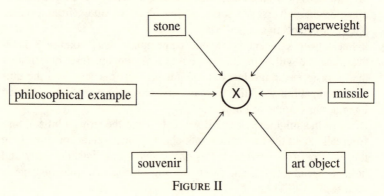

FIGURE II

Now the arrow points inward, ''stone'' has taken a place with the other ''subsidiary'' identities, and the central position formerly occupied by ''stone'' is left undetermined, marked only by an X. (Indeed, if this X on center-stage is never to perform, perhaps we should abandon it and turn the metaphysical charm bracelet of Figure II into an open-ended sequence of diverse and heterogeneous entities.)

What do these changes signify? First, they signify a loss of the notion of proper species or intrinsic identity. That is, no identification of the object X is taken to be essential or intrinsic, with the others merely modifications of that essence. Although it may be our common-sense notion that the object is a stone before it is a paperweight or a missile or a souvenir (or that it is more fundamentally a stone than it is a paperweight, etc.), there is no reason to assign to common sense more weight than it deserves. Common sense tells us many things that are true in an everyday context but false in others. From a common-sense perspective, for example, my wooden desk top is solid and stable (not composed of invisible particles dancing madly in micro-space), and it is motionless (not whirling around the sun at a terrifying speed). From that perspective as well, the largely vertical object outside my window is principally or essentially a tree; only from a secondary or derived perspective is it a weight of so many pounds or kilograms; a restrainer of otherwise erodable soil; a play of cylindrical shapes; and so on. The common-sense view of these objects and phenomena is not wrong; it is simply one view among many, and not a privileged view. Such privilege as we assign to it is almost entirely the result of frequency, since more of our life is spent in the sphere of ''ordinary reality'' than in other spheres. But that doesn't make ordinary reality more real than those others, any more than greater frequency of wear makes my blue jeans more real than my pinstriped suit.

Several points follow from such a surrender of intrinsic or grounding identity. First, the identities of a thing or fact—not its sheer, brute existence, but what it shall count as (is it a souvenir? a missile? or both?)—are multiple and heterogeneous. If something is to be conceived otherwise, ''simplex et unum,'' as Horace put it, then we must see such simplicity and oneness as themselves derived effects, the result of viewing the object in a certain way, and not as features intrinsic to it. Second, the identities of an object are conferred on it by the perspective from which it is viewed or, to change the metaphor, by the set of conceptual and linguistic conventions generating its significance at any point.

For our present purposes, then, the model implied by Figure II grants a much larger place to discourse than the model implied by Figure I. For in II, discourse—if not a creator of thingness or being as such—is nevertheless the creator of the various universes in which a thing may count as a *particular kind* of thing, and without which whatever "uncommitted being" may be thought to reside in a thing can never make itself known anyway, can never appear. That is, it is no real restriction on discourse to say that it cannot create being as such (whatever that is), so long as no particular form or kind of being can exist outside of discourse. If a thing is a thing at all, it is a certain kind of thing.

In the enlarged sense of the term, then, a sense in which linguistic and rhetorical conventions are inseparable from conceptual conventions, discourse is the creator rather than the recorder of the worlds we inhabit. Much of our knowledge, from this perspective, is inescapably textual, and the means of analysis appropriate to the investigation of such knowledge must include textual as well as conceptual tools: instruments for examining argumentative appropriateness, truth, consistency, and implication, certainly, but instruments for examining stylistic and rhetorical structures as well. For what is at stake in our willingness to analyze prose is not just the compositional or aesthetic well-being of our students but their ability to grasp, in detail, the forms of knowing they encounter and the worlds among which they move.

Not every writing instructor, of course, will agree with this account of the textuality of knowledge and the constitutive character of discourse. Some will think it gives too large a place to rhetoric, and that it underplays the role of truth; others will think just the reverse. My own view is that we don't seem to be able to do without either the linguistic or the conceptual. We seem to want, much of the time, to ask two different sorts of question of the texts we read, and these questions imply two different kinds of concern: a concern with rhetoric and a concern with truth.

Neither is dispensable, and in fact each can claim—with reason—to include or serve as ground for the other. The concern with truth can lead us to see the way a particular rhetorical pattern works to disclose, or obscure, the truth. The concern with rhetoric can lead us to see the deployment of a vocabulary of "truth" and "falsity" as itself a significant rhetorical move, and by no means the only available approach to the question the text treats. The view of discourse argued above, then, is at best an accurate account of part of a complex truth.

It is a good thing, therefore, that a commitment to the detailed analysis of prose does not require us to subscribe to that account. Once we concede simply that style and meaning, the conceptual and the rhetorical, are interrelated, the analysis of prose style follows automatically. The next section takes up the basic principles of such analysis.

II. PROSE ANALYSIS

A. *Some Principles*

To analyze prose with some skill and thoroughness, it is necessary to recognize the complexity of its organization. Like other verbal and cultural phenomena, prose is organized in a variety of ways, or at a number of levels. While it is impossible to put aside meaning for long and still discuss prose intelligently, it may be useful to pass over the semantic and the conceptual, for a moment, in order to review some of the other levels that provide prose with the rich variety of patternings that analysis discloses.

First, there is the level of grammar (and syntax) where choices of tense, number, person, voice, mood, phrase, clause, sentence, and so on serve to organize any prose text in a variety of interrelated ways. Then there is the level of rhetoric, the level at which prose is organized by various figures of speech (this is the sense in which "rhetorical" will most often be used here). Insofar as those figures of speech exert their structuring pressure on grammar and syntax, of course, or build on existing grammatical and syntactic structures, the categories of grammar and rhetoric will overlap. Such overlapping is a common phenomenon in stylistic discussions and need not worry us overmuch. It doesn't pose anything like the threat that an effort at terminological hygiene—requiring absolute clarity of terms and distinctness of levels—would pose.

The same goes for "style,'" which is either a relatively restrictive term designating one of the five parts of rhetoric, according to the ancients (the other four being invention, arrangement, memory, and delivery), or a remarkably broad term designating any element of a prose passage viewed as a contributor to the meaning and significance of that passage.

In this second sense, grammatical and syntactic features can also count as elements of style, depending on our perspective. If that perspective is grammatical, we will usually be concerned with a particular passage's relation to the rules of grammaticality in English: with the nature of the first person, for example, or the conventions for agreement of predicate adjectives. If that perspective is stylistic and interpretive, we will usually be concerned with the particular significance—for the passage we are analyzing—of this reliance on the first person or on predicate adjectives *of a certain kind*. The first sort of concern is centrifugal, the second centripetal.

Prose is organized at other levels as well. Patterns of sound and rhythm, and of visual appearance on the page, often contribute significantly to meaning, and detailed stylistic and rhetorical attention will need to take account of these. As we saw in our analysis of Caesar's "Veni, vidi, vici," patterns at a variety of levels (syntactic, phonetic, rhythmic) often converge to create a particularly rich and significant kind of meaning. To that analysis we can add one brief remark on visual patterning. If Caesar's utterance were to be set up on the page as a poem, with line breaks a matter of significance rather than of recurrent arbitrariness (the tyranny of a uniform righthand margin), the meaning might change as well. Consider the following possibility:

> Caesar to the Senate
> Veni, vidi,
> vici.

Here, the isolation of "vici" lends it special emphasis, an emphasis reinforcing its semantic charge but disrupting the prose linearity that subsumed victory in an undifferentiated list of a typical day's activities. The full force of "vici," that is, results precisely from the way the passage—printed as *prose*—seems to take the extraordinariness of that force for granted. Printed as poetry, "vici" has all the unwanted emphasis of an elbow in the ribs or an exaggerately raised eyebrow.

Our first principle, then, is that prose style in the broad sense is a matter of multiple levels of organization. Our second is that features of style are always connected in some way to effects of meaning. This is an assertion of a particular kind. It is not empirical; that is, no one has examined all the stylistic features of all the prose passages ever written (or to be written) and found them to be meaningful. Nor is it a deduction following from the very nature of prose. It is much more like a working hypothesis, an assumption allowing us to undertake such analysis as will show the hypothesis to be correct, or at least enabling and fruitful. If this seems like an odd principle on which to base a large-scale interpretive endeavor, we might recall that the scientist depends on something quite similar, namely, a belief in the meaningfulness of natural phenomena. As in the analysis of style, the belief makes possible the results that would justify our holding it. And, as in the analysis of style, those results are powerful and compelling enough, enough of the time, to keep us from surrendering the principle.

In both cases, moreover, science and prose analysis, the principle can be stated less problematically by being put into a negative form. Instead of asserting that every stylistic element is meaningful (or, worse still, "potentially meaningful"), we can simply claim that no feature of style can be *proven* to be un-meaningful, shown decisively to be non-functional in the generation of meaning. The most we can assert, against the meaningfulness of this or that stylistic trait, is that we have not yet discovered a function for it and we doubt that we will. In science no less than in prose analysis, there are difficulties with such an assumption as this, and we will take up some of these difficulties at appropriate points. It is worth saying right now, though, that the assumption of meaningfulness in the formal features of prose is not an assumption comparable to the belief that tea leaves arrange themselves in cup bottoms so as to figure human destinies. This remark may seem unnecessarily defensive, but it is directed against that parody of "rigorous skepticism" which, in discovering that a particular form of interpretation is guided by assumptions at all, especially assumptions of coherence and meaningfulness in the object under investigation, labels that mode of interpretation "circular" and discounts all of its results. Such skepticism is, of course, haunted by a dream of "pure empiricism" and does not recognize either that the criterion of "working from assumptions and presuppositions" is inadequate to distinguish astrology from astronomy or that astronomy and astrology may yet be distinguished.

Our third basic principle may seem to weaken our second, but in fact it does just the opposite. It is as follows. Although features of style are presumed to be significant—although style and meaning are connected—there is no rule for decisively determining the nature of that connection. This means, for example, that we cannot construct a chart of equivalences between particular rhetorical features and their meanings. The interpretation of style is not a matter of decoding texts according to a set of one-to-one equivalences.

One brief example will suffice. If we tried to construct such a chart of equivalences, we might be tempted to align *alliteration* with likeness or similarity. That is, according to our principle that style and meaning are connected, it makes good sense to assume that a series of terms with the same initial sound might be linked by deeper similarities as well, and this is frequently the case. Campaign slogans, for example, are often built on this presumed correlation of form with meaning, as in the hopeful phrase "Win with Willkie," which sought to connect victory with the candidate by means of alliterative bonding. Such a phrase— whatever the electoral outcome—would indeed be decodable by means of a chart equating alliteration with connectedness or affinity. But phrases like "saint and sinner," or "pleasure and pain," pose a slightly more difficult problem. We can, of course, imagine contexts in which a con- nection between the two terms is precisely the point. One might be arguing, for example, that saints do not differ from sinners so sharply as we commonly suppose, nor pleasure from pain. Or one might wish to suggest that although the terms themselves are opposites, each pair of opposites is part of a single spectrum of discourse or set of values: in one case, a highly traditional spectrum of moral and religious values (saint . . . sinner), in the other, an equally traditional spectrum of feel- ings (pain . . . pleasure). Without such a context, though, our first and proper impulse is to understand the alliteration as a means of distin- guishing the terms—as in "friend or foe?"—rather than as a means of connecting them, even though our hypothetical decoding chart instructs us to translate alliteration as "connection."

The moral of this little demonstration is that even the simplest rhetor- ical or stylistic strategy requires interpretation, and interpretation that takes account of meaning as well as form. While this fact makes our work harder, it also makes it interesting and necessary, as interpreta- tion-by-decoding would assuredly not be. And it reminds us once again that questions of style and questions of meaning cannot really be sepa- rated, even though there is no general rule describing their mode of connection. Like people, style and meaning get together in odd and unpredictable ways.

We have, then, three basic assumptions: that prose is organized at a variety of levels (or in a variety of ways); that style and meaning are significantly connected; and that we cannot specify the nature of this connection except in a given case and on the basis of interpretive analysis.

Despite the warning tone of that last remark, it is possible to make at least a few generalizations about the relation between style and meaning. However numerous and diverse the organizational strategies available to the prose writer, most prose responds to analysis as though the relation between style and meaning were connected, above all, by the principle of analogy or mimesis: as though formal patterns worked chiefly to reinforce patterns of meaning by imitating them or providing analogues to them. Notice that this principle doesn't tell us *how* stylistic or rhetorical features reinforce meaning, only that much of the time they seem to do so. This means, for example, that all of the instances of alliteration discussed above conform to the principle of mimesis, even though they do so in different ways.

B. Applying the Principles

Let's take another example, this time a slightly more extended piece of prose, by E. B. White:

> We received a letter from the Writers' War Board the other day asking for a statement on "The Meaning of Democracy." It presumably is our duty to comply with such a request, and it is certainly our pleasure.
>
> Surely the Board knows what democracy is. It is the line that forms on the right. It is the don't in don't shove. It is the hole in the stuffed shirt through which the sawdust slowly trickles; it is the dent in the high hat. Democracy is the recurrent suspicion that more than half of the people are right more than half of the time. It is the feeling of privacy in the voting booths, the feeling of communion in the libraries, the feeling of vitality everywhere. Democracy is a letter to the editor. Democracy is the score at the beginning of the ninth. It is an idea which hasn't been disproved yet, a song the words of which have not gone bad. It's the mustard on the hot dog and the cream in the rationed coffee. Democracy is a request from a War Board, in the middle of a morning in the middle of a war, wanting to know what democracy is. (13)

If we were to paraphrase White's "definition" of democracy without paying conscious attention to style, we would probably say something about equality and fair play, about skepticism towards emblems of privilege and attitudes of pomposity, about faith in the common man and woman, about a particularly vital mixture of privacy and community (community with one's contemporaries and with one's predecessors). We would mention, too, the right to voice one's opinion, whether in support or protest. Finally, we would say something about small pleasures and innocent luxuries, and about their place—as emblems of freedom—even in the midst of pressing necessities. All this, for White, is implied in the idea of "Democracy."

Yet there are few readers of White's short essay who would not be disappointed by the paraphrase I have offered. What the paraphrase reports it reports fairly accurately, I think, nor does it attribute very much to White that is not implicit in the essay. The trouble is that it leaves out so much. By not paying attention to style, my paraphrase refuses to receive the meaning of one of the essay's ways of existing; it tries to capture White's full-color message on a black-and-white receiver. As a result, certain dimensions of the message appear with great clarity while others are lost entirely.

We can see what some of those lost dimensions are by comparing our paraphrase with the essay itself. The paraphrase is filled with abstractions: equality, fair play, skepticism, privilege, faith, and so on. In contrast, once White's essay gets down to business in the second paragraph, it repeats a single abstraction ("Democracy," or its pronoun surrogate, "it") and links this with a series of fairly concrete terms: the hole in the stuffed shirt, the dent in the high hat, a song, mustard, cream, and a request from the War Board. To be sure, there are abstractions in the essay (suspicion, feeling, idea), but when they appear, they tend to be pretty firmly tied to concrete human experience in voting booths, libraries, and elsewhere.

Moreover, these concrete phrases are tied to the repeated abstraction "democracy" by means of a recurrent structure of equation: *Democracy is X* (where X is usually a concrete noun or noun phrase). Such equations are metaphors, and one way to characterize White's definition of democracy is to say that it is persistently, even doggedly, metaphoric. Why? In part, because *The New Yorker,* where White's piece first appeared in 1943, has always favored prose addressed to the literate non-specialist with an ear for style. It is not the kind of magazine in which one would expect to find a textbook definition of democracy, marked by fussy over-precision and a penchant for latinate abstractions. Prose like White's, moreover, as generations of composition teachers have tirelessly told us, is more lively, vivid, and memorable than the prose of abstract definitions. It stays in the mind and ear longer, and it seems to have been uttered by a person rather than a committee or a robot. Committees don't readily think up phrases like "the cream in the rationed coffee," and readers don't easily forget them.

But White's metaphoric strategy is more than a custom of *The New Yorker* or a bid for memorability. It is an integral part of his conception of democracy. Each of those metaphors is not just an equation but an alchemical process that transforms a single, sterile abstraction ("democracy") into the fruitful concreteness and specificity of every-day reality. Democracy, White's style says, is precisely this, or rather *these:* not an abstract term but a series of lived, concrete experiences. That is why the Writers' War Board "surely . . . knows what democracy is"; it is something the members of the Board live rather than something they define. White's anti-definition merely holds up a mirror—the mirror of metaphor—to that lived reality.

In the world of wars and war boards, of course, metaphor is not highly prized. It is regarded, rather, as something of a luxury, an indulgence. Figurative language, our culture teaches us in ten thousand ways, is ornamental rather than serious, desirable rather than (strictly speaking) necessary. But White's style has two things to say on this question. The first is that metaphor is the only way to say accurately what democracy is. A literal or dictionary definition will not do, because democracy for White is not a matter of dictionaries but of the ways people live and hold their lives. In a sense, we could say that White is not defining the word "democracy" but the reality of democracy, so that a respectable dictionary definition like the following is not so much wrong as irrelevant:

> democracy: government in which the people hold the ruling power either directly or through elected representatives; rule by the ruled.
> (*Webster's New World Dictionary,* 2nd college ed., compressed slightly)

The second thing the essay's style tells us is that man does not live by strict necessity alone. It does not rise to the pitch of King Lear's "reason not the need," but it is pretty explicit about our need for such "luxuries" as cream in coffee, even when the coffee is rationed. The essay presents democracy, that is, as a condition that permits people more than the impoverishments of a siege mentality, even when they are under siege. One of those permitted—indeed, necessary—luxuries is precisely the freedom to request a definition of democracy "in the middle of a morning in the middle of a war." And another is the freedom to answer that request by means of a rich, metaphoric, non-Government Issue prose style.

But of course these two "arguments"—that figurative language is necessary to define democracy, and that democracy permits such luxuries as figurative language—are really two faces of a single argument, an argument defining democracy, in part, as that form of government which recognizes the necessity of certain luxuries. For how can we call mere luxury what is essential to the definition of democracy? In short, metaphor is to prose (realistic, no-nonsense, prosaic prose) what cream is to rationed coffee: that breath of freedom, beyond mere necessity, that is the most needful and serious thing of all. Without it, official "seriousness" would be tedious, colorless, and pointless, and life would be, as Thomas Hobbes said, "solitary, poor, nasty, brutish, and short." What is necessary, then, *strictly speaking,* is precisely something beyond necessity, and White's use of metaphor is both an instance of that something and an implicit argument for its necessity.

We began discussing this essay in connection with the principle of mimesis or analogy, and it may be useful to spell out the connection. In focusing on the role of metaphor in the essay, and on the contrast between abstract and concrete diction, finding in these a principal source of the essay's *meaning* (not its beauty or charm or memorability), we have made a number of assumptions. We have assumed that prose is multiply organized and that patterns at different levels of organization may converge to form a single, complex structure of meaning, as diction and rhetorical figures converge in White's discussion of democracy. We have assumed also that style and meaning are intimately connected, but that there is no automatic procedure for determining the nature of the connection in any given piece of writing. Thus, we did not assume a particular alignment between concrete and abstract diction, on the one hand, and a certain kind of meaning or set of values on the other. It is true that White seems to associate concrete diction with the most fruitful and affirmative aspects of democracy, but we know this only from reading the essay critically. Another essay, even another essay by White might employ an entirely different strategy, aligning concrete diction with, say, barren materialism or thoughtless sensuality, and abstract diction with spiritual or intellectual freedom. Only interpretation can tell us how to take a particular feature of style in a particular passage.

These assumptions led us to see features of style and rhetoric not as embellishments but as carriers of meaning in their own right, not as ornaments but as imitations or analogues or enactments of patterns of significance. In a sense, this means that we read such features symbolically. In this case, moreover, as in many others, the symbolic significance of style and rhetoric does not simply reinforce an argument or theme that the essay otherwise develops more abstractly or (as we often say) more directly. What White's management of diction and metaphor signifies, when interpreted, appears nowhere else in the essay. This is why close attention to style is attention to meaning, and why a reading that ignores style mutilates the meaning of the text, not just its beauty or euphony or "aesthetic appeal."

By "meaning," of course, we do not mean either lexical meaning or literal meaning—what is often called the "plain prose sense"—but something that includes these in a more complex mode of signification that need not reject half of a text's verbal resources in order to label the remaining half basic or essential. Perhaps we could call this "textual meaning" to distinguish it from other accounts of meaning—the reductive paraphrase or the purely conceptual analysis, for example—that do not attempt to take account of the verbal dimension of a text: its stylistic and rhetorical identity, its existence as a structure of words. As Northrop Frye has said, "Anything which makes a functional use of words will always be involved in all the technical problems of words, including rhetorical problems. The only road from grammar to logic . . . runs through the intermediate territory of rhetoric" (331). Textual meaning, then, is the product of an act of reading that does not seek a shortcut from grammar to logic but proceeds through the rich territory of rhetoric—a territory, let us add, that continues to exist even when we choose to ignore it.

C. Style versus Meaning

This distinction between textual and non-textual meaning can help us with one last general topic, which arises in connection with the mimetic or analogical principle. This principle tells us that style can imitate meaning, as when a discussion of discrete, atomistic things is conducted in a highly paratactic and asyndetic style (*parataxis* refers to a style that avoids grammatical subordination; *asyndeton* is the omission of conjunctions), or when two sharply opposed positions are contrasted by means of a strong reliance on patterns of antithesis (syntactic, alliterative, and so on).

It is sometimes said, however, that style can work against meaning as well as with it, and that what is claimed or asserted by a text's meaning can be disclaimed or discredited or undermined by its style. Consider the following brief examples:

> 1. "Don't you just hate questions?"
> 2. "Connection. Interrelation. All part of the same web. Seamless. Spectrum. Smear. No disjunction. No start, no finish. All one."

In the first case, we might say that the meaning of the sentence (a dislike of questions) is countered by the choice of grammatical mood (the interrogative). In the second, a fairly insistent assertion of the indivisibility of something is countered by the fragmentariness of the prose style that conveys it, and by the lack of connections among those fragments. In both cases, it would be plausible to say that style works against meaning.

But not against *textual* meaning. The meaning that style works against in these examples is itself an abstraction from the meaning of the passages taken as a whole, and especially an abstraction from the stylistic and rhetorical—the textual—dimension of the passages. For the full meaning of the first passage is *not* an expressed dislike of questions (a dislike somehow compromised by the interrogative mood), nor of the second passage an assertion of connectedness (somehow compromised by the stylistic disconnection). The style is part of the meaning too. Thus the textual meaning of these passages includes the significance of style and includes, therefore, the tension between propositional or abstracted meaning and the meaning generated by style: the implied dislike of questions *and* the interrogative form, the assertions of continuity *and* the syntactic disconnections. In the artificially limited sense of "meaning," then—text minus style equals meaning—style can certainly work against meaning. But style can never work against textual meaning since the significance of style is already part of that meaning. To assume otherwise is to fall into a category mistake, like assuming that the clothes one wears can "work against" the meaning (not the attractiveness) of one's physical appearance.

The last example, however, suggests one important exception to the claim that style and meaning cannot work at cross purposes. This exception does not have to do with a particular category of text, however, but with a particular stance we can adopt toward texts, an evaluative and "co-authoring" stance. This is the stance we adopt when we advise a friend against wearing a certain shirt or jacket and when we advise a student against using a certain stylistic procedure in an essay. Doing so requires us to guess the intention of the wearer or writer (in a sense, to play his or her role) and to compare that intention with the actual effect of the chosen feature of dress or style. Imagine a student essay, for example, titled "Down with the Wishy-Washy," an essay that attacks various kinds of hedging, compromise, and tentativeness while praising strong opinions and vigorous outspokenness. But imagine, as well, that the student fills his or her essay with all those fussy qualifications that characterize academic prose at its worst:

> It might be asserted that . . .
> Although . . . nevertheless . . .
> To a certain extent . . .
> From one point of view, of course, it might be alleged that . . .
> Despite these qualifications, it to some extent still
>   holds that . . .

If we were to read the essay from an interpretive perspective alone, we would take its meaning as a perhaps complex mixture of affirmed directness and enacted uncertainty. But if we read it from an evaluative and co-authoring perspective (as we would most student essays), we would probably point out to the student, in conference, that the style of the essay "works against" its argument. This might lead the student to do a variety of things: revise the essay for greater unity and directness; rethink his or her position on tentativeness (maybe a little hesitancy isn't such a bad thing, maybe); even defend the essay's procedure as being precisely what he or she aimed to achieve. If we believe this last claim, we will take the real thesis of the essay to be very different from the thesis we had feared the student was stylistically undermining: not "down with the wishy-washy," but something like "uncertainty creeps into the most energetic attempts at boldness." And we will have re-assumed the interpretive perspective.

These two perspectives, the interpretive and the evaluative (in the sense that I have been using it), are themselves at odds with each other. Each looks for different things in a text, and each takes the same things in a different way. Trying to read a text from both perspectives at the same time is a bit like trying to see the duck *and* the rabbit, or the faces *and* the vase, in those drawings that psychology and philosophy texts have made so familiar to us. It's a frustrating experience, or two frustrating experiences (we're never sure which). Fortunately, we don't usually have much trouble keeping them distinct. We adopt the interpretive perspective not just when we are reading a Famous Writer but when we want to reject as little of the text as possible so as to maximize the possibility of discovering meaning. We adopt the evaluative and co-authoring perspective when we want to bring a text in line with an intended meaning that we pretend to know before it achieves full textual embodiment.

This means, of course, that the evaluative perspective re-introduces the container/contained model that the interpretive perspective must reject. The loss of theoretical consistency in this re-introduction, however, is far outweighed by the pedagogical advantage. For if we were to adopt a fully interpretive perspective in reading our students' essays, we would be compelled to treat every feature of those essays as elements—rather than failures—of meaning, and to write such comments as "The vague organization in this nicely captures the movement of a disordered mind," or, "The paucity of supporting evidence here underscores perfectly the untenability of the thesis. Good work." There are times, in short, when an evaluative stance is kindness itself, while to be taken with full interpretive seriousness is to be undone.

There is one other situation in which we commonly put aside full textual interpretation and adopt the evaluative perspective (though not, in this case, the perspective of co-author): when we are teaching a badly written text. Forced, for whatever reasons, to assign stylistically uninteresting or incompetent readings, we do not usually compound the original offense by analyzing those readings in great detail. What we can do is assign texts that are stylistically able, whenever possible; help students to see, through brief analysis, why some texts prove more interesting than others when analyzed; and avoid the error of tediously and over-ingeniously analyzing a text whose prose is just not worth it.

The interpretive perspective is our main concern here, however, and it is time to turn to some practical details of the interpretive analysis of prose.

III. TOOLS OF THE PROSE TRADE: AN ANALYTIC VOCABULARY

This and the following section are the "How To Do It" portions of "Understanding Prose." Section IV will undertake a few sample analyses, putting into action the vocabulary that the present section supplies. In preparation for those analyses, Section III will define a number of terms useful in the analysis of prose, briefly illustrate their usefulness, and divide the complex field of prose structure into the following categories:

Rhetorical Situation
Sentences and Syntactic Patterns
Figurative Language
Diction
Rhythm and Sound

While these are not inescapable categories, frequent experience in the classroom has shown them to be extremely useful. And though that experience is the limited experience of finite and particular instructors, and therefore partial (in both senses), we trust that the categories are reasonable enough, and adaptable enough, to be incorporated into a variety of courses, programs, and styles of teaching.

A. *Rhetorical Situation*

Almost any utterance, we commonly assume, has an utterer, and in everyday life we take the utterer to be the person who is speaking. We assume, beyond this, that the utterer is speaking to someone and about something, and that he or she is taking a particular attitude toward that something. All this is obvious enough. When we are analyzing prose, however, we usually have nothing in front of us but the prose we are analyzing, and this fact turns a common existential or real-life situation into a rhetorical situation: that is, a situation built not out of real people, real objects, and real attitudes, but out of words. The usefulness of a phrase like "rhetorical situation" is that it reminds us of the ultimately verbal character of what often seem to be existential givens.

The speaking voice in prose is sometimes referred to, simply, by the author's name, but it is often given a specifically rhetorical label to remind us that it is a verbal construction. It is sometimes called a *voice,* or a *speaker,* sometimes a *persona* (to remind us that the author, even if he creates a "mask" or assumed character whose opinions are identical to his own, has still reconstructed himself in a purely verbal medium), and at other times an *ethos* (the ancient rhetorical term for the character an orator chooses to assume on a particular occasion). These terms remind us that, just as the role we play in a real-life encounter may be a construction of considerable artifice, though not necessarily one that we would consider false or deceptive, so the "voice" that speaks to us in a piece of prose, the "author" to whom we often respond as to a real person, has no body or mind, no neurons or nagging doubts, but exists only as marks on a page arranged according to certain conventions of linguistic, rhetorical, and semiotic intelligibility.

The same is true, more or less, of those other essentials of the rhetorical situation: the audience, subject (or topic), and attitude (in the language of literary criticism, the speaker's attitude toward his or her subject is often called "tone"). Although it is common to assume that each of these is as real as the speaker, and—when we are reading—that we ourselves are the audience, this is really not the case. Consider the following examples:

1. "You're out!'
2. "My father had a small estate in Nottinghamshire; I was the third of five sons."
3. "Hail, Thargon, prince of Zadd. I am Ploryn from the galaxy Ka-lelp."

It is not difficult for us to determine the speaker, audience, and subject in each of these cases, even though no non-fictional umpire actually uttered *this instance* of "You're out!" to any ballplayer, and even though Ploryn and Thargon are as fictional as Gulliver, and much more recent. Umpire and player called out, Gulliver and reader, Ploryn and Thargon—these are not utterers and audiences using language but (fictional) utterers and audiences *created* by language. Once we make this elementary distinction between a person speaking and the person created by speech or writing, we can begin to analyze the rhetorical—rather than the historical or "real-life"—situation of virtually any piece of written discourse. We will be careful not to confuse author and speaker, or actual audience (ourselves) and dramatic audience, or referent and referential effect of language. We will see, too, that this care is just a matter of making with more consistency and rigor a distinction that we unconsciously make much of the time. When we correctly use what linguists call a deictic or shifter, for example, an utterance whose referent varies with the identity and situation of the utterer—my ''here'' is your ''there,'' my ''now'' is defined by the historical moment in which I speak—we recognize, if only implicitly, that a linguistic structure and a particular historical (or real-life) situation are very different kinds of thing. To extend this recognition, in a mildly systematic way, to as many aspects of a prose utterance as possible is to begin to see the utterance as just that: a piece of prose rather than a slice of life, a rhetorical situation rather than an historical event. Terms such as ''speaker,'' ''dramatic audience,'' and so on simply help us to make this enabling abstraction from all that is, an abstraction that disengages an object of analysis from an endless context and allows a discipline to come into being.

B. Sentences and Syntactic Patterns

Of the many units into which discourse can be divided, the sentence is probably the one most susceptible to close, stylistic analysis. It is long enough to provide a certain amount of conceptual interest and complexity, yet short enough to reveal its formal patterns with great clarity. It is also, by and large, the prose unit that most fully sets the tone of a particular author's style.

SENTENCE LENGTH

There are several ways to classify sentences, depending on the kind of information we seek. First, there is length. A writer's use of predominantly long or short sentences does not, in itself, tell us much, since both long and short sentences can be structured in a great variety of ways. But sentence length can give us an idea of the size, and sometimes of the complexity, of the principal building-blocks of a given piece of discourse. Compare, for example, the following excerpts:

> Montoya knocked on the door and opened it. It was a gloomy room with a little light coming in from the window on the narrow street. There were two beds separated by a monastic partition. The electric light was on. The boy stood very straight and unsmiling in his bull-fighting clothes. His jacket hung over the back of a chair. (Ernest Hemingway, *The Sun Also Rises* 163)

> Fawns, as it had been for him, and as Maggie and Fanny Assingham had both attested, was out of the world, whereas the scene actually about him, with the very sea a mere big booming medium for excursions and aquariums, affected him as so plump in the conscious centre that nothing could have been more complete for representing that pulse of life which they had come to unanimity at home on the subject of their advisedly not hereafter forgetting. (Henry James, *The Golden Bowl* 170)

To be sure, sentence length is only one of the important differences between these two styles, but it is a significant difference. Hemingway uses his sentences as elementary stages in the perceptual construction of a scene, tracing the path by which his character comes to see and know what is before him; James does not seem to be "tracing" anything at all, certainly nothing purely perceptual. Instead, he presents us with a character's understanding of a scene, and a scene whose significance the character grasps by placing it, in part, in a comparative and evaluative context. (In the terms of prose rhetoric, Hemingway often writes in a *running* style and James in a *periodic* style. We will return to those terms later). As Northrop Frye has said:

> The long sentences in the later novels of Henry James are *containing* sentences: all the qualifications and parentheses are fitted in to a pattern, and as one point after another is made, there emerges not a linear process of thought but a simultaneous comprehension. What is explained is turned around and viewed from all aspects, but it is completely there, so to speak, from the beginning. (267)

Part of the reason that James's sentences can contain so much, and can place that so much in a variety of relations, is that they are often very long sentences. Hemingway avoids just that sense of connectedness and pre-existent pattern that James seeks, and his relatively short sentences help to deliver a world more intensely perceptual, more fragmented, and less cogitatively arranged than the world we discover in James.

TENSE, MOOD, AND VOICE

Sentences are of many kinds as well as lengths. The traditional division into *declarative* (making an assertion), *interrogative* (asking a question), and *exclamatory* (making an exclamation) is most useful when we are treating written dialogue, which may use all three kinds of sentence. Most written prose that is not dialogue, however, relies almost exclusively on the declarative sentence while making few exclamations and asking few questions. This is itself, however, a fact of some interest and one to which our awareness of the three kinds of sentence may alert us, for the declarative sentence has its own conventions and its own range of formal significance. This is to say that the norm of the declarative sentence is a bit of rhetorical data, not the absence of such data.

In a standard piece of expository or argumentative writing, the declarative sentence may carry with it a number of conventional assumptions. In contrast to the interrogative sentence, it may intimate a world that is fairly well known and a knower who is fairly secure in his knowledge. And in contrast to the exclamatory sentence, it may stay fairly close to a norm of emotional control. It may also, of course, do neither of these things. The following sentence is certainly declarative, but it does not do what I have been suggesting that a declarative sentence may do:

> I don't know who or what I am, and I am sick with doubt and fear.

This is the declarative sentence adapted not to the norms of a conventional expository style but to those of a rhetoric of conscious suffering. All that one can say with certainty, then, is that the declarative sentence still declares—still makes assertions—and that this fact may be of some interest in a stylistic analysis. There is a difference, for example, between the interrogative "Who am I?" and the declarative "I don't know who I am," the latter implying, in some contexts at least, both a stronger sense of self and a greater analytic distance than the former. If we recall the persistence of assertion in the declarative sentence, then, we can see the particular forms that such assertion takes in a given passage of prose.

Sentences also take much of their tone from the verb-forms they employ. Verb tense, for example, can powerfully affect the meaning and emotional weight of a passage, and it too can function in many ways. To take just one possible contrast, the past tense of historical narration can project the past as something complete and masterable, while the narrative present tense—as in portions of Carlyle's breathless narrative in *The French Revolution*—can underscore the immediacy, unpredictability, and open-endedness of the past, the past as lived rather than as known (it was the present to those who lived it). And the future tense, depending on the assertions it is used to make, can suggest anything from the mild securities of habitual action ("I'll see you at lunch again tomorrow") to the powerful visions of prophecy, whether melodramatic and supernatural or chaste and scientific:

> You and your children will die in agony, foaming and convulsed.

> At some point, these speculations on irreversibility suggest, the universe will simply cease to exist.

The grammatical *mood* of verbs may be even more significant than tense in shaping the character of a sentence or of a larger piece of discourse. The commonest moods in English are the *indicative,* the *subjunctive,* and the *imperative.* Verbs in the indicative mood make assertions or ask questions; verbs in the subjunctive mood indicate that a state or condition is hypothetical or possible or wished for, rather than actually the case; and verbs in the imperative mood give commands. Thus:

> ### indicative mood
> 1. "Do you know who wrote *Middlemarch?*"
> 2. "I do. George Eliot wrote it."
>
> ### subjunctive mood
> 1. "If you were to tell me who wrote *Middlemarch,* I would be very happy."
> 2. "I wish I had written *Middlemarch.*"
>
> ### imperative mood
> 1. "Tell me who wrote *Middlemarch!*"
> 2. "You find out for yourself!"

It is rare to find a sustained stretch of discourse in the imperative mood, though when one turns up, it usually indicates a heightened emotional state of some kind. More often, in expository and argumentative prose at least, an indicative norm is varied by means of the subjunctive, and attention to this pattern can often tell us something about the play between fact and hypothesis, or actuality and desire, or knowledge and imagination in a given piece of prose. It is impossible to predict before the fact just what the significative resources of the indicative or subjunctive moods will be, but once we are alerted to them, we can begin to explore their meaning.

Much the same can be said of *active* and *passive* constructions. As teachers of writing, we often treat these simply as examples of How To Do It and How Not To Do It, respectively, arguing that passive constructions are longer, less emphatic, and likelier to disguise the doer of an action than are active constructions. All this is, of course, true. But the passive voice (like the active) is the name for a structure, not just a fault, and structures have their uses and meanings. The passive voice may be used to suggest an impersonal and perhaps irresistible force in human affairs:.

> Women and men alike were led to pursue their own interests.

Or to focus on the object of an action, when the object is considered more important than the agent:

> Smiling still with that air of world-weary tolerance he had shown throughout the trial, Nelson was led before the judge for the last time.

Or to temper by means of stylistic elevation the emotion that a more direct and informal prose might release:

> It is to be regretted, Father, that the one life you could not refrain from damaging irreparably was that of your own daughter.

Or to bring about numerous other effects. It is doubtless a good idea to urge our students to use the active voice whenever they can. At times, however, they will need the expressive resources of the passive, and they should have some knowledge of the range of those resources. And when we are analyzing rather than correcting prose—adopting the interpretive rather than the evaluative stance—we will usually be asking not whether the passive voice is a good or bad thing but what it contributes to meaning.

SUBORDINATION AND ITS USES

From still another point of view, sentences can be classified as *simple, compound, complex,* or *compound-complex*. Simple sentences contain one main (independent) clause; compound sentences contain two or more such clauses linked by coordinating conjunctions. Complex sentences link a subordinate to an independent clause by means of a subordinating conjunction. And compound-complex sentences, as we might have expected, combine two or more simple sentences with one or more subordinate clauses. Some examples:

simple
Eleanor wrote the essay.

compound
Eleanor wrote the essay and Jennifer returned the books to the library.

complex
Although Eleanor wrote the essay, Jennifer returned the books to the library.

compound-complex
Although Eleanor wrote the essay, Jennifer returned the books to the library and Denise railed against the academic establishment.

What is interesting about this classification of sentence-kinds is that it can alert us to significant relationships. When an independent clause is joined to a dependent clause by means of a subordinating conjunction, we have not just a grammatical or syntactic pattern but also a conceptual relationship in which one element is subordinated to another, whence the difference in meaning between these two sentences:

1. Although Tim is very able, he is extremely arrogant.
2. Although Tim is extremely arrogant, he is very able.

In general, then, a prose style that makes little use of subordination and depends instead on simple or compound sentences will organize the experience it delivers in a relatively unhierarchical (paratactic) manner. A prose style that makes considerable use of subordination—and thus of complex or compound-complex sentences—will organize things in an intensely hierarchical (hypotactic) way. If we recall the passages from Hemingway and James quoted in the earlier discussion of sentence length, we will see that the opposition between parataxis and hypotaxis is a good deal more telling, when we try to distinguish such styles, than the opposition between short and long sentences. When Frye notes that what emerges from James's sentences is "not a linear process of thought but a simultaneous comprehension," he is really calling attention to the hierarchical effects of an intensely hypotactic style. Such a style rearranges linear sequence as hierarchical structure; the yellow brick road becomes a twelve-story hotel. This does not mean that the hypotactic style is intrinsically more elevated, or more formal, or better than the paratactic style, only that it insists on hierarchical relations and interconnections among its elements, relations that it communicates by means of grammatical subordination.

The resources of a paratactic style are different. The "syntactic democracy" of parataxis, as Richard Lanham calls it (33), gives us entities without explicit relations, units of experience without connective tissue. Of course connections may be intimated, left implicit though unmistakable, but that is just the point: the connections are present in parataxis—if at all—only latently, and a latent connection is very different from an overt one. Here is a passage from an essay by Russell Baker on the character of work in corporate America:

> Some jobs in the building require men to fill paper with words. There are persons who type neatly on paper and persons who read paper and jot notes in the margins. Some persons make copies of paper and other persons deliver paper. There are persons who file paper and persons who unfile paper.
>
> Some persons mail paper. Some persons telephone other persons and ask that paper be sent to them. Others telephone to ascertain the whereabouts of paper. Some persons confer about paper. In the grandest offices, men approve of some paper and disapprove of other paper. (386)

The dominant impulse in this passage is paratactic, and the commonest conjunction is the coordinating "and." The effect, here, is one of numbing sameness and of disconnection: all those people doing things with paper, and yet doing them, it seems, in relative isolation from one another.

In Baker as in many writers who use parataxis, moreover, parataxis is reinforced at several points by two other rhetorical patterns: *asyndeton* and *anaphora*. Asyndeton is the omission or avoidance of conjunctions (*polysyndeton,* its opposite, is the use of conjunctions), while anaphora is the repetition of the same word or phrase at the beginning of a series of clauses or sentences. If you think about it, the connection among these three kinds of structure makes good sense. If a style is paratactic, it mostly avoids subordinating conjunctions and sticks to either coordinating conjunctions (*and, but, or,* and so on) or to no conjunctions at all. If the latter, it automatically becomes asyndetic as well. This combination of parataxis and asyndeton gives us a sequence of distinct, disconnected units. Suppose we want to suggest a relation among these units, but a relation based on similarity or analogy rather than connectedness (a paradigmatic rather than syntagmatic relation, as linguistics terms it). We can do so by making the units—or their beginnings, at least—structurally similar, whence anaphora. Look at a few sentences from the Baker passage (the second through the ninth), skeletalized and rearranged to display these structurings visually:

¶I   2. There are some persons who type   and persons who read and jot
      3. Some persons make   and other persons deliver
      4. There are persons who file   and persons who unfile

¶II 5. Some persons mail paper
      6. Some persons telephone and ask
      7. Others telephone to ascertain
      8. Some persons confer
      9. [In the grandest offices,]
              men approve and disapprove

This excerpt is strongly paratactic and often asyndetic as well. Through this pattern, Baker has woven two forms of anaphora: sentences beginning with "there are persons who"(2,4) and those beginning with "Some persons" (3,5,6,8). Only in the final sentence of paragraph two does he vary this pattern of sentence openings with an introductory prepositional phrase—"In the grandest offices"—and this variation is itself ironic (like the substitution of "men" for "persons"), swamped by the equalizing effects of the repetition of "paper" and by the rhetorical patterns we have been discussing (and some we haven't discussed, like *isocolon:* repetition of phrases of equal length and, often, of similar structure).

Baker's ability to evoke an entropic deathliness in the corporate workplace, then, and to portray that workplace as a desert of distinctions without difference, depends on his management of a paratactic style. In particular, it depends on the remorselessly unhierarchical links that such a style is capable of forging, links amounting at times to equal signs.

PERIODIC AND RUNNING SENTENCES

Let us return to hypotaxis once more, and to a kind of sentence closely associated with it: the *periodic* sentence. Long, complicated, marked by patterns of balance and antithesis, variation and repetition, and dependent—for the completion of its sense as for the closure of its syntax—on a crucial element (usually the main verb) that is withheld until the very end and much appreciated when it arrives, the periodic sentence, like an artfully plotted murder mystery or gothic thriller, takes its time in letting us know who done it. What Frye said of James's lengthy sentences applies even to the amateurish example immediately above: "What is explained [here, the periodic sentence itself] is turned around and viewed from all aspects, but it is completely there, so to speak, from the beginning." The periodic sentence shows us the products of thought rather than the act of thinking, an interrelation rather than a sequence of elements. It is thus a special kind of hypotaxis. Kenneth Burke has remarked in *Counter-Statement* that every sentence is, to some degree, a periodic sentence; as Yogi Berra said of a baseball game, "It ain't over until it's over." But the fact remains that much more of both sense and syntax is withheld by the periodic sentence than by the non-periodic.

There is no established name (other than "loose") for the non-periodic or antiperiodic sentence, but this terminological gap need not trouble us. There are pretty clearly two kinds of phenomenon here and the traditional terminology has contrasted their features (at various levels) as follows:

Periodic sentence	*Non-periodic sentence*
Hypotaxis	Parataxis
Ciceronian style	Senecan style
Suspended (and momentarily obscure) syntax	Serial (and continuously perspicuous) syntax

How would my definition of the periodic sentence look rewritten in a less periodic style? "Like an artfully plotted murder mystery or gothic thriller, the periodic sentence takes its time in letting us know who done it. It is long and complicated, and marked by patterns of balance and antithesis, variation and repetition. Moreover, it frequently withholds a crucial element (usually the main verb) and thereby suspends the completion of its sense and the closure of its syntax. When that withheld element arrives, at the very end, it is much appreciated.'' One sentence has become four, in this revision, but that is not important (I could have used semicolons). More significant is the progressive specification, refinement, and working out of a conception that is given in the very first unit of the definition. In this sense, the distinction between the non-periodic sentence and the periodic is analogous to that between the functions (respectively) of the colon and the dash. With the first, we assert and then refine or detail or specify; with the second, we heap up and then assert—and encompass—retrospectively. For example:

> **colon**
> Chroniclers are of many kinds: Froissart and Villehardouin, tree rings and geological strata, the gray hairs on our heads.

> **dash**
> Froissart and Villehardouin, tree rings and geological strata, the gray hairs on our heads—chroniclers are of many kinds.

But we need not stop at the level of the sentence. From the opposition between hypotaxis and parataxis, as Richard Lanham as shown, "emerges the fundamental pairing for prose style, *periodic style* and *running style*" (53, my emphasis). I won't attempt to improve on Lanham's description of these two styles:

> To imitate thus the mind in real-time interaction with the world is to write in some form of running style. The serial syntax registers first the first thing and then the second thing second, simple chronological sequence always calling the tune and beating the tempo. Such a syntax models the mind in the act of coping with the world. The coping is all small-scale, minute-to-minute tactics, not seasonal grand strategy. There is no time to reflect on grand strategy; the reader is on patrol with the writer, sharing immediate dangers and present perplexities. Things happen as they want to, not as we would have them. Circumstances call the tune.
>
> The periodic style reverses all this. The mind shows itself after it has reasoned on the event; after it has sorted by concept and categorized by size; after it has imposed on the temporal flow the shapes through which that flow takes on a beginning, a middle, and an end. The periodic stylist works with balance, antithesis, parallelism, and

careful patterns of repetition; all these dramatize a mind which has dominated experience and reworked it to its liking. It is tempting to say that the periodic style humanizes time and we can say this, so long as we remember that to "go with the flow" is as human as to oppose it, that humankind's bewilderment before raw event is as characteristic as the will to impose order on it. (54)

It is rare to find either style in pure form, but much rarer to find a piece of prose that will not begin to disclose its structure when we examine it in terms of these two grand, and complementary, clusters of patterning energy.

PARALLELISM, ANTITHESIS, CHIASMUS, AND ZEUGMA

At this point, it is almost unnecessary to define *parallelism* and *antithesis,* since the styles we have examined, and our discussions of them, have both exemplified and pointed to these indispensable patterns. Briefly, then, parallelism is the use of similar grammatical, syntactic, or rhetorical structures to enforce similarity of meaning; antithesis is the use of similar grammatical, syntactic, or rhetorical structures to enforce a contrast of meaning (it all depends, that is, on the sense of the terms). A third figure, *chiasmus,* is related to these. If the typical structure of parallelism is AB AB (and that of antithesis too, only in service of an opposition of meaning), chiasmus inverts the second member to create a bilaterally symmetrical pattern, a rhetorical butterfly: AB BA. Chiasmus is purported to be derived from the Greek letter chi, which takes the form of an X. If you label one of the diagonals A A, and the other B B, and then read the letters as though you were reading English (left to right, top to bottom) you will see how it works:

Following is an example of parallelism:

> We are all prompted by the same motives, all deceived by the same fallacies, all animated by hope, obstructed by danger, entangled by desire, and seduced by pleasure. (Samuel Johnson, *Rambler* No. 60)

Diagrammaticially, this becomes:

> We are all
>
> > prompted by the same motives
>
> > all
>
> > deceived by the same fallacies
>
> > all
>
> > animated by hope
> > obstructed by danger
> > entangled by desire
>
> > and
>
> > seduced by pleasure.

Here, from the opening of Charles Dickens's *Tale of Two Cities,* is what might be called a self-diagramming antithesis:

> It was the best of times, it was the worst of times, it was the age of wisdom, it was the age of foolishness, it was the epoch of belief, it was the epoch of incredulity, it was the season of Light, it was the season of Darkness, it was the spring of hope, it was the winter of despair. . . .

And here are a few examples of chiasmus (some based on syntax, some on sound, some on both), with superscript letters pointing up the pattern:

> A B
> Having first been disturbed by a dream, he afterwards grieved that a
> B A
> dream could disturb him. (Samuel Johnson, *Rambler* No. 204)

> A B B A
> When the going gets tough, the tough get going.

> A B B A
> And **M**ichael got the **g**lory, yes, but **G**wendolyn was **m**ine.
> (anon. ballad)

> A B B A
> For as all must die in Adam, so in Christ shall all live again.

As this last example makes clear, chiasmus may at times produce inversion of sentence structure, as may a periodic sentence. An inverted sentence places the predicate before the subject, especially a predicate including the direct object of a transitive verb: " 'Good writing is the prose of the heart' he took to be an inadequate stylistic guide."

Finally, there is the figure called *zeugma* (or "yoking"). It is most easily thought of, perhaps, as a version of parallelism in which a single word governs two other words or phrases each of which brings out (often wittily) one of two different meanings of the single word. The most commonly quoted examples of zeugma come from Alexander Pope's *The Rape of the Lock,* in which a character fears that a young woman may "stain her Honour, or her new Brocade," or that she will "lose her Heart, or Necklace, at a ball" (Canto ii, 106, 608). Here, the yoking of "Honour" and "Brocade" liberates two different senses of "stain," just as "Heart" and "Necklace" call forth the figurative and literal senses of "lose." The effect of zeugma often depends upon some such incongruity in the terms that the single word yokes, and this effect is often ironic.

APHORISMS

With zeugma, syntactic effects shade into figurative language. Before turning to figures of speech, however, we should take note of one more kind of sentence (usually only one sentence, at any rate): the aphorism. Sometimes called a *sententia* (plural: *sententiae*) or maxim, the aphorism is a general truth, or a pithy statement that sounds like a general truth. Some examples:

> Marriage has many pains, but celibacy has no pleasures. (Samuel Johnson, *Rasselas,* Chapter 26)

> Look before you leap.

> Leap Before You Look. (W. H. Auden)

> He who hesitates is lost.

> . . . innocence ends when one is stripped of the delusion that one likes oneself. (Joan Didion, "On Self-Respect")

Self-loathing is an emblem of callowness, self-acceptance a token of
maturity.

These can't all be true at the same time (or applicable to the same
situation), but they all have the ring of truth: general terms, assertive
confidence, the brave authority of the imperative mood or the definition
form. Sententiae are thus one important resource in the development of
an authoritative ethos. Our treating them here—rather than in a discussion of truth—is simply a reminder that while truth is usually taken to
be a matter of correspondence with reality, authoritativeness is often an
effect of syntax. As Northrop Frye has remarked, "what distinguishes,
not simply the epigram, but profundity itself from platitude is very frequently rhetorical wit. In fact it may be doubted whether we ever really
call an idea profound unless we are pleased with the wit of its expression" (329).

C. Figurative Language

Figurative language is as important to prose as it is to poetry, though
its density per cubic sentence is probably somewhat lower. Here, then,
are some brief reminders of the commonest figures of speech.

metaphor: an assertion (or an assumption) of the identity of two different things. Metaphor is often defined as "implied comparison," but
metaphors don't compare, they identify.
example: "Nature is a living temple." Or, less directly: "They sank
to their knees beneath the dome of Nature and offered their specious
prayers."

simile: a comparison using "like" or "as."
example: "Life is like a baseball game." Or, spelling out one of
many possible implications: "Life is like a baseball game; let's hope
it's a double header."

metonymy: substitution of effect for cause, of cause for effect, or of
a thing closely associated with X for X.
example: If a successful presidential candidate spent large sums in

his campaign, and then launched a nuclear war, one might compress this causal chain by means of metonymy and say: "He bought annihilation with campaign funds." Or, conceiving the situation somewhat differently: "Campaign spending kills millions."

synecdoche: the use of a part of something to signify the whole.
example: "All hands on deck." Figures of speech may of course be combined. The effects of a particularly wretched violin concert might be caught by combining metonymy and synecdoche (along with **hyperbole,** or exaggeration): "Never have gut and horsehair given so much pain to so many."

personification: the ascription of human attributes to inanimate or abstract entities.
example: "The typewriter winced as he sat down to write and scholarship dropped a tear."

apostrophe: direct address to an inanimate or abstract entity, or to an absent person.
examples: "History, enroll me in the ranks of your chosen!" "O Time, suspend your flight!"

paradox: a statement that is self-contradictory in one sense, but, in another, perfectly plausible.
example: "Nothing is so palpable and burdensome as nothingness." If the paradox brings together contradictory words, we have the figure **oxymoron.** John Dryden says of a sublimely foolish character that "lambent dullness" played about his face. Oxymoron can also grace humbler texts like restaurant menus, as a student once pointed out: "jumbo shrimp."

D. Diction

Diction is word choice, and English words may be classified in many ways: long or short, abstract or concrete, Latinate or Anglo-Saxon in derivation, current at the time of writing or no longer current *(archaisms),* and so on. (Actually, archaisms don't depend on the time of

writing but on the norm of the discourse as a whole. That is, if I—in
1986—write a text in one of the prose styles of 1750 and use a word no
longer current after 1650, then only that word, textually speaking, is an
archaism.) A writer's diction may also be marked by various kinds of
jargon or, to use a more neutral term, various specialized vocabularies:
the language of heraldry or taxidermy, quantum physics or structural
linguistics. The tone of sprightly amusement that we have come to expect
in Lewis Thomas's prose, for example, is in part the result of a chiastic
linking of diction and subject matter: a "scientific" vocabulary (quan-
titative, definitional, fussily precise, sprinkled with laboratory terms)
used to describe human feeling and motive, and an "anthropomorphic"
vocabulary (emotive and volitional terms, personification, the language
of everyday human social interaction) used to describe nonhuman creatures and inanimate matter. For Thomas, humans collide while neutri-
nos reconsider.

It is difficult to generalize about diction (except for this one generalization, of course) beyond a few obvious reminders. That a style built
on Latinate polysyllabic abstractions is likely to be more formal than a
style built on short, concrete, Anglo-Saxon words. That a persistent set
of cultural conventions associates the first kind of style with intellectual
analysis and abstraction from lived experience, and the second kind of
style with the sensory order and immediate experience. And that these
generalizations (and others) constitute a set of expectations which the
adroit stylist can either show to be false or use to various ends, many of
them comical and parodic. Those lengthy *catalogues* (lists) of learned
abstractions, some coined for the occasion, that we find in Rabelais,
Sterne, or Joyce, for example, are not signs of a mind hovering above
experience in an aether of scholarly irrelevance. Quite the reverse. They
often signify a mind for which scholarly terms, especially scholarly
terms subjected to rhetorical play, are themselves emblems of the world's
fertile abundance, as directly gratifying in their multiplicity and differ-
entness as the plants in a rain forest or the pictures in a gallery or the
features of the women and men who stream by us daily.

Diction, then, must be analyzed patiently and subtly, connected with
other stylistic and rhetorical features, and investigated for its role as a
contributor of meaning in particular passages and works.

E. Rhythm and Sound

The main difference between prose rhythm and verse rhythm is that the former has nothing to do with line length, which is determined in prose not by a principle of metrical recurrence but by the convention of uniform right-hand margins. The line, in prose, is not a significant unit. This means that patterns of prose rhythm will not be recurrent, as certain patterns are recurrent in a poem built of iambic pentameter or trochaic tetrameter lines. Instead, the rhythmic interest of prose is largely *ad hoc* and local, a matter of different kinds of patterning within units of varying length: words, phrases, clauses, sentences, paragraphs, and so on.

When we are dealing with units as large as the paragraph, or larger, "rhythm" is a metaphoric term, a way of talking about patterns of discourse or modes of writing. Thus one can speak of the alternation of narrative and analysis in the case history as a "rhythm" typical of that prose form, or of the "rhythm" of assertion, objection, counter-assertion, counter-objection, and so on, in certain forms of medieval argumentation. "Rhythm," in such cases, is far from a useless term, but it has nothing to do with metrical stress. Within a paragraph, too, one can speak of rhythm in a similarly metaphoric sense: the rhythm of long and short sentences, for example, or of assertion and qualification, or of sentences in verb-style and sentences in noun-style.

When we focus on sentences and their sub-units, however, it becomes practical to use "rhythm" in its more literal sense, as a term describing patterns of stressed and unstressed syllables. These patterns rarely aspire to the regularity of traditional, accentual-syllabic verse, except in demonstration-pieces like this by Robert Graves:

> One doesn't "listen" when reading standard prose; it is only in poetry that one looks out for metre and rhythmic variations on it. The writers of *vers libre* rely on their printers to call your attention to what is called "cadence" or "rhythmic relation" (not easy to follow) which might have escaped you if written as prose; *this* sentence, you'll find, has its thumb to its nose. (8)

At "rely on," this passage slips into regular metrical patterns and, indeed, into two couplets, the first closing on a slack ending of "attention"/ "relation" and the second on the tightly monosyllabic exact rhyme, "prose"/"nose."

Fredric V. Bogel

Much more commonly, rhythmic patterns are less regular and less extended, often working together with sound effects like alliteration and assonance to enforce, and at times create, effects of meaning. At this level, the vocabulary of traditional prosody can be usefully adapted to the analysis of prose. (Prosody refresher follows immediately.)

Standard prosody is the study of verse with attention to two variables: feet (patterns of relatively stressed and unstressed syllables, marked / and x respectively) and number of feet per line. The commonest kinds of feet in English verse are (with a sample word or phrase):

iambic:	x/	(today)
trochaic:	/x	(after)
anapestic:	xx/	(in the past)
dactylic:	/xx	(foolishly)
spondaic:	//	(yes, yes)
pyrrhic:	xx	("on the" in the phrase "she sat on the rug")

(These are the adjectival forms. The noun forms are iamb, trochee, anapest, dactyl, and spondee. A pyrrhic foot is always called a pyrrhic foot.) There are also technical terms for lines containing various numbers of feet:

1 foot/line:	monometer
2 feet/line:	dimeter
3 feet/line:	trimeter
4 feet/line:	tetrameter
5 feet/line:	pentameter
6 feet/line:	hexameter
7 feet/line:	heptameter

To characterize a line of verse, then, we need to specify both the basic kind of foot and the number of those feet per line (assuming that we are treating a poem written in one of the traditional English meters). Here are some examples, with the stressed and unstressed syllables marked (note that some of these lines are not metrically exact. Such inexactness—or variation—is the norm in English, and a good thing too):

a. a poem on fleas in *trochaic monometer.*

    ´ x
Adam

    ´   x
Had'em

b. a line of John Berryman's *iambic pentameter*.

x ´ x ´ x x x ´ x ´
We dream of honor, and we get along. (*77 Dream Songs,* No. 42)

c. two lines of *anapestic trimeter* (they rhyme, so they're called a couplet):

x x ´ x x ´ x x ´
In a time of internecine war,

x x ´ x x ´ x x ´
You must certainly lock every door.

In analyzing prose, we use the names of lines (monometer, etc.) much less frequently than the names of feet; and when we do use them, we do not designate a unit that recurs throughout a piece of prose (as the iambic pentameter lines recurs throughout *Paradise Lost,* for example) but a particular phrase, clause, or sentence that happens to display, if not a fully metrical design, at least some rhythmic stiffening, some spine. The effect may be largely reinforcing, a pleasing adaptation to meaning of one of the sensuous dimensions of prose. When John Updike compares the delights of the old-fashioned beer can (opened with an opener) with the tawdriness of the new (disfigured by "an ugly, shmoo-shaped 'tab' "), his prose rhythm catches the delight he feels. Who can forget, he asks, "the small, symmetrical thrill of those two triangular punctures?" ("Beer Can"). Never mind that "thrill" derives by metathesis from "thirl," meaning a hole or puncture (as in Sylvia Plath's "Cut": "What a thrill—/My thumb instead of an onion"), and thus perfectly fuses opened can and drinker's elation, technology and human feeling. Notice only the near-symmetry, syntactic and rhythmical, of the phrases:

´ x ´ x x ´
small, symmetrical thrill

´ x ´ x x ´ x
two triangular punctures.

Similarly, much of the bite and memorability of the words that open Thomas Paine's *The American Crisis* derives from an artful conjunction of monosyllabic curtness, alliteration, and stressed syllables:

´ x x ´ x ´ ´ ´
These are the times that try men's souls

If this were a line of verse and we had to define its metrical character, we would probably call it iambic tetrameter (the substitution of an initial trochee for an iamb being one of the commonest variations in English). It's close enough to such a line, at any rate, for us to feel the formalizing and formulaic power that Paine's management of stress adds to what might have sounded like mere alarmism.

But the analysis of prose rhythm cannot confine itself to seeking out prose equivalents of verse lines. The continuity of prose requires that we look, instead, for less extended instances of regularity and more kinds of regularity within a given unit of prose. In addition, it is commoner in prose than in verse to find groups of phrases or clauses that have the same, or almost the same, number of stressed syllables but a variable number of unstressed syllables, as in Samuel Johnson's warning, "If you are pleased with prognostics of good, you will be terrified likewise with tokens of evil" (*Rasselas,* Chapter 13). The key phrases of this sentence stand in a loose rhythmic symmetry to each other.

$$\acute{\text{p}}\text{l}\overset{x}{\text{e}}\text{ased } \overset{x}{\text{with }} \acute{\text{p}}\text{r}\overset{x}{\text{o}}\text{gn}\overset{x}{\text{o}}\text{stics of } \acute{\text{good}}$$

$$\acute{\text{t}}\overset{x}{\text{e}}\text{rr}\overset{x}{\text{i}}\text{fied } \acute{\text{l}}\text{ik}\overset{x}{\text{e}}\text{w}\overset{x}{\text{i}}\text{se } \acute{\text{w}}\text{ith } \acute{\text{t}}\overset{x}{\text{o}}\text{k}\overset{x}{\text{e}}\text{ns of } \acute{\text{e}}\overset{x}{\text{vil}}$$

Johnson encourages us to hear this symmetry, of course, by his syntactic parallelism and by the corresponding symmetry of alliterative pattern: p, p, g, set against t, t, e.

As this example may suggest, "rhythm" is used metaphorically—as well as literally—even at the level of words and phrases. That is, the reason we tend to hear phrases like these of Johnson's as balanced, even though they are metrically neither regular nor isomorphic, is that—given the slightest chance—we allegorize syntactic balance as rhythmic balance, especially if it is reinforced by sound patterns, and we minimize the actual difference in pattern of stress. We either abstract from the sentence those units that display rhythmic patterning (ignoring "likewise," for example, as syntactic filler or background) or we treat as insignificant extra unstressed—and sometimes stressed—syllables that are part of the rhythmic unit itself. In short, we permit sense and syntactic structuring to determine which syllables shall count most in a rhythmic configuration.

Consider the famous opening sentence of Johnson's *Rasselas* (arranged and numbered to facilitate rhythmic analysis):

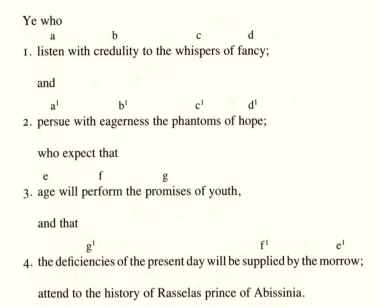

Ye who

     a   b   c   d

1. listen with credulity to the whispers of fancy;

and

    a^1 b^1 c^1 d^1

2. persue with eagerness the phantoms of hope;

who expect that

   e   f   g

3. age will perform the promises of youth,

and that

    g^1 f^1 e^1

4. the deficiencies of the present day will be supplied by the morrow;

attend to the history of Rasselas prince of Abissinia.

Clearly, 1 and 2 are arranged in syntactic parallel, just as 3 and 4 are chiastically ordered (see the superscript letters). If we hear this sentence as rhythmically balanced, moreover, as generations of readers have claimed to do, it must be because we permit the metaphoric "rhythm" of tight syntactic parallelism to override the actual arrangement of stressed and unstressed syllables, which is roughly as follows (I'll mark only units 1 and 2; 3 and 4 are even less regular):

listen with credulity to the whispers of fancy

persue with eagerness the phantoms of hope

There are some tight alignments here ("whispers of" with "phantoms of") but the case for rhythmic congruence rests mainly on the presence of four stressed syllables in each unit and on the tight syntactic parallelism of the central formula: Ye who A with B [to] the C of D (where A is a verb, B is an abstract noun indicating a state of mind, and so on). Given this alignment of stressed syllables and syntactic parallelism, and the further fact that the stresses fall on corresponding words in parallel

phrases, we largely disregard extra unstressed syllables and treat structures of interrelation as patterns of stress: there is rhythm, but it is the
"rhythm" of syntax.

That hybrid phrase can suggest how difficult it is to discuss one dimension of prose without attending to others. The sample analyses in the
next section will aim to demonstrate, among other things, the interrelatedness of those dimensions.

IV. PRACTICAL PROSE ANALYSIS:
TWO SAMPLE ANALYSES

This section will attempt to put some of the terms of Section III to work
in an analysis of two passages of prose. In the course of that analysis it
will also suggest some strategies for using stylistic analysis in undergraduate writing classes and, indeed, in any course that encourages students to pay attention to the language of the texts they study. The
underlying assumption, again, is that such attention to language results
in the discovery of meaning, and that no course—or discipline—can
afford to neglect meaning or to prefer the crudities of gist and paraphrase to the subtlety and exactness of close reading.

Our first passage is the opening paragraph of a review, "Life and the
Novelist," by Virginia Woolf, a review that, typically, became a shrewd
meditation on a significant topic: "the relation of the novelist to life and
what it should be"(46). Such a topic will interest literary critics, certainly, but it will interest many others as well: students of narrative in
disciplines such as history; philosophers concerned with the competing
claims, in aesthetics and elsewhere, of truth to life and formal coherence; psychologists, biographers, and other investigators of the creative
process; and, indeed, any reader who seeks in fiction rewards and challenges that are both formal and, however obliquely, representational.
Woolf's is a text, then, pertinent to a variety of disciplines outside that
of literary criticism.

What Woolf concludes about the novelist's relation to life is that it is
very tricky. On the one hand the novelist "must expose himself to life"
(47), must submit himself to it and seize the impressions it offers. "But
at a certain moment," she concludes, "he must withdraw, alone, to

that mysterious room" where perceptions may be mastered, no longer just received, and "something formidable and enduring created from them" (42).

The essay starts, however, by specifying the novelist's intensely susceptible nature:

> The novelist—it is his distinction and his danger—is terribly exposed to life. Other artists, partially at least, withdraw; they shut themselves up for weeks alone with a dish of apples and a paint-box, or a roll of music paper and a piano. When they emerge it is to forget and distract themselves. But the novelist never forgets and is seldom distracted. He fills his glass and lights his cigarette, he enjoys presumably all the pleasures of talk and table, but always with a sense that he is being stimulated and played upon by the subject-matter of his art. Taste, sound, movement, a few words here, a gesture there, a man coming in, a woman going out, even the motor that passes in the street or the beggar who shuffles along the pavement, and all the reds and blues and lights and shades of the scene claim his attention and rouse his curiosity. He can no more cease to receive impressions than a fish in mid-ocean can cease to let the water rush through his gills. (41)

That susceptibility, Woolf immediately interrupts herself to insist, is double-edged, and the alliteration itself suggests that "distinction" and "danger" may be inseparable in this case. Woolf underscores the distinction, the singularity, of the novelist in several ways. She always describes "other artists" in the plural and "the novelist" (or "he") in the singular. She contrasts the novelist with those other artists by a means of a repetition-with-variation that functions as antithesis: "forget . . . distract"/"never forgets . . . is seldom distracted." She sets the implied self-mastery of certain reflexive verbs ("shut themselves up," "forget and distract themselves") against the un-reflexive verbs associated with the novelist and, indeed, against both passive constructions ("is being stimulated and played upon") and a lengthy periodic sentence in which the novelist is not agent but object while the impressions of everyday life, after ceaselessly accumulating for eight-ninths of a sentence, "claim his attention and rouse his curiosity." In these and other ways, Woolf emphasizes both the intense exposedness of the novelist and the singularity it imposes on him.

The impressions to which the novelist is subject, however, take on an interesting character in this passage, a character communicated less by explicit statement than by certain features of style and structure.

Look again at that long penultimate sentence, arranged diagrammatically this time to disclose some of those features:

```
      ´      ´       ´      x
Taste, sound, movement,
x  ´    x     ´
a few words here,
x   ´   x    ´
a gesture there,
x  ´   x  ´  x   ´
a man coming in,
x   ´   x   ´  x   ´
a woman going out,
```

                                         even

```
x   ´   x   x   ´  x  x    x   ´
the motor that passes in the street
```

                                         or

```
x   ´  x   x    ´  x  x   ´   x    ´    x
the beggar who shuffles along the pavement,
```

                                     and all

```
x   ´   x   ´
the reds and blues
x    ´    x   ´
and lights and shades
```

                                     of the scene

```
   ´   x  x   ´  x
claim his attention                    and
   ´    x   x x´ x x
rouse his curiosity.
```

The sentence is intensely and multiply structured, a series of grammatical, syntactic, and rhythmic parallels and antitheses (even to antitheses—red against blue, light against shade—within parallels). Why? What does such insistent artfulness in the construction of symmetries, categories (unspecified sensations; fragments of human life; humans acting; more remote, specific, and contextualized actions; colors and chiaroscuro), and linguistic shapeliness tell us? It tells us, or shows us through stylistic means, what the essay will later make explicit. That if the registering of random impressions is part of the novelist's task, the shaping of those impressions into a prose that is "formidable and enduring" is another. The novelist, soaking up sensations, may experience that "blooming, buzzing confusion" of which William James wrote. But

Woolf, having written, presents that confusion through the multiple structurings of a studied English prose-style, a prose style whose every sentence—and not just the one we have isolated here—bears the impress of a mind that has actively selected from and imposed order on the experience it seeks to clarify.

The tension between that ordering and those experiences is nicely caught in the style of the sentence we have been considering. On the one hand, it displays the serial accretiveness of the running style (here, asyndetic), and this pattern allegorizes the mind of the Novelist, stage I, in the process of receiving impressions. On the other, those accretions are part of a quasi-periodic sentence—really, an enormously expanded subject wagging a small predicate—whose suspended syntax allegorizes a mind not thinking, but having thought, presenting a structure built from the impressions it had once only received. Such a mind—the mind of the Novelist, stage II—is above all active, shaping its impressions into knowable structures by rhetorical mastery. This is the novelist in his second phase, working in "that mysterious room" to which Woolf later alludes, and the chief exemplar of this phase is the activity of mind whose impress we infer from this paragraph. Woolf, that is, writes the paragraph in the voice of Novelist II.

Novelist I is what she is writing about, and the contrast between them is best caught by putting the insistent mastery of mind that we have been discussing against the climactic image of the paragraph. Here, Novelist I, that poor fish, is condemned to submit passively to the stream that rushes through and by him. The image suggests more than passivity, of course. It strengthens the idea of isolation, which the third person singular had suggested, by locating this fish "in mid-ocean." It underscores the involuntariness of Novelist I's susceptibility. And at the same time it reminds us, without ever quite saying so, that the novelist's life—his life as a novelist, at any rate—depends on that stream of impressions, which is as necessary to his imaginative survival as oxygenated water is to the life of the fish.

Woolf somehow knows this about Novelist I, as she knows of his constant "sense," presumably invisible to others, that "he is being played upon by the subject-matter of his art." She is thus writing a double-portrait of herself as representative novelist, both object and subject, registering sensibility and aggressive stylist, topic under discussion and crafter of shapely paragraphs. In short, the voice which tells us that the novelist is a passive creature "terribly exposed to life" simultaneously shows us, through style and rhetoric, what the novelist must also be: a giver of linguistic form to the impressions she receives. The exposure of the novelist is here part of a double-exposure showing us both dimensions of the artist at once.

In addition to serving as a stylistic demonstration piece, there are many other ways in which Woolf's paragraph might be used in a writing class. For one thing, it is an exemplary model of one kind of paragraph development:

> i. Thesis (sentence 1)
> ii. Clarifying contrast (sent 2–3)
> iii. Development of thesis, with examples (sent. 4–6)
> iv. Conclusion (sent. 7)

For another, the signals of transition from sentence to sentence are so sure and clear that these, too, can serve as a model for student writing. The most obvious of these signals, in each sentence after the first, are as follows:

> 2: "Other artists" (as opposed to the novelist)
> 3: "they" (the "other artists")
> 4: "But," "forgets . . . distracted" (echoing the phrasing of sentence no. 3, but—as the "But" tells us—in order to develop a contrast)
> 5: "He" (the novelist)
> 6: "Taste, sound, movement" etc. (examples of "the subject-matter of his art"); "his" (the novelist's)
> 7: "He" (the novelist)

These signals connect the sentences, and the four main sections of the paragraph, into a smoothly developing whole.

The first and last sentences, moreover, juxtaposed for illustration, can help students see what a proper essay-conclusion (and this excerpt can stand as a one-paragraph essay) should be. Students have very odd ideas about conclusions. Some think they ought to be summaries of the essay (unnecessary and tedious); others think they ought to restate the thesis (ditto); and a few, told by their teachers that an essay should "leave the reader thinking," introduce in their conclusions an entirely new idea. There are many ways to end an essay, of course, but much of the time an argumentative essay ends most effectively with a conclusion that recalls, yet goes beyond, the thesis: drawing out its implications, or demonstrating its full explanatory force, or deepening its import. The movement from thesis to conclusion is thus neither a circling back nor a linear progress but something like a spiral in which the conclusion moves the thesis to a higher level of generalization or lends it an intenser power of implication.

Here are Woolf's thesis and conclusion:

thesis: The novelist—it is his distinction and his danger—is terribly exposed to life.

conclusion: He can no more cease to receive impressions than a fish in mid-ocean can cease to let the water rush through his gills.

What does the conclusion add? First, an arresting concrete image which, by its very nature (here, a simile), solicits consideration and interpretation more forcefully than abstract, discursive summary. Second, those implications discussed above: the novelist's passivity and involuntariness, his solitude (''mid-ocean'' gives us a new sense of the scale of that solitude), and his being always surrounded by ''the subject-matter of his art.'' Third, the idea that the novelist depends, for the continuance of his imaginative life, on that ceaseless stream of impressions. If we redefine breathing as ''incurable oxygen addiction'' we can get some sense of the two-sided situation of the novelist, and the simile of the fish is what brings out the full force of this situation. Woolf's final sentence never really leaves her thesis behind, yet it does much more than simply restate it, and students can profit from a careful analysis of just what it does do. They can also profit, after such analysis, from being asked to imitate the passage in an essay of argumentative definition, an effort to define another sort of figure and to distinguish him or her from other members of the same group: the painter from other artists, say, or the lover from friends, or the concert-mistress from other musicians, or the quarterback from other athletes, and so on.

Our second passage is a very different kind of prose, an excerpt from Chapter 3, ''Conspicuous Leisure,'' of Thorstein Veblen's *The Theory of the Leisure Class*. It is a text likelier to be assigned in an economics or sociology course than in a writing course, but no less likely to reward stylistic analysis in those contexts. To read Veblen's text carefully, with attention to style, is to grasp more precisely and completely its conception of social behavior and social man. Here is the passage:

> Abstention from labour is not only a honorific or meritorious act, but it presently comes to be a requisite of decency. The insistence on property as the basis of reputability is very naive and very imperious during the early stages of the accumulation of wealth. Abstention from labour is the conventional evidence of wealth and is therefore the conventional mark of social standing; and this insistence on the meritoriousness of wealth leads to a more strenuous insistence on leisure. *Nota notae est nota rei ipsius.* [A sign of a sign is a sign of the thing itself.] According to well-established laws of human nature, prescription presently seizes upon this conventional evidence of wealth and fixes it in men's habits of thought as something that is in itself substantially meritorious and ennobling; while productive labour at the same time and by a like process becomes in a double sense intrinsically unworthy. Prescription ends by making labour not only disreputable in the eyes of the community, but morally impossible to the noble, freeborn man, and incompatible with a worthy life.
>
> This tabu on labour has a further consequence in the industrial differentiation of classes. As the population increases in density and the predatory group grows into a settled industrial community, the constituted authorities and the customs governing ownership gain in scope and consistency. It then presently becomes impracticable to accumulate wealth by simple seizure, and, in logical consistency, acquisition by industry is equally impossible for high-minded and impecunious men. The alternative open to them is beggary or privation. Wherever the canon of conspicuous leisure has a chance undisturbed to work out its tendency, there will therefore emerge a secondary, and in a sense spurious, leisure class—abjectly poor and living a precarious life of want and discomfort, but morally unable to stoop to gainful pursuits. The decayed gentleman and the lady who has seen better days are by no means unfamiliar phenomena even now. This pervading sense of the indignity of the slightest manual labour is familiar to all civilised peoples, as well as to peoples of a less advanced pecuniary culture. In persons of delicate sensibility, who have long been habituated to gentle manners, the sense of the shamefulness of manual labour may become so strong that, at a critical juncture, it will even set aside the instinct of self-preservation. So, for instance, we are told of certain Polynesian chiefs, who, under the stress of good form, preferred to starve rather than carry their food to their mouths with their own hands. It is true, this conduct may have been due, at least

in part, to an excessive sanctity or tabu attaching to the chief's person. The tabu would have been communicated by the contact of his hands, and so would have made anything touched by him unfit for human food. But the tabu is itself a derivative of the unworthiness or moral incompatibility of labour; so that even when construed in this sense the conduct of the Polynesian chiefs is truer to the canon of honorific leisure than would at first appear. A better illustration, or at least a more unmistakable one, is afforded by a certain king of France, who is said to have lost his life through an excess of moral stamina in the observance of good form. In the absence of the functionary whose office it was to shift his master's seat, the king sat uncomplaining before the fire and suffered his royal person to be toasted beyond recovery. But in so doing he saved his Most Christian Majesty from menial contamination.

> *Summum crede nefas animam praeferre pudori,*
> *Et propter vitam vivendi perdere causas.* (32–34)
> [Believe it the worst of sins to purchase life with dishonor,
> And in order to live to lose all reason for living.]

This is more difficult than Woolf, for starters, and less obviously attractive as prose. How would a fairly alert undergraduate paraphrase this excerpt if the instructor were to ask, "What is Veblen saying here?" Perhaps like this: "Veblen says that wealth is a sign of your social standing, and that not having to work shows that you're wealthy. So even if you're poor, you can pretend that you have money—and thus a high place in society—by not working, and by making it obvious that you're not working and don't want or need to work." A pretty good discussion-launching summary.

The one curious note, though, is the hypothetical student's use of "you." It sounds overly personal, even intimate, in this context, and the reason it does is not far to seek. There is no "you" in Veblen's passage (not surprising) and, except for the Polynesian chief and the French king, there are scarcely any individuals at all. When one does appear, "the noble, freeborn man," for example, he is a typical rather than an individual figure, like "the decayed gentleman" a little further on, and he is neither the principal agent nor the grammatical subject of the sentence. The student's "you"—an individual who does things, who wants to create certain impressions, and from whose point of view the student speaks—is utterly foreign to the world of Veblen's discourse. In that world, people recede into the background. The foreground is dominated by universal forces—usually represented by abstract nouns—that are both the grammatical subjects of Veblen's sentences and the authentic agents of the social scene he depicts. "Abstention," "insistence," "prescription," "tabu," "the canon of conspicuous leisure"—such forces, often personified, are the real "characters" in Veblen's drama.

For some readers, this demotion of the individual in favor of abstract social forces is precisely what is wrong with the social sciences, and Veblen's prose is just another symptom of the Pretty Pass in which Emile Durkheim and the others have landed us. Those readers would be quite wrong, but they could certainly marshal a lot of stylistic evidence to show that Veblen's discourse is that of sociology itself, and that his prose displays all the signs of rampant sociologese. The bill of indictment might include the following:

1. Nominalization, especially the use of abstract nouns as subjects of sentences where good style would require a human agent and the finite, active verb from which the noun had been made.

2. A high frequency of abstract, latinate diction, generating a good deal of pomposity.

3. Over-reliance on forms of "to be."

4. Passive constructions (though fewer than one would expect, probably because passives still permit the object of the action to remain the subject of the sentence: in "Veblen is analyzed by me," Veblen is still there, despite his fate).

5. Excessive personification, and thus promiscuous reification, of abstractions ("prescription . . . seizes upon this evidence . . .").

6. A vocabulary of causality that mechanizes human behavior and describes it in terms of quasi-scientific necessity: "a further consequence"; "the predatory group grows"; "by a like process"; "a chance undisturbed to work out its tendency"; "well-established laws of human nature." This sense of overly rigid causality is reinforced by the pervasive interrelatedness of forces that Veblen's hypotaxis often suggests.

7. Vague management of the vocabulary of morality (by "moral," Veblen seems often to mean far less than he ought to).

8. Unsure management of levels of diction: "his royal person," for example, clashes ludicrously with "toasted."

These features of style are undoubtedly present, in some form, in the passage, but they do not demonstrate either that Veblen writes badly or that his social-scientific abstraction and neutrality thoughtlessly dehumanize individual men and women. It would be truer to say that Veblen is not neutral at all—that his prose is filled with attitudes, judgments, assessments, and evaluations, that these are frequently ironic (comically and grimly, at times both), and that the "dehumanization" his prose projects is not the result of a methodological stance but of a vision of human nature. Finding that human beings operate as though they lacked individual wills and authentic personal values, Veblen found almost ready-to-hand the perfect style for symbolizing this surrender of selfhood: the coolness and distance of the language of social science. Once the result of certain methodological choices (and ideological forces), this style becomes, in Veblen's hands, an ironic mirror reflecting our actual vacuity. Unlike the more conventional social scientist, Veblen has not "abstracted from" a rich and multiform human reality in order to isolate "trends" and "laws" and "group tendencies." In his ironic vision, that's all there is.

Perhaps this ironic vision of humanity—as a "predatory group" beset by one "tabu" or another—is what led a disciple of Veblen's to term him "a visitor from another world," and to assert that "no other such emancipator of the mind from the subtle tyranny of circumstance has been known in social science, and no other such enlarger of the realm of inquiry" (Benton 40).

From this perspective, our list of Veblen's stylistic "faults" can be rewritten as a repertoire of rhetorical and stylistic means to certain ends:

1. Nominalization: a stylistic means of withdrawing agency from persons and their actions and of ascribing it to large, abstract forces.

2. Abstract, latinate diction (at times, pompous): a reinforcement of nominalization (above) and one source of a detached, ironic tone. This tone is mock-heroic, at times, to designate petty figures caught up in grand processes they scarcely understand, and processes which, for all their scope, are neither dignified, nor moral, nor in the best interests of individuals.

3. Reliance on forms of "to be" and on passive constructions: a way of minimizing human agency, and of insisting on the ineluctability or static intransigence of social forces and structures.

4–5. Personification: a displacement of human agency onto the real agents of human experience in society.

6. A vocabulary of rigid causality and of scientific necessity: a stylistic index of human predictability. If you could set your watch by Kant's strolls, you can found an entire scientific discipline on the behavior of people in societies, Veblen implies.

7. Vague management of moral terms: a stylistic mirror of the human tendency to term "moral" whatever is expedient for social advancement. Such a redefinition of morality is common in Veblen. Government and war, he argues in another passage, are indeed carried on for pecuniary gain, but "it is gain obtained by the honourable method of seizure and conversion. These occupations are of the nature of predatory, not productive, employment" and— this is Veblen's point—that's why they count as honourable.

8. Clashes of diction: part of a pervasive mock-heroic strategy which sets human pretensions to dignity, intelligence, and free will against the actual mechanism of human behavior.

Finally, we can mention Veblen's strategy of quotation. His first Latin tag, *Nota notae est nota rei ipsius,* sounds like a Scholastic maxim, and its taut syntactic neatness reinforces its sense, in this context: that once you have a principle of interpretation, the text (here, society) is an open book. The second quotation is more interesting, especially as it follows on the stories of the chief and the king. Veblen does not identify it (he says in the preface that the few illustrative quotations in his book are "such as will commonly be recognized with sufficient facility without the guidance of citation"). It is from the eighth Satire of the Roman satirist Juvenal, a poem which argues unremittingly that birth and descent should count for nothing since personal merit—character—is the only proper criterion for ranking human beings. Immediately pertinent to the chief and king, the quotation is also more sweepingly ironic when applied to the whole of Veblen's text. Here it clashes with a world in which "personal merit" or "character," like "morality," is a quality we ascribe to those who have effectively, if grotesquely, accommodated themselves to such mindless imperatives as "the canon of conspicuous leisure."

Much more could be said about Veblen's prose: about the comedy in calling "abstention from labour" an "act"; about the parallelism, antithesis, and chiasmus that provide syntactic analogues to the structures that lock individuals into patterns, as in the third sentence of the second paragraph:

a   b   b   a

"impracticable . . . seizure . . . industry . . . impossible";

about the play with audience implied in his claim that "This pervading sense of the indignity of manual labour is familiar to all civilised peoples"; about the use of the present tense to designate actions that are timeless, unvarying, and irresistible; and so on. Enough has been said, however, to show that the paraphrase with which we began is both correct and hopelessly inadequate; that only attention to style can begin to make available the full range of meaning in Veblen's prose; and that this meaning, since it embodies an entire vision of human nature in society, is a kind of meaning that is at least as pertinent to the social scientist or student of social science as it is to the teacher of writing.

V. PROSE ANALYSIS IN THE CLASSROOM

Not every prose passage requires us to wheel out the full arsenal of stylistic analysis. We said very little about Woolf's diction and a good bit about Veblen's. We paid fairly close attention to patterns of balance and antithesis, and to prose rhythm, in Woolf, and not much in Veblen. Choices like these are made for a variety of reasons: because certain things catch our eye while others escape us; because the exhaustive shades readily into the exhausting; and because, at some point in an attentive reading, we decide that analysis of certain features counts for more—explains more powerfully or economically—than analysis of others. Analyzing Woolf's tone and accounting for it in stylistic terms seemed less important than investigating her use of rhetorical patterns and of simile. Veblen's tone, on the other hand, seemed closely bound up with the largest features of his meaning so we probed for its sources in a wide variety of stylistic features. We cannot, and should not, do everything all the time.

Moreover, different texts can suggest different kinds of student exercise. Woolf's, as we have seen, encourages various sorts of work on the paragraph, on the one-paragraph essay, and on the relations between an essay's thesis statement and its conclusion. Veblen, on the other hand, can prompt us to work with students on tone, on diction, on the infusing of attitude into expository and argumentative styles, and of course—ironies aside—on the conceptual framework and rhetorical conventions that characterize the stance of the social scientist.

If a piece of prose is stylistically interesting at all, we might generalize, then its meaning will be more precisely disclosed by analysis of its style, and that analysis can generate a variety of exercises useful to the student writer. In fact, the analysis itself will prove invaluable by making visible, and therefore part of the student's own repertory, some of the innumerable resources of English prose style.

One of the exercises for student writers that analysis can generate, namely, stylistic imitation, requires a bit of elaboration. Long ago, imitation—along with translation from one foreign language into another, and from one style into another—was fairly standard educational fare for young students. There are many reasons why this is no longer the case, one of them of continuing pertinence: the notion that imitation is an essentially passive, mechanical, and therefore stultifying exercise that impedes the liberation of our students' authentic selves and individual voices. The nation that produced Ralph Waldo Emerson and Walt Whitman is not likely to embrace a pedagogy either so ancient or so precedent-honoring as that of stylistic imitation. This (essentially Romantic) argument against imitation, moreover, has considerable force, as well as considerable power to foster self-flattery. It rests on two related notions: that we have an authentic, genuine self buried beneath the encrustations of custom or timidity or laziness or youth, and that the best way to liberate that self is to strip away the structures that confine it. It is clear that imitation will play no large role in a curriculum conceived exclusively according to these principles. Even so un-Romantic a figure as Samuel Johnson harrumphed that "No man was ever great by imitation."

Yet Johnson was no enemy to imitation, or to the idea that such competence and facility as precede greatness could be acquired by imitation. It all comes down to whether you think that originality is achieved by the avoidance of forms or by the mastery and revivification of forms. If you believe the latter—at least some of the time—then imitation may well occupy an important place in your idea of a writing curriculum, for you will conceive it as an enlargement of powers, an acquisition of multiple possibilities, and thus the very condition of whatever freedom a writer is able to achieve. Yet even the instructor who believes in the value of imitation can, all unwittingly, permit it to degenerate into a fairly wooden activity. What follows is a brief attempt to foresee some of the likelier pitfalls and to chart a course around them.

How might an exercise in stylistic imitation proceed? First, the passage to be imitated should be short enough to be examined closely, and it should be read aloud, slowly and well, in class. Then it must be subjected to intense stylistic and rhetorical analysis, but analysis that at every turn connects features of style and rhetoric with the meanings and effects they create (as we will see in subsequent chapters, a given stylistic trait can carry a wide range of meanings and serve a variety of different purposes). Too many exercises in imitation fail because the student has been asked to imitate, say, a certain breathless and under-punctuated passage in Faulkner without being told, or led to notice, that the *subject* of the passage is the relentless pressure of history on the present, or the obstinacy of obsession in a given character's mind. To imitate a style rather than parody it, then, is almost always to imitate a certain kind of subject matter, a certain voice and point of view *(ethos),* a certain relation to one's dramatic audience, and a certain rhetorical purpose. These should be spelled out in classroom analysis.

That analysis might even conclude with a summary list (on the blackboard) of principal stylistic, rhetorical, and other features of the passage, a kind of recipe for writing like this or that author. Then, perhaps, a discussion of other topics suitable for such an imitation. At this point, a portion of class time can be given over to writing: three or four introductory sentences, a trying-on of the style to be imitated. After a short discussion of some of these (volunteers can read theirs aloud), the class can be asked to complete the imitation for the next meeting, or the next but one, leaving the instructor time to duplicate a few finished products for the entire class.

In that subsequent class, students can discuss particular features of the duplicated imitations or excerpts: the passages that get the original style just right (and the stylistic means for doing so), and those that display instructive near misses. The *next* writing assignment might then take one of three forms: a revision of the imitation; an analytic essay treating one student imitation and its relation to the original (an exercise in close analysis for which the students are now extremely well prepared); or a slightly longer essay in the same *mode* as the imitation, but not itself an imitation. This latter assignment is designed to take the rhetorical and stylistic skills developed in the imitation work and begin to integrate them into the student's prose repertory.

Such a sequence of assignments, only one of many that might be devised, demonstrates the role of imitation by conducting students into the detailed mimicry of another writer's habits and then beyond, into a new measure of rhetorical freedom acquired from that mimicry. The process is well known to confirmed improvisers like jazz musicians, who are often less sentimental than some of their fans about the "pure spontaneity" of jazz performance or the alleged restrictiveness of imitation. As the distinguished alto saxophonist and teacher, Lee Konitz, has put it: "I often tell my students to learn this or that Charlie Parker solo. He created our études, and to learn a Charlie Parker solo can change your life" (quoted by Whitney Balliett, 76). In taking students through these stages, the imitative sequence also demonstrates one natural connection between close reading and thoughtful writing, and thus between textual analysis in a given field and the effort to improve student writing.

WORKS CITED

Entries marked with an asterisk are described in Chapter 8, "A Bibliographical Guide to the Profession."

Auden, W. H. "Leap Before You Look." *W. H. Auden: Collected Poems.* Edited by Edward Mendelson 244. New York: Random House, 1968.

Baker, Russell. *Poor Russell's Almanac.* Garden City, N.Y.: Doubleday, 1972. Selection reprinted as "Work in Corporate America" in *The Bedford Reader.* Edited by X.J. Kennedy and Dorothy M. Kennedy. 384–86. New York: St. Martin's, 1982.

Balliett, Whitney. "Jazz." *The New Yorker* Aug. 16, 1982: 76–83.

Benton, William. "Veblen, Thorstein." *Encyclopedia Britannica: Macropedia.* 1974.

Berryman, John. *77 Dream Songs,* No. 42. *The Dream Songs.* New York: Farrar, Straus and Giroux, 1969.

Burke, Kenneth. *Counter-Statement.* New York: Harcourt Brace, 1931.

Dickens, Charles. *A Tale of Two Cities.* Edited by George Woodcock. London: Penguin English Library Series, 1970.

Didion, Joan. "On Self-Respect." *Slouching Towards Bethlehem.* 142–48, New

York: Farrar, Straus and Giroux, 1961, 1968.

Frye, Northrop. *Anatomy of Criticism: Four Essays.* Princeton: Princeton Univ. Press, 1957.

Goodman, Nelson. *Ways of Worldmaking.* Indianapolis: Hackett, 1978.

Graves, Robert. *The Common Asphodel: Collected Essays on Poetry, 1922– 1949.* London: Hamish Hamilton, 1949.

Hemingway, Ernest. *The Sun Also Rises.* New York: Scribner's, 1954.

James, Henry. *The Golden Bowl.* Great Britain: Penguin Classics, 1966.

Johnson, Samuel. *Rambler.* Vols. 3–5. *The Yale Edition of the Works of Samuel Johnson.* 12 vols. New Haven: Yale Univ. Press, 1969.

———. *The History of Rasselas, Prince of Abyssinia.* Edited by J. P. Hardy. Great Britain: Oxford Univ. Press, 1968.

*Lanham, Richard A. *Analyzing Prose.* New York: Scribner's, 1983.

Newman, John Henry, Cardinal. *The Idea of a University.* Edited by I. T. Ker. Great Britain: Oxford Clarendon Press, 1976.

Paine, Thomas. *The American Crisis.* 1776. Franklin, Pa.: Franklin Library, 1979.

Plath, Sylvia. "Cut." *Ariel,* 23–24. London: Faber and Faber, 1968.

Updike, John. "Beer Can." *Assorted Prose,* 115. New York: Knopf, 1965.

Veblen, Thorstein. *The Theory of the Leisure Class.* New York: Modern Library, 1961.

White, E. B. "Democracy." *The New Yorker,* 3 July 1943; 13.

Woolf, Virginia. "Life and the Novelist." *Granite and Rainbow,* 41–47. London: Hogarth Press, 1958.

7

Improving Sentences: Common Sentence Problems and Common Terms

DIANE P. FREEDMAN

I. INTRODUCTION: WHY TALK ABOUT GRAMMAR?

As many people remember from their own schooling, grammar books more often administered prescriptions than provided the descriptions that linguists—as opposed to language-teachers—originally sought. Rather than neutrally describing how native speakers generate English sentences, traditional grammar books listed rules for the proper way to write or speak English. They thus implied a social program of linguistic conformity as they set out to make students speak and write the way educated speakers and writers of English do. Preservers of a norm of English prose style, they pretended to purvey the spoken vernacular. They rarely questioned or announced their sources for the "correct" English they wanted reproduced, and they rarely acceded to the trends and predilections of everyday English users, especially English speakers. While this chapter will to some extent follow this practice, it recognizes the problems in teaching traditional grammar even as it suggests reasons for and means of resurrecting it in the college curriculum.

Yet even those teachers shocked by freshman subject-verb disagreements, faulty parallelism, or variable verb tenses argue against teaching writing by teaching grammar. They are suspicious of late-in-life sentence parsing, grammar drill, and grammar exercises as ways of teaching students to write well. They themselves became good writers almost unconsciously, they argue; by being read to as children, reading still, and trusting their ears, they spontaneously acquired the most beautiful (and "correct") cadences of their language. They need no select group of educated souls telling them not to say "It's me."

Why, then, should writing teachers who believe in writing-as-process, in practice not preaching, and who are proud of the diverse idioms and images of their writing students' work subscribe to old terms and old methods?

One reason is that a knowledge of traditional grammar is socially potent. When contemporary students learn the "rules" and conventions of English grammar, they are better able to communicate with those schooled in a similar mode—business people, artisans, politicians, poets, teachers, and others. They fit in rather than stand out. They get the job. While a good many students have been privy intuitively to these rules without the textbooks, others have missed out. Providing these latter students with overt ear-training and grammar instruction, even as late in their linguistic lives as college, can help their writing (and their careers), while more natively skilled students may need work with only the finer points of grammar and usage.

There is little evidence that detailed knowledge of the infrastructure of English will systematically help students write better, just as it is probably unnecessary and perhaps not even useful for beginning drivers to understand how the pistons and points of a car engine work. But letting students peek at the undercarriage and finish of prose can give them the confidence that comes with familiarity. It can make them aware of the existence—even in so-called Non-Standard English—of such a structure in the first place. The chapter on "Understanding Prose" makes this argument more extensively since it illustrates the usefulness of rhetorical terminology, a terminology grounded in a knowledge of grammar.

Furthermore, a solid understanding of terms such as *dependent clause, parallel structure, gerund, appositive,* or *pronoun-antecedent agreement* helps teachers comment on or correct student papers, and helps even students uninterested in mechanics learn to edit and improve their own papers. Naming the problem makes a vaguely-sensed difficulty visible and more remediable. Finally, students come to writing class with certain expectations, among them that they will be expected to talk grammar and that class will be dull. Fulfill the former but explode the latter. If the teacher cannot answer student questions about "me" vs. "I" or "who" vs. "whom"—whether such questions are in earnest or are teacher tests—students will lose confidence in the whole proposition of an English class. They will become distracted by worries about whether they are getting what they paid for. (A professor of cognitive psychology confided at a recent writing conference that he had to bait his students with "speed-reading" techniques and machines the first few weeks of class before they would settle back to absorb what he really had to offer in "Developmental Reading," something quite different from the principles of speed-reading.) Even instructors convinced that grammar instruction is for naught should be able to prove that they know grammar well enough to get beyond it. After that, the trick is to make writing class interesting, whatever the teaching methods and terminology. I hope that the demonstrations, explanations, and teaching tips to follow will help, especially if traditional grammar figures in your syllabus and classroom nomenclature.

Described first are the most common sentence problems beginning writers have (Section II); a review of the parts of speech and related phenomena follows (Section III). Since discussions of problems of style and usage (Section II) often invoke the terms and concepts of traditional grammar, I provide Section III as a detailed review some readers might prefer to examine first. In any case, Section III is cross-referenced with Section II, and the actual order in which you teach or come upon the subjects of either section will depend on your own classes.

II. COMMON SENTENCE PROBLEMS IN BEGINNERS' WRITING

A. *Recognizing the Sentence Unit*

I. THE SENTENCE FRAGMENT

The sentence fragment is one of the most common student errors. If a group of words makes little sense without the sentence next to it or leaves unanswered Who did what? X did what? the string of words is a fragment, an incomplete sentence. Some authors use the sentence fragment to create variety, an informal tone, or a breathless style, especially in narrative writing. Advertising copywriters use it for emphasis or because they think their readers have very short attention spans. Most academic writers use the fragment sparingly, usually for emphasis. Too many fragments become an annoying tic, a cheap trick.

Students usually need to be reminded that a complete sentence minimally consists of one subject (a noun or pronoun usually appearing before the verb) and one predicate or verb (statement of action or existence). When a sentence lacks either of these parts, or when it is a dependent clause (begun with a subordinator), it is a fragment.

> 1. Got out of bed to check on the yogurt. *(no subject)*
>
> 2. Sam, being the oldest of the dogs. *(no predicate)* (Many student fragments begin with or depend on "being"; if students avoid "being" in favor of "is" or "are"—or opt for action verbs instead— the problem goes away, and the sentences turn livelier.)
>
> 3. Which was a good plan. *(relative clause)*
>
> 4. If he were to marry. *(dependent clause)* (Students should be reminded that clauses beginning, *if, since,* or *when* need to be coupled with a clause beginning with "then" or some other independent clause.)

Students do not usually compose fragments on purpose. Having been taught to avoid comma splices (the second-most common student error), they end their sentences and then, as an afterthought, begin what look like new sentences (to them). "He had finished his essay two days early. Which was a good plan," or "He had finished his essay two days early. A plan his teacher recommended." The student does not recognize the relative clause or summative modifier as dependent. If you explain to students why or how they have made the error, and then demonstrate the comma that goes with a "which" or a summative modifier like "plan," students will be able to avoid, not merely revise, fragments.

Rather than make up hypothetical examples or use these, you can cull fragments from the first round of student essays you collect. Type them up on a ditto, and have your class amend or rewrite them as best they can.

2. FUSED SENTENCES OR THE COMMA SPLICE

The fused sentence consists of two independent clauses stuck together, sometimes with a comma (the splice), as if they were one sentence. Ask students with comma-splice troubles to read their sentences aloud, reading right through commas and pausing only at periods; they will suddenly hear that there aren't enough stops. They can begin to fix the run-ons with a coordinating conjunction, a subordinating conjunction, a semicolon, or a period.

Comma splice:
Hamlet noticed that the Queen was not wearing black, instead she was attired in her normal clothing.
Correct:
1. Hamlet noticed that the Queen was not wearing black; instead, she was attired in her normal clothing.
2. Hamlet noticed that the Queen was not wearing black. Instead, she was attired in her normal clothing.

Comma splice:
He had a heart attack, he did not die.
Correct:
1. Although he had a heart attack, he did not die. *(subordinating conjunction)*
2. He had a heart attack; however, he did not die. *(conjunctive adverb)*
3. He had a heart attack, but he did not die. *(coordinating conjunction)*
4. He had a heart attack; he did not die. *(semicolon)*
5. He had a heart attack. He did not die. *(period)*

Many students believe that *however, thus,* and *rather* are simple (coordinating) conjunctions; these students must learn that these words cannot connect two independent clauses as *and, or, but, for, yet,* and *so* can when preceded by a comma (see example 3 directly above). Instead, words like *however* (*consequently, moreover, therefore,* etc.)— sometimes called "logic" words—are usually preceded by a semicolon when they join two complete sentences, as in example 2 directly above. Furthermore, clauses beginning with *although, after, because, unless, whenever,* etc. are punctuated with or without commas, as demonstrated below, but not with semicolons:

> Whenever the sun shines, I want to run outside.
> I want to run outside whenever the sun shines.

(See also "Checking Punctuation," p. 240.) For fuller lists of subordinators and coordinators, see Section III.

As with fragments, when you find a class having a great many commasplice problems, distribute a ditto of poorly punctuated sentences culled from student papers. Have students edit these sentences, with your help, in class. Before students turn in each of their subsequent papers, have them look over a neighbor's paper for five minutes, editing out comma splices, especially those caused by misuse of *however* or *rather.* When you return corrected papers, have your students fix any sentence you've marked "run-on" or CS (commonly used correction symbols) and return the corrected sentences to you at your next class meeting. Avoid rewriting the fused sentences yourself. Eventually, students will edit their own sentences as they compose them.

B. Choosing Subjects and Verbs

I. OVERUSE OF THE PASSIVE VOICE

Using the passive voice can often create problems of organization and argument, as Joseph Williams explains in *Style: Ten Lessons in Clarity and Grace.* To be sure, the passive voice is sometimes effective or necessary, but to write clearly we should usually prefer action verbs in the active voice.

1. The harbor was mined. *(truncated passive)*
2. The harbor was mined by the CIA. *(passive)*
3. The CIA mined the harbor. *(active)*

"The harbor was mined" is passive; the agent (the one who actually acts, the true—not merely grammatical—subject) is not in the sentence at all. The harbor itself is not doing anything; it is having something done to it (by some invisible agent left out of the sentence). Sentence 2 relegates the agent, the CIA, to the "by" phrase (prepositional phrase) while the direct object, or the passive recipient of the action, "the harbor,'' appears in the subject slot. ''The harbor'' is grammatically the subject but logically the object, just as ''the CIA'' is grammatically the object of the preposition but logically the subject. Sentence 3, the active version, puts the agent up front where we can see, criticize, or question it. When we let our sentences run counter to our meaning, we tend to fuzz the logic of our argument or observation. Our readers are left wondering who or what is the causal agent.

Choosing between active and passive voice in writing is not a matter of correctness but of style. The passive voice, as is pointed out in Chapter 5, ''Responding to Student Essays,'' is in most cases less vigorous than the active voice. It is also less interesting, and sometimes subversive—the real (logical) agent is ''faceless . . . written out of the sentence,'' asserted Alfred E. Kahn in a Cornell lecture (1982) as he criticized ''bureaucratese,'' the language of bureaucrats. People use the passive voice because they think it sounds more polite than telling the whole story: ''The Vietnamese countryside was defoliated'' (by whom?). Or, as Kahn went on to say, because they want to withhold information, avoid responsibility, and sound distant and authoritative: ''The MX missiles were deployed.''

As Kahn's comments suggest, writing style is more than a matter of rules and convention; the way we write reflects and affects the way we think—the ways those who read our writing think and understand. When we opt for the active voice, we often achieve better organization and better argument, along with the greater honesty Kahn would have us seek.

Beginning writers need, then, to ask themselves: ''Do I know who or what the real agent is? Do I have the real agent up front doing something? Is there a logical or political reason the object should appear in the subject slot?'' If your friend is wounded at war, the salient fact is ''My friend was wounded''; you may not immediately care about who or what hurt him as much as you care about his health. We commonly use the passive then, and when we do not know who or what the real agent is. Your students should be able to decide consciously to use one form over the other.

Students sometimes switch back and forth from the active to the passive voice in a misguided attempt to vary sentence structure or words: ''Reagan wants to convince the American people that we should take an active part in Central American politics. The nation can be persuaded to this belief if his appearances on television are frequent enough.'' In the second sentence here, Reagan has almost disappeared—and so has the focus on him. While learning to use the active voice, students can also learn to keep their argumentative focus. If they worry about beginning sentences too often with the same word, teach them to avoid landing on the same word in the same place by using a subordinate clause to change the rhythm of their sentences: "Reagan wants to convince the American people that we should take an active part in Central American politics. If he appears frequently enough on television, he will probably succeed." (With such an example, you can remind students that introductory dependent clauses are followed by a comma. See also "Checking Punctuation," p. 240.)

Students also resort to the passive voice because of their valiant attempts to avoid "I" as the subject of sentences. They should know that most composition teachers (and readers) no longer ban the first-person pronoun in expository prose. Such a relaxation of the rules formerly calling for "this writer" over "I" should help students produce more personal and perhaps compelling active prose.

Students can fairly easily identify the passive voice, especially if you ask them to look for the tell-tale "by" phrase, or have them consider whether the noun or pronoun in the subject slot is in fact the agent of the action the sentence describes. A passive without the "by" phrase is called (as labelled above) a truncated passive, the "by X" portion being left off for brevity or because the agent's identity is unknown. (When the agent or subject is unknown, the passive legitimately may be the only way to cast a sentence.). If the agent is known, however, ask students to rewrite their sentences with it up front.

You can select passive-verb sentences from student papers and put them on a ditto or a blackboard for an in-class editing session. Or ask students to bring in textbook selections or handouts from their social science classes. Even city planners dedicated to meeting the needs of government, community, and individuals often leave out people of any sort in their discourse: "Realistic goals can be created with rational planning."

2. OVERUSE OF NOMINALIZATIONS (AND EUPHEMISMS)

Nominalizations are verbs turned into nouns (or adjectives turned into nouns) and often end in "t / ion":

There is considerable belief in intervention in Central America.

Nominalized verbs, like passives, usually leave unanswered "Who did what?" They hurt the causes of clarity and brevity, because, like passives, they often conceal the true subject and verb in a barrage of words. Joseph Williams speaks at length about the advantage of verbs over nominalizations: "Although we cannot always express crucial actions in verbs, in the clearest and most vigorous sentences we usually do" (*Style* 9–10). Action covers "many notions: movement, feeling, process, change, activity, condition—physical or mental, literal or figurative" (*Style* 9).

Have students recast their inactive sentences and put "the crucial action in the verb." Tell them to replace "intervention" with "intervene" and make up an agent or at least think about whether they want to dispose of the agent. Thus, they can change the example sentence to: "Reagan believes the CIA should intervene in Central America" (or, with as many specifics announced as possible: "Reagan and the U.S. Congress will give military aid to the Contras").

Junk mail and bank- or electric-company brochures can yield luminous examples of nominalized prose for your class to revise. Ask each of your students to bring in for revision an example from the newspaper, television news, or a course textbook. Further examples: "The allegations were unsubstantiated," vs. "He didn't tell the truth." "Acceleration of spending occurred" vs. "The U.S. military spent more in the last six months of 1983 than in the first six months." "Revenue enhancement was instituted" vs. "Congress raised our taxes."

The last example brings up the question of euphemisms such as "revenue enhancement," words intended to sweeten a sour situation. Many euphemisms have become clichés in our language, serving perhaps a useful social function; when we speak of our dear uncle "passing away" or our dog Joey being "put to sleep," we are trying to insulate ourselves from a reality that starker language might make unavoidable. As with passives, you can have students decide whether the situation really calls for such greeting-card gentleness or whether the writing and its emotions would be more powerful told "like it is." Often they don't know what it is like until they try in earnest—and actively—to tell it.

3. STRINGS OF PREPOSITIONS AND THE UBIQUITOUS "TO BE"

In *Revising Prose* (1–6), Richard Lanham proposes another set of strategies for eliminating nominalizations and the passive voice. Like Williams and the writers of other recent writing texts, he urges writers to use active verbs and put the true subject up front in the sentences. Answer directly "Who's kicking who?" Write, for example, "Jim kicks Bill," and not, Lanham says, exaggerating to make his point, "One can easily see that a kicking situation is taking place between Bill and Jim." Lanham suggests we avoid strings of prepositional phrases "glued together by that all-purpose epoxy 'is.' " He provides a neat, useful formula for avoiding ambiguity and fixing such sentences as "This sentence is in need of an active verb":

1. Circle the prepositions.
2. Circle the "is" forms.
3. Ask "who is kicking who?" [who or what acts on whom]
4. Put this "kicking" [or other] action in a simple (not compound) active verb.
5. Start fast—no mindless introductions.

Thus, he replaces the example above with "This sentence needs an active verb."

Each time an essay draft or final version is due, ask your students to spend ten minutes working on the grammar or usage issue of the week (or their own recurrent problem as diagnosed by you). Circulate around the room one such day helping students circle prepositions and forms of "to be," locate the true subject and the perhaps hidden verb, and then eliminate what Lanham would call the fat in their sentences. Ask students to murmur their revised sentences aloud. Has the rhythm improved? How many fewer words are at work now? I have even assigned my students the first chapter of Lanham's book and then dittoed off examples from their essays with the examples *Revising Prose* provides as a prelude to this student paper-correcting exercise. With a little practice, as Lanham argues, students will compose more directly right away without such a need for in-class revision and instructor assistance.

C. Making Subjects and Verbs Agree

A subject and a verb agree if both are singular or both are plural in form. Pronouns and their antecedents (see "Pronouns," p. 254) should agree in number and in gender. The first sentence below illustrates a subject-verb error and the second a pronoun-antecedent error:

1. The senators' vote on the bills were unanimous.
2. Each student took their seat.

A word that refers to one person or thing is singular in number; a word referring to more than one thing is plural. Singular subjects take singular verbs (non-native speakers are often confused by the fact that most singular verbs end in "s," as do most plural nouns): "The Displaywriter ingests disks." Plural subjects take plural verbs (in English, these verbs usually do not end in "s"): "Birds ingest worms." (See also "Verbs," p. 247.) Not many students have trouble distinguishing between the singular and plural forms of nouns and pronouns, but some have trouble using the right verb forms.

Rules Governing Subject-Verb Agreement

Students most frequently fail to make subject and verb agree when intervening phrases and clauses separate a noun from its verb, as in the incorrect sentence, "The senators' vote on the bills were unanimous." Practice, and awareness of the following rules, will help them.

a) The number of the subject is not changed by a phrase or clause following the subject, nor can the (grammatical) subject of a sentence appear in a prepositional phrase. This means, for example, that in the sentence, "The group of blue horses in Chagall's painting still gambols in my mind," "group," not "blue horses," is the subject (because "blue horses" appears in a prepositional phrase beginning with "of"). The verb ("gambols") thus agrees with the singular subject ("group") in number.

b) Subjects joined by *and* take a plural verb: "Tom and Alice drink bitter coffee."

c) Singular subjects joined by *or* or *nor* take a singular verb (and singular pronoun): "Has your brother or your monster written his life story yet?" (Note that what may look silly or too cute in print—

such as an example like this—often works surprisingly well in front of a class.)

    d) When a singular subject and a plural subject are joined by *or* or *nor,* the verb agrees with the nearer subject: "Neither my brother nor his friends write regularly." (If this sounds awkward, rewrite the sentence: "My brother doesn't write regularly, and neither do his friends.")

    e) When the subject and the predicate nominative (see "Nouns," p. 245) are different in number, the verb agrees with the subject: "One of the first signs of spring is crocuses." (See also "Pronoun-Antecedent Agreement," p. 227.)

If agreement errors are class-wide, you can choose problem sentences from student essays for in-class review, or distribute dittoes of made-up sentences with two choices of verb forms:

Exercise:
Underline the correct verb form in the parenthesis.
1. The sum total of raspberries this year (stagger, staggers) me.

For collective nouns that go either way and other special problems in agreement, have your students consult one of the grammar handbooks listed in Chapter 8, "A Bibliographical Guide to the Profession." Many handbooks and workbooks provide exercises students can work on independently: see for example pp. 351 ff. of Heffernan and Lincoln's *Writing—A College Handbook* (described in "A Bibliographical Guide to the Profession").

D. *Working with Pronouns*

1. PRONOUN-ANTECEDENT AGREEMENT AND GENDER PROBLEMS

Like subjects and verbs, antecedents (words to which pronouns refer or for which they stand) and pronouns should agree in number. When the antecedent is singular, the pronoun is too; when the antecedent is plural, the pronoun is plural. Pronouns also agree with their antecedents in gender. A pronoun is masculine *(he, him, his)* when its antecedent is masculine, but it is feminine *(she, her, hers)* when its antecedent is feminine, and neuter *(it, its)* when its antecedent is neuter.

1. Grammar has taken its fair share of criticism. *(neuter)*
2. Evangeline has escaped on her charger. *(feminine)*
3. The students took their seats. *(plural)*

This is clear so far. But what if the singular subject could be either male or female, as in the sentence, "The writer took (his, her) work home"? The eight writers of this book repeatedly faced questions such as this—and found varying solutions. Traditionally, the masculine pronoun has been used when the antecedent may be either masculine or feminine, but this convention is being challenged, by some writers of this book among others. *His* is being replaced with *his or her,* just *her,* or even more creative, if clumsy, constructions such as *s / he* or *his / her.* Often I suggest that my students use *she* and *her* for a while in order to change their readers'—and their own—perspective. Exposing students to the other options currently available often leads to useful student conjectures about how language shapes our world view.

We refer to indefinite pronouns *(each, either, neither, one, everyone, everybody, nobody, anyone, anybody, someone,* and *somebody)* with singular pronouns *(he, him, she, her,* etc.). Conventionally, we treat *everybody* as a singular subject: "Everybody take her seat, please." But this convention has all but disappeared in spoken English and is fast disappearing in writing. Decide how much of a stickler for the old (formal) convention you wish to be—or tell your students to decide on a norm depending on the audience they want to reach at the time. I prohibit "The school gives anybody their diploma," if only to remind students that some rhetorical situations will continue to demand the traditional form. Your students can avoid offending either the formal reader or their informal peers, however. Tell them to rewrite each *everyone* out of their sentences: "Everyone took her seat" can easily become "The students all took their seats."

We treat most collective nouns *(family, class, audience, jury, committee)* as singular subjects in American English (while many such nouns are plural in British English). We say, "The jury had its lunch outdoors." If this sounds awkward to your students, however, have them recast the sentence to read instead, "The jurors took their lunch outdoors."

2. PROBLEMS WITH PRONOUN CASE

Nouns and pronouns have three case functions: the nominative, the objective, and the possessive. Except in the possessive, nouns do not show case by change of form and consequently do not present any problems of case to students. The case of pronouns, however, often gives students difficulty.

Nominative	Objective	Possessive
I	me	my
you	you	your
he, she	him, her	his, hers
it	it	its
we	us	our
you	you	your
they	them	their

Uses of the Nominative Case

a) for the subject of a verb: "He will relent."

b) for the predicate nominative: "It is I"; "The winners are he and I."

c) for an appositive of the subject or of the predicate nominative: "When the victors, Tom and she, perform, the audience is spellbound"; "The victors are 'Diamond and Rust,' Tom and she."

d) for the subject of an understood verb in a clause of comparison: "No one is as goofy as she [is]."

e) if the pronoun in question appears in an emphatic construction like this: "We women are hard workers."

Uses of the Objective Case

a) when the pronoun is the direct or indirect object of the verb: "Jeronimo hit me."

b) for the object of a preposition: "Eleanor moved towards them then." (If the pronoun after a preposition is the relative pronoun *who / whom* and is itself the subject of a verb, however, we write "Bring the floppy disks to whoever *[nominative form]* wants them," not "Bring the floppy disks to whomever *[objective form]* wants them.")

c) for the subject of an infinitive: "The Yankees expect him to be elated."

If students are still confused about whether to use *I* or *me* in a sentence such as "The award was shared by Pythagoras and _____" have them eliminate "Pythagoras." *I* will sound wrong; *me* will be the apparent (and correct) choice—even after "Pythagoras" is returned to the sentence.

Uses of the Possessive Case

a) to show ownership: "You never doff your hat."

b) with a noun or gerund, a verbal acting as a noun: "I would appreciate your lending me three dollars." (Not *"you* lending." The object of the verb "appreciate" is the noun/gerund, "lending"; *your* is then the possessive adjective modifying this gerund. Most students do not know this rule; the more sophisticated writers will enjoy learning it.)

Notice that the personal and relative pronouns form their possessives without the apostrophe: "The cat lost its collar"; "The fellow whose car I covet drives carelessly." Students often confuse the contraction *it's* with the possessive *its;* drill them or give them a quiz on the two forms (along with *their / there, too / to,* and *here / hear*) if you need to.

3. WEAK OR AMBIGUOUS REFERENCE

The word to which a pronoun refers should always be clear to the reader. Because a pronoun may be used with grammatical correctness and still be confusing or misleading, it is sometimes necessary to remind students to repeat their antecedents or to recast an entire sentence for clarity.

Ambiguous Reference

"Henrietta told her sister that her house was on fire." The first *her* is clear enough, but the second one could refer to either "Henrietta" or "her sister." Such a sentence can be revised any number of ways; " 'Your house is on fire,' Henrietta shouted to her sister" is one. In Chapter 5, "Responding to Student Essays," Harry Shaw suggests that rewriting for students gets in the way; instead, spell out the ambiguity: "This is

ambiguous; do you mean 'x' or 'y'." Make your students submit to you
an unambiguous revision.

Broad Reference

"She rattled on about her car, and this was annoying." Usually a
pronoun should not refer broadly to the whole idea of the preceding
clause, as *this* does in the sentence above. Supply a definite antecedent
or substitute a noun for the pronoun in such a sentence: "She rattled on
about her car, and this chatter was annoying"; "Her rattling on about
her car annoyed me." Harry Shaw prohibits his students from using
what he calls " 'the lonely this' (that is, 'this' instead of 'this person,'
'this idea,' and so on)." (See p. 135, Chapter 5, "Responding to Student Essays.")

Students frequently use the *and this* sentence structure because they
haven't learned to revise. They write their papers while thinking linearly, and then do not go back to put sophisticated relationships into
necessarily (grammatically) complex sentences. Sentence-combining
work—learning the complex syntax with which complex ideas can be
expressed—will help students naturally to grow away from the mental
helplessness of "and this." (See "Combining Sentences," p. 234.)

Another strategy for avoiding broad reference is to use a summative
or resumptive modifier in place of a lonely *this* or a vague *which.* "With
a summative modifier, you end a segment of a sentence with a comma,
sum up in a noun or noun phrase what you have just said, and then
continue with a relative clause"*(Style* 136): "We have been told a Sandinista incursion took place, a *charge* that may soon be proven fiction."
With a resumptive modifier, you "[s]imply repeat a key noun, verb, or
adjective and then resume the line of thought, elaborating on what went
before" (*Style* 135): "We have heard about the Sandinista incursion,
an incursion disputed by Honduran, Nicaraguan, and U.S. officials alike."

Weak Reference

"My uncle is a doctor. That is a profession I admire." The antecedent of "that" is "medicine," which is implied in "doctor" but not
actually stated. Traditional grammar insists that the sentence should state
the actual antecedent or substitute a noun for the weak pronoun: "My
uncle is in medicine. That is a profession I admire"; "My uncle is a
doctor. Medicine is a profession I admire."

For exercises in clear pronoun reference and the case of pronouns, consult the section on "Handbooks" in Chapter 8, "A Bibliographical Guide to the Profession." As usual, you may well want to supplement such exercises with work on sentences drawn from your students' essays.

E. *Working with Modifiers*

I. DISTINGUISHING RESTRICTION FROM NONRESTRICTION

Concern with restrictive and nonrestrictive modifiers usually develops when students maneuver commas unsuccessfully because of them. It's then necessary to share the following information with your students:

A restrictive modifier is essential to the meaning of the noun it modifies and is thus necessary to the meaning of the sentence. A nonrestrictive modifier is not essential to the noun it modifies; it is not essential to the meaning of the sentence. Consider it an aside.

The nonrestrictive modifier is set off with two commas (unless the last word of it ends the sentence and thus appears with a period). The restrictive modifier is not set off with commas. (Elements appearing between commas can be unpinned from their sentences; the sentence is less fancy without them, but it still makes sense.)

Adjective clauses:
   Boys who eat worms are disgusting. *(restrictive)*
   Sam, who ate a jar of worms, is now ill. *(nonrestrictive)*

Adjective phrases:
   The boy with green hair made a movie. *(restrictive)*
   The trophy for excellence in spelling, engraved in gold, had a typographical error. *(nonrestrictive)*

Incorrect punctuation:
   Boys, who eat worms, are disgusting.
   Boys who eats worms, are disgusting.
   Sam who ate a jar of worms is now ill.

The first correct sentence above ("Boys who eat worms are disgusting") specifies that those boys who eat worms are disgusting. The restrictive modifier "who eat worms" is essential to identifying the subject, essential to the sentence. The first incorrect sentence above ("Boys, who eat worms, are disgusting.") makes too large a claim, is logically and grammatically incorrect. Punctuated as it is, the sentence says that, in fact, all boys eat worms and all boys are (thus) disgusting. Since this isn't what the speaker presumably means to say, the punctuation must be changed.

All three kinds of incorrect sentence are common in student work: students use pairs of commas where they shouldn't; they use only one comma (incorrectly separating the subject from the verb of the sentence); or they neglect to use commas to set off extra sentence parts, extra information about a subject. Provide practice from their own sentences, from your imagination, or from an assigned handbook.

2. DANGLING OR MISPLACED MODIFIERS

A misplaced modifier is one that does not clearly point to the noun or pronoun (or phrase) it modifies. The resulting sentence is ambiguous or distorted: "Teresa found a Jack-in-the-Pulpit walking in the woods." The participial phrase, "walking in the woods," describes Teresa, not a Jack-in-the-Pulpit. The modifier needs to be placed nearer its head noun: "Walking in the woods, Teresa found a Jack-in-the-Pulpit."

A dangling modifier has nothing in a sentence to "hang on to": "Driving around the curve, the moon looked huge." Some person, not the moon, must be doing the driving. The participial phrase, "Driving around the curve," dangles. Provide students with example corrections: "As I drove around the curve, the moon looked huge to me." Or: "Driving around the curve, I noticed the huge moon."

Give students a sheet of ambiguous, perhaps humorous ("Did you see my briefcase walking down the hall?") sentences to correct. Have them write sentences following modifying phrases: "Giggling hysterically, _____." Lastly, show students in their sentence-combining work how to use participles and other modifiers well (see the following section).

Some students avoid using participles because they so often have led to error: "Dangling participle!" Since "Combining Sentences" (following) emphasizes success rather than failure, it should help your students gain faith and competence. Other students give up on participles because they don't know how to find the true subjects of their sentences, the subjects required by their verbs. If they have been working on nominalizations and the passive voice, which require an interest in subjects, they will be less likely to find themselves with dangling participles, which often occur because of a switch to the passive voice: "Wishing to end the war quickly, Cambodia was bombed." A student aware of the passive will probably write: "Wishing to end the war quickly, Nixon bombed Cambodia."

F. Combining Sentences (for Subordination and Style)

Sentence-combining exercises, even courses, are in vogue in high schools and colleges today. They are a good idea; diverse readers polled assert that a complex or "mature" prose style full of subordination and free modifiers is much more "interesting" than a staccato, primer prose style ("Jane has a dog. His name is Spot. Spot and Jane are friends."). More important, research shows that frequent practice with sophisticated syntax leads to subtler argumentation: rather than depending on a narrative framework ("Orwell says") or setting down ideas as they occur (writer- rather than reader-oriented prose), students are encouraged to discover and demonstrate relationships between ideas. "Orwell says we must improve our use of the English language. He says language can help us think clearly" may become "Orwell claims we must improve our use of the English language, because doing so will help us think clearly."

Almost all of our public writing explains or asserts something, or tries more generally to win the reader over. An array of observations noted in short sentences or connected only by a series of *and's* gluts the reader's senses and requires him or her to work to order them. We need to direct readers through a series of observations towards a reasonable goal or conclusion. Writers direct the traffic of their readers' thoughts with signals (sometimes called "transition" words), whether spatial (*where?* five miles away), chronological (*after, as long as),* or logical (*in order that, since,* etc.). Writers thereby purposefully subordinate one idea or event to another, sort out the wheat from the chaff, depict a hierarchy, or at least illustrate what relations (if not hierarchies) are in play. (See Chapter 6, "Understanding Prose," for further amplification of the relationship between syntax and meaning.)

Sentence-combining exercises teach students something concrete to do to improve their writing. They thus quiet whatever panic may be rising in their minds over the usefulness of learning to identify the parts of speech or sentence "errors." Instead of short, choppy sentences like those in children's readers, these exercises produce complex sentences. (See "Clauses and Phrases," p. 258.) Information a writer decides is less important appears in a dependent clause, while the information he or she wants featured appears in the independent, or main, clause. Or the subordinate information goes into a phrase (verbal, adverbial, absolute). The structures of subordination themselves, their shapes, contribute to the meanings. Such un-primerlike structures can also make prose much more musical than can a series of simple sentences.

Some students already use complex sentences skillfully as a result of a rich language life of reading and listening; too often, however, their high school experience with writing has taught them to play it safe by sticking to simple sentences. Other students are just not familiar with the kinds of sentence patterns that will help them logically organize, and display, their own thoughts. Occasionally, students are surprised to learn that it is all right to begin a sentence with a participial phrase or "because." Once students learn, through imitation and exercises, the kinds of structures that are both available and acceptable, they gladly begin to use them, pleased with their new space and freedom. (You can designate a particular essay an occasion for extensive experimentation and showing-off, thereby freeing students from some of their former fear of semicolons and subordination. Have them spend ten minutes of the day an essay is due underlining their complex sentences and putting question marks by the ones they think need help or approval.) Some examples of sentence-combining exercises follow (and you can consult a text such as William Strong's *Sentence Combining: A Composing Book* for further help and examples).

Exercise 1:

In a rough draft of your next paper, substitute a subordinating conjunction (see "Conjunctions," p. 257) or a relative pronoun (see "Pronouns," p. 254) for the *and* (a coordinating conjuction), overused as a joiner of words and thoughts. Instead of *and,* an indefinite because egalitarian connector, choose from the words below in order to depict one of the corresponding relationships:

Relationship	Connectors
Time	*when, after, before, until, as long as*
Place	*where*
Cause	*since, because*
Concession	*although*
Condition	*unless, if, provided that*
Exception	*except*
Purpose	*in order that, to*
Description	relative pronoun: *who, which, that*
	appositive: Sam, the ursurper, went

Students can try this kind of sentence combining at any stage of the writing process. Sentence combining also provides a good focus for collaborative work, as students are often more easily able to locate occasions for sentence combining in their peers' work than in their own.

Exercise 2:
Combine the following short, choppy sentences with a connector from the above chart.

> a. Loretta was a poor coalminer's daughter. She won a song-writing contest at the Grand Ole Opry. (Not "Loretta was a poor coalminer's daughter and she won a songwriting contest at the Grand Old Opry" but "Loretta was a poor coalminer's daughter until she won a songwriting contest at the Grand Ole Opry.")
>
> b. The boat was in the harbor. It caught fire. Most of the children escaped. ("Although the boat in the harbor caught fire, most of the children escaped.")

Exercises like this one are easily created: simply type up sentences from a student essay that should have been combined (an entire paragraph may work best) and put students to work. Or you can work on a badly written text from your syllabus.

Exercise 3:
Another kind of exercise asks students to embed asides, or extra-added-attractions, in prepositional, participial, absolute, or gerundic phrases; to use appositives, free modifiers, or even parentheses. These add-on exercises can teach the proper punctuation of restrictive (non-subordinating) and nonrestrictive clauses and phrases; of various coor-

dinators and subordinators; of parenthetical remarks and interjections.

Exercise a: In each of the numbered sentences below, put some of the information into a new sentence's main clause and subordinate some of the less essential information by moving it into prepositional, participial, gerundic, absolute, or free-modifier phrases. [Students need not know all these terms; they need only imitate the examples you supply. They will get the idea.]

Examples:

Prepositional: He went, in cross-gartered yellow stockings, to Lady Olivia. *(adjectival)*

Participial: Singing to himself, Jerry went to meet Tom. *(adjectival)*

Gerundic: Caring for elephants was Hannibal's hobby. *(noun, subject)*

Absolute: His leg having snapped in that fall, Todd could never forgive Brad.

Free Modifier: Wimp was a cat of powerful haunches, driven by a voracious appetite and charmed forever by the cat next door. *(uses past participles)*

Adverbial: Wherever she goes, Lulu has friends.

1. Sally is a spy. Sally has broken a leg. Sally made a run for it. A trench-coated assailant pursued her. (Try: "Pursued by a trench-coated assailant, Sally, a spy with a broken leg, made a run for it." Or: "Despite having broken a leg, Sally, a spy, made a run for it, a trench-coated assailant in hot pursuit.")

2. The truck was moving. The truck carried groceries. There was an accident. The truck hit a Cadillac.

3. The labrador was old and small. He ran slowly down the hill. He moved a little from side to side in his gait. He moved with the switching motion and proud posture of a wrestler.

Exercise b: The passage below comes from Scott Elledge's biography of E. B. White, but it has been converted into simple sentences. Study it, then improve it by combining the sentences into *one:* you may change the order of words, and omit words too often repeated, but try to include all the information. Then compare your sentence to Elledge's. How close did you get?

Scott Elledge is describing a visit to E. B. White, in the course of which Elledge views the dachshund Fred's grave.

1. I accepted Mr. White's invitation.
2. The invitation was to visit him and his wife.
3. In the course of a memorable day I saw Fred's grave.
4. The grave was near the private dump.
5. The dump existed "with its useless junk of all kinds including a wrong-size crank for a broken ice-cream freezer."
6. I saw the boat house and Allen Cove.
7. Allen Cove was where *Charlotte's Web* was written.
8. I saw the barn in whose cellar Wilbur met Charlotte.
9. I saw the house where White has lived.
10. The house is large. It is comfortable. It is handsome.
11. It is a late-eighteenth-century farmhouse.
12. The house is where White has lived, off and on, for fifty years.

Scott Elledge's version:

I accepted Mr. White's invitation to visit him and his wife, and in the course of a memorable day I saw not only Fred's grave near the private dump "with its useless junk of all kinds including a wrong-size crank for a broken ice-cream freezer," but the boathouse on Allen Cove where *Charlotte's Web* was written, the barn in whose cellar Wilbur met Charlotte, and the large, comfortable, and handsome late-eighteenth-century farmhouse where White has lived, off and on, for fifty years. (3)

You and your students can turn to their essays or to texts on the syllabus to locate well-written sentences full of subordination. These can then be analyzed or rewritten into a series of short, primer-style sentences (as above) to see how very many separate "thoughts" may be gracefully embedded in one another.

Exercise c: Write a story in which each sentence begins with a different letter of the alphabet. The first sentence should begin with an "A," the second with a "B," and so on. [Students will be inclined to vary the subject-verb-object sentence pattern, especially if you tell them not to begin every sentence with a noun.]

Exercise d: Type up sentences or whole paragraphs containing various instances of subordination. Allow time in class for students to imitate the structure of these sentences and then to read the imitation aloud to the class. Then point out sentences or passages in the assigned texts for students to imitate at home. You might assign students a minimum of one sentence a week for imitation. *The Norton Reader's* "Prose Forms: An Album of Styles" is a good place to find sentences for your initial imitation exercises.

G. Handling Parallelism

A result of sentence combining can be increased interest in parallelism, the need for which often arises when short sentences must be linked. But students often avoid parallelism, for a variety of reasons (many of which have made work with sentence combining necessary): they want to keep their sentences short (i.e., safe and correct); they want to avoid error (faulty use of *not only . . . but also*); they don't recognize or comfortably handle the often longer and more sophisticated forms demanded by parallelism. There's nothing any more mysterious about parallelism than about mathematical equations, however. Remove the mystery and you may be surprised to find that students enjoy analyzing parallel structures and then trying them in some sentence-combining exercises. You've put them in control of an important tool, as parallelism effects the greater coordination of words, phrases, and clauses in a sentence; it at once underscores meaning and contributes elegance.

A parallel construction consists of two or more sentence elements that are grammatically alike. When there are two or more items in a list, a series, a choice, a contract, a statement of equivalence, or a comparison, all of the items should usually be expressed in the same grammatical form (part of speech, word order, number).

Examples:

a) *List:* Helen's dog was black, sleek, and spunky. *(three adjectives)*

b) *Series:* To find him, she'd climb mountains, ford rivers, comb valleys. *(three transitive action verbs in the active voice; also, three geographical features as direct objects)*

c) *Choice:* You can serve chicken baked in wine and mushrooms or sauteed with Chinese vegetables. *(two participial phrases)*

d) *Contrast:* They wrote their essays slowly but happily. *(two adverbs)*

e) *Equivalence:* God is a metaphor. *(two singular nouns, subject-linking verb-predicate nominative construction)*

f) *Comparison:* The pen is mightier than the sword. *(two monosyllabic, concrete nouns).*

A balanced sentence contains two main clauses that are parallel and in a kind of logical agreement with each other: "To move is to exist: to dance is to live."

A sentence with two parallel main clauses containing information is called an antithetical sentence: "To take flowers to a woman is to look forward; to take flowers to a grave is to look back."

Exercises:

Sentence-combining exercises can be combined with work in parallelism. You might ask your students to combine a set of sentences into one or two sentences, using parallelism where possible:

The sheep in the meadow are lost.
The cow in the corn is lowing and lost.
The shepherd is in a forest of trees.
The shepherd is weeping.
By consequence, they are all sad.
Each species is alone, too.

(The sheep, the cow, and the shepherd are lost; the sheep is in the meadow, the cow in the corn, the shepherd in a forest of trees. Each alone, each sad, the cow lows and the shepherd weeps.)

H. Checking Punctuation

Some students appear not to have problems with punctuation: that may be because they never use semicolons, colons, or dashes, rarely use the comma, and trust to short sentences to get the periods right (the teacher will catch the missing apostrophes). The following alphabetical review of commonly misused punctuation suggests ways to encourage use and understanding of such liberating marks as the colon, dash, and semicolon, punctuation crucial for students who wish to build better sentences.

Apostrophes

Apostrophes signal contractions and possessives.

a) The rule for contracting two words into one is to use the apostrophe in place of missing letters. You'd be surprised how many students write *coul'dnt* or *wo'nt* instead of *couldn't* and *won't*. (In the first few weeks of class, hand out a ditto sheet listing the correct versions of apostrophe and other errors common to your class. Insist that students proofread each subsequent essay using this handout as a style guide.)

b) There are two ways to express possession in English; we can write either the "hat of the cook" or "the cook's hat." In general, we use the first method for nouns that stand for something inanimate and the second for nouns representing something animate (the "s" form does help to eliminate the piling up of prepositional phrases, however, and recent writers are using it for inanimate possessives).

Animate: Willie's room; Martha's dictionary.

Inanimate: the leg of the table; the end of the poem.

c) To form the possessive of irregular nouns, add "s": "Children's Song." The rule is optional with proper names ending in "s": "Dickens' novel," "Keats's poem."

d) In a compound noun, the last word takes "s": "sister-in-law's coat."

e) Place the "s" after the last item in a series of nouns to indicate joint ownership but after each item to show individual possession: "We went to Mary and Al's wedding"; "We borrowed Mary's and Al's golf clubs."

Colons

In my experience, students often shy away from using colons—or simply haven't thought about what they can do for a sentence.

a) Colons introduce a series of items explained in the main clause of the sentence. "For spring training, we need plenty of equipment: bats, softballs, softball mitts, a catcher's mitt, and four bases.''

b) Colons point the reader to a final fact, an upshot, a punchline. ''You have all you need: jazz.''

c) Colons introduce a direct quotation of some length: *''Their Eyes Were Watching God* describes the black woman's plight: 'Maybe it's some place way off in de ocean where de black man is in power, but we don't know nothing but what we see. So de white man throw down de load and tell de nigger tuh pick it up. . . .' ''

An independent clause must precede the colon. The following use of the colon is not correct: ''For spring training we need: bats, softballs, and bases.''

Commas

The comma is the most frequently used of all punctuation marks; it signals an addition or an aside that interrupts the main statement. Commas are used less frequently than ever before, especially in technical writing; still, students can enjoy flexing various stylistic muscles after closely examining comma-laden passages by Faulkner, James, Wolfe, or Dickens.

a) Commas separate independent clauses joined by coordinating conjunctions (see ''Fused Sentences or the Comma Splice,'' p. 220 and ''Conjunctions,'' p. 257): ''We have travelled far and wide, and we have purchased too many souvenirs.'' The comma may be left out between short independent clauses.

b) Commas separate items (nouns, phrases, or short clauses) in a series: ''In the U.S.S.R., we went to the Bolshoi Ballet, Pushkin's palace, and a park in Kiev.'' Modern writers use either the ''x, y, and z'' (two commas) or the ''x, y and z'' (one comma) formula. I teach my students to use the first formula so that they can reserve the second for a noun followed by a pair of adjectives (''We bought her a great car, red and racy'') or for three items, the last two of which have an especially close relation: ''I ate toast, eggs and bacon.''

c) Commas separate introductory elements (words, phrases, clauses, or transitions) from the rest of a sentence: ''Before he went to Michigan, Tom labored in Pittsburgh Steel Mills''; ''Thus, Belle won the bet.''

d) Commas set off parenthetical elements (appositives, nonrestrictive modifiers—see "Combining Sentences," p. 234 and "Distinguishing Restriction from Nonrestriction," 232:

1. Cecil Taylor, the performer in green gloves, plays jazz piano. *(appositive)*
2. A pigeon, alas, is on the grass. *(parenthetical element)*
3. The team, which formed but a week ago, has already racked up two successes. *(non-restrictive element)*

No commas are necessary with *that:* "The team that won the trophy last year is at it again."

Dashes

Dashes separate as commas and parentheses do but they add emphasis. They are also often considered informal. On a typewriter, form the dash with two hyphens, leaving no spaces between them and the words before and after.

a) Dashes set off a series of items separated by commas from the rest of a sentence. They are especially useful for clarity in sentences employing several commas: "Beauty, age, goodness, size—these are the kinds of adjectives that should precede the noun in French."

b) Dashes can set off final appositives: "The professor never told us how important Levi-Strauss' work was in related disciplines—linguistics, literature, or philosophy."

c) They can set off nonrestrictive appositives for emphasis or clarity: "Three dogs—Tom, Dick, and Harry—won ribbons in sit-stay class" vs. the more confusing "Three dogs, Tom, Dick, and Harry, won ribbons in sit-stay class." In the latter sentence, we cannot be sure that Tom, Dick, and Harry are not human pet-owners given ribbons along with three dogs.

d) They can set off parenthetical interruptions: "So this searching for symbols—this taking the world too personally, you might say—started early, as Judy helped me see."

Periods

Periods mark the end of complete sentences, but note that, like closing commas, they go inside closing quotation marks (semicolons go outside): "The narrator remarks, 'I cry at nothing, and cry most of the time.' '' Students need to be reminded to space twice after typing periods or colons; space once after typing commas or semicolons.

Semicolons

Semicolons, like periods, signal the end of an independent clause, but one beyond which the sentence continues.

a) They can separate independent clauses with or without a conjunctive adverb (*moreover, nonetheless,* etc.): ''Living in upstate New York spoiled me; the only good apples in Washington are the Gravensteins that grow in my new backyard, but they don't last''; ''I miss New York state apples; moreover, I miss Ithaca's rolling hills.'' (See also ''Fused Sentences or the Comma Splice,'' p. 220.)

b) They separate items in a series if they are lengthy or contain other forms of punctuation: ''We collected bats, balls, gloves, and bases for baseball; a ball, shoulder pads, jerseys, and helmets for football; skis, poles, and pairs of goggles for skiing.''

Punctuation exercises:

Encourage your students to use a particular essay assignment to experiment with dashes and colons or semicolons and commas. Have them trade papers with a neighbor on the day the essay is due. Instruct them to underline with a straight line experiments they like and which they believe worked and to underline with a squiggly line places they are not sure work well. Let the pair talk over their respective responses and call you over when they cannot resolve their questions or differences.

One of the best ways to teach both an appreciation for and the uses of punctuation is to have students hand copy, word-for-word and triple-spaced, a passage full of interesting punctuation. Ask students to substitute their own words for the original, but to retain each mark of punctuation. Choose passages from ''An Album of Styles'' in *The Norton Reader,* or bring in Dickens' description of Mrs. Tulkinghorn in *Bleak House* or passages from contemporary non-fiction writers such as Annie Dillard and John McPhee. Or remove all the punctuation from a paragraph of assigned reading and have the students supply it. They will learn a great deal from discussion of possible correct choices and from a comparison of their decisions with the author's.

You can also have your students closely examine one paragraph of a text on your syllabus. Go around the room until each student has read aloud one complete sentence and explained the effectiveness of its internal punctuation. How could sentences have been punctuated differently?

For information about other forms of punctuation—question marks, exclamation points, parentheses, quotation marks, ellipses, and so on— consult any one of the grammar handbooks listed in Chapter 8, "A Bibliographical Guide to the Profession."

II. A QUICK REVIEW OF SENTENCE PARTS

A. Nouns

A discussion of nouns may be suitable for a class untutored in grammar, unconfident, or just curious. The discussion below could substitute for, or supplement, the discussion in any of a number of conventional grammar handbooks. It can be abridged, certainly, as needed.

Nouns are naming words (in fact, their name means "name"). They name a person, place, thing, or idea: *Sally, Chicago, city hall, brouhaha, noun.* Nouns may be replaced by a personal pronoun: *I, you, he, him, she, her, it, they, them.*

They usually have different forms of the plural and the singular. That is, nouns can show number, usually through an ending of *-s* or *-es: cat, cats; daisy, daisies.* Exceptions: *deer, deer; fish, fish* (do not show number); *phenomenon, phenomena; child, children* (irregular plural ending). Thus, one way to recognize (regular) nouns is by their linguistic shape.

Nouns fit into certain slots of a sentence—a *the* or a *this* might come before a noun which in turn comes before a verb, or a noun marker *(a, an, the)* and its noun will line up directly after a verb. Depending on the sentence, nouns (or pronouns) can act as subjects, direct or indirect objects, objects of prepositions, predicate nominatives, or appositives. Notice the sentence slot each kind of noun occupies below:

1) Dance moves me. (*subject*, comes before a verb)

2) I despise dance. (*direct object*, comes after action verb)

3) Tom gave the dance a new twist. (*indirect object*, comes before the direct object it cannot appear without, answers "to what?" in "Gave what to what?" See "Verbs," following)

4) Bobby Jo ran to the dance. *(object of preposition, to)*

5) Her hobby is dance. *(predicate nominative*, renames "hobby" and appears after the linking verb *is)*

6) Her first love, dance, was abandoned in 1968. (*appositive* renaming "first love" is surrounded by commas)

Sometimes whole groups of words act as a noun. In the sentence, "Surviving without a compass isn't easy," "surviving without a compass" is a noun phrase acting as a subject.

Types of Nouns

a) There are *common nouns* (uncapitalized: *boys, table, hope*) and *proper nouns* (capitalized: *Mrs. Dixon, Esperanto, Christian Dior*). You might discriminate between the two types when students capitalize incorrectly. When they address their mothers and thus refer to her by a proper name, *Mom,* or *Mother,* they should capitalize. When they say *my mother,* however, they should not. The direct-address mode makes *Mom* into a proper name like *Mrs. Dixon,* while the generic mode, "My mom went to work today," presents *mom* as a common noun.

b) There are *concrete nouns* (nouns whose referents can be apprehended by the senses: *table, contact paper, jellybeans*) and *abstract nouns (love, dissatisfaction, direction).* Explore this distinction when you discuss effective word choices with your class; ask them to write concretely, where possible, in both creative and expository writing.

c) *Collective nouns* usually act like singular nouns, but imply a group *(audience, crowd, committee, group, collective).* These words get writers in awkward jams: "The crowd took their (?) seats"; or "The crowd took its (?) seat." "The crowd sat down" (easiest). (See "Making Subjects and Verbs Agree," p. 226.)

d) *Mass nouns (water, spumoni, bread, population, salt)* are opposed to

e) *Count nouns (person, egg, pencil).* Students sometimes confuse one category with the other, writing *fewer furniture,* when they mean less furniture—furniture is a mass noun, not a count noun.

Ask students who need or want to know more about nouns to underline the nouns in a ditto-sheet of sentences; label subjects, direct objects, predicate nominatives, and so on; turn verbs or adjectives into noun forms (as a preparation for turning nominalizations—non-nouns changed into nouns—back into their original, more vigorous, parts of speech—see "Overuse of Nominalizations [and Euphemisms]," p. 223).

You should of course feel no obligation to know or go into the entire catechism of the noun, but you could, if you wished, use an elaborate discussion of nouns to talk about diction and word choice, sentence variety, subject-verb agreement, the use of the colon before a list (of nouns), and so forth.

B. Verbs

Verbs convey the action or existence of the subject of a sentence or connect the subject to a complement (direct object, indirect object, predicate nominative, predicate adjective).

Verb Forms: Tenses and Moods

Verbs are inflected; that is, they have different endings depending on whether their subject is plural or singular. They also change form (tense) depending on the time of the action described. We can express, then, different time relations with these different verbs forms:

present:	He dances.
past:	He danced.
future:	He will dance.
present perfect:	He has danced.
past perfect:	He had danced.
future perfect:	He will have danced.
present progressive:	He is dancing.
present perfect progressive:	He has been dancing.
past perfect progressive:	He had been dancing.
future perfect progressive:	He will have been dancing.

Students often mix tenses inappropriately in their prose or fail to use the "historical present" where convention dictates they should. We write about literature, for example, as if the events we speak of were still unfolding, would forever unfold; thus, recounting part of the plot of the novel *Middlemarch,* we say: "Dorothea discovers Ladislaw alone with Mrs. Lydgate," not "Dorothea discovered Ladislaw alone with Mrs. Lydgate."

Verbs also show whether a subject is acting or having action done to it because verbs can be in the active or passive voice. (See "Overuse of the Passive Voice," p. 221.) And verbs can be in different moods:

a) *informative (indicative):* I hate Cheerios. Time goes slowly.

b) *commanding (imperative):* Archaeologist #1: "Get out of my site!"

c) *contrary to fact, wishful (subjunctive):* If I were Queen, I'd go out in my coach, and all the people would wave. (Many students don't know anything about the subjunctive; you will have to teach them and help them get the habit of "If . . . were.")

Every verb has an infinitive *(to* plus the verb: *to munch)* and three principal parts (present, past, and past participle). An infinitive can act as a noun ("To dance is to live"), as an adjective (*"Flatland* is the book to read") or an adverb ("Harry went home to eat". Why did Harry go home?) Adverbs answer "why"—or when, where, how, to what extent, how often; see "Adverbs," p. 252. The principal parts are used alone or combined with helping (auxiliary) verbs to form the various tenses.

Verb Types: Helping and Linking

Helping verbs are used with other verbs to form the many tenses of English. There are two kinds:

a) *regular helping or auxiliary:* I *am* learning the mazurka on Mondays. Sarah *had* inspected her attic.

Standing alone, they are *main verbs:* I *am* a wonderful dancer. Sarah *had* ghosts in her garret.

b) *modal auxiliary,* which can not stand alone as main verbs *(can, could, will, would, may, might, must, should):* Sarah *can* eradicate ghosts in our lifetime. You *should* learn the lindy.

Modal verbs affect the meaning of the main verbs and are used as abbreviations of a main verb phrase only in casual conversation: "Did Sarah call the exterminators?" "She should." (Note that to form questions in English, we split the helping verb from the main verb and put it up front: "Sarah did call the exterminators" becomes "Did Sarah call the exterminators?" Or we put in a "dummy" helping verb when there is none: "They run quickly" thus becomes "Do they run quickly?" or "Can they run quickly?") See the figure below for a Venn diagram of verbs:

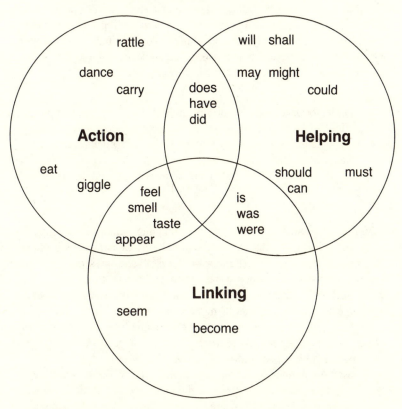

Students also overuse and abuse the conditional, perhaps out of uncertainty about themselves as writers or as thinkers. As a result, they introduce more auxiliaries than needed: "A typical outfit I might wear would be blue jeans, sneakers, and a button-down Oxford-cloth shirt." The student could say more directly and naturally, "I usually wear blue jeans, sneakers, and a button-down Oxford-cloth shirt."

Linking verbs, a kind of main verb, connect the subject to another noun (the predicate nominative) or an adjective in the predicate (the predicate adjective). We contrast linking verbs with action verbs, the latter being preferable wherever possible, as active-voice sentences are more vigorous than those in passive voice. (See "Overuse of the Passive Voice," p. 221.)

To test for a linking verb, students can try to substitute a form of "to be" for the word in question. "The soup tasted salty" equals "The soup was salty." The sentences below contain linking verbs followed by either a predicate adjective or a predicate nominative. (Predicate adjectives and nominatives are also called subject complements, while direct and indirect objects are known as object complements.)

a) Trapeze artists became my idols. (*idols* is a predicate nominative)

b) Circuses still seem enormously popular. (*popular* is a predicate adjective)

c) Elephants still are enormous. (*enormous* is a predictive adjective)

Verbs, like nouns, are either plural or singular in number. A singular verb goes with a singular subject; a plural verb accompanies a plural subject: "Tommy runs" (singular verb) vs. "The boys run" (plural verb). Students occasionally use the wrong verb forms, particularly when the subject of the verb is several words away from the verb. (See "Making Subjects and Verbs Agree," p. 226.)

Regular verbs form the past and past participle by adding a suffix of *-d, -e,* or *-t (jolt, jolted; lose, lost);* while *teach, feel, be,* and others are irregular *(teach, taught; feel, felt; am, was, been).*

Verbs form present participles by adding *-ing* to the present tense. Present and past participles, because they are used sometimes as adjectives and sometimes as nouns, are called verbals—they look like verbs but act as adjectives or nouns. When they act as adjectives they are called participles—a confusing use of the generic term "participle" for the specific adjective-participle "participle." (See also "Adjectives," p. 251.) When present participles function as nouns, they are called gerunds. (Gerunds always have *-ing* endings.) A verbal, whether participle or gerund, cannot be used as the main verb of a sentence. (See also "Combining Sentences," p. 234.)

Verb Types: Transitive and Intransitive

Action verbs are transitive if they need objects to complete their meaning: "The minister baptized the child." Since linking verbs never have subject complements, they are constitutionally intransitive.

Intransitive action verbs make sense without objects: "The desert rat jumped." Many verbs go either way, however: "I sang cheerfully" (intransitive); "I sang 'The Music Goes Round and Round' " (transitive).

The more verb-conscious students become, the better. Teach them that the direct version surpasses the wordy, turgid ones below.

1) I see what to do. *(simple verb, infinitive)*

2) I am seeing what to do. *(helping verb, present participle, infinitive)*

3) It is apparent that seeing what to do is meaningful. *(linking verb, gerund, infinitive, linking verb)*

4) It is apparent that the sight of what to do is meaningful. *(linking verb, nominalization of verb, infinitive, linking verb)*

Writers who can make choices among verb forms can control their sentences; they are less likely to lapse into bad habits such as relying on nominalizations.

C. Adjectives

Adjectives describe or "modify" nouns or pronouns. They answer the questions "How many?" "Which one?" "What kind?" *(twelve, this, red).*

Adjectives often change in degree to show comparative quantity or quality *(good, better, best; ugly, uglier, ugliest; beautiful, more beautiful, most beautiful; few, more, many).* You may occasionally need to give students a review of which adjectives take *-er* and *-est* and which take *more* and *most*.

If an adjective comes after the verb, it functions as a predicate adjective: "The book was red." Present or past participles (see "Verbs," p. 247) can act as adjectives: "Wind-blown hair is hard to comb"; "The singing sands stung my feet." (See also "Dangling or Misplaced Modifiers," p. 233.)

Because they modify nouns, we class noun determiners (*the, an, you,* etc.) as adjectives.

D. Adverbs

Adverbs describe or modify verbs, adjectives, or other adverbs. They answer one of the following questions: "How?" "To what extent?" "When?" "Where?" "Why?":

She read the book rapidly.

"Rapidly" modifies the verb "read" and answers the adverb question "How?"

Many adverbs end in *-ily* or *-ly (happily, fluently, shyly),* endings that can turn many adjectives *(happy, fluent, shy, polite)* into adverbs. All words ending in *-ly,* however, are not adverbs (*friendly* is an adjective, for example, *comply* is a verb, and *butterfly* is a noun).

Kinds of Adverbs

One kind of adverb is the *intensifier.* These words modify only adjectives or adverbs: "rather quietly"; "too nosy"; "very disgustingly." Intensifiers often answer the adverb question "To what extent?" Yet students who rely on *very* for emphasis should learn to intensify through subordination, syntax, or varied diction instead. Compare "It is very important that Congress vote on the bill" to "Congress must vote 'Yes' on the bill if inflation is to stop." Students also misuse *so* in place of *very,* with an often accompanying overuse of exclamation: "That bill is so important to the country's economy!"

Conjunctive adverbs join clauses without making the clauses that follow them dependent as subordinating conjunctions do. Common conjunctive adverbs include *however, thus, therefore, consequently, indeed,* and *furthermore.* Conjunctive adverbs create both sentence logic and sentence variety. (See also "Fused Sentences or the Comma Splice," p. 220, "Combining Sentences," p. 234, and "Checking Punctuation," p. 240.)

1. He delivered the ice cream cake; consequently, the party was a success.
2. She delights in music; nonetheless, she hates the ballet.

Point out to students that in such sentences as those above, a semicolon precedes the conjunctive adverb and separates the two sentences. A period could also, of course, correctly precede the adverb: "She delights in music. Nonetheless, she hates the ballet." Sometimes a conjunctive adverb interrupts a single sentence (independent clause). Remind students that in such a case the adverb must be surrounded by commas: "He went, however, to the Baltimore Zoo."

Paired commas often serve to mark off the less essential part of a sentence, the aside, from the central grammatical and lexical elements, "He went to the Baltimore Zoo." The "however" adds argument and tone, but the sentence conforms to one of the five basic indicative sentence patterns without it (see "Clauses and Phrases," p. 258).

Some adverbs, like some adjectives, have comparative and superlative forms. *(ran fast, ran faster, ran fastest)*. Students often incorrectly use adjectives for adverbs or adverbs for adjectives. Have them decide whether the word in the parentheses should modify the subject (in which case an adjective is appropriate) or the verb (in which case an adverb is correct):

Exercise:
1. He drove up the hill (quick, quickly).

   [How did he drive? Choose "quickly," the adverb.]
2. He feels (bad, badly).

   [If he has numb fingertips, he might feel (action verb) badly (adverb). If his state of being isn't good, if he's in ill health, he feels bad (adjective). Chances are good that "bad" is the correct choice here.]

Adverbs are the most moveable part of speech, so the slots they occupy vary greatly: "Now Sam will go home." "Sam now will go home." "Sam will now go home." "Sam will go home now." Sometimes the meaning will change when the adverb is moved; students can have fun playing on that fact: "Only Jack ate the potroast." "Jack ate only the potroast."

Adverbials are other parts of speech or groups of words that act as adverbs in a sentence. Sometimes an infinitive phrase is an adverbial:

"I finished college *to impress my hometown honey.*" The italicized phrase answers the adverb question "why?" Prepositional phrases and nouns can also act as adverbs.

An adverb clause includes a noun and a verb and answers questions about the main clause of a sentence: *"While Mary repaired the porch,* John built the castle of his dreams.*"* The italicized (dependent) clause answers the adverb question "When?"

E. Pronouns

The parts of speech discussed so far—nouns, verbs, adjectives, and adverbs—make up the open word classes. New nouns, verbs, adjectives, and adverbs get born every day (though some are less lively than others—compare "interface" with "scarf" as in "to scarf a pizza"). The parts of speech about to be discussed—pronouns, prepositions, and conjunctions—are function words in closed word classes. New prepositions, conjunctions, or pronouns are not likely to be coined.

A pronoun takes the place of a noun and is therefore a nominal. Pronouns substitute for nouns when nouns would be too awkward or repetitious in a sentence. The noun that a pronoun substitutes for is its antecedent (see "Pronoun-Antecedent Agreement and Gender Problems," p. 227).

    1. Sammy took Sammy's bat to the plate. *(without pronouns)*
        Sammy took his bat to the plate *(pronoun acting as possessive adjective)*
    2. Sammy had a bad batting record. Sammy's bad batting record made Sammy very nervous every game. *(without pronouns)*
        Sammy had a bad batting record which made him very nervous every game. *(with relative and objective pronouns)*

Students sometimes need reminding that pronouns help avoid choppy sentences, too much repetition, and the sense that each sentence is the first one in an essay.

Types of Pronouns
    a) *Personal pronouns* include the following nominals and possessives:

	Singular	**Plural**
First Person	I	we
	me	us
	my, mine	our, ours
Second Person	you	you
	you	you
	your, yours	your, yours
Third Person	he, she, it	they
	him, her, it	them
	his, her, hers, its	their, theirs

Students often make the stylistic mistake of mixing ''persons'' in their papers, switching from *I* to *you* to *we* or the formal, third-indefinite pronoun *one*. Urge them to be consistent, suggesting that *I* is acceptable. *We* often sounds royal or forced, *you* may sound too know-it-all familiar, while *one* may be just right or too formal, depending on the writing occasion. As long as students determine for themselves which voice they mean to adopt and then stick with an appropriate pronoun throughout an essay, they'll be writing ''correctly.''

b) *Relative pronouns (who, which, whose, that)* introduce subordinate clauses: ''The rose that you gave me was never to bloom.'' (See also ''Distinguishing Restriction from Nonrestriction,'' p. 232 and ''Checking Punctuation,'' p. 240.)

c) *Demonstrative pronouns* point at objects: ''Look at that!'' ''Give me those!'' If *this, that, these,* or *those* come before a noun, however, they perform the job of adjective. Similarly, if a possessive pronoun comes before a noun rather than standing alone (''I gave him his due'' vs. ''I gave him his''), it is acting as an adjective and not merely as a pronoun.

d) *Reflexive pronouns* are sometimes also emphatic or intensive pronouns. Reflexive: ''I was washing myself.'' Emphatic or intensive: ''Mother, I'd really rather do it myself!''

e) *Interrogative pronouns (who, whom, which)* form questions.

f) *Indefinite pronouns* refer generally rather than specifically to persons, places, or things *(all, any, anybody, anyone, both, each, either, everybody, everyone, everything, few, many, more, much, neither, nobody, none, no one, one, several, some, somebody, someone, such)*. Students sometimes use plural pronouns following singular indefinite pronouns, as in the incorrect sentence, "Everyone loves their mother." (See also "Pronoun-Antecedent Agreement and Gender Problems," p. 227.)

F. Prepositions

Prepositions are used with nouns or pronouns, which are called objects of prepositions, to form prepositional phrases. Prepositional phrases then function as adjectives or adverbs:

1) The boy with green hair ran away from home. *(adjective)*
2) The horse galloped into the artist's loft. *(adverb)*

Most prepositions are single words *(by, for, into, of, with, near),* but some consist of more *(as well as, according to, on account of).* There are some seventy-five prepositions in all. To help students learn to recognize which words are prepositions, tell students they are "relating" words that demonstrate the relationship between a noun or pronoun and another word or group of words:

> The bee goes *around* the hive, *towards* the hive, *into* the hive, *under* the hive, *above* the hive, *beside* the hive, and so forth.

Some verbs, called phrasal verbs, have as part of the verb what would in other sentences be described as prepositions or adverbs. The expression "to look up a word in the dictionary" contains the phrasal verb "to look up"; the only preposition present in the utterance is "in." "To look up the stairs," on the other hand, contains the infinitive "to look" plus the preposition "up" followed by its object, "the stairs." Other phrasal verbs include "run away," "run over," "put up," and "shut up." Note that the second word in each construction could in other contexts act as either a preposition or an adverb.

Non-native speakers often have trouble choosing the right preposition for an idiomatic English expression. There are no rules that will help them choose correctly. Instead, feel free to edit their incorrect sentences so as to provide ear (and eye) training for these students. Ask them to pay closer attention to how native speakers of English use prepositions. They will eventually write idiomatically.

G. *Conjunctions*

Conjunctions join words, phrases, or clauses.

a) *Coordinating conjunctions (and, or, for, but, nor, so, yet)* enable us to make things grammatically and lexically equal: "Sally ate peanuts and guzzled beer."

Students tend to overuse these connectors, especially "and," as is discussed in "Combining Sentences," p. 234. When student sentences are only weakly joined to one another, student paragraphs and papers exhibit little development, and little momentum or lovely inevitability in their arguments.

b) *Correlative or paired conjunctions (either . . . or, neither . . . nor, both . . . and, not only . . . but also)* act like *and* and *or* but are more emphatic: "Both German and French are required for the Ph.D." Students using correlative conjunctions occasionally need a review of subject-verb agreement rules (see "Making Subjects and Verbs Agree," p. 226).

c) *Subordinating conjunctions (after, although, as, as if, as long as, as soon as, as though, because, before, how, in order that, unless, wherever, that, than, since, so that, where, while, and so forth)*. Some of these may be other parts of speech in other contexts. For example, *after* can begin a prepositional phrase that functions as an adverb—"He went home after dinner"—or appear as an adverb—"And Jack came tumbling after." Subordinating conjunctions contribute to sentence logic and variety (see also "Combining Sentences," p. 234, and the discussion of parataxis and hypotaxis in Chapter 6, "Understanding Prose").

H. *Interjections*

Interjections refer to something "thrown in" a sentence. Not functional parts of sentences as such, they are interrupters and mood-makers and are more often used in dialogue than in expository prose. They include exclamations and expletives (those words that don't directly contribute to the paraphraseable meaning of a sentence): "Damn! I hurt my finger"; "A pigeon on the grass, alas." They are followed by exclamation marks, periods, or commas. If they don't begin a sentence, they are usually preceded by commas.

I. Clauses and Phrases

A phrase is a group of related words unable to stand alone as a sentence. There are *noun phrases* ("the fat red Cadillac"), *verb phrases* ("horridly heaves and lurches"), *adjective phrases* ("wearing the red carnation"), *adverb phrases* ("tomorrow at the latest"), *prepositional phrases* ("of cabbages and kings"), and *absolute phrases* ("having broken her leg").

A clause contains a verb and its subject, whereas—as you can see if you examine the phrases above—a phrase lacks at least one of these. Clauses can be independent ("Anthony went for a drive") or dependent—that is, incomplete, subordinate ("While Anthony went for a drive"). Two independent clauses joined by a coordinator make a compound clause or compound sentence: "Anthony went for a drive and I did my income taxes." A combination of a dependent and an independent clause makes up a complex sentence: "While Anthony went for a drive, I did my income taxes." A sentence with two or more independent clauses and one or more dependent clauses is called a compound-complex sentence: "While Anthony went for a drive and I did my income taxes, Steve, who was bored to tears, made five long-distance phone calls." One independent clause constitutes a simple sentence: "I went for a drive." See Chapter 6, "Understanding Prose," for a discussion of sentence types and style.

Indicative sentences inform or assert; traditional grammarians contrast them with questions, exclamations, and imperatives. Five basic indicative sentence patterns follow.

1. *Subject–verb:* He runs.
2. *Subject–verb–direct object:* They eat potatoes.
3. *Subject–linking verb–predicate nominative:* Sasha is a labrador retriever.

4. *Subject–linking verb–predicate adjective:* The harvest moon is golden.

5. *Subject–verb–indirect object–direct object:* Eudora gave me her short story.

For further reading and reviewing, and for exercises in style and logic, see the texts described in Chapter 8, ''A Bibliographical Guide to the Profession.'' In general, grammar texts are a good source for fine points once the principles have been taught or reviewed. For students flailing in an otherwise competent class, a handbook or workbook can be especially helpful. Instead of taking up class time with usage issues problematic for only one or two students, insist that these students buy a handbook you recommend and perform whatever text and applied exercises you assign them (extra corrections or revisions of their own sentences, for example).

And a word of caution to pass on to your students: All teachers—and writers—hold some usage rules more sacred than others. In addition, as every stylist and enunciator of usage rules admits, rules are only guidelines and are made eventually to be broken. Grammatical disasters often become mere infelicities when a piece of writing has—in spite of these ''errors''—coherence, integrity, and rhetorical power. Joseph Williams published an article laden with so-called errors he knew his readers would not notice until he drew their attention to them at the very end of the article. If everything else is working for a piece of writing, some kinds of errors won't matter terribly. But for beginning writers, this is usually not the case; errors not only are prevalent but are often both magnified and caused by correspondingly weak arguments and voices. Grammar still has its place in the writing curriculum.

WORKS CITED

Entries marked with an asterisk are described in Chapter 8, ''A Bibliographical Guide to the Profession.''

Eastman, Arthur M., ed. *The Norton Reader: An Anthology of Expository Prose.* 6th ed. New York: Norton, 1984.
Elledge, Scott. *E. B. White: A Biography.* New York: Norton, 1984.

*Lanham, Richard. *Revising Prose*. 2nd ed. New York: Macmillan, 1987.

*Strong, William. *Sentence Combining: A Composing Book*. 2nd ed. New York: Random House, 1983.

Williams, Joseph. "The Phenomenology of Error." *CCC* (1981): 152–68.

*————. *Style: Ten Lessons in Clarity and Grace*. 2nd ed. Glenview, Ill.: Scott, Foresman, 1985.

8

A Bibliographical Guide to the Profession

KEITH HJORTSHOJ

I. INTRODUCTION: ALLIES OR INTERLOPERS?

Finding appropriate textbooks for a writing course should be an easier task than it is, considering the number and variety of books in print. Every major publisher in the field offers at least one college handbook, along with rhetorics, readers, workbooks, and more specialized volumes that focus on particular aspects of writing, particular types of writing, or the needs of particular types of students. Several new titles and revised editions appear every spring, uniformly promoted with claims that the authors have developed the perfect formula for literary excellence, based on the latest research on composition and pedagogy, and tested in the classroom with astonishing success. Like remedies for obesity, baldness, impotence, and other intractable maladies, writing texts often promise quick and painless, almost miraculous cures for bad prose, which almost everyone now considers an endemic disease. If even one-tenth of these claims were valid, of course, there would be far fewer composition texts on the market and writing problems would vanish like smallpox in a single term. We know this is impossible, and that the struggles with language that our students bring to the classroom can't be fully alleviated by formulas in a single semester. But in this complicated, often discouraging profession, students almost invariably make less progress than we had hoped, and this hope with which we begin each term sustains the belief that there must be a better method, and a better textbook, than the one we used last semester. In turn, this dissatisfaction sustains a growing, regenerative, yet peculiarly redundant sector of the publishing industry. In what other sector of this industry can one find essentially the same information (e.g., rules for the use of the semicolon, or an acceptable format for documentation) in two or three hundred separate publications that all, like laundry detergents, claim to be newer and more powerful than the rest?

In spite of our efforts and those of publishers and authors, very few of us who teach writing as a profession have discovered the ideal writing text: the book that neatly corresponds with our specific courses and teaching styles, and that effectively addresses all, or even most, of our students' needs. When we ignore hopes and claims for miraculous cure, the reason is fairly obvious. Almost all composition texts address students directly, but when you read these books try to imagine their audience. When I do so, with very few exceptions I see rows of amorphous, silent creatures with blank faces, listening and following instructions—composing the same essay, correcting the same errors. Now if I think of a particular batch of students I have worked with, the problems involved in writing these textbooks and the problems we face in using them become mutually intelligible. In this real class I recall a student who wrote in simple assertions as though he were stringing beads and another whose sentences were usually overstructured and tentative, like card houses. One student tried to defend his two-page, triple-spaced paper by swearing that his mind was as empty and silent on the subject as a plundered tomb, while another had tried to pack a dozen interesting but conflicting ideas into a single essay. A native speaker of Chinese in the class could recognize and name all verb forms but consistently misused them, while the native speakers of English used them correctly without recognizing any but the simple present and past tenses.

This was not an unusually diverse or difficult class, but when I think of it I recall a collection of individuals who wrote in particular styles and voices, with particular backgrounds and preconceptions, strengths and weaknesses. How could any textbook address all of them at once, or lead them hand-in-hand to a collective liberation from their difficulties with composition? If you allow them to run your course for you, the most regimented textbooks might create an illusion of uniform progress, and they will certainly simplify class preparation, but they can never replace the attentiveness to individual students and to specific uses of language, or the investment in real communication between teachers and students, essential to good writing instruction.

Only the writing teacher can supply and stimulate these essential qualities in a writing course. The best textbooks will supplement your efforts, help you to structure a course of your own design, and shift some of the burden of instruction to the students by supplying references and guidance they can consult on their own. A textbook should never interfere with your work, take charge of our class for you, or make you feel obliged to assign chapters simply because you forced students to buy it.

If they are chosen and used carefully, however, textbooks can help you accomplish much more in a single term than you could accomplish without them, particularly because class and conference time is so limited. Use of a comprehensive handbook as a companion text, for example, will allow you to refer students to constructions and explanations you can't address in paper comments and shouldn't have to address in class, especially if the problem applies only to a few of our students. Other types of references can help you not only identify problems in a sentence and paragraph but also teach students to identify these problems and reconstruct their sentences and paragraphs on their own. In this respect, textbooks can be ultimately more valuable than teachers in the classroom. Most of us probably spend too much time editing and revising student writing and too little time teaching students to develop their own, independent skills and resources. After all, when they leave our courses and colleges students can take good references with them, but they can't keep an English teacher around, and probably wouldn't want to even if they could.

Rhetorics and rhetorical sections in good handbooks can help you understand and discuss the complexity of the writing process, the stylistic and rhetorical variations in student papers and readings, the rhetorical demands of writing in different contexts and disciplines, the uses of voice and methods of integrating the voices of other writers—distinctions and skills that can be taught and are essential to writing and reading in college work but are not taught in most high school classes. In general, the best references on writing and teaching can help you liberate students from the romantic and hopeless notion that the ability to write well is a mysterious gift, and from the grim, deadening belief that good writing results primarily from obeying rules and avoiding errors.

A good textbook for someone else's course, however, might be a miserable failure in yours. In the process of selecting a book you should first get examination copies from the publishers and read them, with your students in mind, and with attention to format and function, tone and voice. Even a straight handbook, the most detached type of writing text, will address your students in a particular way, and when you choose a book you have, in effect, invited another teacher into your class, to help you run your course. Obviously you will want to work with someone you can get along with: an author who shares your basic assumptions about writing, respects your approach to teaching, and holds similar views of students—one who complements, rather than usurps or undermines, your role in the classroom. Some of these authors are content to remain in the background, providing information, exercises, assignments, or readings when you need them. Others want very much to take charge of your class and use you as their teaching assistant and grader. Sections of their books that you might wish to use for your own purposes are so inextricably locked into an integrated course plan and discourse that you won't be able to extract them without confusing your students. Some of the most innovative and carefully designed books are virtually useless unless you are willing to subject yourself and your class to the entire course plan they prescribe.

Writing texts should also be models of good writing that demonstrate awareness of and respect for their audiences. On these rhetorical and stylistic grounds, probably more often than on any other, composition texts often fail. Because communication is the subject of a writing course, good instruction relies upon lively discussion and inquiry, the exchange of ideas and information among students and between the students and their teacher. The authors of textbooks want very much to participate in this interaction, but they really can't. And because in the process of writing they have to address a hypothetical audience that cannot ask or answer questions, express confusion, complain, suggest alternative viewpoints, or in any way respond, the tones and voices in which these authors address students often sound very peculiar, like one-sided conversations. They tend, on the whole, to be bossy and patronizing, a bit frantic, and excessively didactic. Some are written almost entirely in imperatives. Others attempt to engage their silent audiences with strings of rhetorical questions and informal patter, intended to stimulate thought in presumably blank minds. In contrast with the dense blocks of prose and lists of injunctions in traditional rhetorics, new textbooks are often loaded with "visuals": inspirational photographs, magazine ads, cartoons, and drawings intended, as one promotional brochure tells us, to "really grab students' attention and spark interest." Not necessarily a noble aim, but certainly a practical one, if we think of our students as a generation of television addicts who can't read a long paragraph in a single typeface without intellectual fatigue, and who can't really understand anything without a picture.

Whether these visuals, schematics, type changes, color codes, and keys are valuable or not, they often distract us from more substantial questions about the strengths and weaknesses of a book, and from the real aims of writing instruction. Can a textbook teach students to write sustained, coherent passages of prose if it doesn't contain any? In their attempt to be popular and entertaining, authors and publishers frequently aim too low, I believe, and you will often find that a book intended for college freshmen sounds and looks as though it were designed for junior high school students with particularly short attention spans. If you want most of all to keep your students amused for a semester, books of this sort might do the trick. But if you want to get somewhere—to make students more aware of their own potential and of the potential intricacy, subtlety, and power of the English language—you should choose a textbook that is aimed a bit above your students' level over one that concedes to their misgivings about language and tries most of all to make writing seem easy and fun. Writing that we take seriously is rarely easy and fun, even when it gives us a different kind of pleasure and gratification.

Throughout the following sections on books for the classroom I have assumed that teachers have the power to choose textbooks and other materials for their courses, even though I realize that many of you are obliged to use books chosen by your departments or supervisors, according to course plans that are often quite rigid. Even in the most tightly structured courses, however, the people who make decisions usually welcome discussion of course designs and materials, and they often form textbook selection committees that include teaching staff. In any case, teachers must claim a course as their own in some positive way in order to teach it well, and few courses are so rigidly structured that they admit no innovation, interpretation, or supplementary material. And teachers are always empowered by recognition of alternatives, even if they can't pursue these alternatives with complete freedom. Books listed in Section II of this chapter will expand your awareness of theories and methods for teaching composition in ways you can apply at some level in any course, regardless of the textbooks you use, and other sections may provide supplementary teaching materials and guidance, even if you are not responsible for course design and textbook selection.

For obvious reasons I haven't attempted in this chapter to provide a comprehensive survey of the books currently available for and about teaching writing. Instead, this chapter will serve as a guide to some of the best books on the market, and to the variations, strengths, and weaknesses among them. In the process of compiling these references I excluded books of very limited interest to a general audience of writing teachers, along with books I thoroughly dislike. In this preface and in the introduction to this book I have already revealed some of my criteria and biases, and I will no doubt reveal others in following sections. Even so, there are more valuable textbooks than I could include here, and omission does not signify condemnation. In the category of handbooks, for example, formats and contents are so similar that the choices were almost arbitrary.

II. BOOKS ABOUT WRITING AND TEACHING

In an article called "The Winds of Change: Thomas Kuhn and the Revolution in the Teaching of Writing," Maxine Hairston suggested in 1982 that our profession was in the midst of a "paradigm shift" analogous to the radical transformation in physics and astronomy that Thomas Kuhn described in *The Structure of Scientific Revolutions*. The traditional paradigm for teaching writing, of course, dictated concern with finished products; the new, emerging paradigm, in the most simple terms, attends to the writing process. At the vanguard of this revolution, Hairston contends, are the authors of new textbooks, teaching guides, and professional articles, whose enlightenment will gradually filter down to the benighted masses of composition teachers who still employ archaic methods because they are too busy teaching to attend conferences and read professional journals.

On this last point, Hairston is at least partly correct, though she underestimates both the ingenuity and the diversity of writing teachers who invent their own courses and methods for their own students, without benefit of revolutionary ideology. Even so, all of us can benefit from fresh ideas and communication with other teachers, and few of us who teach even moderate course loads can find time to keep in touch with more than a small fraction of the recent literature, in books and in journals, addressed to writing instructors. In this section, therefore, I have listed some of the most valuable books about composition and teaching, presented in two categories. The first includes books on the theory and practice of writing instruction. Several of these guides to teaching attempt to synthesize and implement recent scholarship in the field. In the second part I have listed collections of some of the most important articles from professional journals, including relevant work in fields such as cognitive psychology, linguistics, sociology, and education. Books in both categories often include extensive bibliographies for further reference.

In surveying this literature I found little evidence of an emerging "paradigm" beyond the obligatory incantation of a few stock phrases. A new set of platitudes in the service of wildly conflicting theories and methods was not, I suspect, what Thomas Kuhn had in mind. Nor am I convinced that we should look forward to a new paradigm, a new orthodoxy and "normal" mode of teaching writing, even if one does acquire substance, consistency, and prescriptive authority. The value of the material cited below lies in its diversity, particularly evident in the practical advice about preparing assignments, responding to student writing, dealing with error, teaching the analysis of style, and other work in the classroom. While it would be difficult now to find a single author who would dare to deny the importance of the writing process or revision, it would be equally difficult to find a specific method, in the books cited below, that is not contradicted by another. And while those who wish to develop the profession into an academic discipline must find this virtual chaos in the ranks discouraging, it provides an exciting and inexhaustible supply of ideas for individual teachers.

A. Guides to Teaching Writing

BERTHOFF, ANN. *The Making of Meaning: Metaphors, Models, and Maxims For Writing Teachers*. Montclair, N.J.: Boynton / Cook, 1981.

In this collection of her own essays and passages from other writers, Ann Berthoff presents an engaging philosophy for teaching writing, synthesized from the work of other philosophers, writers, and teachers (such as I. A. Richards, Suzanne Langer, Paulo Freire, Sylvia Ashton-Warner, Leo Tolstoy, and William James.) The principles of Berthoff's philosophy do not differ dramatically from those one will find in other discussions of modern rhetoric. She advises us to teach writing as a process and as a way of knowing rather than as a set of skills and forms. She suggests that we "reclaim the imagination" and recognize that writing instruction is "a matter chiefly of teaching critical thinking." Like most theorists, Berthoff offers little direct advice about the practice of teaching.

Yet this is among the most attractive and rewarding of theoretical books for teachers, partly because Berthoff recognizes that teachers must reinvent theory in the classroom. She is very critical of theorists and research specialists who view the writing instructor as the footsoldier of the profession, who should follow orders from above, and of authors and teachers who use the principles of modern rhetoric to assert prescriptive authority. Berthoff's viewpoint is rich and complex, and it will introduce her readers to other work of great significance to the profession.

COLES, WILLIAM, JR. *The Plural I—The Teaching of Writing*. New York: Holt, Rinehart and Winston, 1978.

This is a narrative account of an English class in which Coles attempts to break through the dead patterns of conventional response and teach his students to write with voices of their own, with recognition that writing can be a process of exploration beyond the confines of "Themewriting."

Few of you will choose his approach on the whole, but the book raises important questions about what we are doing when we teach writing and what students are doing when they write papers for us. *The Plural I* will be especially useful for those of you who feel increasing distance from your students, or see increasing formality and stiffness in their writing.

DONOVAN, TIMOTHY, AND BEN MCCLELLAND, EDS. *Eight Approaches to Teaching Writing*. Urbana: NCTE, 1980.

Beginning with an excellent essay by Donald Murray, "Writing as Process: How Writing Finds Its Own Meaning," the chapters in this volume describe most of the general approaches to teaching composition used at the college level. The titles are for the most part self-explanatory: "The Prose Models Approach: Using Products in the Process"; "The Experiential Approach"; "The Rhetorical Approach: Stages of Writing and Strategies for Writers"; "The Epistemic Approach" (teaching writing as a "means of knowing," a way of developing a new understanding of a subject); "Basic Writing" (teaching weak writers); "The Writing Conference"; and "Writing in the Total Curriculum: A Program for Cross-Disciplinary Cooperation."

ELBOW, PETER. *Writing Without Teachers.* New York: Oxford Univ. Press, 1973.

The title seems naive in undergraduate education, but the techniques Elbow describes can be useful in any writing class. This book advocates "freewriting": exercises in spontaneous, continuous writing that can generate ideas and help students overcome some types of writing blocks. This was one of the first of the books concerned primarily with the writing process (with the ways in which people actually think and act when they write) rather than the final product, and one of the first to admit that this process is extremely messy.

IRMSCHER, WILLIAM F. *Teaching Expository Writing.* New York: Holt, Rinehart and Winston, 1979.

Irmscher presents concise, honest, and useful advice, especially valuable for inexperienced teachers. The book contains general discussion of teaching and writing, along with sections on course planning, assignments, ways of generating material, organization, diction, mechanics, style, and the evaluation of student writing.

Teaching Expository Writing is so concise that you could easily read through it in an evening, and the experience would resemble a long, relaxed conversation with an extremely amiable, experienced teacher. The most valuable chapters are those (the first five especially) in which Irmscher writes directly from his own experience, for in these passages he often makes informal observations about writing and teaching that represent wisdom and insight. Irmscher knows that writing and teaching writing cannot be schematized; his book is least valuable, then, when he forgets this and presents lists, charts, and outlines for teaching.

JUDY, STEPHEN, AND SUSAN JUDY. *An Introduction to the Teaching of Writing.* New York: Wiley, 1981.

This book is a brief guide to course design, teaching methods, and evaluation of student writing, particularly useful for inexperienced teachers or those who need to reassess their methods.

The authors begin by surveying points of general agreement and conflict among current approaches. Following chapters discuss methods of teaching the composing process, assignments and exercises, interdisciplinary writing, revising and editing (with emphasis on peer editing and discussion of student writing), questions of audience, general course designs, and the assessment and evaluation of student writing. These chapters are too brief to cover their subjects in depth, but they will suggest lots of ideas for teaching that you can develop and apply in your own fashion.

KLAUS, CARL, AND NANCY JONES, EDS. *Courses for Change in Writing: A Selection from the NEH Iowa Institute.* Montclair, N.J.: Boynton / Cook, 1984.

Courses for Change might serve as an antidote to course manuals and teaching guides that offer generic models for teaching all students at all institutions. This selection of 16 course plans developed at the Institute on Writing at the University of Iowa reminds us of the extraordinary diversity among student writers, teaching styles, theories of composition, colleges, and curricula in which writing instruction occurs. *Courses for Change* includes course plans for "basic writers" and advanced students at a wide variety of institutions (liberal arts colleges, technical colleges, the U. S. Air Force Academy . . .). Subject areas include literature, regional studies, history, psychology, linguistics, problem-solving, and personal experience.

Because each course description is limited to a brief explanation and a sequence of assignments, *Courses for Change* won't tell you much about classroom strategies and responding to student writing, but it contains a wealth of ideas for assignments and course design. In this respect it resembles a good cookbook that an imaginative chef can plunder for ideas. The 16 course plans are followed by a series of brief essays on teacher training and staff workshops, especially for writing across the curriculum.

KNOBLAUCH, C. H., AND LIL BRANNON. *Rhetorical Traditions and the Teaching of Writing.* Montclair, N.J.: Boynton / Cook, 1984.

With a kind of energy and conviction available only to writers who have embraced a doctrine, Knoblauch and Brannon argue that writing teachers "must become philosophers in order to carry out the work of improving writing instruction by first improving the theoretical under-pinnings of instruction." To carry out this task, teachers must purge from their minds and methods all vestiges of classical philosophy and rhetoric in favor of thoroughly modern principles and approaches for teaching writing as a way of knowing, a "process of organizing expe-rience through symbolic action."

Unlike many of their colleagues, Knoblauch and Brannon make abso-lute distinctions between classical and modern rhetoric, and in this book they frequently attack classical revivalists, such as James Kinneavy, along with "closet traditionalists" who superficially promote modern teaching methods in taxonomic and prescriptive forms that betray their archaic assumptions about writing and writing instruction. Although *Rhetorical Traditions* itself is most often prescriptive and "directive" rather than "facilitative," it contains some penetrating discussion of the history and implications of philosophical choices we too often fail to examine when we design and teach writing courses. And while most of this book addresses theoretical issues in writing instruction, the last three chapters apply what the authors consider the "pure" principles of mod-ern rhetoric to the classroom. Even these chapters remain rather general and abstract, but they do provide some guidelines and examples for teaching strategies one should cultivate or avoid. Their ideal writing class (crudely simplified) is a student-centered workshop, an "authentic context for writing," in which students can engage in "verbal confron-tation with the world" rather than attempting to approximate their teacher's notion of an Ideal Text.

LANHAM, RICHARD. *Style—An Anti-Textbook*. New Haven: Yale Univ. Press, 1974.

" 'It is the thought that really matters.' This illusion runs deep in American society. It may account for the pervasive stylelessness of American life. It certainly explains the stylelessness of American prose."

Lanham is something of a renegade English teacher, and his book challenges many of the most widely accepted notions about what English instruction and good writing are supposed to be. Lanham specifically attacks the premise that the cardinal virtues of an elegant prose style are "clarity, plainness, and sincerity." He argues that this premise is a false antidote to the "prose problem" in America, because it suggests that language is simply a packaging of ideas, and because it denies all the pleasure, playfulness, and subtlety we discover, both as writers and as readers, in truly fine prose. "Style," Lanham says, "must be taught for and as what it is—a pleasure, a grace, a joy, a delight. Pleasure will not, it is true, teach the dumb to speak, the stupid to write, or the bad to practice goodness. But neither will anything else."

These statements apply to Lanham's book as well. It won't tell you in much detail how you should teach a writing course, but it will make you think carefully about the way you define good writing for your students.

LINDEMANN, ERIKA. *A Rhetoric for Writing Teachers.* Cambridge: Oxford Univ. Press, 1982.

Lindemann has written a general introduction to rhetoric that will be most valuable for beginning teachers or those who would benefit from a brief survey of developments in rhetoric and pedagogy over the past twenty years, including some relevant theory and research in cognitive psychology and linguistics.

In the first chapter Lindemann tells us that her book emphasizes practical implementation rather than theory, but only the last fifty pages directly discuss course design and assignments, and even these sections reduce work in the classroom to communication triangles and lists of suggestions. The rest of *A Rhetoric for Writing Teachers* moves rapidly and somewhat superficially through the history of rhetoric and the stages of the writing process, and leaves the problems of implementing these perspectives almost entirely to the teacher's imagination. The book is most useful as a quick way of learning about the major approaches to teaching writing now in vogue.

PONSOT, MARIE, AND ROSEMARY DEEN. *Beat Not the Poor Desk. Writing: What to Teach, How to Teach It, and Why.* Montclair, N.J.: Boynton / Cook, 1982.

Beat Not the Poor Desk tells us to abandon our roles as dictators and judges of writing skills and to shift our efforts "from the passivity of the student to the activity of the writer." In other words, we should stop talking about our own expectations and spend this time helping students to write, revise, comment, and evaluate on their own and as a class. In addition, we should always work with whole structures rather than addressing particular aspects of grammar and composition analytically.

Excellent advice, in general, supported with some interesting, detailed descriptions of activities in the classroom. These general principles and specific methods are sufficient to recommend the book, even though you might find its tone rather offensive and its prescriptions too narrow for your students and programs. In their enthusiasm and in their certainty that they have developed the Correct Approach, Ponsot and Deen often forget that their audience includes experienced teachers in a wide variety of institutions and curricula, and that their course plan covers a very narrow range of rhetorical situations, isolated from any particular context or discipline. Although they ban adverse criticism in the classroom and insist that writing practice can't be done wrong, they frequently criticize student writing styles and attitudes that they attribute to the influence of former, unenlightened teachers. They also make some very enigmatic, absolute assertions. Try this one: "In our experience and the experience of those we know, there is no essential difference between writing a poem and writing an essay, except, as we must often say, that writing a poem is easier, its conventions being so much clearer and more plentiful."

SHAUGHNESSY, MINA. *Errors and Expectations.* New York: Oxford Univ. Press, 1977.

Although it is based on Shaughnessy's work with extremely weak writers in open admissions at CCNY, this book has instructed and inspired teachers at every level. Shaughnessy argues and then demonstrates that most of the errors we find in student writing are not simply random flaws on the surface of prose, but patterned, and in their own ways logical, uses of language. If we want to help students to learn *from* their mistakes, therefore, we should attempt to understand these errors and not simply mark them.

With this objective, Shaughnessy analyzes and illustrates the most common difficulties that weak writers face with handwriting and punctuation, syntax, grammar and usage, vocabulary, and sequences of sentences. Although most of these errors are characteristic of "basic writers," whose grasp of standard English is considerably weaker than that of the average college freshman, you can learn a great deal from Shaughnessy's general approach and from her methods of analysis. Her introduction and the last two chapters, "Beyond the Sentence" and

"Expectations," describe a general approach to teaching composition that is remarkably intelligent, perceptive, and humane. Shaughnessy also writes beautifully.

WALVOORD, BARBARA E. FASSLER. *Helping Students Write Well: A Guide for Teachers in All Disciplines.* The Modern Language Association, 1982.

As the title of her book indicates, Walvoord addresses teachers who assign writing in a wide variety of courses other than English composition, and especially those who haven't found comfortable or effective methods for dealing with student writing in their courses. The first and longest section, "The Writing Process," offers advice on writing assignments, helping students through stages of the writing process, and responding to student writing. The second section is a brief guide to teaching mechanics—too brief, in fact, to use as a handbook, but valuable for the conceptual material on the sources and significance of various patterns of mechanical error most common in student writing.

Parts of this book will be useful and enlightening to teachers who haven't come to grips with the fact that they are, or should be, teaching writing in conjunction with history, psychology, or biology. For the most part, however, Walvoord explains concepts and methods that English teachers have developed for teaching writing in English composition courses, without much attention to the diverse rhetorical and pedagogical problems that teachers and students face in other disciplines. This common weakness in literature on writing across the curriculum tends to enforce rather than diminish the separation between writing instruction and other academic endeavors. Because Walvoord largely ignores these rhetorical variations in writing across the curriculum, yet writes in a didactic style, *Helping Students Write Well* is a how-to-do-it manual without a clear sense of what "it" might actually be.

B. Collections of Articles on Teaching and Composition

COOPER, CHARLES, AND LEE ODELL, EDS. *Research on Composing.* Urbana, Ill.: NCTE, 1978.

This is a collection of essays on various aspects of the composing process and various types of composition, some directly relevant to teaching writing and some not. The first three chapters serve as an introduction to current (or almost current) theory and research on composition and its departure from traditional rhetoric. "Some Implications of Cognitive-Developmental Psychology" explores the relevance of theory in this field (particularly that of Piaget and his followers) to our understanding of the composing process. Janet Emig's essay, "Hand, Eye, Brain: Some 'Basics' in the Writing Process," explains the implications and coordination of physical, visual, and cognitive activity in writing. This is a particularly interesting article, and one that students might enjoy. Donald Murray's essay, "Internal Revision: A Process of Discovery," emphasizes the importance of substantial revision, especially as a process of rethinking a subject. The essay concludes with a long series of quotations in which established writers describe the sense of mystery and discovery at the heart of their work.

GEBHARDT, RICHARD, ED. *Composition and Its Teaching: Articles from* College Composition and Communication *During the Editorship of Edward P. J. Corbett.* Ohio Council of Teachers of English Language Arts, 1979.

The 21 articles included in this anthology represent a wide range of statements about writing and teaching, both practical and theoretical. "Writing as a Mode of Learning," "Losing One's Mind," and "Write Before Writing" provide some insight into the composing process. Other essays discuss approaches to teaching rhetoric, Kenneth Burke's dramatic approach to composition, error analysis, student-teacher conferences, and skill levels in the composing process.

GRAVES, RICHARD L. *Rhetoric and Composition: A Sourcebook for Teachers and Writers.* 2nd ed. Montclair, N.J.: Boynton / Cook, 1984.

If you want to purchase one book to help you catch up on modern theory and research on composition and teaching, this would be a good choice. The 38 essays in this volume are among the most important published in major professional journals over the past fifteen years or so. If you can afford two books for this purpose you might add Gary Tate's sourcebook (listed below), which contains more material on the practice of teaching. Some of the essays in *Rhetoric and Composition* are highly specialized, especially in the section on the sentence, but few of them address practical concerns in the classroom.

HORNER, WINIFRED BRYAN, ED. *Composition and Literature: Bridging the Gap*. Chicago: Univ. of Chicago Press, 1983.

The twelve essays in this volume followed discussions in the "Teaching of Writing Division" at the Modern Language Association meetings in 1980 and 1981. As the title suggests, the theme of this collection is the uneasy and ambiguous relationship between the study of literature and the teaching of composition in the university, and particularly within English departments. Most of the authors represented in this volume (Richard Lanham, Wayne Booth, Elaine Maimon, Frederick Crews, Nancy Comley, Edward Corbett, et al.) are major theorists and authors of composition textbooks, and most of them suggest reconciliations between literature and composition—within the English department, in the classroom, or simply in theory.

These essays will be most interesting for instructors who are teaching literature courses, and for graduate students who are being trained as specialists in literature but expect to spend most of their time teaching composition. Elaine Maimon's "Maps and Genres," Walter Ong's "Literacy and Orality in Our Times," and E. D. Hirsch's "Reading, Writing, and Cultural Literacy" address broader concerns about the uses of language and the teaching of composition within the university as a whole.

OHMANN, RICHARD, AND W. B. COLEY, EDS. *Ideas for English 101— Teaching Writing in College*. Urbana, Ill.: NCTE, 1975.

A collection of 23 articles on course design and classroom strategies from various issues of *College English*, 1964–1975—a decade of innovation and of dissatisfaction with traditional composition classes.

Essays in the first half of the book describe various approaches to teaching freshman writing (e.g., as communication in the open classroom, and through collaborative learning). Essays in the second section discuss "tactics" for teaching writing. The section begins with two essays on invention, the more interesting by Ross Winterowd. "Teaching Relationships" (as opposed to absolutes), "The Circle of Implication," and "Teaching Without Judging" are also worth reading. "Teaching Freshman Comp to New York Cops" is an engaging period piece.

STOCK, PATRICIA, ED. *fforum: Essays on Theory and Practice in the Teaching of Writing*. Montclair, N.J.: Boynton / Cook, 1983.

In this volume Patricia Stock has collected 50 essays, revised versions of articles that originally appeared in *fforum,* the newsletter of the English Composition Board at the University of Michigan. These essays cover a broader range of subjects than the title of the collection suggests and depart in several directions beyond the core of literature addressed to college writing teachers. The five sections of the book include discussions of literacy and language acquisition; the relationship between speech, reading, and writing; dialects; and the uses of language in various professions and disciplines, in addition to essays more directly focused on writing in the college composition class. Several essays concern writing across the curriculum, in Britain and the United States.

TATE, GARY, AND EDWARD CORBETT, EDS. *The Writing Teacher's Sourcebook.* New York: Oxford Univ. Press, 1981.

Thirty-two articles on the theory and practice of teaching composition, by leading authorities on writing instruction.

Following four general discussions of literacy and English instruction, the essays in this collection are presented in two categories: "Theory" and "Practice." The most valuable essay in the first category, I believe, is Janet Emig's "Writing as a Mode of Learning." Essays on "Practice" cover the use of rhetorical invention, planning assignments, "Seeing Students As Writers," problems of teaching grammar and addressing errors, paragraph development, coherence, style, and sentence combining. The subsections of the *Sourcebook* are supplemented with bibliographies.

III. TEXTBOOKS

These are books you might consider adopting as writing texts for your courses, to help you teach writing in conjunction with your own assignments and course material, and to give students access, while they are writing, to clear, reliable information about the structure of the language. You can use these books as background references for teaching: to refresh your memory of terms and constructions or to help you discuss and analyze writing in class.

All of the books I have included are designed for students at intermediate to advanced levels, appropriate for college-level writing courses, including those offered in high schools, but they differ radically in design and function. To provide you with a guide to the broadest range of variation, I have sorted these writing texts into six categories: handbooks, rhetoric-handbooks, rhetorics, books designed for writing across the curriculum, style manuals, and readers. Within these categories I will describe further variations and the qualities of specific texts, to the extent that I can do so in brief comments. To be certain that a book meets your needs, of course, you will have to examine it carefully and consider its potential value in your course.

A. Handbooks

The textbooks listed in this category are primarily handbooks of grammar, sentence structure, punctuation, and usage; they include little or no discussion of composition. They are most appropriate, therefore, if you plan to teach composition on your own and simply need a reference for handling errors and constructions. For a more concise teaching guide to patterns of error and structure most common in freshman writing, consult Chapter 7, "Improving Sentences."

Your students will need to review the basic structure of the language to varying degrees, but you shouldn't have to spend hours of class time defining clauses, parts of speech, and sentence types, or explaining rules of pronoun usage and punctuation that half your students already know, or do not need to know because they use the language correctly. A good handbook, used as a required text, will help you shift most of the burden of review from your shoulders to your students' if you refer them to specific sections. They will not tend to use it on their own. A good handbook will also allow you to distribute this burden according to the individual needs of your students. I am not suggesting, however, that a handbook will eliminate the relevance of pronoun usage or punctuation when you discuss writing in class, since the basic elements of language remain important in the most subtle variations of tone and style. But if you assign the appropriate section of a handbook in advance, you can discuss the ways in which passive and active constructions, for example, affect the clarity, tone, and emphasis of a passage without having to spend the first half of the class teaching students to identify passive and active verb forms.

All of the handbooks listed below include information about writing research papers, a sample research paper, and formats for documentation. Although they often include brief discussions of composition, especially at the level of the paragraph, these are insufficient to provide substantial instruction. Most of all, these books need to be clear and easy to use. I have picked out five of the best ones, and because they are so similar in design I will simply list them.

CREWS, FREDERICK, AND SANDRA SCHOR. *The Borzoi Handbook for Writers*. New York: Knopf, 1985.

ELSBREE, LANGDON, et al. *The Health Handbook of Composition*. 11th ed. Lexington, Mass.: D. C. Heath, 1986.

GEFVERT, CONSTANCE J. *The Confident Writer—A Norton Handbook*. New York: Norton, 1985.

HODGES, JOHN C., AND MARY E. WHITTEN. *Harbrace College Handbook*. 10th ed. New York: Harcourt Brace Jovanovich, 1986.

KRISZNER, LAURIE, AND STEPHEN MANDELL. *The Holt Handbook*. New York: Holt, Rinehart and Winston, 1986.

LEGGETT, GLEN, et al. *Prentice-Hall Handbook for Writers*. 9th ed. Englewood Cliffs, N.J.: Prentice Hall, 1985.

B. Rhetoric-Handbooks

Some of these textbooks are also called "handbooks" or "guides to writing" at the college level, but they cover both composition and the structure of the language, usually in approximately equal proportions. The handbook sections of the books listed below are not always as thorough as the straight handbooks, and they tend to present discussions of the structure of the language and lists of the most crucial points of grammar and usage rather than elaborate, schematic indices to English. In most cases, however, these handbook sections are adequate for the needs of college and advanced high school students, and I will indicate those that are the most thorough.

If you choose a text of this type, you should look carefully at the chapters on composition, which vary a great deal in tone and approach from one book to another. Some of these books are based on traditional rhetoric, and present a taxonomy of forms and strategies as models for composition. Others emphasize the writing process with little or no attention to modes for discourse. A few texts attempt to combine these approaches. Although the newest editions of these guides to college writing have almost routinely added or expanded sections on the writing process, these are often hastily and awkwardly superimposed upon the material carried over from older editions. I will describe these approaches briefly under each reference, but their usefulness will vary from one writing course to another. If most of the assignments in your course require arguments, for example, large sections of the books based on modes of discourse will be of very limited value to your students, at least in the context of your course. An appropriate text will continually support your teaching and help students complete your assignments successfully.

AXELROD, RISE B., AND CHARLES R. COOPER. *The St. Martin's Guide to Writing*. New York: St. Martin's, 1985.

This first edition guide to writing employs the "New Rhetoric" in an interesting and unique format. Following an introductory chapter on invention and the writing process, the book is divided into four parts. Part One, "Writing Activities," supplies several model essays for each of nine types of prose (including varieties of autobiographical writing, reports, proposals, evaluations, and literary criticism), followed by discussion of this type of writing, strategies for invention, and a sample of the way a particular student developed an essay of this type from first thoughts to finished product. Part Two, "Writing Strategies," provides a more traditional discussion of modes of discourse (description, narration, and so on). Part Three covers writing based on research, with an emphasis on invention found throughout this textbook, and Part Four contains a "Handbook" of grammar, usage, style, and mechanics, roughly 100 pages long and generally adequate for college classes.

Because Part One is by far the longest section and contains 38 short, professional essays in addition to samples of student writing, *The St. Martin's Guide* attempts more than other listings in this section to provide a comprehensive course plan. Although the organization based on specific forms of the essay seems excessively categorical, examples of the writing process in student work do a great deal to compensate for this excessive formality and might be very useful in the classroom.

A short edition of *The St. Martin's Guide* is also available, without the handbook section, and in paperback.

CREWS, FREDERICK. *The Random House Handbook.* 4th ed. New York: Random House, 1984.

Crews has tried to provide an all-purpose college writing text, with solid, balanced sections on composition, style, documentation, grammar, and usage. The six sections of this handbook cover modes of discourse; the composing process and revision; organization and style; grammar, usage, and mechanics; research and documentation; and (very briefly) business writing.

The Random House Handbook has been widely used in college classes because it is thorough, clear, direct, and supported with excellent examples and exercises. Some teachers dislike Crews's tone, which is brisk and often imperative ("Say no more than you mean." "Support your most important assertions."), but the new edition seems to be more friendly.

HEFFERNAN, JAMES, AND JOHN LINCOLN. *Writing—A College Handbook.* 2nd ed. New York: Norton, 1986.

Writing is extremely clear, reliable, and easy to use as a general reference for college writing. The format is superb. At least half of the book, again, covers grammar, usage, documentation, punctuation, and sentence structure, and these sections strike just the right balance between schematic representation and discussion of the structure of English. Heffernan and Lincoln address their readers as intelligent adults, in a tone that is direct and dignified. Discussion of the composing process has been expanded in the new edition to five chapters on prewriting, freewriting, organization, revision, and editing—all somewhat prescriptive and formal. These chapters, and the two that follow on modes of discourse, emphasize logic, patterns, and strategy. They encourage awareness of the structural, rather than generative, features of composition.

Writing is probably the easiest general handbook for students to use on their own, if you refer them to specific sections.

IRMSCHER, WILLIAM. *The Holt Guide to English.* 3rd ed. New York: Holt, Rinehart and Winston, 1981.

The Holt Guide is in its own way as thorough as the *Random House Handbook* and other general texts in this section, but it differs substantially in tone, content, and approach—especially in the sections on composition. About half of the book is devoted to grammar, sentence structure, usage, punctuation, and documentation.

Irmscher addresses the reader in a relaxed, almost conversational tone, and he discusses writing and methods for producing good writing in full passages of clear, sensible explanation. Influenced by new approaches to rhetoric and the composing process, he emphasizes the purposes of writing and varieties of writer-audience relationships in different types of discourse. In the chapter called "Generating a Topic," he uses Kenneth Burke's "pentad"—action, agent, scene, means, purpose—as a set of questions for developing an idea and provides an interesting example of the use of this heuristic. Irmscher also includes an extensive, effective chapter on revision and proofreading, and approximately 100 pages on special problems in writing about literature. This book would be an excellent choice, therefore, as a general writing text for a literature course.

McCRIMMON, JAMES. *Writing with a Purpose.* 8th ed. Revised by Joseph Trimmer and Nancy Sommers. Boston: Houghton Mifflin, 1984.

Writing with a Purpose is one of the most popular textbooks for general college composition classes, but you should note that it is primarily a course plan rather than a reference book. In other words, to make substantial use of the book you will have to teach with it: assign and discuss chapters in conjunction with your own writing assignments. The "Handbook" section at the end (about one-fifth of the book) briefly covers the areas of grammar and usage that college students most often need to review, but it will not meet the needs of weak writers or nonnative speakers of English. *Writing with a Purpose* is primarily a rhetoric, with a short handbook attached.

McCrimmon views writing as purposeful communication; he is concerned with the aims of the essay and with the relationship between writer and audience, and he stresses the implications of these concerns at different stages of the writing process. Earlier editions reduced this process to a linear sequence of three stages—prewriting, writing, and rewriting—but in the 1984 edition Trimmer and Sommers reorganized the book, adding a 150-page section that attempts to coordinate

McCrimmon's emphasis on purpose with new perspectives in composition theory.

The style of *Writing with a Purpose* is discursive rather than schematic (i.e., McCrimmon discusses stages and strategies, presenting examples and exercises along the way). If you choose to assign this textbook for your class you should share McCrimmon's view of writing as a process of determining and fulfilling particular aims in communication.

MEMERING, DEAN, AND FRANK O'HARE. *The Writer's Work: Guide to Effective Composition.* 2nd ed. Englewood Cliffs, N.J.: Prentice-Hall, 1984.

The Writer's Work departs more radically than most of the other texts listed in this section from the forms and standards of traditional rhetoric, and is devoted instead (at least in the half of the book called "Writing") "to the writing process and invention procedures that will help you find your own ideas." The first half of *The Writer's Work* discusses the composing process with reference to personal writing, exposition, and "reasoned writing," with a concluding section on writing with sources. Like McCrimmon's book, this is designed as a course text and must be used as one. It addresses the student in the second person with such familiarity and immediacy, in fact, that you might feel you are being pushed out of the classroom altogether.

The second half of the book is called "Skills" and includes general information on sentences, paragraphing, grammar, and usage. One special strength of *The Writer's Work* is the material on sentence combining. These are the exercises O'Hare developed for teaching students to write more effective and complex sentences without formal grammar instruction (discussed at greater length in Section IV. B. of the present chapter).

C. Rhetorics

The books in this category focus almost entirely on composition, and although they usually include chapters on word choice and sentence structure (as aspects of "style"), they contain little or no material on grammar, punctuation, and usage. Their main objective, in other words, is to teach students standards and methods for composing good essays, but their approaches to this task vary radically in tone, theory, and design.

If you consider using a composition text as a required book for your writing class, the most common limitation is that their authors assume too much and know too little about your course, your students, and your approach to teaching. Some rhetorics are more adaptable than others in this respect, because they tend to discuss composition in general, without reference to specific course designs and sequences of assignments. At the opposite extreme, many rhetorics are designed for teachers who would like to buy a pre-packaged writing course, complete with short readings, assignments, discussion questions, and exercises. Because their authors really want to teach the course for you, they address your students directly, in tones often borrowed from scoutmasters, newscasters, used car salesmen, bankers, drill sergeants, or anxious parents. Although this type of rhetoric often contains excellent ideas for teaching composition, it will usually interfere with the real work of teaching writing, which is based on perceptions of individual students, specific compositions, and specific uses of language. For this reason I have listed the books that seem the most flexible and the least bossy, since the purpose of this chapter, and of our book in general, is to help you develop your own course designs and teaching methods—not to encourage you to buy someone else's. Some of these rhetorics might be useful as references for teaching: as sources of ideas, distinctions, and methods for course planning, rather than as required texts.

To varying degrees, however, all rhetorics prescribe particular course designs and approaches to teaching. Although the teaching methods they suggest differ a great deal, virtually all of the books I have listed in Part C are designed for use in general English composition classes, from high school Advanced Placement courses to advanced college courses in expository writing. In Part D, I have included some of the textbooks that have appeared with increasing frequency over the past three years or so for writing courses that attempt to span the college curriculum and avoid the traditional American inclination to view writing instruction as an exclusive function of the English Department.

BROOKS, CLEANTH, AND ROBERT PENN WARREN. *Modern Rhetoric.* 4th ed. New York: Harcourt Brace Jovanovich, 1979.

Modern Rhetoric is probably the most solid and useful of the traditional rhetorics: those concerned primarily with products and their formal variations. Brooks and Warren present this view of discourse with a pervasive sense of order and logic. Their book is divided into three main sections: "Forms of Discourse" (with descriptions and examples of exposition, persuasion, argument, description, and narration); "Special Problems of Discourse" (including chapters on paragraphs, sentences, diction, metaphor, and tone); and "Research and Critical Papers." The book concludes with an excellent appendix on deductive reasoning. In general, this is an excellent text for teaching logic in composition.

CORDER, JIM. *Contemporary Writing: Process and Practice.* 2nd ed. Glenview, Ill.: Scott, Foresman, 1983.

Contemporary Writing is a process-oriented rhetoric divided into three mains sections. The first section, "The Process of Writing," contains separate chapters on finding, exploring, and "claiming" a subject for composition and then discusses the "communication triangle" of author, subject, and audience. Chapters six through eleven in this first section, which constitutes more than half of the book, cover organization and development, diction, sentence structure, paragraphs, and "An Interlude on Style" (simply an illustration of several styles, without substantial comment.)

"Occasions and Choices," the second section, emphasizes the context of writing of several general types: letters, reports, arguments, and critical writing.

"Reference Materials for Writing" presents an extremely brief, virtually useless discussion of research writing and concludes with an equally brief "Guide to Grammar, Punctuation, and Usage," insufficient for students who need substantial review.

Contemporary Writing is most valuable, then, as a guide to the writing process and to considerations of audience, viewpoint, and development.

HAIRSTON, MAXINE. *Successful Writing: A Rhetoric for Advanced Composition.* 2nd ed. New York: Norton, 1986.

"Successful Writing," the author notes in her preface, "is a text for students who have mastered the basic writing skills and are now ready and motivated to learn more about the writing process."

Hairston's book is "advanced" in the sense that it aims for thoroughly competent writing at the college level and addresses problems of organization, reasoning, and style in a thoroughly mature tone. Hairston has also written a larger rhetoric, but the conciseness of *Successful Writing* (238 pages) might recommend it as a companion text for teachers who want to avoid the long, often tedious, discussions of composition in more comprehensive textbooks.

Hairston is a staunch advocate of the new rhetoric, and she might have written this book as an alternative to Brooks and Warren's *Modern Rhetoric,* which is equally concise. Rather than presenting forms of the essay, in other words, she discusses the considerations and processes through which one arrives at various patterns of organization, as matters of choice, strategy, and awareness of audience. Some sections are so brief that they are little more than bits of good advice. One of these sections provides rare and useful guidelines for avoiding sexist language.

HORTON, SUSAN. *Thinking Through Writing.* Baltimore: Johns Hopkins Univ. Press, 1982.

"Jean-Paul Sartre gave up writing entirely when his left eye was hemorrhaging (his right eye had been bad from birth), because, he said, 'I cannot see what I write.' For him, writing was a way of seeing what he was thinking. I think writing works this way for everyone. . . ."

Dozens of textbook writers now tell students that writing is a complicated process that involves thinking in particular ways, but Horton comes closer than any other author I have read to a clear and useful description of the ways in which writers think while they write. Horton is concerned with what she calls "the real basics": not grammar, but the ways in which writing both represents and informs thought—"what writing is and is for, how you get an idea, and how and why each idea demands its own kind of organization, how ideas turn into essays, and, even more basic . . . how your mind forms ideas in the first place."

To make students aware of these "real basics," Horton focuses upon concepts, their formation, and their relation to language. Almost the entire book, therefore, concerns the stages of writing prior to the final draft—stages of thinking and rethinking, writing, reading, and rewriting.

The central purpose of this genuinely innovative textbook is to help students think for themselves as writers, and for this reason *Thinking Through Writing* could be an excellent companion text for reading and writing in any field.

WINTEROWD, W. ROSS. *The Contemporary Writer.* 2nd ed. New York: Harcourt Brace Jovanovich, 1981.

Winterowd states in his preface that *The Contemporary Writer* is a "real book," rather than simply a reference book for writing; in other words, one should be able to read it with pleasure and with a sense of intellectual engagement, because it is conceptually rich and thoroughly composed and illustrated.

I tend to agree, but I'm not sure I could convince my freshman students, who are even less inclined than I am to read rhetorics for pleasure, and who want very much to believe that writing can be orderly and efficient. Because Winterowd avoids simple prescriptions and writes with a full appreciation for the richness and complexity of the language, *The Contemporary Writer* is probably the longest rhetoric on the market. His discussions of invention strategies, outlining, diction, sentence structure, and writing about literature are more thorough, therefore, than those in most rhetorics, and they rely more explicitly on contemporary theory in rhetoric and linguistics. As a consequence, Winterowd's book is a particularly rich source of ideas and information for teaching, but might be too extensive to use as a textbook in a course that involves other reading.

D. Books for Writing and Reading Across the Curriculum

A student from Trinidad told me recently that when she is given multiple choice and short answer examinations in her social science courses she requests essay examinations or papers instead, on the grounds that so-called "objective" tests cannot adequately measure her understanding of the subject. Her attitude toward writing and education captures the spirit and part of the history of recent interest in "writing across the curriculum" in American education. Before she came to the United States this student was educated in British schools, where she wrote examination papers even in her science classes and became accustomed to the premise that knowledge acquired through language can be measured only through language. Writing and speech were already more thoroughly integrated into British education than they were (and are) in

America when, around 1970, James Britton and Douglas Barnes advocated greater attention in British schools to the relation between *Language and Learning,* the title of Britton's book on the subject. Recent interest in interdisciplinary language instruction derives, to a great extent, from these developments in England.

In America, attention to writing is comparatively isolated as the province of the English class and English Department, where students are supposed to learn and practice the language skills they might have to apply in earnest in other courses and in their professions. Because American educators tend to view language simply as a vehicle for knowledge (and an unreliable vehicle among growing numbers of weak writers), interdisciplinary writing instruction has taken root very slowly, and writing practice has even declined in many disciplines. Due in part to the growing influence of modern rhetoric and its recognition that "writing is a way of knowing," however, interdisciplinary writing programs and writing classes have become more popular, and with them new textbooks for writing across the curriculum.

In some respects almost all rhetorics and readers are interdisciplinary, simply because the English composition class has no subject matter of its own unless it focuses on literature or selects, more or less arbitrarily, some other topic. Most readers, therefore, include essays by scholars in a variety of fields, along with the work of journalists, politicians, novelists, poets, and others. But these essays are chosen and arranged as examples of particular rhetorical forms, styles, or broad ranges of content that English teachers use to make their own distinctions about writing—distinctions that bear little or no relation to differences among criteria for successful writing in other fields. Even when one of these essays happens to have been written by a psychologist, or a biologist, it will very rarely represent the literary traditions and constraints of that discipline, much less illuminate them. Instead, it will represent the narrow range of writing by psychologists or biologists that English teachers can appreciate as "good writing": the kind of writing that suggests that psychologists and biologists (or at least the "good writers" among them) are really humanists at heart.

Textbooks for writing across the curriculum attempt to make different kinds of distinctions with some of the same material, and often, I'm afraid, with the same effect. A full program for writing across the curriculum—one that distributes responsibility for writing instruction among departments and disciplines—does not need interdisciplinary rhetorics and readers, because the writing and reading in a particular course is already lodged in a particular discipline. (See Appendix 2, on strategies for teaching "Writing in the Non-Writing Class.") As a consequence, the interdisciplinary textbooks on the market are designed for the inter-disciplinary writing course, offered in the English Department or else-where, in which a single teacher or course staff attempts to illuminate variations in academic writing.

A challenging task, given the complexity of these variations among and within disciplines, and one that raises many difficult, but important questions. Are there general standards for "good writing" that apply to all disciplines within the university? Are there really sociological styles as opposed to anthropological or psychological ones, or, for that matter, social scientific styles distinct from humanistic ones? If there are, what are their foundations and how can we distinguish them?

Most of the books I have listed below do not attempt to answer these questions with much authority, and we should not expect them to do so, for an author and scholar of sufficient stature for this task would hold nothing less than the key to the entire universe of academic discourse. With readings organized according to broad categories of academic work or around specific topics, these books do illustrate for undergraduates that scholars in diverse fields address different problems, or look at the same problems from different angles. Many composition teachers will find this approach to language in undergraduate education an effective compromise between contradictory notions of academic writing: that the same standards for "good writing" apply to all disciplines, and that these standards vary altogether from one field and occasion to another.

BEHRENS, LAURENCE, AND LEONARD ROSEN. *Writing and Reading Across the Curriculum.* 2nd ed. Boston: Little, Brown, 1985.
This plump paperback consolidates most of the discussion of rhetoric into the first 120 pages, in the section called "How to Write Summaries, Syntheses, and Critiques." The authors illustrate the process for writing each of these three forms of the student essay by demonstrating responses to sample readings. The rest of the book (another 500 pages) is "An Anthology of Readings," organized not by field but around eight specific topics: morality and the movies, the business of college sports, artificial intelligence, the "Cinderella" tale (its versions and interpretation), obedience to authority, death and dying, nuclear war, and Orwell's *Animal Farm*. Under each topic the authors present sev-

eral essays, along with review and discussion questions, writing suggestions, possible research topics, and a bibliography for further reading. The section on "Obedience to Authority," for example, begins with a description of the Milgram experiments on obedience and disobedience, followed by exchanges between Milgram and other psychologists, an essay on responsibility and obedience in the military, and two opposing views of civil disobedience.

This topical approach encourages sustained discussion, interpretation, and comparison, in the classroom and in student writing, because it establishes a frame of reference that most collections of readings fail to provide. "Death and Dying" might not be a topic of choice for college freshmen, but there are so many essays and additional references for each topic that one could easily organize an entire course around two or three of them. Behrens and Rosen provide excellent material for teaching and further innovation without dictating a course plan.

BECKER, HOWARD. *Writing for Social Scientists: How to Start and Finish Your Thesis, Book, or Article.* Chicago: Univ. of Chicago Press, 1986.

As a professor of sociology at Northwestern University, Howard Becker wrote this remarkable little book primarily for graduate students in the social sciences, but his advice and his descriptions of the composing process are so unusual, honest, and valuable that I can imagine using his book even in a freshman course on writing across the curriculum, or on social scientific prose. Undergraduates look ahead, first of all, to the challenges of graduate school or professional life, and I think they would be very interested in the struggles with language that occur in the process of writing theses, books, and journal articles. Second, large sections of this book discuss and attempt to alleviate fear of writing and revising academic prose—fear among graduate students and scholars that begins, I believe, in the subjection to texts, disciplines, and language that students feel even in secondary schools, and certainly in their first years of college.

Becker also brings a unique combination of perspectives to this book. He is an excellent writer and editor who has written extensively in his field and thought carefully about uses of language in the social sciences; as a sociologist he has studied student and academic life; he has also read extensively through the literature on modern rhetoric and applied these concepts to his own writing courses. In this book he conveys these perspectives by documenting his own experiences and development as a writer, and those of his students. One chapter, "Risk," is written by a former student, Pamela Richards, who explains the sources of her fear of writing and revising in the intensely competitive context of the university.

COMLEY, NANCY R., et al. *Fields of Writing: Readings Across the Disciplines.* 2nd ed. New York: St. Martin's, 1987.

This reader contains short essays, articles, and excerpts organized according to four rhetorical categories—Reporting, Explaining, Arguing, and Reflecting—and according to three curriculum areas: Arts and Humanities, Social Sciences and Public Affairs, and Sciences and Technologies.

Fields of Writing is an excellent source for model essays in a wide variety of styles and on a wide variety of subjects, though most of the samples the authors have chosen do not really represent academic writing in sociology, for example, or biology, but humanistic perspectives on sociological or biological concerns. For the most part, these are the authors routinely cited as evidence that scientists and social scientists are occasionally good writers as well (e.g., Loren Eiseley, Margaret Mead, Lewis Thomas, Bruno Bettelheim, J. Robert Oppenheimer, and Stephen Jay Gould), to the extent that their work is appealing and intelligible to English teachers. All of these readings will be interesting and enjoyable for freshman writers, and suitable for almost any general composition class that requires a book of readings. Brief, almost negligible comments on "Reporting" or "Arguing" precede each major section of the book, and apart from these the sequence of readings is broken only by a few of the typical questions textbook authors insert after essays, to tell students they are supposed to be thinking.

GRINOLS, ANNE BRADSTREET. *Critical Thinking: Reading Across the Curriculum.* Ithaca: Cornell Univ. Press, 1984.

Anne Grinols developed *Critical Thinking* in conjunction with a very effective reading and study skills course that she teaches at Cornell, particularly for students who have difficulty coping with the volume and complexity of reading and writing assignments they encounter. Brief introductory comments addressed to the student explain strategies for analytical reading. The rest of the book is composed of 35 short essays, almost all of them by Cornell faculty, gathered into three categories:

Physical Sciences, Social Sciences, and Humanities. Comprehension questions and analysis questions follow each essay, and a page of comparative analysis questions follows each section.

Although *Critical Thinking* is designed for a reading course, analytical reading skills are such an essential foundation for writing in academic work that this book might work equally well in a composition class. If anything, the discussion of "Critical Reading and Learning in College" is too brief, considering its importance. You might find the essays too brief as well, but they do represent an unusually broad and authentic range of the subjects and styles students have to contend with in the university.

MAIMON, ELAINE, et al. *Readings in the Arts and Sciences.* Boston: Little, Brown, 1984.

The five authors of this book are professors of English, History, Biology, Psychology, and Philosophy who collaborated on a reader intended for writing courses that approach composition as an interdisciplinary activity. *Readings in the Arts and Sciences* can be used independently or as a companion text with the interdisciplinary rhetoric *Writing in the Arts and Sciences,* listed below.

Readings in the Arts and Sciences begins with an interesting chapter on the process through which the Declaration of Independence was actually composed, including all the major drafts and revisions. Subsequent chapters provide well-written essays and passages in many fields of the humanities, social sciences, and natural sciences, drawn from central books in these fields, textbooks, professional journals, and popular magazines. Brief discussion questions and exercises follow each article or essay. Many of the readings included in this volume are more technical and authentic representations of specialized prose styles than the readings in *Fields of Writing,* for example, but they are not too difficult or specialized for a freshman composition class.

MAIMON, ELAINE, et al. *Writing in the Arts and Sciences.* Cambridge, Mass.: Winthrop, 1981.

On theoretical foundations derived from the work of Mina Shaughnessy, James Kinneavy, and Kenneth Bruffee, Maimon and her colleagues in other disciplines designed this rhetoric to help teachers in English composition classes illuminate the varying rhetorical and stylistic demands of writing in academic fields. According to the authors, these are differences of perspective, audience, and literary behavior more than differences of subject matter.

The first section of the book covers invention, the writing process, and contexts for academic writing in a fashion similar to that of general process-oriented rhetorics. The next three sections discuss particular rhetorical problems, analytical approaches, and formal variations in the humanities, social sciences, and natural sciences respectively. Throughout these sections the authors emphasize the importance of revision and awareness of rhetorical variation; they illustrate these variations with numerous examples of specific writing tasks, student essays, collections of data, formats, graphs, and other representations of actual circumstances in which students compose. This is very much a student-oriented rhetoric, designed to help novice writers cope with the peculiar and diverse demands of writing in academic disciplines.

MILLER, ROBERT K. *The Informed Argument: A Multidisciplinary Reader and Guide*. New York: Harcourt Brace Jovanovich, 1986.

The "guide" sections of this textbook are confined to a brief discussion of argument at the beginning and a 40-page "Guide to Research and Documentation" at the end. For the most part, therefore, *The Informed Argument* is an interdisciplinary reader that one could use in many different ways—not just in a course on argument. Like Behrens and Rosen (listed above), Miller has organized readings according to topics rather than disciplines, and provides seven or eight essays on each of eight topics. Unfortunately, most of these are the standard "controversial issues" that students have been resorting to, for lack of more original ideas, since the seventh grade. I would not like to count, much less to read, all the student research papers on the subjects of gun control, capital punishment, censorship, animal rights, abortion, and nuclear power—six of the eight subject areas in this book.

E. Books on Style

In Chapter 6, "Understanding Prose," Fredric Bogel emphasizes the most fundamental reason for which considerations of style, in student writing and in readings, are crucial to writing instruction. With regard to prose, the term "style" is not, as most of your students will believe, equivalent to "fashion" in the clothing industry: a concern with appearances, packaging, and embellishment. Because style refers to the ways in which particular uses of language deliver particular meanings and effects to the reader, the examination of style extends to the heart of a text and its meaning. And because larger elements of a text are composed of smaller ones—the qualities of words and phrases, their arrangement in sentences, and the development of short passages—when you examine writing in detail you are looking at style, even if you call it something else. Concern with writing at this level is not just fussiness, but an affirmation of the importance and potential power of language itself.

Another, related reason for stylistic analysis is that responses to student writing consisting entirely of corrected errors and critical broadsides ("This paper is badly organized." "What is your thesis?") support students' suspicions that writing well is a matter of following procedures, avoiding errors, and, in general, meeting the narrow-minded demands of writing teachers. By contrast, close examination of the uses of language will teach students that writing is above all a matter of making meaningful choices—that a sentence is not merely right or wrong, but instead a complex of these meaningful choices that can be altered and rearranged with differing effects.

Almost every handbook and rhetoric contains chapters on style (under the headings of diction and phrasing, sentences, metaphor, wordiness, sound, etc.), but these often define style as embellishment or present a pathology of stylistic ailments. The rhetorics by Irmscher and Winterowd, listed above, represent two of the most useful and positive approaches. The references listed below are full volumes on style, though they interpret the term in radically different ways.

FOLLETT, WILSON. *Modern American Usage.* Edited and completed by Jacques Barzun. New York: Warner, 1966.
This is a dictionary of American usage, in its own way as useful to writers as a standard dictionary. It is also useful for teaching, especially for answering difficult questions of usage and determining why a specific word or phrase in a paper sounds wrong. Fowler's or Longman's usage dictionaries would serve the same purposes.

GRAVES, ROBERT, AND ALAN HODGE. *The Reader Over Your Shoulder.* 2nd ed. New York: Vintage, 1979.

"Our practice was to pick up every book or paper we found lying about and, whenever our reading pace was checked by some difficulty of expression, to note the cause. Eventually we formulated our principles after cataloguing the difficulties under forty-one general headings—twenty-five concerned with clarity of statement, and sixteen with grace of expression."

The result is more useful and enjoyable to read than you might expect. These "Principles" make up the core of the book, preceded by engaging essays on the development of English as a vernacular, its current condition, and its official abuse, and followed by some examples of the critical methods described above. The latter are in refreshing contrast to the usual examples of weak student writing, since the authors attack passages from T. S. Eliot, Bertrand Russell, G. B. Shaw, A. N. Whitehead, and various other scholars and British dignitaries. These critical passages would be fun to use in class.

LANHAM, RICHARD. *Analyzing Prose.* New York: Scribners, 1983.

"Every statement about style is, if we know how to interpret it, a statement about behavior. Thus the study of style is not a peripheral or cosmetic accompaniment to the exposition of self-standing ideas but a choreography of the whole dance of human consciousness, a dance in which practical purpose and information form but one part."

In his introduction to *Analyzing Prose,* Lanham advocates descriptive, rather than evaluative, approaches to prose analysis and argues that our emphasis on the values of "Clarity, Brevity, and Sincerity" has almost replaced descriptive appreciation of the extraordinary power, subtlety, variety, and complexity of English prose.

Following this introduction, then, Lanham applies descriptive analysis in a taxonomy of prose styles, illustrated with examples drawn from a wide variety of published sources, scholarly and popular. Five chapters describe contrasting prose styles in pairs: noun / verb, parataxis / hypotaxis, periodic / running, voiced / unvoiced, opaque / transparent. Other chapters cover visual considerations of style, persuasion, "high, middle, and low styles," and exhaustive methods of stylistic analysis, applied to a passage from Tom Wolfe and to the Gettysburg Address. In the final chapter, "Value Judgments," Lanham argues that descriptive analysis provides a matrix for informed evaluation of prose style, with recognition that specific styles work or fail to work within specific contexts.

Analyzing Prose is not designed as a freshman composition text, and Lanham's methods of descriptive analysis are in most respects inappropriate to the task of evaluating student writing. The general lesson Lanham presents, however, is that we should look at prose rather than through it, and that a genuine understanding of its qualities must result from detailed observation, not from the application of narrow preconceptions about good writing. This general lesson does apply to freshman writing instruction, and the analytical distinctions Lanham makes might allow you to recognize characteristics and qualities in student writing, and in readings, that you could not see before.

Lanham's own prose style makes his detailed analysis of texts engaging—for some readers infuriating—for his writing is always charged, it seems, with a peculiar mixture of anger and delight, with which he gleefully explodes myths wherever he finds them.

MARIUS, RICHARD. *A Writer's Companion*. New York: Knopf, 1985.

This brief, cheerful guide to writing contains short sections on the writing process, organization, and arguments, along with 15 pages on grammar and mechanics, but it is most valuable as a collection of rules and guidelines on usage and style, composed by an excellent writer who enjoys his work. Marius explains that he wrote *The Writer's Companion* "for advanced writers, and so it abounds with rules. Beginning writers should probably stay away from books about writing." Instead, he suggests, they should write constantly without worrying about rules until writing becomes a habit. Then they can turn to rules to improve what they have already learned to do.

With this advice, and his good-natured discussion of the way writers think and compose. Marius manages to present lists of rules and stylistic injunctions without conveying the moralistic illusion that they are prescriptions for good writing. The advice he offers on usage, diction, and sentence structure is particularly valuable for revision and editing, and although *The Writer's Companion* would be most appropriate for an advanced writing class one could also use it as a supplementary textbook in freshman composition, or in other courses that involve extensive writing. My favorite chapter, considering the misconceptions my students bring with them from previous writing classes, is called "False Rules and What Is True About Them."

STRUNK, WILLIAM AND E. B. WHITE. *The Elements of Style*. 3rd ed. New York: Macmillan, 1979.

The Elements of Style is especially popular at Cornell, its birthplace, where stacks of these tiny volumes sell like hotcakes at the Campus Store, and where faculty and students often announce with a glow of virtue that they have read it cover–to–cover and that it did them a world of good, as though it were the New Testament. My own view is that *The Elements of Style* demonstrates E. B. White's remarkable skill at drawing readers into compelling little myths about ordinary things. The myth in this case is that White, with the ghostly voice of William Strunk still ringing in his ears, miraculously condensed everything everyone needs to know about writing into 85 pages, available for the price of a plain pizza. We all wish it were true.

Setting the myth aside, if that is even possible, we have a little book of useful rules, terse and cranky in a charming way. If you assign it, your students will feel someone has finally taken their sloppy writing in hand—given it the good caning it deserves. Catching the spirit of Strunk's economy and righteousness, you can then use his numbering system to tell students which rules they have broken. They will know they are bad, but will always come back for more.

WILLIAMS, JOSEPH M. *Style: Ten Lessons in Clarity and Grace.* 2nd ed. Glenview, Ill.: Scott, Foresman, 1985.

"This is a short book based on a simple thesis: It's good to write clearly, and anyone can."

Williams attempts in this book to teach all writers (not only students) to revise and clarify their own prose, almost entirely at the level of individual sentences. He delivers this instruction in ten compact chapters that cover such categories as "The Grammar of Clarity" (avoiding excessive nominalization and dead verbs), wordiness, sprawling sentences, balance and metaphor, usage, and punctuation. These chapters are extensively subdivided according to specific problems and patterns, illustrated with thousands of sample sentences and occasional exercises.

Because it is a practical guide to revision, *Style* will be much easier to use as a textbook than *Analyzing Prose,* though Lanham has published another, more practical text that I have included in the section on sentences. Although *Style* is "a short book based on a simple thesis," its organization is sufficiently dense and complex that you will have to help students use it effectively in conjunction with their own writing.

F. Readers

There are dozens of college readers available for general composition courses—so many, so similar in design and purpose, that I have no grounds for choosing particular ones to recommend other than my own preferences among the essays they include. And because your preferences are the only relevant ones when you consider collections of readings for your courses, I won't list in this section any of the general readers that every major publisher offers, though I have included a few in Section VI. B. below. The most traditional readers organize their contents according to modes of discourse; others arrange model essays according to prevailing themes (Life, Death, Sex, Politics . . .). Few of them resist the temptation to add a few stimulating questions at the end of each entry, presumably to slap students back to consciousness, but they contain little or no discussion of rhetoric and style. You should get examination copies and determine which collection will provide the most interesting writing assignments and discussions in your course.

Here I have included a few titles that focus on particular subject areas or types of writing.

CLARK, VIRGINIA, et al. *Language: Introductory Readings.* 4th ed. New York: St. Martin's, 1985.

If you were to choose any single subject area for a writing course, a focus on language might be the best candidate, and this large collection of essays from various branches of linguistics would provide more than enough material. Contributors include the most prominent linguists, and although these are serious, scholarly essays, most of them are readily understandable by non-specialists. Sections of the book include essays on animal communication, the history of English, diction and dictionaries, systems of grammar, regional dialects, social variations in language, and body language.

ESCHHOLZ, PAUL, et al. *Language Awareness.* 3rd ed. New York: St. Martin's, 1982.

"Few of us," the authors of *Language Awareness* contend, "are conscious of the extent to which language is used to mislead and manipulate us or of the ways in which our own use of language, however well intentioned, affects others. Still fewer of us recognize that our very perceptions of the world are influenced, and our thoughts at least partially shaped, by language.''

The 40 essays in this collection cover diverse aspects of the uses and effects of language in speech, politics, advertising, journalism, and academic work. This is a particularly lively, interesting, and entertaining anthology that will make students more aware of the intricacy, power, danger, or absurdity of particular uses of language. Some of the contributions offer serious views of the relation between language and prejudice, propaganda, judgment, and social status; others are light-hearted discussions of ''Tips of the Slongue,'' malapropisms, euphemisms, and language play. My favorite is William Safire's ''I Led the Pigeons to the Flag.''

JACOBUS, LEE. *A World of Ideas.* 2nd ed. New York: St. Martin's, 1986.

This is a collection of particularly important essays and excerpts, ancient and modern, on politics and society, psychology, the sciences, philosophy, and art. It includes passages from Machiavelli, Marx, William James, Darwin, Jung, Plato and twenty or thirty other luminaries. *A World of Ideas* is specialized only in the sense that it might have been called *Great Minds of Western Civilization.* The readings it includes are also longer (about fifteen pages each) and more substantial than those in the typical college reader.

McQUADE, DONALD, AND ROBERT ATWAN. *Popular Writing in America: The Interaction of Style and Audience.* 3rd ed. New York: Oxford Univ. Press, 1985.

Popular Writing is a very large reader, solidly packed with examples of the kinds of prose to which Americans are most commonly exposed, and were in the past. The first section covers advertising, with extensive illustration. Following sections provide numerous examples of writing from the press, magazines, best sellers, classic popular literature, and various types of scripts. Old and recent material is interwoven in these sections.

In their preface McQuade and Atwan explain that their choice of material is ''intended in part to generate lively and productive discussions about writing and to help students become more analytically familiar with the diversity of styles and strategies that develop within a contemporary system of communications increasingly dependent upon corporate enterprise, mass audiences, interlocking media industries, and vast outlays of money.'' Beyond this and a few other introductory comments about the purpose of the book, this rich and fascinating anthology is unencumbered by commentary, and can be used in the classroom with great flexibility. The authors do provide a rhetorical table of contents and a key to ''linked selections,'' to help teachers and students locate interconnections for writing tasks and discussion.

SOMMERS, NANCY, AND DONALD MCQUADE, EDS. *Student Writers at Work: and in the Company of Other Writers*. The Bedford Prizes. Second Series. New York: St. Martin's, 1986.

The First (1984) and Second Series of Student Writers at Work present collections of student essays chosen as winners of the Bedford Contest from freshman composition classes throughout the country. Along with the finished essays, the editors provide extensive comments from these students about their methods, complete preliminary notes and drafts for two of the selections, a chapter on the ways in which peer editing contributed to final versions, and further revisions of two essays under the guidance of a professional editor. This expanded version adds to the Second Series of Bedford Prize essays a conventional collection of professional essays of the sort one can buy by the dozen in college readers.

I don't know why the editors attached this collection of professional writing to the student essays, since it bears no obvious relation to the first part and contains none of the valuable material on the writing process that supplements and enhances *Student Writers at Work*. In any case, the student essays and the supplements to them are by far the most valuable and rare among textbooks for writing instruction, and you can still buy the Second Series of student essays separately.

STEVENS, MARTIN, AND JEFFRY KLUEWER. *In Print: Critical Reading and Writing*. New York: Longman, 1983.

In Print attempts to enliven the writing class by providing readings from ''the most popular print media'': all sorts of newspaper stories and columns (even obituaries), advertising, movie reviews, articles from popular magazines, and selections from popular books. The readings themselves do provide relief from the deadly serious or terribly clever essays one finds in most readers, and they might provoke interesting discussions and writing assignments on the types of prose with which Americans are most relentlessly bombarded. These readings are nested, however, in a tangle of rhetorical advice, introductory remarks, review questions, and exercises that might interfere seriously with other attempts to use this material creatively in the classroom.

IV. REFERENCES FOR SENTENCE REVISION

If any of your students do not write in complete sentences or frequently write sentences that contain serious structural errors, they will probably need exercises and review on sentence structure and sentence division of the sort one can find in any college handbook. The rest of your students will need to correct minor errors and learn to revise sentences: to pay closer attention to their internal qualities, their contributions to the quality of a passage, and the interconnections among them. These are primarily concerns with style, in the broadest sense of the term. All style manuals and all sections on style within handbooks and rhetorics address the qualities of sentences.

Sentences patterns and problems with sentence structure differ substantially from one student writer to another, however, and for this reason I have divided references on sentence structure into three categories: "Revising Complex Sentences," "Sentence Combining," and "The Grammar of Sentence Types."

Joseph Williams's *Style* and Richard Lanham's *Revising Prose* are most useful for writers who tend to produce unnecessarily long, complex sentences that are indirect and vague. In his note "To Teachers" at the beginning of *Style,* however, Williams feels obliged to justify this emphasis, since "many undergraduates have a problem precisely opposite to that which most of this book addresses—a style characterized by one fifteen-word sentence after another." Williams notes that none of the "adult" writers he teaches still write in this choppy, disconnected style. He argues, then, that student writers will soon outgrow this phase of syntactic immaturity and produce the long, opaque, garbled sentences of the educated American adult. Meanwhile, he suggests, his book will administer preventive treatment and indirectly teach students to use more complex sentences.

Williams is partly right, and his book does cover problems with sentence structure appropriate for many college students. It seems obvious, however, that we should attempt to teach all of our students what they need to learn now, rather than addressing difficulties they might face in four or five years. Many college freshmen are unable to write cohesive, sustained passages because they work almost entirely with the most elementary sentence types, composed of one or two clauses with very little subordination, transition, or punctuation. Some students are unable to construct more complex sentences, and others are reluctant to risk making errors, often because previous English teachers told them their sentences were too long, labelled all complex sentences ''run-ons,'' or advised them to repair all comma splices with periods. Regardless of the causes of this problem, the sentence combining exercises listed in the second part of this section are designed to help students overcome ''syntactic immaturity'' and write more fluent, sustained passages without recourse to formal grammar instruction. These exercises also help students to recognize that their statements are composed of distinguishable parts that can be dismantled and recombined in dozens of different ways.

Sentence combining exercises work best, however, for students who already know how to construct and connect various kinds of clauses and need to be prodded to take risks with language and revision. Other students will need or want more formal instruction in grammar and sentence structure, and for this reason I have added some references on sentence analysis and diagramming.

A. Revising Complex Sentences

LANHAM, RICHARD. *Revising Prose*. New York: Scribners, 1979.

Revising Prose provides diagnosis and cures for a specific but epidemic range of stylistic maladies that Lanham calls ''the Official Style'': the ponderous, circumspect, and monotonous passages that students read constantly in academic and administrative prose, and often imitate as models of sophisticated writing: ''These examples *of* unusual appropriateness *of* the sense *of* adequacy to the situation suggest the primary signification *of* rhyme *in* the usual run *of* lyric poetry.''

Lanham's first two chapters teach students to identify and eliminate the central problems in sentences like the one above: the leaden emphasis on nouns strung together with prepositional phrases and weak verbs. Although this book is less comprehensive than *Style* as a guide to revising sentences, *Revising Prose* is more lively and easier to use as a guide to specific kinds of revision, including sentence length, rhythm, and voice. Lanham also works with the revision of sentences within passages, and provides many good illustrations of his methods.

WILLIAMS, JOSEPH M. *Style: Ten Lessons in Clarity and Grace.* 2nd ed. Glenview, Ill.: Scott, Foresman, 1985.

I provided a general description of this book in Section III. E., on style manuals. Williams addresses style and revision almost exclusively in terms of sentence patterns, with an emphasis on clarity and conciseness. In most of his chapters, Williams shows us how to make sentences shorter, clearer, and more direct, rather than longer and more complex. In Lesson Seven and Lesson Eight, however, he explains methods for sustaining longer sentences and addresses questions of balance, emphasis, rhythm, and imagery—questions of eloquence.

Style is especially useful as a reference for teaching, and to use it effectively, in any case, you will have to read it carefully, and apply it to specific problems.

B. Sentence Combining

Frank O'Hare developed sentence combining exercises in a research project described in *Sentence Combining: Improving Student Writing Without Formal Grammar Instruction* (an NCTE Report, 1973). O'Hare's exercises teach students methods for building complex sentences by supplying visual cues to the use of punctuation, subordination, conjunctions, and other devices for connecting and elaborating clauses. O'Hare and Dean Memering have published a version of these exercises in *The Writer's Work* (272-312).

Other books provide sentence combining exercises that leave strategies for combining up to the student, and rely on a basic sense for sentence building, without conscious reference to grammar, that students have derived from reading:

CLIFFORD, JOHN, AND ROBERT WATERHOUSE. *Sentence Combining: Shaping Ideas for Better Style.* Indianapolis: Bobbs-Merrill, 1983.

STRONG, WILLIAM. *Sentence Combining: A Composing Book.* 2nd ed. New York: Random House, 1983.

If you examine the methods used in these books, however, you can easily construct your own sentence combining exercises, using readings for your course or, more effective, student writing. For example, have students break a passage of their own writing into independent clauses and then, without reference to the original, recombine these clauses in two or three different versions. Spend some time reading these out loud, noting variations in meaning, clarity, and sound.

C. The Grammar of Sentence Types

EMERY, DONALD. *Sentence Analysis.* New York: Holt, Rinehart and Winston, 1961.
Emery's book teaches sentence structure through sentence diagrams, that old-fashioned but valuable method of illustrating sentence structure that you might remember from elementary school.

FAULKNER, CLAUDE W. *Writing Good Sentences: A Functional Approach to Sentence Structure, Grammar, and Punctuation.* 3rd ed. New York: Scribner's, 1973.
In the first half of his book, Faulkner provides extremely detailed explanations and examples of parts of speech, tense, phrases and clauses, modification, and the functions of these sentence elements within a wide range of sentence types. The second half provides brief exercises for each topic.

ROMINE, JACK S. *Writing Sentences: A Self-Teaching Guide to Grammar, Structure, and Sentence Combining.* 2nd ed. New York: Holt, Rinehart and Winston, 1979.
Beginning with a diagnostic test on sentence structure and punctua-

tion, Romine combines exercises and explanation in a workbook format, organized according to potential problems with sentence boundaries and syntax, verb forms and agreement, pronouns, and mechanics.

V. TWO APPROACHES TO PARAGRAPHS

If you ask your students what they learned about writing essays before they came to college, you will discover that most of them were taught to write some variety of the five-paragraph theme or Sheridan Baker's "keyhole" essay (22–35), and that they will describe the model essay almost entirely in terms of paragraphs. According to the standard formula, essays are composed of three types of paragraphs: introductions, body paragraphs, and conclusions. Introductory paragraphs are shaped like funnels because they begin with general statements and gradually narrow to a thesis statement at the end. Each body paragraph must represent a subcategory of the general theme and have its own topic sentence, usually at the beginning. The conclusion is an inverted funnel that begins with a rephrasing of the thesis statement and then, in Baker's description,

> . . . pours out broader and broader implications and finer emphases. The end paragraph reiterates, summarizes, and emphasizes with decorous fervor. This is your last chance. This is what your readers will carry away—and if you can carry *them* away, so much the better. All within decent intellectual bounds, of course. You are the person of reason still, but the person of reason supercharged with conviction, sure of your idea and sure of its importance. (30)

This approach to composition is almost uniform in American junior high and high schools, and you will encounter its effects continually in student writing. Your students might not conclude their papers "with decorous fervor" or remain "within decent intellectual bounds," but they will tend to view both the paragraph and the whole essay as containers for subject matter, containers that one can visualize in the abstract as ideal forms, with external shapes and, to varying degrees, internal structures. Form, in this view, precedes content. Writing an essay, therefore, is a process of filling prefabricated forms with substance, comparable to the process of constructing a five-story building with poured, reinforced concrete. I don't believe this is exactly the image Sheridan Baker had in mind, but all of us—teachers, students, and text-book writers alike—wish that writing could be easier and more systematic than it is.

Your students will also know by this time, or at least suspect, that this approach to writing doesn't always work, doesn't describe the way they actually write, and won't apply to most of the writing they will have to do in college. They will expect that you, as a college writing teacher, will show them new, more sophisticated methods for building paragraphs and putting them together in complex ways. Until you either teach them such methods or lead a revolution in the way they think about writing paragraphs and writing in general, you can expect to read many drawn and quartered versions of the five-paragraph theme—for the three to four page essays assigned in most freshman composition classes are just long enough to torture the logic of this method without killing it outright. The first paragraph of an essay will often begin with empty generalizations (a type of introduction that Roger Sale, in his book *On Writing,* characterized as "a clearing of the throat" [87–88]) and meander dutifully to a thesis statement that leaps out at the reader like an arm bearing a club. "Body paragraphs" will frequently be amorphous clumps of sentences sorted into categories, or short sequences of statements rather than discussions—brief lay-overs on the restless journey from beginning to end. The final paragraph will simply rephrase the introduction, present a précis of the entire essay, or say, in effect, "The End."

Composition texts for college students approach these problems with paragraphs in two fundamentally different ways, so I will present these references in separate categories. The approach that is easiest to identify and convey to students involves various elaborations of what students already know about paragraphs: that they should have specific functions and patterns of internal organization within the essay as a whole. These are generally descriptions of effective paragraphs of various types, used as models or prescriptions for writing effective paragraphs. The second approach emphasizes that the paragraph is not a container for writing but the result of writing: a representation of sustained thought.

A. *Paragraph Structures and Functions*

The following references describe what good paragraphs do within a larger composition and how they are put together as little compositions in themselves. They are most useful for making students conscious that every paragraph they write should have a clear purpose as well as internal development and cohesion. These references provide models, therefore, for writing, for serious revision, and for the analysis of the way finished writing works or fails to work. Virtually every rhetoric and handbook discusses paragraphs; these are just a few good examples.

HARTWELL, PATRICK. *Open to Language: A New College Rhetoric.* New York: Oxford Univ. Press, 1982.

Hartwell's chapter on paragraphs attempts to break away from the standard emphasis on the objective qualities of good paragraphs (unity, coherence, completeness, etc.) and focuses instead on "commitment and response": the writer's obligation to elaborate and clarify a stated aim. His accounts of the ways in which this obligation can be fulfilled are schematic and nicely illustrated. They include discussion of levels of generality, coordinate and subordinate frameworks, and more complex structures.

The tone of this book, however, is peculiar. Read it and translate it into your own terms. I don't think your students will be able to follow the explanations on their own.

HEFFERNAN, JAMES, AND JOHN LINCOLN. *Writing—A College Handbook.* 2nd ed. New York: Norton, 1986.

The chapter called "Writing Paragraphs" is both concise and useful. It begins with explanation and examples of paragraph division and then turns to paragraph organization, which the authors describe in terms of two strategies: list structures and chain structures. In list structure, the topic sentence introduces a sequence of points. Chain structure, as the name implies, develops through a series of logical and verbal links established by internal transitions. Both of these strategies are clearly illustrated, and the latter is finally applied to the revision of a chaotic paragraph presented at the beginning of the chapter.

IRMSCHER, WILLIAM. *The Holt Guide to English.* 3rd ed. New York: Holt, Rinehart and Winston, 1981.

Irmscher describes a greater variety of paragraph functions than most authors, and he presents descriptions and examples of six types of paragraph organization. He also discusses levels of generality in the paragraph and includes a useful checklist for determining whether a paragraph is effective or not.

McCRIMMON, JAMES. *Writing With a Purpose.* 8th ed. Revised by Joseph Trimmer and Nancy Sommers. Boston: Houghton Mifflin, 1984.

In his chapter on paragraphs, McCrimmon emphasizes four qualities of effective paragraphs: unity, completeness, order and movement, and coherence. Most of the chapter is devoted to illustration of these qualities, with lots of examples and sensible explanation. The section on paragraph movement describes four types of development: general to particular; particular to general; whole to parts; and question to answer/ effect to cause. The section on coherence is particularly useful, because it illustrates types of logical connection within paragraphs and, in one case, among several paragraphs in sequence. The chapter ends with discussion and examples of effective introductions, conclusions, and transition paragraphs.

PARKS, A. FRANKLIN, et al. *Structuring Paragraphs: A Guide to Effective Writing.* New York: St. Martin's Press, 1981.

Structuring Paragraphs is an elaboration of the discussions cited in the other references in this section, based on the assertion that "the most efficient way to teach the basic principles of good expository writing is to focus on the paragraph." Individual chapters focus on levels of generality, unity and structure, methods of development, coherence, the functions of paragraphs within longer essays, and revision. This approach to the paragraph is comparable to the chapter in McCrimmon cited above. The only advantage in Parks's discussion is that there is more of it: a greater variety of paragraph functions, more extensive examples and analyses of paragraph structure, and a longer, more thorough checklist for revision.

B. Paragraphs as Passages

The references listed above provide excellent descriptions and examples of successful paragraphs, useful as models for raising students' expectations of what their own paragraphs can and should do, and perhaps most valuable as guides to revision. When you use these approaches in class, however, you should emphasize that they are descriptions of good paragraphs rather than prescriptions for writing paragraphs according to elaborate formulas.

In practice, "paragraph problems" are not as easy to isolate and remedy as most writing texts suggest, and all of those separate chapters on the paragraph, however useful they might be as collections of models, are probably elements of a false, though alluring, taxonomy. Students who write in short, undeveloped sentences, for example, also tend to write short, undeveloped paragraphs in short, undeveloped essays. Students who tend to write vague, convoluted sentences, in turn, often have difficulty linking these sentences in cohesive paragraphs and tend to write disorganized essays. At which level of construction does the *real* problem lie?

At the beginning of her chapter "Beyond the Sentence," in *Errors and Expectations,* Mina Shaughnessy states that "the mature writer is recognized not so much by the quality of his individual sentences as by his ability to relate sentences in such a way as to create a flow of sentences, a pattern of thought that is produced, one suspects, according to the principles of yet another kind of grammar—a grammar, let us say, of passages" (226). Immature writers, according to Shaughnessy, do not necessarily lack ideas. The mark of their immaturity as writers, instead, is that their thought "often seems to halt at the boundary of each sentence rather than move on, by gradations of subsequent comment, to an elaboration of the sentence." In other words, they compose in "sentences of thought" rather than in "passages of thought" (227).

Shaughnessy refers to "passages" rather than to "paragraphs" because the development of an idea does not necessarily end with the last word of a paragraph, any more than it must end with the last word of a sentence. Instead, sentences and paragraphs are elements of discourse with which mature writers shape and sustain ideas rather than isolate and abandon them. And although the paragraph is in many ways the most convenient unit of composition for purposes of analyzing prose and observing the development of ideas, we can only observe that paragraphs have or lack structure and cohesion after they have been written. We actually write paragraphs, as "passages," by using language to formulate, develop, support, and sustain ideas that did not fully exist until they were put into words, either in the mind or on paper. Teachers and textbooks ultimately mislead and discourage students when they suggest that this process is mechanical rather than intellectual.

In Shaughnessy's terms of literary maturity and immaturity, we find most college freshmen (and usually leave them) in various stages of adolescence. To varying degrees, in other words, they sustain thoughts beyond the sentence to paragraphs and relations among paragraphs, but they often fail to examine and pursue ideas in fully developed passages, even though they are usually capable of doing so. If we view paragraphs as passages and elements of discourse, undeveloped or disorganized paragraphs are usually the symptoms of a more fundamental problem: the writer has not spent enough time thinking and writing, rethinking and rewriting, to produce full, cohesive paragraphs in the process of composition.

The implications of this problem, in turn, vary radically from one paragraph, essay, and writer to another, in ways that often demand that we look beyond the structure of the paragraph to its substance. In *Language in Thought and Action,* for example, S. I. Hayakawa observes that students often write in conclusions and premature judgments rather than presenting the information and observations that lead to reasonable conclusions (40–41). Unless they result from discourse, conclusions and judgments "stop thought" altogether and leave the writer with nothing else to say. As a consequence, the broadest, most complex subjects often produce the shortest and least developed paragraphs and essays, because the writer can't begin to examine the issues involved and must settle for strings of flat assertions. If this is the case and you simply note in your comments that "paragraphs are too short and undeveloped," you have described the obvious symptoms of the problem but failed to address its cause or to provide guidance for revision. If you ask students to examine assertions they have simply stated, revision might involve more than the development of an individual paragraph; sometimes it will require the transformation of the subject of a single paragraph into an entire essay.

Because paragraphs encompass concerns with sentence structure and style, function as primary units of organization in an essay, and represent "passages of thought," the references presented in other sections of this chapter refer directly and indirectly to the qualities of paragraphs as well. Books entirely devoted to the paragraph, therefore, tend to be elementary composition texts, and authors who view writing as an intellectual process seldom make reference to paragraphs at all, since they assume that paragraph divisions will emerge naturally in discourse, as a type of punctuation for units of thought. Deductive approaches to paragraph development and form provide students, especially weak writers, with examples of effective paragraph organization and illustrations of various ways in which good paragraphs work, but students should also recognize that accomplished writers do not produce cohesive paragraphs and essays by consciously selecting and filling in one of a dozen templates from their store of literary devices.

The following article challenges almost everything you will read about paragraphs in composition texts:

STERN, ARTHUR. "When is a Paragraph?" *The Writing Teacher's Sourcebook.* Edited by Gary Tate and Edward Corbett. 294–300. New York: Oxford Univ. Press, 1981.

In this brief essay, Stern argues that most of the deductive statements teachers offer students about paragraphs as units are false. The paragraph is not a logical unit, Stern says. It does not necessarily begin with a topic sentence or cover a distinct topic. Nor is the paragraph a miniature composition. In practice, approaches to paragraphing differ a great deal from one writer to another, and they have also changed a great deal over the past century. Stern concludes, then, that the paragraph "is not an independent, self-contained whole but a functioning part of discourse; its boundaries are not sealed but open to the surrounding text; it links as often as it divides . . . the paragraph is a flexible, expressive rhetorical instrument."

VI. LOGIC, EVIDENCE, AND ORGANIZATION

Writing teachers and others who assign writing in their classes often assert that they can do nothing for students who do not think clearly, and in some respects this is certainly true. We are not obliged to impart wisdom to our students, raise their intelligence, supply the ideas in their writing, or make certain they have their wits about them when they sit down to write a paper. In any case, writing is not a clear window to the mind, and when we examine student writing we are not directly examining the way students think.

Unless teachers imagine that writing is simply a set of mechanical skills somehow separable from its meaning, however, they must continually address the ways in which language represents thought. In the preceding section, for example, I mentioned S. I. Hayakawa's observation that "judgments stop thought," an example of the correlation between thought and composition that you might encounter dozens of times in a single batch of papers. And regardless of the direction from which you approach this problem, if you require revision rather than simply make an observation, you will always affect both sides of this correlation. If you tell the writer to develop the paragraph, in other words, you will indirectly call for alteration of the idea; if you tell the writer to develop the idea, you will indirectly call for alteration of the paragraph. If you explain the ways in which these problems of development are related, you will provide writing instruction in the fullest sense of the term and still leave the student with the intellectual burden of composition.

College freshmen are usually bright enough to identify the specific strengths and weaknesses of an argument they are analyzing, but they are much less inclined to apply these critical skills to their own writing, which they tend to view as an unalterable chunk of the self. They are also almost totally unfamiliar with the principles of formal logic and the uses of evidence. Neither their science teachers nor their English teachers, it seems, have taught them the difference between induction and deduction, or shown them how to distinguish assertions, opinions, assumptions, inferences, and other elements of thought in argumentation and problem-solving. They will not understand very clearly what an argument is, or for that matter an analysis, or criticism. Many will believe, until you tell them otherwise, that argument and criticism always have to be against something. Others will base their view of argument on their experience on the debate team: there are always two sides; pick one; defend it with your life. These misconceptions and their effects on student writing are not reliable evidence of stupidity, but represent understandable ignorance of terms, concepts, and strategies that we can teach to students.

The principles of logic and evidence in discourse have always been the domain of traditional rhetoric, which is concerned almost entirely with the formal qualities of finished writing. Every good essay, from this perspective, should have a logical structure, represented in sequences of statements within individual paragraphs and in sequences of paragraphs that constitute the organizational framework and "strategy" of the essay as a whole. In Part A of this section I have listed some references on the principles of formal logic and evidence, invariably presented within chapters on "argument" or "persuasion" in traditional and contemporary rhetorics. These chapters will not provide your students with brilliant ideas or transform them into reasonable people, but they do make fundamental distinctions that might help students evaluate and revise their own arguments, and analyze those of other writers.

Rhetoric readers based upon traditional rhetoric provide model essays, generally from published work of various kinds, arranged according to a classification of rhetorical forms and functions: definition, comparison and contrast, classification, cause and effect, process analysis, analogy, exemplification, argument, and others that vary from one reader to another. In Part B. I have listed a few of the rhetoric readers that provide some explanation of the organizational strategies involved in these forms, along with the usual suggestions for classroom discussion. These are useful resources if you need to find an essay of a certain type, to illustrate a specific approach to organization. Ignore the broader suggestion that essays always fall into one of these categories, and that essays should be purely of one form or another. "Classification," for example, is rarely a type of essay, as traditional rhetorics and readers often suggest, but is more fundamentally a type of thought and a variety of organization that one can apply to many different kinds of writing, including "argument" and "process analysis."

The patterns of thought represented in finished essays or outlines, however, do not fully describe the relationship between thought and language in the process of composition. In Part C., I have listed the work of a few writers who have attempted to address the complexity of this process and help students through its initial and often most difficult stages. These references describe strategies for invention, development, and organization, or present more general discussions of the relationship between thought and language in composition.

A. *Formal Logic and Organization*

All of the following references discuss the principles of reasoning within chapters on "argument" or "persuasion." The uses of these two terms differ to some extent from one textbook to another. Typically, these chapters will discuss the nature of assertions or propositions, the distinction between induction and deduction, the uses and varieties of evidence, the use of analogy, and the types of fallacy.

Most of these books also view logic as the foundation of organization. Variations in logic and intent, therefore, govern variations among rhetorical forms and patterns of organization. Sections on "comparison and contrast," "cause and effect," "classification," and "definition" describe these specific forms of the essay as specific forms of thought.

BROOKS, CLEANTH, AND ROBERT PENN WARREN. *Modern Rhetoric*. 4th ed. New York: Harcourt Brace Jovanovich, 1979.

You can read the description of traditional rhetorics above as a description of *Modern Rhetoric*, which, perhaps more than any writing text in print, views all good writing as the result of reasonable and orderly thought. In these terms, the writing in *Modern Rhetoric* itself is extremely good—clear and precise, with well-chosen examples.

Brooks and Warren discuss reasoning, evidence, and fallacy in their chapter on "argument." If you need one concise source of reasoning in argument, this is probably the best.

D'ANGELO, FRANK. *Process and Thought in Composition*. 2nd ed. Cambridge, Mass.: Winthrop, 1980.

In the second edition (not in the first), D'Angelo includes two chapters on "Persuasion as an Aim." The first of these chapters, "Induction and Deduction," covers various strategies for developing arguments (e.g., the use of description, analogy, comparison, example, and authority). Most of these sections include discussion of specific types of faulty reasoning.

"The Syllogism and the Enthymeme" illustrates methods of generating arguments from the logical relations among sequences of statements of various types, described at length. While syllogism is at least potentially a very useful tool in writing, the weakness of this chapter is that it remains almost totally absorbed in logic itself, without much direct reference to writing. The examples ("If you inject heroin you will die. You inject heroin. Therefore, you will die.") do not hold much promise for generating essays, but you can apply the methods to issues in your course.

KANE, THOMAS, *The Oxford Guide to Writing*. New York: Oxford Univ. Press, 1983.

You will find discussions of reasoning in the section called "Persuasion," which is divided into chapters on "Argument" and "Persuasion: Nonrational modes." The latter is relevant because it contains most of the discussion of fallacy.

Like D'Angelo, Kane uses classical rhetoric as a guide to the discussion of reasoning, but he does a better job of extending the use of syllogism, for example, to the process of composition. In the chapter on argument, he illustrates most of the methods under discussion in the development of a sample essay, accompanied by analysis of reasoning in the beginning, middle, and end of the sample composition.

B. Rhetoric Readers

With the exception of McDonald's *The Language of Argument,* these readers are so similar in format and range of content that I will simply list them. If you need an essay of a particular type, you can simply check the table of contents under the form you have in mind until you find a sample essay that suits your purposes. All of these books include some discussion of the rhetorical forms represented in sample essays.

CLAYES, STANLEY, et al. *Contexts for Composition.* 5th ed. Englewood Cliffs, N.J.: Prentice-Hall, 1979.

LEVIN, GERALD, *Prose Models.* 6th ed. New York: Harcourt Brace Jovanovich, 1984.

McDONALD, DANIEL. *The Language of Argument.* 4th ed. New York: Harper and Row, 1983.
The Language of Argument is not a typical reader, since it focuses entirely on argument and uses sample essays to illustrate both strategies and fallacies. I include it primarily because the choices of sample essays are particularly interesting. Most readers contain a standard range of clever, polished, and often rather slippery essays from reputable writers and reputable publications. Here you will find "Astounding New Discoveries About the Bible," distributed by the Southwest Radio Church of the Air in Oklahoma City, and the transcript of a speech in favor of nuclear power delivered to a Rotary Club meeting in Sherbrooke, Quebec. The contrast is refreshing. These are essays your students can easily confront.

NICHOLAS, J. KARL, AND JAMES R. NICHOLL. *Rhetorical Models for Effective Writing*. 3rd ed. Cambridge, Mass.: Winthrop, 1985.

ROSA, ALFRED, AND PAUL ESCHOLZ. *Models for Writers*. New York: St. Martin's, 1982.

ZENDER, KARL, AND LINDA MORRIS. *Persuasive Writing*. New York: Harcourt Brace Jovanovich, 1981.

C. Invention, Development, and Organization

COHEN, B. BERNARD. *Writing About Literature*. 2nd ed. Glenview, Ill.: Scott, Foresman, 1973.

This book will be particularly useful in writing courses on literature, but three of the central chapters provide guidance of general value in the process of focusing and developing themes: "Thesis Statement as Related to Content and Structure," "Solidity of Content," and "Organization." The second of these chapters makes effective distinctions between generalization and analysis, and summary and analysis.

FAHNESTOCK, JEANNE, AND MARIE SECOR. *A Rhetoric of Argument*. New York: Random House, 1982.

A Rhetoric of Argument abandons the use of classical logic for describing arguments in favor of an emphasis on "categorical propositions": the ways in which we formulate and support them, the kinds of questions we can ask about them, and the kinds of questions they attempt to answer. Although this is primarily a rhetoric, and a good one for a course devoted to argument, several of the fifteen chapters include short readings to illustrate the type of argument under discussion.

HAIRSTON, MAXINE. *Successful Writing: A Rhetoric for Advanced Composition*. 2nd ed. New York: Norton, 1986.

Chapters Three through Six in *Successful Writing* (13–102) provide useful guidance for the process of finding and developing topics and organizing essays. Chapters Three and Four describe writing as a process of creative problem solving and introduce considerations of "Audience, Purpose, Persona, and Message." Chapter Five, "Getting Started," explains the use of generative statements and illustrates several methods of organization. "Holding Your Reader" explains techniques for making an organizational strategy clear to the reader through effective transitions and "directional signals."

HAYAKAWA, S. I. *Language in Thought and Action*. 4th ed. New York: Harcourt Brace Jovanovich, 1978.

As one might expect, Hayakawa mixes semantics, ethics, and political philosophy in this loosely organized discussion of "language as both an intellectual and a moral discipline," but you do not have to share his general premises to benefit from specific discussions of the power of language to convey, inform, and deform perception.

I include *Language in Thought and Action* in this section because much of the book concerns the use and misuse of logic, types of fallacy, judgments and inferences, the language of prejudice, levels of abstraction, and other topics relevant to the construction and criticism of arguments. The chapters appear to have been thrown together at random, but Hayakawa's discussions of language and logic are generally more lively and interesting, and sometimes of more immediate value in writing, than the abstract, dispassionate advice offered in most rhetorics. Note particularly the chapters on "Reports, Inferences, Judgments," "How We Know What We Know," "Classification," "The Two-Valued Orientation," and "The Multi-Valued Orientation."

HORTON, SUSAN. *Thinking Through Writing*. Baltimore: Johns Hopkins Univ. Press, 1982.

Horton's entire book concerns the way people think when they write and the ways in which writing enhances thought. Horton helps students recognize and examine concepts for the purpose of writing and in the process of writing. The first four chapters—"What is Writing?", "What is an Essay?", "What is a Concept?", and "How Does Your Mind Work?"—provide an excellent introduction to the task of composition and the intellectual processes this task involves. Although my description sounds abstract, Horton addresses these questions in language students can understand, and she discusses problems they actually face while they are writing.

IRMSCHER, WILLIAM F. *The Holt Guide to English*. 3rd ed. New York: Holt, Rinehart and Winston, 1981.

Irmscher includes two chapters on the task of finding a subject and developing it in a logical, coherent fashion. The first, called "The Subject: Generating a Topic," presents an elaborate illustration of Kenneth Burke's "dramatistic pentad" of questions one can ask about a subject. Irmscher explains this method and then applies it to the development of several sample essays on a painting, Edward Hopper's *Nighthawks*. The second chapter, "Order, Logic, and Mode," explores strategies for developing an essay in different modes, with attention to particular problems of development in the beginning, middle, and end.

SMITH, CHARLES KAY. *Styles and Structures*. New York: Norton, 1974.

Smith's interesting book is based on the premise "that patterns of writing enact patterns of thinking, that by finding and practicing different ways of writing we can literally think different things." Most of the book is devoted, then, to discussion and illustration of the ways in which "form and content work together" in various styles of writing; it includes examples and explanation of the underlying logic of organization.

The four sections of *Styles and Structures* cover narrative and descriptive styles, the logical foundations of seven different types of definition, the use of assumptions and dialectic, and "A Rhetoric of Reperception," on the use of writing as a creative process of questioning conventional perception.

WINTEROWD, W. ROSS. *The Contemporary Writer*. 2nd ed. New York: Harcourt Brace Jovanovich, 1981.

Winterowd includes several chapters on methods of discovering and developing coherent themes. The first of these chapters is a "Survey of the Composing Process," followed by a separate chapter on "Prewriting" in which Winterowd describes and illustrates several methods of finding and exploring ideas for papers. In addition to Burke's "pentad," these include long lists of strategies for problem-solving and angles from which one can view a subject. In his chapter on persuasion, Winterowd uses the classical six-part structure of the persuasive essay as a heuristic device for developing a subject. All of these discussions include examples you might find useful in class.

VII. PUNCTUATION:
BEYOND RULES AND ERRORS

Punctuation has been more thoroughly codified than any other aspect of the language, and for this reason you should not have to teach students the rules for punctuation as such. They can find these rules, along with examples of correct and incorrect usage, in any college handbook. They will not tend to do so, however, unless you use a handbook as a required text and refer students to specific sections when you correct punctuation errors in their papers. Otherwise they will simply wince at these corrections in passing, without noticing patterns among them, and leave you with the responsibility for punctuating their papers correctly each week.

Another possibility, even if you do refer them to a required handbook, is that students will use less punctuation and fewer types of punctuation to reduce the risk of error. This reaction is a symptom of a problem more fundamental than ignorance of the rules, and one you should address as a writing teacher. The central problem, I believe, is that most teachers and writing texts, and therefore most students as well, view punctuation as a matter of "mechanics" or as a legal code of misdemeanors. After all, college freshmen have had more than a decade to learn the functions of fewer than a dozen punctuation marks. If they still use only six or seven, and use these inaccurately, we might conclude that they view punctuation as a matter of minor importance in writing, or perhaps that they have been trained to avoid it as much as possible. The observation that students read punctuation accurately supports this conclusion. When they are reading, they usually recognize the meanings and effects of commas, semicolons, colons, dashes, and other marks that they often avoid or use incorrectly when they write. In other words, they read punctuation marks as pieces of language, with specific meanings and values; they tend to write with punctuation marks as minor formalities and potential errors.

Some types of punctuation (such as the placement of apostrophes and quotation marks, or the uses of capitals and underlining) are simply a matter of following rules. For the most common forms of punctuation, however, rules represent, rather than dictate, the collaboration of eye and ear by means of which fluent writers use punctuation marks as essential instruments in the process of shaping a passage, controlling its pace and rhythm, distinguishing and connecting its parts, embedding or emphasizing its meanings. We develop this ear and eye for punctuation almost entirely from reading, and you can help students transfer their reading knowledge of punctuation to writing by making them more conscious of the functions and effects of punctuation in the process of analyzing passages.

The few sources listed at the end of this section will clarify the general functions of punctuation marks, help students appreciate the importance of punctuation, provide special help for students who have tin ears, and give you some background for addressing and answering questions. The most valuable exercise in punctuation usage, however, is simply a matter of explaining and discussing the specific effects of punctuation in a piece of writing (for a more detailed discussion of such punctuation exercise, see ''Checking Punctuation' in Chapter 7.

As preparation for this type of exercise, however, your students should become more conscious of the general functions and values of specific punctuation marks: that we generally use commas, for example, where we can hear natural pauses, or that a semicolon is not in any sense half of a colon but usually a weak period used between sentences that lean into each other. To help clarify these functions, I have listed two references that classify and describe the general uses of punctuation marks, along with a more subjective account of their qualities as pieces of language.

In the questions that emerge from the discussion of punctuation strategies you will discover another reason why students do not follow all the rules for punctuation. They can't understand them. The injunction against comma splices will make little sense to a student who can't identify an independent clause. And when someone in the class asks, ''Why can't I put a comma before 'that' in the third sentence?'' you should be prepared to explain the differences between restrictive and nonrestrictive clauses and modifiers, among other structural charactersitics of the language that suddenly become relevant in ways they would never be if you explained them in the abstract. For this reason, I have also included some references that address punctuation in the context of sentence structure. (See also ''Common Sentence Problems in Beginners' Writing'' in Chapter 7.)

A. *Functions and Qualities of Punctuation Marks*

IRMSCHER, WILLIAM F. *Teaching Expository Writing.* New York: Holt, Rinehart and Winston, 1979.

In the chapter called "Teaching Mechanics," Irmscher presents a method for simplifying and clarifying the uses of punctuation. The foundation of this method is a chart that lists punctuation marks under four general functions: to terminate and separate; to combine and separate; to introduce; to enclose. This chart and the comparisons that it establishes allow students to view punctuation as a matter of function and choice rather than as the application, in an "additive" fashion, of a complex system of rules.

THOMAS, LEWIS. "Notes on Punctuation." *The Medusa and the Snail.* New York: Viking Penguin, 1979.

You will also find this essay in *The Norton Reader* of expository prose and in Rosa and Escholz's *Models for Writers.*

"Notes on Punctuation" is a wonderful essay to use in class, because it is both playful and instructive, and because it defeats the common notion that punctuation is the most fussy and boring of all aspects of language. Thomas is a scientist who loves language, and in this essay he describes punctuation marks in terms of what we might call their personalities. Because he illustrates the use of a punctuation mark in the passage in which he describes it, your students will have to see this essay to appreciate it—and they should see it.

WHITEHALL, HAROLD. "The System of Punctuation." *Essays on Language and Usage.* Edited by Leonard Dean and Kenneth Wilson. 223–233. 2nd ed. New York: Oxford Univ. Press, 1963.

Whitehall begins with a brief history of punctuation and then, like Irmscher, divides the functions of punctuation marks into four categories: to *link* sentences and part of words; to *separate* sentences and parts of sentences; to *enclose* parts of sentences; and to *indicate omissions.* He then lists the types of punctuation that fulfill these functions and illustrates their use with sample sentences.

Whitehall's system is more thorough than Irmscher's, because it includes a greater variety of punctuation and clearer explanations, and I also think his categories are easier to understand. He is less concerned, however, with the problems of teaching punctuation.

B. Punctuation and Sentence Structure

ELCAN, RUTH. *Elements of College Writing.* 2nd ed. Boston: Little, Brown, 1980.

Elcan's chapter on punctuation provides brief exercises for punctuation with specific types of clauses, along with exercises for avoiding comma splices.

REINKING, JAMES, et al. *Improving College Writing: A Book of Exercises.* New York: St. Martin's, 1981.

Reinking provides a large section on "Learning to Punctuate and Use Mechanics Properly," subdivided into chapters on specific punctuation marks and functions. "Commas to Separate" and "Commas to Set Off" therefore represent separate functions. Each chapter includes an explanation of patterns of usage in terms of sentence structure, followed by exercises. There is an answer key at the end of the book.

WILLIAMS, JOSEPH M. *Style: Ten Lessons in Clarity and Grace.* 2nd ed. Glenview, Ill.: Scott, Foresman, 1985.

In his chapter on "Style and Punctuation," Williams classifies punctuation usage according to position in the sentence, providing rules and explanations when possible or necessary, and offering advice about strategies in terms of style. At the end of this section he presents two passages (one by James Baldwin, the other by J. Robert Oppenheimer) from which he has removed all punctuation except spaces at the end of grammatical sentences. You could use these effectively for the exercise I described at the beginning of this section. The chapter concludes with a summary of "Reasonable Punctuation," which describes choices and limitations at particular points in a sentence. This list is more concise and useful than the rules you will find in most handbooks.

VIII. SPECIAL INSTRUCTION FOR NON-NATIVE SPEAKERS OF ENGLISH

Many writing classes will include foreign or American students who use English as a second, occasionally as a third or fourth language, and some of these students will need special references or special types of instruction.

I am not referring to students who need basic, intensive instruction in English as a foreign or second language. Most high schools and colleges have methods of identifying these students and provide special programs and courses taught by people who have training in EFL and ESL instruction. If students in your class have serious difficulties with English syntax, can't understand the readings in the course, or make extraordinary numbers and varieties of errors that require special instruction, you should investigate special programs and get these students transferred to a more appropriate course as early in the term as possible. At many institutions cultural diversity is a rare asset that teachers are reluctant to sacrifice in a writing class, but we ultimately do non-native speakers of English a disservice if we allow them to remain in a course that can't deliver the instruction they need.

This section applies to non-native speakers of English who are nearly fluent, but have lingering problems with the language that often differ radically from, but are not necessarily more serious or intractable than, the comma splices, sentence fragments, punctuation errors, ambiguous pronouns, awkward passive constructions, dangling phrases, foggy diction, and other abuses of English that we have learned to expect as the normal range of error and ambiguity in student writing. Errors that appear to represent fundamentally flawed or ''broken'' English, simply because native speakers rarely make them, are often the last and most stubborn obstacles to full fluency—obstacles that, with some special materials, methods, and understanding, you can help these students overcome. We do a different kind of disservice to students who are nearly fluent in English if we throw up our hands in despair over relatively minor errors simply because they are unfamiliar to us. These advanced non-native speakers often have problems with writing identical to those of native speakers (difficulties with sentence division, paragraph development, organization, etc.), but in this section I will focus only on the difficulties that result from learning English as a foreign or second language, since writing texts designed for native speakers tend to ignore these problems.

Non-native speakers tend to have the most difficulty with aspects of English that one must learn almost entirely through usage, and with those that do not exist in their native languages. For example, almost everyone who has learned English as a foreign language will have lingering difficulties with prepositions, because the use of a particular preposition in English is linked in the specific instance to specific verbs and objects in ways that often defy reason and for which there are no reliable rules. Learning to use prepositions accurately, therefore, is a process of mastering a complex vocabulary of phrases and contexts ("I got *to* the airport on time"; "I arrived *at* the airport on time")—a vocabulary native speakers have learned in the process of learning to speak. For students who have learned English largely through formal instruction, prepositions are ungoverned parts of speech, their uses chaotic and idiomatic.

Asian students have particular difficulties with articles, verb tenses, and subject-verb-pronoun agreement: aspects of English that have no comparable forms in most Asian languages. A sentence with missing or extra articles ("In morning I am going to the New York City") sounds crippled and incomprehensible, but articles are probably the least important parts of speech in terms of establishing clarity. They are also among the last elements of English that Asian students learn to master, and you will discover the reason if you try to explain, or ask other native speakers to explain, how and why we use articles in particular cases. Students whose native language is Spanish face other obstacles as they approach fluency in English. Because Spanish syntax is more flexible and allows for longer, more loosely structured sentences, these students often write in what we consider rambling, run-on sentences. Numerous Spanish-English cognates create problems with diction and usage (which students can sometimes remedy by using an English-English rather than a Spanish-English dictionary), and differences in pronunciation lead Spanish speaking students to confuse words such as "this" and "these." Following conventions in Spanish, they will sometimes drop the meaningless subject "It" and begin a sentence with "Is," attempt to pluralize adjectives, or place adjectives after the nouns they modify.

English grammars and handbooks designed for native speakers are of limited value for addressing these problems. Although college handbooks do present descriptions and explanations of verb tenses and verbal forms, rules of agreement, and other descriptions of the structure of English, Asian students educated abroad, for example, already know these rules and structures, often more thoroughly than any of your other students. Their problems, in many cases, is that they haven't mastered the peculiar logic with which we use these constructions in writing. Standard grammars and handbooks also tend to dismiss articles, prepositions, and other elements of English that native speakers use without difficulty. As a consequence, the most thorough, detailed (and in some cases massive and expensive) grammars of English available are those designed for ESL/EFL instructors and linguists. And because they cover virtually every aspect of the language (at least of structure and usage), they are excellent references for all teachers, and for work with all types of students. The largest ones, however, are designed almost exclusively for teachers, and here I have included more concise grammars that both students and teachers might find useful.

Most of the references listed below, therefore, are designed for non-native speakers at advanced levels, who often enroll in composition classes designed for native speakers of English. Some of these students will need to buy or consult a thorough grammar and usage text designed for non-native speakers. Others will need exercises designed to give students practice with specific patterns of usage and sentence structure. For this reason, I have divided these references into two categories. Because I had very limited familiarity with this material, for help with this section I consulted Ingrid Arnesen, who teaches ESL/EFL courses in the Division of Modern Languages and Linguistics at Cornell.

A. Grammar and Usage Texts

ARONSON, TRUDY. *English Grammar Digest*. Englewood Cliffs. N.J.: Prentice-Hall, 1984.

English Grammar Digest is a concise grammar review book for advanced ESL/EFL students, designed partly to help them prepare for the grammar and usage section of the TOEFL (Test on English as a Foreign Language). Aronson's book actually belongs as appropriately in the next category as well, since it combines grammar instruction with exercises on the most common areas of difficulty that advanced students face. Although its conciseness necessarily compromises sections on complex parts of speech and usage (such as articles and prepositions), *English Grammar Digest* would be a useful, comparatively inexpensive choice for students who need limited review of grammar and syntax— especially if they have trouble with verbs. It includes sample tests for the TOEFL, with an answer key.

FRANK, MARCELLA. *Modern English: A Practical Reference Guide.* Englewood Cliffs, N.J.: Prentice-Hall, 1972.

Modern English is one of the best general references available for non-native speakers, especially at advanced levels. It is a comprehensive description of the structure of English, with special emphasis on the forms that give non-native speakers the most trouble: articles, prepositions, verb tenses and sequences, verbals, idioms, and word order. Frank attempts to reduce the mysteries of articles and prepositions, for example, through elaborate classifications and illustrations of usage, far beyond anything you will find in a standard handbook. Some students might want to buy this book if you tell them about it. A comprehensive ESL grammar of this type would also be a useful reference to have on hand for your own purposes if you work extensively, or even occasionally, with non-native speakers of English.

FRANK, MARCELLA. *Writer's Companion.* Englewood Cliffs, N.J.: Prentice-Hall, 1983.

Writer's Companion is an extremely concise (146 page) index to usage and rhetoric for advanced non-native speakers, with a section for grammar and review practice at the end. Because it is so tightly condensed and schematic, this book is less useful as a reference for specific problems than *Modern English* (listed above), but it would be a good reference to own and carry around for quick consultation.

HEFFERNAN, JAMES, AND JOHN LINCOLN. *Writing—A College Handbook.* 2nd ed. New York: Norton, 1986.

Although it is not an ESL text and does not cover articles and prepositions, *Writing* offers particularly clear explanations of the tense, voice, mood, and sequence of verbs (365–406)), subject-verb agreement (351–364), and pronoun usage (327–350) sufficient for most advanced non-native speakers of English.

LEECH, GEOFFREY, AND JAN SVARTVIK. *A Communicative Grammar of English.* Singapore: Longman, 1975.

This "communicative" (as opposed to structural) grammar of English presents aspects of grammar and usage according to their functions in written and spoken communication. In other words, it explains to students the kinds of situations in which particular constructions apply. It is designed, then, for advanced students of the sort you might find in your classes, and who might suffer from what the authors call "grammar fatigue": they have spent years studying the structure of the language but still have problems with usage that structural grammars cannot address. In its own way, then, *A Communicative Grammar of English* is quite thorough, even though it is a compact and comparatively inexpensive paperback.

QUIRK, RANDOLPH, AND SIDNEY GREENBAUM. *A Concise Grammar of Contemporary English.* New York: Harcourt Brace Jovanovich, 1973.

A condensed, but still substantial version of *A Grammar of Contemporary English* (one of the most thorough grammars for linguists and ESL teachers), this concise version is sufficiently clear and detailed to serve as a primary reference for advanced non-native speakers of English, or as a reference for teachers who need to learn about constructions with which these students have difficulty. This is a structural grammar, organized according to parts of speech, and types of phrases, clauses, and sentences.

B. Exercises

Non-native speakers need focused exercises on a specific problem if they have persistent difficulty and can't reliably proofread for particular patterns of error. Exercises give students practice in applying rules, to the extent that these rules exist, and help them develop an ear and eye for other patterns of usage that do not clearly conform to rules. In the references listed below, you will find specific exercises for virtually every pattern of error you can distinguish in student writing, and it is important that you identify these patterns as clearly as possible. For example, students who have mastered most of the verb forms in English often have remaining difficulty identifying and constructing passives, because these forms shift the expression of tense from the main verb to some form of the verb "to be." Among the references below, then, you will find specific exercises on passives, more focused and useful for these students than a full, 75-page dose of exercises on verbs in general.

AZAR, BETTY SCHRAMPFER. *Understanding and Using English Grammar.* Englewood Cliffs, N.J.: Prentice-Hall, Inc., 1981.

A compact but thorough book of explanations and exercises for intermediate to advanced ESL students. Azar covers all of the most common areas of difficulty, though sections on articles and prepositions are very brief, especially when compared with those in Frank (below). Her book is most useful for problems with verbs and agreement. Some of you might find irritating the stereotypes among the sample sentences, and especially in the little drawings sprinkled here and there in the text.

Cook, Mary Jane. *Trouble Spots of English Grammar: A Text-Workbook for ESL*. 2 vols. New York: Harcourt Brace Jovanovich, 1983.

These are large, thorough paperbacks, most useful as workbooks, but with enough explanation for each aspect of the language to serve as grammar review and instruction as well. Volume I includes a review of English syntax and extensive work with the uses of verbs of all kinds within phrases and sentences. Volume II covers the remaining parts of speech, once again within sentence patterns, and includes long sections on articles and prepositions—two areas of usage that cause the most trouble but most often get inadequate treatment in concise grammars and workbooks.

Frank, Marcella. *Modern English: Exercises for Non-Native Speakers*. 2nd ed. 2 vols. Englewood Cliffs, N.J.: Prentice-Hall, 1986.

These two volumes of exercises are companion texts to the *Practical Reference Guide* cited in Section VII. A., but they are self-contained instruction tools, with brief explanations preceding each exercise.

Part I: Parts of Speech is the more useful of the two volumes, because it contains extensive exercises on verbs, articles, prepositions, nouns, pronouns, adjectives, and adverbs—subdivided and focused upon the types of usage that give non-native speakers the most trouble. The section on prepositions, for example, begins with a classification of preposition functions, connections with other parts of speech, and types of prepositional phrases, followed by exercises that ask students to fill in the appropriate prepositions in a sequence of sentences, using a key to their specific functions. Other exercises in the book follow roughly the same pattern: brief explanations and keys followed by fill-in or transformation exercises that focus on a specific function, tense, or structural feature of the part of speech in question.

Part II: Sentences and Complex Structures provides exercises that illustrate the uses of specific types of clauses and phrases, along with basic sentence types and parallel constructions. Again, these exercises begin with brief definitions of the clause or phrase in question, followed by sentences in which the student must fill in, transform, or combine sentence elements.

These two volumes do not provide answer keys. Although most of the exercises give students enough information to do the work on their own, you will have to check it for errors.

REYNOLDS, AUDREY L. *Exploring Written English: A Guide for Basic Writers*. Boston: Little, Brown, 1983.

Exploring Written English was designed both for ESL students and for "basic writers" among native speakers of English. The first five chapters constitute a rudimentary rhetoric with a few exercises, but I include Reynolds's book in this section because of the numerous and effective exercises she provides on sentence division, agreement, verb forms, and especially proofreading. Students who make these types of errors can learn to correct everything *you* see and point out to them, but until they train their own eyes and ears to catch errors without you the problems will persist. Good proofreading exercises are hard to find.

RIZZO, BETTY. *The Writer's Studio: Exercises for Grammar, Proofreading and Composition*. 2nd ed. New York: Harper and Row, 1982.

The Writer's Studio includes elaborate exercises on all types of subject-verb-pronoun agreement, verbs, sentence structure, and punctuation. It is less thorough on prepositions and makes no reference to articles.

Although Rizzo uses some sentence exercises, at least half of the exercises ask students to correct, punctuate, or identify parts of speech, clauses, and phrases in full passages, including poems. This makes the work a bit more interesting than the transformation or completion of individual sentences. This type of exercise is especially effective as practice in proofreading for subject-verb agreement.

Because *The Writer's Studio* is designed as a course plan, with overlapping exercises and review sections that involve several different procedures at once, exercises for a specific problem are somewhat more difficult to locate than they are in Frank's *Modern English,* but the exercises are worth looking for. You can find them without much trouble by checking the index and table of contents.

At the end of the book there are answers to all of the exercises.

IX. COPYRIGHT LAWS CONCERNING REPRODUCTION OF PUBLISHED MATERIAL

Before 1976, the copyright laws failed to define the exact limits within which teachers could reproduce published material and use it in the classroom without permission from publishers. The new laws, however, are fairly explicit and allow for limited use of published material while attempting, at least, to protect the rights of publishers and authors. I will summarize these laws briefly, not only to help you avoid violating them when you consider using published material in the classroom, but also to explain the extent to which you can use copies of published material legally.

The current laws allow teachers to make one copy of an excerpt, essay, story, article, or poem for their own use and one copy for each of their students in one course, within the following limitations:

1. Poetry: You may copy a complete poem of fewer than 250 words, or an excerpt of fewer than 250 words from a volume of poems.

2. Prose: You may copy a complete article, essay, story, etc. of fewer than 2500 words, or an excerpt of 1000 words or ten percent of the volume, whichever is less.

3. Your use of this material should be "spontaneous"; i.e., it should not be a matter of course policy or planning, but at the "instance and inspiration of the individual teacher" when there is not sufficient time to request permission to use this material.

4. Without permission, you may use this material only in one course for one term.

5. You may use only two excerpts or one poem or essay by a particular author or from a particular volume each term.

6. You may use no more than nine of these from different sources per course per term.

7. You are not allowed to compile these photocopied materials, to make your own little textbook, without permission from the publishers.

8. The right to reproduce published material excludes publications intended to be "consumable," such as workbooks and exercise sheets.

9. Each copy should include a notice of copyright.

10. You may not charge your students more than the cost of copying.

If you do need to get permission from publishers to use copied material or to compile this material for your class, the reference librarians at your institution will probably have sample letters for this purpose, and they will also steer you to more complete explanations of the copyright laws.

ALPHABETICAL LIST OF WORKS DESCRIBED

At the end of each entry I have listed the chapter section/s in which the text is discussed (e.g., [§ VIII. A]).

Aronson, Trudy. *English Grammar Digest.* Englewood Cliffs, N.J.: Prentice-Hall, 1984. [§ VIII. A]

Axelrod, Rise B., and Charles R. Cooper. *The St. Martin's Guide to Writing.* New York: St. Martin's, 1985. [§ III. B]

Azar, Betty Schrampfer. *Understanding and Using English Grammar.* Englewood Cliffs, N.J.: Prentice-Hall, 1981. [§ VIII. B]

Becker, Howard, *Writing for Social Scientists: How to Start and Finish Your Thesis, Book, or Article.* Chicago: Univ. of Chicago Press, 1986. [§ III. D]

Behrens, Laurence, and Leonard Rosen. *Writing and Reading Across the Curriculum.* 2nd ed. Boston: Little, Brown, 1985. [§ III. D]

Berthoff, Ann. *The Making of Meaning: Metaphors, Models, and Maxims For Writing Teachers.* Montclair, N.J.: Boynton/Cook, 1981. [§ II. A]

Brooks, Cleanth, and Robert Penn Warren. *Modern Rhetoric.* 4th ed. New York: Harcourt Brace Jovanovich, 1979. [§s III. C and VI. A]

Clark, Virginia, et al. *Language: Introductory Readings.* 4th ed. New York: St. Martin's, 1985. [§ III. F]

Clayes, Stanley, et al. *Contexts for Composition.* 5th ed. Englewood Cliffs, N.J.: Prentice-Hall, 1979. [§ VI. B]

Clifford, John, and Robert Waterhouse. *Sentence Combining: Shaping Ideas for Better Style.* Indianapolis: Bobbs-Merrill, 1983. [§ IV. B]

Cohen, B. Bernard. *Writing About Literature.* 2nd ed. Glenview, Ill.: Scott, Foresman, 1973. [§ VI. C]

Coles, William, Jr. *The Plural I—The Teaching of Writing.* New York: Holt, Rinehart and Winston, 1978. [§ II. A]

Comley, Nancy R., et al. *Fields of Writing: Reading Across the Disciplines.*
    2nd ed. New York: St. Martin's, 1987. [§ III. D]

Cook, Mary Jane. *Trouble Spots of English Grammar: A Text-Workbook
    for ESL.* 2 vols. New York: Harcourt Brace Jovanovich, 1983.
    [§ VIII. B]

Cooper, Charles, and Lee Odell, eds. *Research on Composing: Points of
    Departure.* Urbana, Ill.: NCTE, 1978. [§ II. B]

Corder, Jim. *Contemporary Writing: Process and Practice.* 2nd ed. Glenview,
    Ill.: Scott, Foresman, 1983. [§ III. C]

Crews, Frederick, and Sandra Schor. *The Borzoi Handbook for Writers.* New
    York: Knopf, 1985. [§ III. A]

Crews, Frederick, *The Random House Handbook.* 4th ed. New York: Random
    House, 1984 [§ III. B]

D'Angelo, Frank. *Process and Thought in Composition.* 2nd ed. Cambridge,
    Mass.: Winthrop, 1980. [§ VI. A]

Donovan, Timothy, and Ben McClelland, eds. *Eight Approaches to Teaching
    Writing.* Urbana: NCTE, 1980. [§ II. A]

Elbow, Peter. *Writing Without Teachers.* New York: Oxford Univ. Press, 1973.
    [§ II. A]

Elcan, Ruth. *Elements of College Writing.* 2nd ed. Boston: Little, Brown, 1980.
    [§ VII. B]

Elsbree, Langdon, et al. *The Heath Handbook of Composition.* 11th ed. Lex-
    ington, Mass.: D. C. Heath, 1986. [§ III. A]

Emery, Donald. *Sentence Analysis.* New York: Holt, Rinehart and Winston,
    1961. [§ IV. C]

Escholz, Paul, et al. *Language Awareness.* 3rd ed. New York: St. Martin's,
    1982. [§ III. F]

Fahnestock, Jeanne, and Marie Secor. *A Rhetoric of Argument.* New York:
    Random House, 1982. [§ VI. C]

Faulkner, Claude W. *Writing Good Sentences: A Functional Approach to Sen-
    tence Structure, Grammar, and Punctuation.* 3rd ed. New York: Scrib-
    ners, 1973. [§ IV. C]

Follett, Wilson. *Modern American Usage.* Edited and completed by Jacques
    Barzun. New York: Warner, 1966. [§ III. E]

Frank, Marcella. *Modern English: A Practical Reference Guide.* Englewood
    Cliffs, N.J.: Prentice-Hall, 1972. [§ VIII. A]

————. *Modern English: Exercises for Non-Native Speakers.* 2nd ed. 2 vols.
    Englewood Cliffs, N.J.: Prentice-Hall, 1986. [§ VIII. B]

————. *Writer's Companion.* Englewood Cliffs, N.J.: Prentice-Hall, 1983. [§
    VIII. A]

Gebhardt, Richard, ed. *Composition and Its Teaching: Articles from* College
    Composition and Communication *During the Editorship of Edward P. J.*

Corbett. Ohio Council of Teachers of English Language Arts, 1979. [§ II. B]

Gefvert, Constance J. *The Confident Writer—A Norton Handbook*. New York: Norton, 1985 [§ III. A]

Graves, Richard L. *Rhetoric and Composition: A Sourcebook for Teachers and Writers*. Montclair, N.J.: Boynton/Cook, 1984. [§ II. B]

Graves, Robert, and Alan Hodge. *The Reader Over Your Shoulder: A Handbook for Writers of English Prose*. 2nd ed. New York: Vintage, 1979. [§ III. E]

Grinols, Anne Bradstreet. *Critical Thinking: Reading Across the Curriculum*. Ithaca: Cornell Univ. Press, 1984. [§ III. D]

Hairston, Maxine. *Successful Writing: A Rhetoric for Advanced Composition*. 2nd ed. New York: Norton, 1986. [§s III. C and VI. C]

Hartwell, Patrick. *Open to Language: A New College Rhetoric*. New York: Oxford Univ. Press, 1982. [§ V. A]

Hayakawa, S. I. *Language in Thought and Action*. 4th ed. New York: Harcourt Brace Jovanovich, 1978. [§ VI. C]

Heffernan, James, and John Lincoln. *Writing—A College Handbook*. 2nd ed. New York: Norton, 1986. [§s III. B, V. A and VIII. A]

Hodges, John C., and Mary E. Whitten. *Harbrace College Handbook*. 10th ed. New York: Harcourt Brace Jovanovich, 1986. [§ III. A]

Horner, Winifred Bryan, ed. *Composition and Literature: Bridging the Gap*. Chicago: Univ. of Chicago Press, 1983. [§ II. B]

Horton, Susan. *Thinking Through Writing*. Baltimore: Johns Hopkins Univ. Press, 1982. [§s III. C and VI. C]

Irmscher, William F. *Teaching Expository Writing*. New York: Holt, Rinehart and Winston, 1979. [§s II. A and VII. A]

———. *The Holt Guide to English*. 3rd ed. New York: Holt, Rinehart and Winston, 1981. [§s III. B, V. A and VI. C]

Jacobus, Lee. *A World of Ideas: Essential Readings for College Writers*. 2nd ed. New York: St. Martin's, 1986. [§ III. F]

Judy, Stephen, and Susan Judy. *An Introduction to the Teaching of Writing*. New York: Wiley, 1981. [§ II. A]

Kane, Thomas. *The Oxford Guide to Writing: A Rhetoric and Handbook for College Students*. New York: Oxford Univ. Press, 1983. [§ VI. A]

Kirszner, Laurie, and Stephen Mandell. *The Holt Handbook*. New York: Holt, Rinehart and Winston, 1986. [§ III. A]

Klaus, Carl, and Nancy Jones, eds. *Courses for Change in Writing: A Selection from the NEH Iowa Institute*. Montclair, N.J.: Boynton/Cook, 1984. [§ II. A]

Knoblauch, C. H., and Lil Brannon. *Rhetorical Traditions and the Teaching of Writing*. Montclair, N.J.: Boynton / Cook, 1984. [§ II. A]

Lanham, Richard. *Analyzing Prose*. New York: Scribner's, 1983. [§ III. E]

————. *Revising Prose*. New York: Scribners, 1979. [§ IV. A]

————. *Style—An Anti-Textbook*. New Haven: Yale Univ. Press, 1974. [§ II. A]

Leech, Geoffrey, and Jan Svartvik. *A Communicative Grammar of English*. Singapore: Longman, 1975. [§ VIII. A]

Leggett, Glen, et al. *Prentice-Hall Handbook for Writers*. 9th ed. Englewood Cliffs, N.J.: Prentice-Hall, 1985. [§ III. A]

Levin, Gerald. *Prose Models*. 6th ed. New York: Harcourt Brace Jovanovich, 1984. [§ VI. B]

Lindemann, Erika. *A Rhetoric for Writing Teachers*. Cambridge: Oxford Univ. Press, 1982. [§ II. A]

Maimon, Elaine, et al. *Readings in the Arts and Sciences*. Boston: Little, Brown, 1984. [§ III. D]

————. *Writing in the Arts and Sciences*. Cambridge: Winthrop, 1981. [§ III. D]

Marius, Richard. *A Writer's Companion*. New York: Knopf, 1985. [§ III. E]

McCrimmon, James. *Writing with a Purpose*. 8th ed. Revised by Joseph Trimmer and Nancy Sommers. Boston: Houghton Mifflin, 1984. [§ III. B and V. A]

McDonald, Daniel. *The Language of Argument*. 4th ed. New York: Harper and Row, 1983. [§ VI. B]

McQuade, Donald, and Robert Atwan. *Popular Writing in America: The Interaction of Style and Audience*. 3rd ed. New York: Oxford Univ. Press, 1985. [§ III. F]

Memering, Dean, and Frank O'Hare. *The Writer's Work: Guide to Effective Composition*. 2nd ed. Englewood Cliffs, N.J.: Prentice-Hall, 1984. [§ III. B]

Miller, Robert K. *The Informed Argument: A Multidisciplinary Reader and Guide*. New York: Harcourt Brace Jovanovich, 1986. [§ III. D]

Nicolas, J. Karl, and James R. Nicholl. *Rhetorical Models for Effective Writing*. 3rd ed. Cambridge, Mass.: Winthrop, 1985. [§ VI. B]

Ohmann, Richard, and W. B. Coley, eds. *Ideas for English 101—Teaching Writing in College*. Urbana: NCTE, 1975. [§ II. B]

Parks, A. Franklin, et al. *Structuring Paragraphs: A Guide to Effective Writing*. New York: St. Martin's, 1981. [§ V. A]

Ponsot, Marie, and Rosemary Deen. *Beat Not the Poor Desk. Writing: What to Teach, How to Teach It, and Why*. Montclair, N.J.: Boynton/Cook, 1982. [§ II. A]

Quirk, Randolph, and Sidney Greenbaum. *A Concise Grammer of Contemporary English*. New York: Harcourt Brace Jovanovich, 1973. [§ VIII. A]

Reinking, James, et al. *Improving College Writing: A Book of Exercises*. New

York: St. Martin's, 1981. [§ VII. B]

Reynolds, Audrey L. *Exploring Written English: A Guide for Basic Writers.* Boston: Little, Brown, 1983. [§ VIII. B]

Rizzo, Betty. *The Writer's Studio: Exercises for Grammar, Proofreading and Composition.* 2nd ed. New York: Harper and Row, 1982. [§ VIII. B]

Romine, Jack S. *Writing Sentences: A Self-Teaching Guide to Grammar, Structure, and Sentence Combining.* 2nd ed. New York: Holt, Rinehart and Winston, 1979. [§ IV. C]

Rosa, Alfred, and Paul Escholz. *Models for Writers: Short Essays for Composition.* New York: St. Martin's, 1982. [§ VI. B]

Shaughnessy, Mina. *Errors and Expectations: A Guide for the Teacher of Basic Writing.* New York: Oxford Univ. Press, 1977. [§ II. A]

Smith, Charles Kay. *Styles and Structures: Alternative Approaches to College Writing.* New York: Norton, 1974. [§ VI. C]

Sommers, Nancy, and Donald McQuade, eds. *Student Writers at Work: and in the Company of Other Writers.* The Bedford Prizes. Second Series. New York: St. Martin's, 1986. [§ III. F]

Stern, Arthur. "When is a Paragraph?" *The Writing Teacher's Sourcebook.* Edited by Gary Tate and Edward Corbett. 294–300. New York: Oxford Univ. Press, 1981. [§ V. B]

Stevens, Martin, and Jeffry Kluewer. *In Print: Critical Reading and Writing.* New York: Longman, 1983. [§ III. F]

Stock, Patricia, ed. *fforum: Essays on Theory and Practice in the Teaching of Writing.* Montclair, N.J.: Boynton/Cook, 1983. [§ II. B]

Strong, William. *Sentence Combining: A Composing Book.* 2nd ed. New York: Random House, 1983. [§ IV. B]

Strunk, William, and E. B. White. *The Elements of Style.* 3rd ed. New York: Macmillan, 1979. [§ III. E]

Tate, Gary, and Edward Corbett, eds. *The Writing Teacher's Sourcebook.* New York: Oxford Univ. Press, 1981. [§ II. B]

Thomas, Lewis. "Notes on Punctuation." *The Medusa and the Snail.* New York: Viking Penguin, 1979. (Rpt. in *The Norton Reader: An Anthology of Expository Prose.* 6th ed. Edited by Arthur M. Eastman. 339–41. New York: Norton, 1984.) [§ VII. A]

Walvoord, Barbara E. Fassler. *Helping Students Write Well: A Guide for Teachers in All Disciplines.* The Modern Language Association, 1982. [§ II. A]

Whitehall, Harold. "The System of Punctuation."' *Essays on Language and Usage.* Edited by Leonard Dean and Kenneth Wilson. 223–33. 2nd ed. New York: Oxford Univ. Press, 1963. [§ VII. A]

Williams, Joseph M. *Style: Ten Lessons in Clarity and Grace.* 2nd ed. Glenview, Ill.: Scott, Foresman, 1985. [§s III. E, IV. A, and VII. B]

Winterowd, W. Ross. *The Contemporary Writer: A Practical Rhetoric.* 2nd ed.

New York: Harcourt Brace Jovanovich, 1981. [§s III. C and VI. C]

Zender, Karl, and Linda Morris. *Persuasive Writing: A College Reader*. New York: Harcourt Brace Jovanovich, 1981. [§ VI. B]

Works Cited

Baker, Sheridan. *The Practical Stylist*. 5th ed. New York: Harper and Row, 1981.

Britton, James, and Douglas Barnes. *Language and Learning*. Harmondsworth: Pelican, 1972.

Eastman, Arthur M., ed. *The Norton Reader*. 6th ed. New York: Norton, 1984.

Hairston, Maxine. "The Winds of Change: Thomas Kuhn and the Revolution in the Teaching of Writing." *CCC* 33 (Feb. 1982): 76–88.

Kuhn, Thomas. *The Structure of Scientific Revolutions*. Vol. II, No. 2. *International Encyclopedia of Unified Science*. 2nd ed. Chicago: Univ. of Chicago Press, 1970.

Sale, Roger. *On Writing*. New York: Random House, 1970.

APPENDIX 1

The Ragged Interface: Computers and the Teaching of Writing[1]

STUART DAVIS

I. INTRODUCTION: WRITERS' NEEDS AND MACHINES' POWERS

There are, to be sure, no quick fixes. That is a little hard to remember in the current rush of enthusiasm for computers in education—and in the face of a campaign by the commercial sector fiercer and more inevitable than any sales effort since Islam conquered the East. Computers do, however, promise some enchanting *partial* "fixes" in a teaching discipline which, in theory and practice, is abandoning many of its older fixities. Several of their current uses offer means of modifying the scene of writing instruction in accordance with the more promising thought of the last two decades about composition teaching. In one central role— as word processors—they are very prominently on the scene already and need to be reckoned with. This appendix will survey some regions of that scene where word-processors have already made an appearance, describing a few of their typical roles and suggesting ways of casting and directing them effectively. It will look at some issues in composition theory and teaching practice on which the use of machines seems to shed light. And it will offer some minimal information about the machines themselves and their applications[2]—not in order to review products, and not to proclaim the state of the art—but to illustrate my own timebound and far from authoritative proposals.

Right now, computers present writing teachers with a *conditional* imperative: to use them, if we do, in ways consistent with their limits, our aims, their potential, and our reasonable expectations of our students. "Principled use" is the motto of Lillian Bridwell and her co-workers at the University of Minnesota; for them it is a summons to systematic study of the ways in which processors can meet writers' needs ("The Writing Process" 383). For us, it might name a more modest project: to learn something about the current use of machines in writing and consider a few principles implied by their use. Yet that project does not seem wholly simple when we realize that the uses of computers in writing instruction are already several, various, and disparate, and when we resist (as we should) the idea that any computer application that does or might exist will answer a real "need" of writers without deflecting or transforming it. Currently available computer applications are scattered across the field of writing instruction almost as unevenly as the machines themselves are scattered across the scene of higher education.[3] And that is largely because the interface between machines' power and writers' needs is ragged and intermittent. It is hard, for example, not to be struck by the oddness of the still probationary marriage between the craft of controlling computer machinery and the trade of helping students to write well—to write, in just that medium where computers work with even more tortuous difficulty than some students do: natural language. Computer applications that do something with language provide and require widely differing investments of machine and human intelligence. In the word processor we have a lavishly powerful and mature application—nimble, versatile, and with great teaching potential, but fundamentally stupid; the intelligence comes from its users. Word processors, to which Sections II and III of this appendix are devoted, require a good deal of supplementary intelligence from those who would use them well for learning and teaching. Then there are a host of applications striving to use computers in "smarter" ways—to stimulate and pace students' discovery of what they have to say, to help them organize their work, to check writers' prose for stylistic and grammatical flaws and merits, and the like; some of these struggle with (and some try to circumvent) the very stringent limits to machines' power for dealing intelligently with language. Few of them can do without word processors, and some have been combined with word processors. And some teachers and developers have tried to extend or exploit word processors' power without direct appeal to machines' linguistic "intelligence." I'll look over a variety of these alternative applications in Section IV, for they offer to loosen machines' present limitations in ways that may eventually change our means of meeting our students' needs and perhaps alter those needs themselves, reshaping the interface and smoothing it a bit.

But not (so I hope) too quickly or with too much modish unction. Writer's needs, especially when those writers are students, are so variously defined by different pedagogies and by the brute expediencies of teaching that a sudden match of tool and "need" may be as much a cause for suspicion as for rejoicing. Consider the five-paragraph argumentative essay. In the early 1980s, at one of those conferences on Computers and Education or Composition which have multiplied since then, two teachers presented a program for stimulating and controlling the progress of such an essay. It was hard for a BASIC programmer and writing teacher not to share their pride in an application which they had programmed themselves and which offered to reduce to an obvious sequence the risks and messiness of composing a paper. They had pet names for sentences. The program prompted students to enter the thesis sentence (I don't remember its name). Then it prompted for the "grabber"—the very first sentence of the introductory paragraph, which was to end with the thesis. Then it prompted for the "zinger"—the first or last sentence of the *final* paragraph. And then, of course, for the three reasons or causes or occasions or topics which would create the topic sentences of paragraphs 2, 3, and 4. And then the program would display the created outline of the essay, and the student would write it.

Just what offends us here? Is it the sheer formalism, the dogged insistence on the supremacy of topic sentences, the idolatry of the outline? Is it the implied denial that the writer could possibly discover a concrete basis for her essay's form in her own experience of living and of writing? These estranging features add up to what Richard Ohmann found abundantly in the writing textbooks of the last decade and called "administered"—and alienated—"thought." The five-paragraph-theme routine was already embedded in this teaching discipline; the machines only raised it to the level of caricature, helped by teachers who should have recognized that too close a fit between machine power and writers' needs may indicate that those needs have already been systematically distorted. And an even more powerful version of the same routine survives in a widely distributed package of writers' aids that I discuss in Section IV.

Administered thought is appropriated thought, and appropriation is the trade's besetting temptation. (Write it like this, we say, meaning: write it as I would if I were writing your essay and I were . . . me, and you too.) And yet: *"We are the only profession,"* writes Geoffrey Hartman, *"that asks people to do their own writing—and reading"* (185). His essay, "The Humanities, Literacy, and Communication," wars gently not on computers but on speed and specialization, especially in the teaching of "skills" or "composition" (as well as, I think, on McLuhanite dreams of immediate communication).

> Writing is an activity that takes place in time and cannot leave time. . . . Composition may be a skill, editing may be a skill, but writing is something more. We can teach composition, and we can give courses—bigger and better—in expository prose: but it all remains a come-on to introduce the student to the discipline of writing by making it habitual. (187)

Speed is what has made computers' fortunes. Specialization—an algorithmic conformity to the requirements of machines, by which one thing must be done, completely, at one step—is what makes them work. Computer use often seems to require us to do something other than writing (in Hartman's very emphatic sense of that word) or threatens to take away from us elements of our *own* writing (the full execution, the slow struggle with the material medium) in exchange for speed and power of communication. Or efficiency in teaching.

Judiciously used, of course, computers may appropriate nothing of the teacher's or the student's own; but they may disguise or heighten paradoxes in both roles that are already there. I want to suggest that machines, in addition to their instrumental value, have one more "use" for teachers of writing: as perspectival devices, means of looking twice at writing and at teaching writing—no less in the discrepancies between them and the needs of writers than the serviceable congruities we discover. "Principled use" challenges us to look both "at" and "through" machines: to look *at* them and their functions in writing instruction, seeing what they do best and least well, and to look *through* them to the theories and practices they may facilitate, favor, supplement, replace, or offer to transform. They are partial mirrors and models of what we do. For that reason, Section II looks more closely at "process" theories of writing and at what is known about students' revising habits than an unwavering gaze "at" the machine might warrant; Section III, likewise, addresses the teaching of revision as an exemplary case where machines facilitate teaching practices that can, indeed, be carried out without their aid.

And for us and our students, of course, computers are also immensely alluring "come-ons" to the discipline of writing. We need daring and sagacity to use them to make that discipline habitual and autonomous.

II. THE WORD PROCESSOR AND THE WRITING PROCESS

A. Seeing Writing . . . as Process

Early converts to word processing promptly wrote books or articles on word processing, or at least talked enthusiastically to those who were writing them. These conversion stories often testified to the machine's benign effects on their authors' work habits, style, and gastric health, or, more interestingly, to the *aesthetic* appeal of text emerging on the screen—an appeal that most people who write with machines will recognize. Phrases and sentences take shape in the frictionless, cool medium of phosphorescence or on the pleasingly grainy ground of the high-resolution black and white monitor; text pours or flows from line to line to the paragraph's end, offering a visual pledge of that fluency of expression we laboriously seek; and pages scroll past in a magic band that, however often wounded, heals itself instantly like the limbs of a Miltonic angel. Work on the text gains rhythm, pacing activity with orderly closure.

> The screen became a dancing sea of revisions and repairs. Long sentences suddenly vanished, but left no hole—the remaining sentences closed the gap and rearranged themselves as if nothing had been removed. Everything was instantly made tidy. (Zinsser 17)

Excrescence and ugliness disappear on command.

> [To write this way] is . . . satisfying to the soul, because each maimed
> and misconceived passage can be made to vanish instantly, by the
> word or by the paragraph, leaving a pristine green field on which to
> make the next attempt. (Fallows 86)

And the text itself becomes "fluid," not only on its surface but in its
emergence from the depths of the writing process—as it may always
have been for creative writers like Robert Coover, who have discovered
a new vehicle for that fluidity in the file structure of a word processor.

> I'm no longer just collecting material, I'm moving the collected mate-
> rial—the vague ideas, that is, plus the information that I've gath-
> ered—a step toward the actual writing experience. I'm beginning to
> see the elements that look most interesting, the ones that look less so.
> Ideas that seem disconnected at one point suddenly have some rele-
> vance and I draw them up and link them to these thoughts, and they
> begin to shape themselves into a show of sorts. And this is actually
> creative activity, this activity between the collection, the preparation,
> and the actual writing of the line. (quoted in Catano, "Computer-
> Based Writing" 312)

The electronic powers that make such experiences possible have led
many people to expect that machines will work their magic *directly* on
those who write, helping them (as William Zinsser, an early proselyte,
anticipated) to "clean up their sentences by focusing their mind on the
act of writing and revising"; to learn, through the machine's new lucidity, the connection between thinking clearly and writing clearly; and to
discover the professional writer's secret:

> . . . That rewriting is the essence of writing—that their first draft is
> probably poor and that they have a second and a third chance to make
> it better. . . .
> Seeing is a key to writing. What the word processor could do is
> revolutionize the way we think about words by displaying them for
> our consideration and giving us an instant chance to reconsider them.
> (23, 25-6)

Indeed, rewriting is the essence of writing—a lesson that is at least
as hard for college students to learn as for those "professional men and
women" Zinsser has in mind. Teachers may want to offer students
something more than the functional clarity that Zinsser favors as a criterion of style, and of course they *must* offer students something more
in order to help them attain even that.

What teachers do offer, at their best, is a more deeply considered ideal of "writing," both as text to be read with heightened awareness of its rhetorical efficacy and as a "process" in or through which texts come into being. "The writing process"—the term, at least—has not lost its hold on the thinking of writing teachers and researchers after two decades of currency, as several sections of this book testify. "Process" militates against both an exclusive valuation of written products and a discredited model of what happens, or should happen, when writers write: the following of "a linear sequence of rational procedures for packaging ideas in language, according to prescribed forms," as Chapter 1 has it (5). It speaks *for* intimately serious attention to writers' experience of their developing tasks and texts in the real time of composition. But beyond these concerns, "writing process" is the site of rival theorizings, acknowledged paradoxes, and divergent practices. If there is *a* writing process, is it recursive or linear? Both (Sommers, "The Need for Theory" 46): there is no more sense in describing it as a linear series of stages than as an eternal loop. Are its critical moments sudden intuitions of discovery, or are they results of methodized planning? Both: writers' testimony on each side of the question is compelling (Gebhardt). "The writing process" names theorists' attempts at finding a comprehensive theory or paradigm from which teaching practices can be deduced; its contradictions show nothing so much as that the ideal is elusive and vulnerable. Vulnerable, above all, to debasement. "The writing process" may be cultivated for its own sake, and "process" work and perhaps navel-gazing may come to dominate the classroom. Or it may be "dismantled" into discrete successive stages (prewriting, writing, rewriting; prevision, vision, revision), as some textbooks and some theory have done, subjecting it to mechanical administration (Rose). Unsurprisingly but strikingly, the strongest process model to stand up against the "linear stage" one—that of Linda Flower and John Hayes—is based on the problem-solving theory that lies behind much thinking in cognitive science and is potentially apt for the new writing environment provided by the machine.

B. The Computer's Promise for Process: The Fluid Text

Then will computers clarify our thought about The Process and help us explore and control it? After all, the writing "processor" may put us and our students in closer touch with that process because of the way it restructures writing work, abridging some phases of it and raising others to visibility and control. Anything, in principle, can be done with that fluid text at any time with the machine, just as in Flower's and Hayes's "cognitive process" model any of the procedures into which the process is analyzed ("generating," "organizing," "translating" into written copy, "reviewing") can be called up at any point and put in the service of a comprehensive, goal-directed activity. But if "process" and processor share some of the same promise, they risk the same fate: they may license undisciplined or mindless practice or decay into a means of routinization.

Yet: "Seeing is a key to writing," and *seeing*—seeing immediately what is written—is surely where the potential of the word processor begins, for good or ill. Hopes for the machine's direct impact on students have rested on four main ways in which it modifies the work of writing, and if these are often figuratively discussed as powers of the machine or features of the text, teacher-theorists are really interested in the new relations which these powers and features may create among writers, tools, texts, and tasks. First is the visual *perspicuity* of the text entered from the keyboard, its surface lucidity and order. On the screen there is no tangle or blur, no doubt about what is and what isn't written. Nor is there the opportunity that handwriting provides for the chronically blocked writer or self-deprecating anti-writer to foul his own nest with scrawl. Displayed writing can be *read,* immediately placing the writer in a reader's relation to her text; it looks mature and published, a stimulus to pride, and invites comparison with the mature and published writing of others.

Next, this lucidity and order are *dynamic and interactive.* Word processors open "a direct path from the mind to the page," favoring "fingertip thinking," in the words of a popular word processing/writing cookbook (Fluegelman and Hewes 151); writers project their words into an instantly responsive environment which may strip away the physical and cognitive constraints that attend writing by hand or typewriter and may induce them to write more (and more fluent) prose. Common experience suggests that computers favor an inherently, even addictively pleasurable work/play rhythm (witness the allure of video games and of "hacking" in BASIC); that rhythm may be reclaimed from such reprobate activities as these and diverted to writing instruction. For such a hope there are more informed, or studied, explanations. Colette Daiute, a learning psychologist who champions computer use at every level of writing instruction, finds the machine intrinsically, if "subtly," inter-active, offering feedback from a system that may even become a kind of surrogate audience. She expects the word processor's speed and flex-ibility—and its power to delete, reorder, recall, and transform text—to unload writers' short-term memories of the otherwise simultaneous demands of the writing act, allowing them to suspend some demands and fulfill others and sequence their work as more experienced writers do.

The writer's new freedom to review text, of course, has trained the hopes of teachers on the machine's vast power to support and stimulate revision, which depends in turn on two of its other features: the *mobility* it offers writers to course back and forth through their own text, work-ing on any part of it at any time and addressing it at any level ("sur-face" or "deep"; conceptual or rhetorical; word, sentence, paragraph, or beyond), and the *duplicability* of texts of any size that the machine makes possible. Writers can copy versions of a sentence, a passage, or an essay to the limits of document length or storage space, each one a specimen for a new experiment or an artifact to be broken and remade in a new way—above all, without loss of the prototype. The same power spares writers the task of recopying; the word processor frees students from the chief material constraint on productive revision to focus their attention on passages needing change or to release their faculties for creative elaboration. By this account, the machine offers the best of all possibilities: challenge, surprise, an invitation to risk-taking—*but* with the security of a stable text; the option of infinite variations, pauses, revisions—*but* all woven into one ultimately continuous and recupera-ble writing process.

Here the writing-place provided by the word processor is surely the utopia of the "fluid" text, "open" to the writing process in all dimen-sions at once. To say the least, this prospect places considerable demands on the imagination and experience of the user—demands which can be rather easily ignored or evaded with the help of the machine itself. The word processor may challenge users to explore its transformative pow-ers; it also lures them to "process the process" with new and unreflec-tive immediacy, showing that what might have been an enrichment of process is really a relapse into mass production. What is lost is the salutary tension that the new technology *can* help to create between expressive facility and resistance, perhaps or between "process"- and "product"-thinking.

C. Realities: Students and Word Processors

Unreflective use of the word processor shows what happens when the tension is lost. Despite its technical powers, despite the resources it offers practiced writers for doing gratifyingly and sometimes quickly what they already know how to do, the word processor offers very ambivalent help as an isolated learning device. My experience and a certain amount of published research (I think of the studies and proposals of Bean, Bridwell et al., Harris, Hawisher, Hitchcock, Hull, Moulthrop, and Prufahl) indicate that merely providing students with word processors doesn't, as a rule, change their writing patterns for the better or improve their prose. Some of the machine's virtues turn against the value of its product; others are ignored or one-sidedly exploited; and the net effect, while sometimes the stimulation of new resources of invention and expression, is more often the entrenchment of old habits of composing. Here are some effects on writing processes and products that unmediated computer use seems to encourage—effects that you should be able to recognize in the work at least of new converts to the word processor.

1. Students write more. Almost everyone does. The fact is fascinating; constraints fall and the machine draws us on and on, "interactively" prompting for more words, showing no pity for the forests that will have to be destroyed. This is not an unmixed curse; with the right students, in the right circumstances, it can be an absolute marvel. The freshman writer who has hitherto written about 2000 words a year, with some difficulty, suddenly discovers electronic license for prolixity—and now for the first time there is text for student and reader to work with. Students sophisticated enough to use "prewriting" strategies on their own to generate what they *know* is a first draft find headlong composition a valuable step toward a more concise, better organized version. But the same license lends itself to padding, repetition, and the mechanical elaboration of local structure without gain in substance.

2. Casual error proliferates. In spite of their new perspicuity or perhaps because of it, texts can grow surprisingly spotty at the local level; they may become rife with typographical mistakes, doublings, elisions, and fossils of words and abandoned syntactic structures. Why? For one thing, writing that actually conceals manifold flaws may look perfect on the screen and may lend itself to instant visual approval, not careful proofreading. (Call this the "whited sepulchre" effect.) For another, the new ease of "spot" revision or editing, performed without recopying, encourages neglect of the syntactic consequences. The following sentence is an archaeological record of the revisions of a writer who had evidently forgotten how to use the "cut" command.

> It is the curriculum that must, despite traditionalists' arguments for the values of the old liberal arts, that must change to include a strong requirement in non-Western culture, must be added to the curriculum.

3. Coherence declines. Along with the expansion (but also without it), there may come defects in global structure and "sinew"—and for roughly the same reasons for which subjects and verb lose their amity and sentences their coherence. For me, this effect is the most striking clue that a student whose work I know has just switched over from manual composition to word processing. I see a sudden vagueness in long-range reference, an oblique or confused restatement of earlier ideas, quick departures from an established design, or a general stringiness of transitions, together with astonishing logical lapses. Something similar seems to have happened in Stuart Moulthrop's large and well-controlled study at Yale in 1984–1985, which showed rather striking deficiencies in "organization and persuasiveness" in the work of computer writers (as against manual composers) as scored by blind evaluators. (In a second review of the same study, Moulthrop views these shortcomings as evidence of his students' discovery "of the flexibility and richness of the writing process itself" ["Computers and Writing" 6–7]).

An easy explanation is the limit the computer screen places on an essay's immediate visibility; at any *one* point, the writer sees 18 to 24 lines of text and lacks the chance of continuous self-cueing (and self-orientation) that access to already-written material laid out in a paper copy provides. Of course "scrolling" and other movement commands can provide the scope that is lacking, but these operations may darken counsel in another way: electronic text which is viewed as a band or scroll of paragraphs may take on a new linearity and may be that much harder to imagine as the realization of a two- or three-dimensional design. Perhaps, too (*pace* Daiute), the word processor does not seem to supply an "audience" worth addressing; and coping with its mere functional complexities may make writing an even more solitary activity than it usually is.

Effects like these (and we could mention a few more, such as increased

monotony of basic sentence structures and repetition of sentence openings) may be predictable in light of the way word processors shape
work, but their intensity is sometimes surprising. Together they may
attest to a kind of tyranny of the bodily eye, a ''funneling'' of vision
that one researcher urges teachers strenuously to counteract with more
emphasis on writers' powers of abstraction and on ''the larger vision of
the work'' (Hitchcock 8).

4. And large-scale revision? ''The larger vision of work'' is just
what early observers of students' word processor use did not find. Dis-
mayingly, the students they left alone with word processors did not
undertake the large-scale revisions that the machines should have freed
them, even solicited them, to attempt. Most of the resulting studies
agree: word processors have often excited students and increased their
enthusiasm for writing, and students have sometimes been impressed
with their own ability to get thought on paper rapidly. But the students'
revising practices—measured against either their own manual performance or those of their peers—have not changed for the better. Word-
processing students may make more changes in their texts, sometimes
to the point of endlessly altering words and phrases, and (less frequently) sentences. Or they may make significantly different kinds of
sentence-level changes, doing more adding and reordering and less mere
substitution and deletion. They may also, when measured against manual revisers, make rather *fewer* changes because deprived of the stimulus of recopying the work (see Hawisher 157). But they do not, typically,
use machines to reorganize sections or resequence paragraphs (and adjust
transitions) or draw new aims for or conceptions of their work from old
versions of it—no more, at least, than they do when they type or write
by hand. They may sometimes add significantly more material to written work between one state and another, but corresponding deletion is
relatively rare. And finally, *no one* has been able to show that the increased
frequency of local revision and such more general rewriting as takes
place improves the product, whether in grammatical, stylistic, rhetorical, or intellectual terms.

Yet the students who used and use machines to write this way are of
course fulfilling the first aims of the technology; word processors were
developed as machines for speed copying *and only secondarily* for speed
composition, let alone for considered composition—for local editing,
mechanical and lexical, and not for global reconstruction of a piece of
writing. The machines dramatize, with particular force, how relatively

specialized is our idea of "writing" (and of "doing *one's own* writing," in Hartman's sense), as well as our idea of "revision," and how far from obvious those senses may be to student writers. And they also point up the real diversity of actual writers' "writing processes": student and "professional" (code for: studied, mature, thoughtful) writing does not emerge by the same channels, for many circumstances separate the professional writer from the amateur:

> a wider range of experiences to draw upon in writing, a larger storehouse of world knowledge to use in developing ideas, a larger number of writing strategies available during composing, a more finely developed sense of when to call on them, and a greater degree of control over the processes themselves. (Witte 253)

Observations of students at work with word-processors should, then, call our attention to studies of writing and revising processes at large—first, perhaps, to Nancy Sommers' "Revision Strategies of Student Writers and Experienced Adult Writers," a dispassionate demonstration of what her student writers showed that they *didn't* know about revision. The students Sommers studied didn't know even the word, preferring "scratching out and doing over" or "redoing" to designate the chiefly sanitary and lexical operations they performed on a paper when they rewrote:

> [S]tudents understand the revision process as a rewording activity. . . . They approach the revision process with what could be labeled as a "thesaurus philosophy of writing." . . . What is revealed in the students' use of the thesaurus is a governing attitude toward their writing: that the meaning communicated is already there, already finished, already produced, ready to be communicated, and all that is necessary is a better word "rightly worded." (381–382)

What characterized the work of Sommers' "experienced adult" writers (is age essential or accidental?) was above all a sense of timing. For them, a first version was, or became, a *first* one, the starting point of a continuing activity and a matrix in which to discover the seeds and to anticipate the fruits of ongoing cultivation. In the experienced writers' sense of what to expect and when to expect it lay the kinds of awareness she ascribed to them: "the adoption of a holistic perspective and the perception that revision is a recursive process."

"Student" and "experienced" writers are of course types; not all beginning students are as radically innocent as Sommers' and few "experienced" writers are satisfied with their effective control of a whole vision of their work, and it is one of the merits of Lillian Bridwell's and her colleagues' studies of writers of the two types to have shown both the real diversity of individuals' composing patterns and the tenacity with which they hold to them when first exposed to word processors. Some are and remain laborious planners, some spontaneous composers; some can rough-write a spotty text and return to amend it, while some need to perfect a relatively "finished" draft sentence by sentence before proceeding; and some—one imagines—share Robert Coover's evident pleasure in the "intermediate activity . . . between the collection, the preparation, and the actual writing of the line." Worth noting, too, is the fact that almost all the *students* whose first acquaintance with computers was studied were as new to college writing as they were to machines; the unpleasant effects I've listed are most conspicuous among neophytes, while students I teach in upper-level writing courses occasionally *do* transform their writing—both stylistically and in the clarity and coherence of its design—in a first paper or two written at the terminal, validating hopes that the computer's own resources can work directly on the writer's perceptions and powers. Transfer these recognitions to "the writing process" at large, and you will have a "process"-concept far more complex and nuanced than mere incantation of the term suggests. *Or* you may conclude that there is no "*the* writing process," but a congeries of habits and strategies characteristic of individuals' work and forming some patterns that we can learn from and selectively try to change.

D. The Need for Guides and Models

From watching writers of varying abilities and backgrounds (and particularly, perhaps, yourself) at work on word processors, you may reach further conclusions.

Like writing, writing-with-a-word-processor has to be learned, and someone has to teach it if machine use is to supplement a writing course. In the next section I suggest some teaching strategies for those who want to exploit machines' resources for individual composition and group study of writing. But how effectively we teach the use of those resources depends rather markedly on the way we think about that "interface" between writers' needs and machines' powers. To assume a perfect fit between the two is at best to accept an office-manager's view of the production of written work—or, in the case of beginning writing students, to experience a fine instance of the congruence of human and computer *limits*.

Yet a strong case can be made for the power of word processors to support an enhanced process-pedagogy; its elements are found in subsections A and B above. To "model" it in such a way that its promise becomes clearer is the writing teacher's responsibility. The suggestions I offer in the next section amount to a scissors-and-tape, *ad hoc* model, but there are more radical ones, dramatizing the allure of such a pedagogy through projections of the "process" ideal into new dimensions of time and space. Characteristically they take the form of talk about the text.

> The malleability of [the] electronic text must . . . give it a status closer to the spoken word than all other kinds of "written" texts, since it can be reconsidered and restructured in much the same way spoken text can (i.e., instantly, on the spot). Conversely, the printed version of a word processed text bears the look of a finished statement, thereby suggesting a greater finality than handwritten or even typewritten statements. In short, word processing technology spreads the notion of writing backward toward speech and forward toward print—and so makes the concept of writing less clear and less definitive. (160)

Brian Gallagher's prophecy projects the machine's processive powers into a future world of discourse, reflecting—but also clarifying—his interest in the communal writing experience offered by a collaborative, computer-equipped classroom. You may not be too comfortable with the logic of his assimilation of writing to speech or his near-dissolution of the concept "writing." You may be more intrigued by an alternative that inscribes "process" within the space of the machine: Diane Balestri's conception of "softcopy," anticipated successor of the "hard" copy churned out by line printers or typewriters. Softcopy is fluid and malleable, of course, the result of "writing to the screen" rather than "writing to the printer." But it is not amorphous, for Balestri's screen is no two-dimensional surface for the display, up and down, fast or slow, of text; it is inherently structured by ordering resources of the word processor like split-screen capabilities and file management routines and of more specialized applications like a few discussed in Section IV below. Her screen offers the student multiple perspectives on the "copy" in process, making the text a site for organized exploration of its own possibilities. The writing space so envisioned comes a little closer to the utopia sketched out earlier, where linear and recursive process-models could be realized together. To pause, to identify the available structures, to think through their application to students' needs— all these are major challenges.

You may conclude that putting machines and models to work in the writing classroom right now depends on our very gradually changing experience of writing processes and products alike and of the balance in which we have to hold them to satisfy ourselves and our students' needs. The "experienced" writers featured in Sommers' and Bridwell's studies may differ from the inexperienced in their knowledge of products, not only of processes—there, and in their understanding of how to look at those products in the right ways. Writing processes, that is, are in part reading processes, a fact that will not change as machines grow more powerful and familiar, capable of supporting the activities of a generation bred up to their use. Some of the adverse effects reviewed above surely stem from the fact that inexperienced writers are either trying and failing or simply not trying to read their work in a new way— in the glow of a cathode ray tube, of course, but also in a new combination of immediacy (to the self and its powers) and remoteness.

"Alienation" is visited by all technologies on their beneficiaries, but if some alienation is now present in everyone's experience of machine writing, that may not be wholly detrimental. Among the many enthusiastic student initiates to the word processor have been dissenters; one, a frequent reviser on paper who made far fewer changes on the machine (which she disliked), is worth listening to. "It's awfully hard for me to look at the screen and want to edit anything," she explained. "My paper seems so far away, almost abstract. . . . I thought I didn't have any right to edit that. It's not mine" (Harris 327-1328). Of course more experience would have (and presumably has) made her a more effective word processor user and allowed her to reappropriate her own writing.

But an alienation-effect may be no more a liability in the writing classroom than on the Brechtian stage; it may offer teachers an opportunity to change, not merely to perpetuate, writers' practices by affecting their ways of seeing as well as their ways of doing. For if you want to defamiliarize a common object or practice, you may put it in a new context, and if you want someone to look "at" as well as "through" something, you can start by showing it to him from different perspectives, in different media—and then encouraging him to reconstruct it. For this purpose, I suggest, the word processor is now rather well suited, as a generator of "hardcopy" as well as of "softcopy." At the borders of our awareness, perhaps, our experience of writing is being transformed. If so, the change will grow out of the new tension and intimacy the machine creates between written products and writing processes, and that is an effect we should exploit.

III. TEACHING WITH WORD PROCESSORS

A. *The Opportunities*

So: What can teachers do and what must they do in order to maximize machines' usefulness to students and to themselves and to achieve something like that intimate tension between process and product that word processors rightly used seem to favor?

Through the ordinary exchange of papers and comments, they can require of students more drafting and more revision with greater certainty that the work can be done within the time available. Machines, after all, help teachers shed certain inhibitions of their own: their reluctance, for example, to urge yet another task of recopying typescript on a student whose typing skills are minimal; their reluctance, in the other case, to labor through hopelessly patched and scrawled drafts and "rewritings," trying to figure out where their authors are headed or what they've done with a version already submitted and reviewed. By "phasing" assignments thoughtfully, teachers can look at emerging essays at any point they please, responding to what they see in ways appropriate to the student's achievement and supplying the audience that is normally absent at most stages of writing, responding to local and general features of writing, experimenting with text, and prompting changes themselves or letting students, individually or as a group, work on highly visible problem texts. Here the machine may replace, respectively, the scraps of paper on which we hurriedly sketch out examples during conferences, and the blackboard, cruelest pedagogic device since the pandybat.

In class (again, with appropriate equipment) teachers can work through each phase of a "generic" writing process, setting up exercises or activities in planning, composing, revising, and editing. "Exercises," of course, is not really what these must be. Workbook tasks performed in isolation tend to be stultifying because they are workbook tasks, "worked" on writing that is not the writer's own and "corrected" after a lapse of time. But when similar operations are carried out in public, often with students' own texts and in an improvisational spirit (and in an instantly responsive medium), they can gain a different character, social and ludic rather than disciplinary.

Most generally, computers can help teach writing as a product-directed process, regardless of which term (product, process) the teacher's preferences and the course's design favor. Teachers can plan their work—in responding to papers, in conference, and in class—so as to reveal the variety of options open to writers at each point in the process of composition and to try to defeat the common linearity of the process and the dominance of the static text. And if word processors give a new fluidity to students' writing, teachers *must* supply new paradigms of order and orientation—to limit its volatility, to keep the fluid from turning into gas.

All these claims may say little more than that you can use machines to accomplish, rapidly and rather dramatically, most of the teaching aims featured in this book; if so, few of them need much illustration, nor will they receive it. The new ingredient is of course the word processor, with its peculiar constraints and opportunities.

B. Constraints and Preparations

The opportunities at *your* disposal, of course, will impose some limits on what you can do. Colleges—and within colleges, programs and departments—differ widely in the amount of computer time they can make available to students. Some, still wedded to mainframes or common time-limited microcomputer labs, may not allow writing students a real chance to use machines for discovery and rewriting as well as for the production of final drafts. At others, students can count on ample or even generous word processing time, perhaps in facilities reserved for writers, perhaps in their own rooms. Again, "compatibility" may be a problem at campuses that do not link all student machines to main-frames or involve them in minicomputer networks; divisions and departments may have "bought in" to batches of Apples, DEC's, Commodores, or IBM-PC's and may have created a kind of patchwork of microcomputers across campus. Some options will be closed to you if half your class is writing on Displaywriters and the other half on Macintoshes—and if you have a nice old TRS-80 that has seen you through college and graduate school.

Finally, you may be teaching in a traditional classroom with no computer support while your students do their writing elsewhere; if so, your opportunities for group use of machines will be limited. For purposes of discussion, this appendix will assume that your campus supports minimally adequate computer use for you and your students and that you and they can write on the same kinds of machine and system. It assumes, too, that you have decided to require your students to do at least some of their writing on machines, if only so that they can submit their written work on disk and revise it speedily and freely. And finally, it allows for the possibility that your own and institutional schedules will permit at least some *class time* to be spent in a room where computer facilities can be shared and made the focus of collective activity. That room may be a lab with computers networked in such a way that one document can be displayed on everyone's screen—or it may be one with stand-alone terminals favoring individual work but also exposing it to peer discussion and your own intervention. (The teaching opportunities created by networked *campuses* and electronic mail are beyond the scope of this discussion.) Or it may be a classroom with a single machine and the hardware necessary to project its output on a large screen or monitor that everyone can see.

One opportunity or obligation—technical instruction of students in the use of machines—is a little more nearly under your control. I've suggested that as a writing teacher you should intervene in your students' commerce with machines, exploiting the teaching opportunities they offer. But how much technical guidance should you provide? Word processors differ widely in their hospitality to first-time users. Novices can pick up Bank Street Writer or Apple's MacWrite with an hour of instruction and some experimenting; "heavier" systems (the widely used Wordstar for the IBM-PC or Microsoft Word for the MacIntosh are good examples) demand much more learning time to allow users to perform basic functions. One answer is this: unless you are teaching a course in word processing *and* writing (and such combinations are becoming more frequent in specialized areas like technical and business communication) you should not have to carry the burden of technical instruction. Doing so can cut deeply into valuable class time and send an undesirable message to your students about the course's priorities and your own. Your program or computer lab should give introductory workshops on using the system, and it should provide technical assistance whenever the working facility is open. (Here student aides, working at the usual risible work-study wage, can be particularly helpful.)

And yet, for your own purposes, you should understand the system being used reasonably well, and if you are going to ask students to write on machines you had better be able to do some trouble-shooting to speed the production of written work. In practice, you may be playing a composite role: part teacher of writing, occasional technical consultant and machine *writing* specialist. And in the first and last capacities you will want to emphasize some features of machines and some ways of using them at the expense of others. Here are a few suggestions.

1. Know the machine. Assess the word processor that's available and learn it well yourself. You should identify its potential snags and obstacles for novices and the special features that may influence the writing of your students. You should be able to demystify the components of the machine for curious students—the hardware, the operating system, and the word processor proper; you should understand the file handling procedures of your particular system (for this is where nine out of ten word processing disasters occur); and you should be able to reassure anxious students about how little damage they and their software can do to the "hard" parts of the machine and warn them of the few sources of real damage which their carelessness can do to their own work—chiefly bad disk care or ill-timed interruptions in the work process.

2. Simplify the documentation. Don't expect your students to rely for guidance on the documentation that accompanies commercial word processors: some of it is obscure or almost illiterate; all of it is longer than anything you can reasonably expect your students to master in order to write papers. If your technical support people haven't done so, prepare a *short (3 to 4 page MAXIMUM)* list of step-by-step instructions for the most fundamental moves student users must make to call up the word processor; to write, edit, and print papers; and to save files. Don't bother with the refinements; students will learn these from each other, from watching you, or from dipping into the documentation.

3. Show students how to "move" text. One "refinement" *is* worth bothering with. On most word processors, entering and deleting text are intuitively clear operations—at least at the end of a growing document and usually in the middle. The user puts the cursor or the insertion point wherever he wants it and just types; in most cases the characters to the right of that point obligingly slide or march along to make room for the new material. But "block move" operations are not so simple. Because such "moves" are never single-keystroke operations or binary choices, different word processors handle them very differently. Such procedures are particularly important to you, for you'll want to fight students' preference for local over global changes and machines' willingness to indulge it. You'll want a student to be able to carve out a chunk of text of any size from, say, page 4 of an essay and carry it to page 1 with a minimum of effort, disorientation, or anxiety about where the chunk may be when it's no longer *here* but not yet *there*. Here you might step in and teach one word processing skill in direct conjunction with a writing exercise. Ask students to combine two short (not tiny) texts using block move commands only. For example: give them a two- or three-paragraph text that alludes to, but does not quote from, a passage in another text—perhaps a poem or part of a novel; on the same disk, give them the passage. Then ask them to carry a sizeable part of the passage into the first text, making it an effectively "blocked" quotation—and then, with more basic editorial commands, adjust context appropriately, introducing and commenting on the quotation. When they become comfortable with "cut and paste" operations like these, you can urge them to be bolder in making major changes in the organization of their own work.

4. De-emphasize formatting tricks. Almost all word processors offer a wide variety of formatting commands and procedures, and you should waste no time exploring these with your students. Of course you may wish to specify a standard format for student work, including margin-settings, spacing, headers, and page numbers (very frequently forgotten by machine writers). But if inexperienced writers tend to ignore "deep" problems of structure, logic, organization, and rhetoric on behalf of local lexical fiddling, they are all the more likely to get fixated on the most superficial features of a text.

Broadly speaking, word processors handle these features in two markedly different ways, depending on their age and the lineage of their design. Some systems seem to want you to concentrate on typing in text, *then* to concern yourself with readying it for the printer—or, if you insist on doing these things simultaneously, to look at a screen cluttered with special symbols and commands that won't print but will tell the printer what to do. For example, a student essay formatted for printing by Perfect Writer (for the IBM-PC) might begin this way on the screen:

> STYLE(leftmargin 10 chars, rightmargin 15 chars, spacing 2 lines)
> Alice Liddell
> English 101
> May 4, 1892
> Professor Dodgson
>
> @ CENTER) UN (Ravens and Writing-Desks)
> An Essay in Comparison and Contrast)

In much the same way, the old screen editors added formatting commands for a separate program to handle. In the micro world, systems like these are called "print-oriented." The alternative is a "screen-oriented" program which invites you to format as you go along with keystrokes and menu choices and *hides* most if not all of your format commands—maintaining the so-called WYSIWYG principle (What You See Is What You Get) and its corollary: what you don't get in the final printed copy, you shouldn't have to see on the screen. The distinction between these types isn't absolute, but their tendencies are clear—and the trend in more recently developed applications for the more powerful machines is toward the "screen" end of the spectrum and toward the WYSIWYG principle. Wordstar Professional for the IBM-PC, for example, strives for WYSIWYG but stops short when it comes to underlining, boldfacing, and other typeface features; to bold and underscore a title I must key in the right symbols:

> ∧B∧SQuoth the Raven: "Comparisons Are Odious"∧S∧B

WordPerfect for the IBM suppresses these marks, substituting color and/ or highlighting to let the user know what choices she's made, but its screen doesn't show some other features that may be chosen—the "justification" of type, for example, or changes in type fonts. MacWrite and other word processors for the Apple Macintosh take advantage of the machine's high-resolution screen, its proportional letter-spacing, and its intrinsic typefacing functions to display the user's document almost exactly as she'll see it in print.

From a writing teacher's point of view, there is a lot to be said for the so-called "print-oriented" systems: more exotic and distracting formatting decisions can be quietly ignored, while those commands which are minimally necessary (margin and spacing settings, indents, and underlinings) are highly conspicuous and easy to change. For first drafts, moreover, such systems usually have adequate "default" settings that will deliver text in legible form. On the other hand, if you can counteract the technical temptations they present, "screen-oriented" systems help to break down artificial partitions in the process of writing. By not expressly marking the point of closure in the preparation of a text, they better serve the ideal of a revision-based writing course in which the future of an essay is always open to review. And the screen of a once-formatted document is simply more legible.

5. SAVE THE TEXT! You should insist, again and again, that the most important command is the one that "saves" a document in the machine to its assigned place on the disk (or in another form of external storage); advise students to "save" their work every ten minutes or so, not just at the end of a work session. ("Saving" doesn't normally interrupt writing, nor does it gobble up new disk space. It merely recopies the working document from main memory into the space occupied by the previous version of itself.) You should insist, too, that students "back up" (duplicate) single copies of essay files on separate "archive" disks, both for security and to preserve copies of the term's work. Such procedures aren't just logistical conveniences; they can serve the writing process in an important way. If students are going to do more revision—both under your guidance and (one hopes) on their own—they'll want multiple copies of essays in distinct stages of development, and they'll want the freedom to reject an hour's worth of revising work and go back to the last complete state of the text.

Most systems control the saving and filing of documents by file *names;* copying a document involves changing its name, as does saving a new version of an old document. Particularly if you are asking students to submit work on disk, you may want to lay down simple naming conventions for distinguishing students, essays, and versions. On an IBM-PC-like system (different systems have different rules for naming files), "PSMITH1.2" might be the second version of Paul Smith's first essay. If you have helped Smith discover how to get from ".1" to ".2" with significant improvement, a method like this will help him go back to see in detail just how he's done it.

6. Require printed drafts. Finally, printed copy retains a central place in the process of writing and shouldn't be allowed to fade into artificial obsolescence. (The computer revolution, with its mass of writing about machines and its new opportunities for "desktop publishing," has flatly falsified prophecies about "the death of paper.") Of course students should "print out" to protect their essays yet once again, and if you're accepting student work on disk, you should for your own convenience ask for the same work on paper. But for more fundamental reasons, you should *require your students to print out at some point in the process of composition, to read the printed copy closely and mark it up for changes, and then to return to the machine to make these changes.* A printout may help to compensate not only for "screen hypnosis" and rush-writing habits but for the alienation some users may feel from what they see. And—if the process / product tension is a genuine source of the insight machines offer—printing out and viewing the hardcopy essay as a whole is also a writer's essential means for gaining all of the critical perspective on his words that the machine has to offer him.

C. Teacher, Student, and Machine: Guiding Revision

Technical preparations will get you only so far. How can you best use word processors to shape your exchange of written work with your students?

If you are teaching what I've loosely called a "conventional" and not a "workshop" or laboratory course, you may gain some of the advantages of the alternative format by asking students to submit written work on disk as well as on paper and by conferring frequently with them in the presence of a machine or by returning work quickly with requests for change or suggestions for development. Just how much of this immediately interactive counseling you can do will depend on the limits to your own time and energy; just when and how you intervene— at the point of "prewriting" or with a drafted or (provisionally) finished essay on hand—will depend on your philosophy of intervention and on the *kind* of writing course you are teaching. First, reading and evaluating student work on disk may or may not save you time. You will gain some time from the opportunity to key in comments swiftly, and your remarks will be sharply legible, whether you return them on disk or print them out. You may lose time to the machine's inevitable sloth in loading and displaying successive text files and, interestingly, to your own tendency to *write more* when composing on a machine. You may be able to control that last infirmity of noble mind; if so, experiment, finding your own pace and style. (Or you may be tempted by an application like *Writewell* or *PROSE,* described in Section IV, which automatically keys comments to passages in student texts.)

The larger issue—when and how to intervene—is so deeply involved with the role *revision* plays in writing courses and processes that revision deserves some comment for its own sake; moreover, our notions of revision help shape our use of machines.

Revision is that "point" (never a single point, of course) where teachers' concerns with process and product come to grips with each other; it is also that phase in the teaching of writing with which computers are peculiarly well adapted to deal—because of the fluidity of the text they generate and its luminous or printed fixity alike. Here I take "revision" not as a metaphor for the whole process of writing (as one might do in pointing out that every envisionment of a subject is a reenvisionment, every beginning an inaugural repetition, and so forth), nor as a way of accounting for that immediately recursive dialogue between a good writer and her emerging text by which a re-vision of what is being written spurs discovery. (These refined or extended senses of the word mark the goal of teaching: the good writer's integration of the work of rewriting in the process of composition.) I mean "revision" in its ordinary sense of rewriting an existing text to fulfill or redirect its original intention, and I have in mind the kind of revision guided by some more or less assertive intervention on the teacher's part. For something to be re-seen, there must be something to see. Revision, in this sense, also has the advantage of lying beyond some academic disputes about the *fundamental* nature of the "process" (linear? recursive? simultaneous? successive?) and of rather swiftly forcing practical decisions on us. Now, here, there is a text in the machine, almost infinitely plastic; what shall we and the writer do with it?

Nothing, perhaps. We can start making bricks without straw, but we need a little clay. If the essay is a tenement of straw, an assembly of forms of discourse more or less competently put together but without a foundation in real thought or in the student's real interests, we should commend it (if commendation it deserves) and let it blow away. With such an essay the "product"-oriented teacher will be no happier than her "process"-oriented colleague (see "Writing: Product or Process?" in Harry Shaw's Chapter 5) but at least she will be able to get the student going on something else without feeling obliged to help him to rebuild the essay from the ground, or the sub-basement, up. Surely this is a general rule: an essay is eligible for revision as against editing just as far as it shows strengths, whether actual or potential. That presumably is why Shaw suggests we follow the "seemingly paradoxical" path of encouraging students to revise stronger rather than weaker papers. Of course there is no principled reason for limiting that advice to "product"-oriented courses. If revision is an art worth learning, the "process" course too should be teaching it with the richest materials at hand, not the poorest.

Yet "process" and "product" teachers tend to view revision so very differently that the difference all but defines their opposing approaches. The "process" philosophy favors repeated rewriting prompted by open-ended, "facilitative" responses to student papers. In fact if not in principle, it extends "revision" back into the heuristic, prewriting phase of composition. At the extreme represented by Knoblauch and Brannon's *Rhetorical Traditions and the Teaching of Writing,* teachers' commentary on a text seems to aim at giving the student room and wingspace to turn and turn again, deciding *what* she wants to say (the "how" is plainly secondary); it may indeed result in the invention of a new essay, or several, sharing little textual matter with the old. "Product" commentary of the kind Shaw prefers tends to address student writing with more directive tasks and to encourage far more selective revision. "Process" teachers like Knoblauch and Brannon try to plumb students' minds to find the foundation of real intellectual concern or interest that will suffice for a paper; they seek to inspire a radical re-envisionment of the sources or the goal of writing. A "product" approach like Shaw's tries to work faster; it presumes or provides some of the same foundation and invites students to erect the superstructure; then it may challenge them to reform and strengthen the edifice, partially or as a whole. The difference, although not absolute, is no accident of professorial whim. It stems from disparate philosophies of composition teaching; it has a certain ethical basis in the teacher's willingness or reluctance to "appropriate" students' expression; and it is also determined in the last instance by real-life limits of time and energy.

Word processors, in their idiot impartiality, favor neither approach. But, perhaps paradoxically, I suggest that the "product" teacher has most to gain and least to lose from machine application in the kind of "conventional" course and classroom I have in mind. Machines may, obviously, loosen time- and energy-constraints just enough to give a greater revisionary dimension to a "product" course, allowing the instructor to teach the revision of whole essays and to ask students for more frequent rewriting than might otherwise be possible. Moreover, the "product" approach guarantees that there will be something to rewrite—an artifact that, however provisionally, has entered the public sphere and can be read alongside the readings typically assigned by the "product" course and according to the stylistic and rhetorical categories applied to those; it can be read, moreover, as evidence of the processes that produced it and that may, if appropriately guided, produce another, better, and more nearly "final" version.

Such reading is of course the essence of that "evaluative and co-authoring" stance which we take toward most student writing (see "Style versus Meaning," Bogel, Chapter 6, 173). It looks for "strengths" relative to the writer's abilities and the level of the course and finds their potential not in "meaning" or in "form" alone but in the way in which the meanings conveyed by statement and style alike conflict or exclude one another, opening avenues for development. Such reading becomes an effective cue to revision (1) when we can *specify* the source of strength in the existing text, and (2) when we can convince the writer that the weaknesses impeding its realization have a certain logic or pattern of their own. In the fanciful case Bogel asks us to imagine—the polemic against "the Wishy-Washy" whose own expression teems with wishy-washy hedges and selfqualifications (175)—the reader faces not so much a weakness or failure of meaning as a plethora of meanings in conflict, a problem which came into being during the writing process and which, by its own logic, needs to be solved by an extension of that process. To point out to the writer that his style works against his argument—Bogel's imagined cue—is really to point *to* a set of textual features that *do* work systematically together, however badly (the passives, the expletive subjects, the adversative and concessive conjunctions), and for our remark to have an effect we must have helped the student understand this stylistic pattern. That is a kind of interpretation; it rests on our understanding of the systematicity even of bad writing—on, if you will, a kind of poetics of imperfect prose.

That understanding is fairly easy to come by in the ordinary course of reading student papers. We notice how frequently a pattern of weak verbs, dummy subjects, and nominalizations accompanies ambiguous thought; how random topicalization often signals a conflict of directions or purposes; how a sequence of "this"-headed sentences can reinforce false inferences (because all things and categories are leveled by being "thissed"); and how failures of subordination at the sentence-level may reproduce similar failures in the organization of a piece of writing and the coherence of its thought. These are "product"-features, but they reflect events or tendencies in the writing process that *may* be changed by thoughtful intervention.

Take a case more concrete than Bogel's and more generally characteristic of papers by inexperienced writers: the short essay that begins with a perfunctory introduction and develops its thought late without ever fully discovering it. The instance I have at hand is a paper on Stanley Kubrick's *A Clockwork Orange* and its battle with the MPPA's rating system ("X" or "R"?); the writer had seen the film and read the 1968 rating code as well as its 1930 predecessor. Please follow me through a few of its intricacies. The first paragraph indicates some planning but more stalling:

> In Stanley Kubrick's film *A Clockwork Orange,* we are presented with a violent and sexually explicit drama. In that drama, our sympathies are drawn to a convicted murderer and rapist, something that seems totally backwards to our way of thinking and ultimately leads us to wonder what the moral standards of our society have become.

Two features of style evident here—the passives and the loose reference ("something")—pervade the essay. Yet in the course of the paper several substantial arguments emerge: that *Clockwork* deserves an "X," not the "R" it received, under the 1968 code; that watching the film had desensitized the writer himself to the sexual violence it presented (and could be counted on to do that to other viewers); that the film would have been found even more offensive under the stricter 1930 code; that the change in codes points to a change in public morality *BUT* that the similarity of the codes points to the public's refusal to acknowledge that change; and finally—a late recognition—that the picture is a deliberate challenge to just this hypocrisy.

> Stanley Kubrick's underlying idea was to make a statement about our morality today and where it is going. Using graphic sex and violence, Kubrick pointed out that we have been living a great paradox and probably will for some time to come.

The process behind this product is pretty transparent. Lacking any very clear idea about the connection between *Clockwork*'s sex and violence and the decline in public morality, the writer wrote away, discovering the stages of a rather interesting argument as he went along. The key discovery was one of agency and intention: Kubrick *meant* the film to do what the film does to us. Agency and intention, of course, are just what are lacking in the first paragraph's stylistic gaps. One way of prompting the fairly radical revision that this essay needs is to urge the writer to create a strong first paragraph, marked by active verbs and "tight" references, and then to reorganize the essay accordingly. We might also point out to him a logical problem shrouded by the disorder of the first version (what is there *in the picture* that shows that Kubrick was aware of the "great paradox"?), and we might leave that as a problem to be solved. We would, in short, prompt a revision beginning in a stylistic problem and leading to a substantive question about argument. We'd be addressing "product" features, but as evidence of the history of "process" to date and a starting point for renewing the process of revision and of discovery. And we'd be doing it on the "strength" of the student's developing thought, which in the context of his course and the assignment was recognizably original and which issued in that striking phrase in the final sentence: "living a great paradox." A thought, I would suggest, worth rethinking—on the student's time and ours.

D. Teaching Classes with Machines

We can teach revision to individual writers by asking them to revise under informed guidance. We can teach the more general skills of reading and reconstruction to classes by demonstrating or "performing" them, with or without computers, in hopes that more spontaneous and disciplined self-scrutiny will take place *before* we see papers. For some kinds of demonstration, classroom equipment such as a projector, a large monitor, or a network is particularly valuable, if only because it allows larger units of text to be displayed and manipulated far more rapidly than a blackboard or an overhead projector. But what text?

Text in development, first of all. You can start with a class and a machine and move through the initial phases of composition by collective "brainstorming," outlining, paragraph-development, and the "flagging" of key points of cohesion in a developing essay. If you play a somewhat reserved role as moderator and class secretary you'll find that you can get a great deal of writing on the screen rapidly, but you'll also find that unless you take editorial control you won't be able to produce a lot of well-formed text in the limits of a normal class period. Machine performance, like any other kind, favors preparation, and that is why you can probably get further in the time at your disposal by working with material already on hand—above all, material that lends itself to rapid alteration in restricted ways that emphasize the *multiple* possibilities afforded students by their commitment to writing and their use of machines.

Text that you have prepared—fodder for "exercises," if you will—is a starting point for such activity. Of such collective exercises I can suggest a handful that seem particularly well-suited to capitalizing on machines' strength or counteracting some of their temptations.

Exercises with texts:

1. *Local transformation of sentences and sentential units,* from passive to active, from weakly to strongly topicalized, from simple to compound and complex. Making such changes is easy (and fun) on machines, especially because the resulting text is legible—and there's always room on the infinitely expanding screen for another version.

2. *Graphic analysis*—in the space of the computer display, with whatever resources of emphasis the machine offers (color, highlighting, facing and font changes)—of sentences' grammatical and stylistic structure.

3. *Stylistic imitation,* either as recommended in earlier chapters or with a twist of ventriloquism. Assign George Orwell's "Shooting an Elephant" and Clifford Geertz's "Notes on the Balinese Cockfight"; how would Geertz have written the opening paragraphs of Orwell's essay—and vice versa? Machines greatly facilitate this work: the original text can remain visible in one window while the student works in another; the student can insert revised

text either into the original text, say by changing parts of a sentence, or immediately after the sentence. In fact, with machines, the student can line up as many versions as she wants, before deciding which to delete.

4. *"Decomposition": breaking and remaking texts.* Take a highly paratactic text and start supplying conjunctions and transitions. Hemingway's most concise vignette from *In Our Time*—the one beginning "They shot the six cabinet ministers . . ."—is useful because in its original form it illustrates a near-perfect progression from simple to compound to (minimally) complex sentence types. Or take a highly hypotactic text from the course reading and break it down, purging all relational words; then let your students build it up again, finally comparing it with the original. Exercises like these alert students to the real basis of styles in writers' purposes, as well as to the elements of styles themselves.

5. *Mutilation.* Open holes in texts by students or published authors (eliminate suites of reasoning or series of instances) and let your group fill them. A microstructural version of this maneuver is called "clozing," and it tells writers something about their prose and readers something about their reading habits. Starting with a student essay, count off the first 100 words and then knock out every fifth, sixth, or seventh word; replace it with a five-character-length blank and then invite readers to fill in the blanks. A high degree of accuracy in guessing the writer's original words—50 to 70 percent—tells her that her syntax is probably carrying a healthy amount of her meaning. Lower success rates on the part of a community of readers suggests either that word choice is erratic or that syntax *isn't* doing its job of orientation and guidance.

6. *"Tightening," condensation.* Moulthrop, in a paper mentioned above, remarks: "The computer made our students more willing to take their prose apart. The problem was that they did not know how to put it back together." So show them. Take a loosely written text that your students have had a chance to read and go to work on it, fast: strike out verbiage and irrelevance; combine sentences; reinforce cohesional devices.

7. *Varying* possible forms that a single text can take—e.g., a first paragraph. Many students come to college convinced that an essay's first paragraph is a funnel into which the blandest generalities must first be poured; finally, a golden drop of Thesis will issue

from the nether tip. Prepare a *good* funnel introduction with several generalizations and several potential thesis statements, and perhaps a quotation; then reconstruct it several times in the period.

But the material that is bound to be "on hand" in a writing course—and on disk, if you have requested it—is completed student writing. One kind of writing course requires each member of the group to duplicate and distribute an essay at some point in the term; other students come to class prepared to discuss it. When the product can be projected from a machine, critique can move into active intervention. A thorough rewrite of the *Clockwork Orange* essay (indeed, a complex case) would be out of the question in a normal class period and perhaps undesirable anyway; it's the student's own essay and he should be doing the bulk of the revision. A good strategy would be to copy the first and last paragraphs, move to free space at the bottom of the file, juxtapose them, and set about composing the strongly organized first paragraph that the essay seems to need; with good timing, the class could get that done and suggest tactics for reorganization (without carrying them out) before the end of the period. With other student essays you can carry out other, equally selective operations: outlining the essay anew on the basis of the text at hand (and then asking the writer to compare the structure readers find with the one he intended to give it); creating a "barebones" version of the essay by cutting all but one or two (topic?) sentences from every paragraph and then displaying the result; throwing transitions into relief by stripping away all but the first and last sentences of each paragraph; tracing the use and repetition of key terms throughout the essay by highlighting or boldfacing them, depending on the resources of your computer's user interface. Each operation could lead to as much active revision as time allows.

In each case you'd be throwing a particular piece of prose into a new perspective and calling attention to those more general categories of discourse to which its features belong. You might also take the trouble to perform these tasks using special functions shared by most word processors, thus teaching students to use them on their own: split-screen capabilities for comparing and copying documents, the "search" command for hunting up terms and problem words, footnotes for entering comments and possible revisions. More generally, you'd be letting the technology, through its dramatic heightening of the relation between the writing process and the written product, deliver the message that prose is both static and dynamic, both final and mutable—and that the decision to regard it in one way or the other is very much within the writer's own power.

IV. FURTHER PROGRAMS FOR TEACHING WRITING

A. *Toward the Integrated Writing Environment*

Word processors are bound to remain the primary computer applications for college writers and for those writing instructors who teach with them. But they won't necessarily be the same word processors, nor will they be those that offer only "more of the same" powers that commercial or general-purpose word processors provide today: greater multitasking abilities, for example, or greater document lengths, more elegant command structures, or nearer approximations to the WYSIWYG ideal. Programs are emerging that try to address the needs of specific writing constituencies: academic scholars (for whom Dragonfly Software's *Nota Bene* has been designed), beginning college writers, students who wish to write up and organize their curricular knowledge, teachers who want a special medium in which to comment on student papers, and undergraduate writers at various levels who want a serviceable writing and research tool.

Broadly, developers have followed several courses, sometimes simultaneously, to achieve such customization: (1) *packaging* word processors with a variety of separately existing teaching applications or research tools; 2) *exploiting* the peculiar configuration of space, time, and memory (and sometimes the graphics capabilities) of the single terminal or microcomputers; and (3) *interfacing* word processors with other applications to extend their range through telephone lines or optical fiber networks into online databases and other computers' spheres, opening external channels of research and communication. Each approach seems to me a move toward integration, for whether it expands or concentrates the functions of the general-purpose word processor, each one seeks to produce a whole application adapted to a newly defined range of writing tasks.

In this section I want to look toward some of the writing "environ-ments" that are on the horizon for microcomputers, discussing a few systems that have already appeared and a few others that are in the testing stage as of September 1986. Omitting the complexities of net-works, telecommunications devices, and database managers, I'll con-centrate on a few of the "packages" and "exploitations." First I'll look at a few of the parts of which some bundles are made.

B. Machine Intelligence and College Writers: Some Existing Software

What have machines traditionally done with college writing training or with the writing of college students?

COMPUTER-ASSISTED INSTRUCTION

Software developed for education has typically been one species or another of computer-assisted instruction, and much CAI has stopped short of providing learners with anything approaching full word-pro-cessing resources either because they aren't needed (as in the case of drill-and-practice applications, simulations, and tools for scientific and mathematical study) or because they aren't available. The most obvious model of machine teaching is a "closed" transaction between the user and the machine: the user enters some information and the machine evaluates it and responds accordingly: by calculating, by returning information to the user, by answering or questioning "interactively." The most basic rule governing this transaction is the simplest: if you want a machine functioning in this way to be "intelligent" after its fashion, let it control what the user does with it, limiting his options as stringently as possible. You may, of course, loosen that control with increasingly complex and sophisticated programming designed to trap "freer" user input, but you have to go very far indeed to accept rela-tively unconstrained natural-language responses or instructions. The zero case is the multiple-choice exam, answered with a number-two pencil on papers forms or by single-digit choices among possible answers displayed on a monitor: complete control, absolute (machine) "intelligence."

Next on the ladder of adaptation to teaching purposes are drills and tutorials, programs that instruct and test by querying and evoking replies that, when evaluated, can be the basis for further queries and replies. Control prevails and "intelligence" can be high; well-made CAI applications branch and loop with impressive flexibility, assessing students' strengths and weaknesses and adjusting instruction accordingly. But the activity, however well-planned and tactfully prompted, is not really the student's own, and for most purposes of writing instruction that fact is decisive. Traditional drill-and-practice programs, which typically try to teach the elements of grammar and mechanics, isolate the learner not only from his "own" product but from a context resembling the context of use. (The popularity of computers in foreign language and ESL teaching surely owes something to the fact that in these fields the context of use *is* an acknowledged context of instruction. The same may be the case with such a carefully designed and comprehensive program as Michael Southwell's *GrammarLab,* which tutors basic writing students in the syntax of English "as if it were an entirely new language" [Southwell 92].) The isolation typical of most such programs makes them useless for most college students who, however faulty their writing, belong to their language (whether or not it belongs fully to them) and need above all to write, with a view to appropriating the product and the process.

INVENTION PROGRAMS

There is another way of loosening the constraints that make interactive CAI irrelevant to the teaching of writing: abandon the "closed" model and use the machine to stimulate responses that the machine only very partially evaluates, if at all—to create, in the words of Major Hugh Burns, "an 'open' instructional system . . . , a computer-based package which does not have an associated body of content from which to draw appropriate answers" (Burns and Culp 9). That is the aim of Burns' applications *TOPOI, BURKE,* and *TAGI,* which combine prompting and questioning routines with questions based on several "heuristic" schemes appropriate to different kinds of writing: Aristotle's enthymeme topics for persuasive writing, Kenneth Burke's "pentad" for reportage, and the "tagmemic matrix" of Young, Becker, and Pike for exploratory and informative prose. The programs allow a student user to explore his own knowledge of his subject. After some preparatory questions about that subject and his purpose or interest in it, *TOPOI* begins the sequence of "topical" inquiries, asking about the causes of the subject, its results, its opposites, what has been decided about it, and so forth, as well—significantly—as what the writer does *not* know about it. Major Burns has prevented the sequence from becoming purely formal and monotonous with a certain mixture of personalized hokum ("SUPER, EDDIE! ANYTHING ELSE?") and flexible programming—a mixture that prompts students for more response to a question until a certain limit is reached, answers students' demands for clarification, and turns aside questions with which the program cannot cope.

Of course there's well-intentioned subterfuge here reminiscent of the clever-Hans games played by Joseph Weizenbaum's *ELIZA* and other early Artificial Intelligence conversation makers, but *TOPOI* and its siblings do not even pretend to evaluate the yield; the student, if he has set out by achieving what Burns calls "a *most willing* suspension of disbelief," goes home with a good deal of raw material for an essay on the fear of death, terrorism, gymshoes, or whatever his announced concern may be. Two facts about invention programs have not escaped other developers: first, that the focus of prompts and questions can be restricted even further according to genre and subject-matter, with an apparent gain in relevance to a certain type of writing or an assignment (and such programs have been developed for journalism and for specific rhetorical forms of the essay); and second, that even Burns's level of "intelligent" machine response isn't strictly necessary for stimulating invention—or trying to. (Stephen Marcus's *Disk Script,* a portion of his *Computer Writing Resource Kit,* is simply a series of heuristic templates involving no interaction, to be filled in under a word processor.) As invention programs reach the currently available packages, they tend further and further toward a kind of formalism of which the five-paragraph essay template mentioned in Section I is the most striking example. *HBJWriter,* by Morton Friedman and colleagues, has one planning routine that prompts for sentence after sentence and then gives the student the opportunity to rearrange sentences to build the skeleton of an essay. A procedure in William Wresch's *Writer's Helper* elicits the student's subject, audience, thesis statement, topic sentences, and paragraph support and then (in the words of its documentation) "actually writes the essay for the student." These are discouragingly mechanical procedures, but it is true that they supplement more open and / or imaginative "prewriting" modules in each package: a kind of randomized comparison-prompter in *Writer's Helper,* and freewriting and invisible writing routines in *HBJWriter*.

FEATURE FINDERS AND "STYLE ANALYSTS"

Another class of applications uses machine intelligence in an entirely different way—to review or "analyze" finished drafts in order to call writers' attention to mechanical, grammatical, and stylistic features (mostly flaws). Traditionally such programs have run alone, accepting documents as disk files and delivering the results of their analysis as displayed or printed summaries or with notations in the texts themselves; users have then moved their documents back into the word processors that created them and revised. But word processor manufacturers soon found good reason to pack spelling checkers into their applications, and, with the recent growth of microcomputer memories, systems such as *The ALPS Writing lab* and *HBJWriter* have combined with their word processors modest but not negligible arsenals of "checkers" for other features. (Other packages of checkers, like Eva Thury's *Tools for Writers* and William Wresch's *Writer's Helper,* include text editors that make possible some immediate revisions.) Further packaging of this sort is very likely; it is desirable if the checkers or analysts deliver valuable results to writing students.

The "if" is a big one, for here we approach the limitations of machine intelligence not obliquely but frontally. What can the existing applications do with freely entered discourse—a student essay, a piece of text over whose subject-matter and form the machine has no control? Start with the obvious. Working in a one-by-one (or "local") mode, the machine can search the text for instances of words or expressions banked in a "dictionary" in its memory; it can rapidly identify words for which there is no "match" in the dictionary and point out the failure to the user, perhaps suggesting other more or less similarly spelled words that might be appropriate. This operation isn't a "spelling check" but merely the preparation for one; the user has to decide in each instance whether the word flagged is (a) correctly spelled, but absent from the dictionary; (b) a typographical error; or (c) a real misspelling. Although the dictionaries for these operations can become very bulky, routines for searching them and the text are svelte and often lightning quick. Spelling checkers abound on the market, and, if used with a dictionary, they can probably even help students learn how to spell—if only students can be persuaded to use them. Faint hope.

Still in the local mode, but relying on more selective dictionaries, machines can go hunting for chronically misformed, misused, or often stylistically undesirable words and phrases, again bringing them to the user's attention, normally with a brief explanation or suggestion keyed to the dictionary entry. Programs for these tasks are "usage checkers," and they exercise a wider appeal, as they look for a much more varied range of features and make some claim to affecting the correctness, clarity, and appropriateness of the writer's language. But they work with a margin of error or irrelevance similar to those of spelling checkers. On their hit lists are often a small number of manifest errors *(alot, alright);* a larger class of frequently confused or misused words *(their / they're / there, affect / effect, imply / infer);* and yet larger and often heterogeneous lists of expressions that *may* be stylistically offensive in most contexts because they are "vague," "abstract," "inflated," or "overused" or because they lend themselves to wordiness. The further into this third class usage checkers go, the less frequently their identifications will be helpful. Of course such applications promise to locate only potential, not actual, trouble spots, and they stand a chance of coming up with useful information even if they may harass writers with frequently irrelevant advice. But warning messages are typically cryptic or indiscriminate. Few users of Bell Laboratories' *Writer's Workbench,* for example, appreciate finding every *which* flagged with the dubious reminder that *which* is for nonrestrictive modifiers, *that* for restrictive. Some users of *Tools for Writers* may be baffled to see such a range of words as *thing, it, problem, such,* and *whole* repeatedly marked with the message "Be more specific. Give examples."

Potential errors and infelicities are not all that computers can flag. They can mark members of a few classes of words (conjunctions, as does *Tools for Writers;* transitional expressions, as does *HBJWriter*) that writers may profit from having called to their attention simultaneously or in succession. To see a screenful of text with all transitionals highlighted may give users the chance to plot the direction of an argument or notice the lack of it. But here style analysts verge on delivering information of other sorts. Working generally, not locally, they can count certain surface features of a text; compute totals, averages, and deviations, and return these to the user with interpretive messages; they can also mark patterns of these features conspicuously in copies of the text itself. The volume and kinds of information they deliver are abundant, and they force on us questions about its basis, its applicability to written discourse, and its usefulness to student writers. Summarily, style analysts now running on microcomputers can compute the frequencies of expressions with stylistic relevance (*be* verbs, nominalizations with standard endings, prepositions, and the like); they may list the frequencies of words, calculating the ratios of "types" or "unique words" to "tokens" of them (i.e. the ratio of the number of words on the list to the number of times they are used in the document); they may measure the lengths of sentences and paragraphs, averaging them and figuring the range of variation; they may assign readability levels to texts on the basis of sentence-lengths and syllabic lengths of words; and of course they may return this information to users with more or less helpful interpretations and more or less prescriptive advice.

As should be evident, information like this comes from the merest surface of the text; a computer working at this level uses nothing but its counting abilities and small dictionaries for flagging a few word types, and it is utterly insensitive to meaning, to context, and to almost all dimensions of syntax. Indeed, "surface" is almost a misnomer here in light of the word's meaning(s) to linguists, for a human being who worked this way would be flagging, grouping, and counting strings of graphemes without even realizing that they represented a language. Even to arrive, occasionally, at the real surface of language requires more substantial programming than microcomputers support at the moment, or a willingness to take risks, or both. Decisionware's *Rightwriter* (a style-checker for general, not specificially educational use) works with heftier-than-usual dictionaries to deliver a "strength index" and a "descriptive index," based on rough part-of-speech identifications, for a piece of writing; it descends to the local level to make judgments as nearly grammatical as it dares, flagging a sentence as incomplete or as "missing [a] comma" because the sentence lacks a "predicate verb" that *Rightwriter* recognizes *or* because it begins with a subordinating conjunction and lacks the comma supposedly necessary to set off a subordinate clause, even a short one.

Bell Laboratories' *Writer's Workbench* positions itself more firmly on the surface and offers the writer not only the information summarized above—frequencies, lengths, and readability-scores—but a mass

of additional data on parts of speech, sentence types, sentence beginnings, and other quasi-grammatical elements of a text. The *Workbench*
is not a microcomputer application (it's just too bulky) and it was not
originally designed for education (having been devised to police the
prose of technical writers at Bell). But it remains the industry standard
and has found educational application.[4] It is of interest to us because its
ability to deal with natural language stands at the limit of a certain kind
of programming; on the other side of that limit lies the far more complex
and laborious task of parsing syntactic structure (i.e., assigning a functional category to each part of a sentence and thus preparing, as it were,
to make sense of it). The typical subset of *Writer's Workbench* programs (they are myriad) includes a program which makes part-of-speech
assignments for all words in a text and several others which interpret its
data. The assignments are right about 90 percent of the time, and when
they're not, the errors rarely affect the program's assessment of the text
because that is delivered in percentages of the whole.

> Writing teachers stress that no more than 75% of the sentences in a
> text should begin with the subject of the sentence; [the sentences in
> your essay] start with the subject 92% of the time. Try starting more
> of your sentences with prepositions, adverbs, or conjunctions. This
> change will have the added benefit of adding variety of sentence-
> length and type.

Is this the result of a parse? Not really. *WWB*'s program PARTS works
through a lookup of function words, a check of inflections, and a match
with word sequences that are necessary or probable in English sentences. The above message's reference to ''the subject'' is indeed a
functional assignment, but the message happens to be a pretty safe guess
that is not backed up by full syntactic analysis; even so, the application
wisely refrains from identifying any one sentence as certainly beginning
with the subject.[5]

Much more to the point, of how much value is this information—
word-frequencies, sentence-lengths, readability-levels, percentages of
sentence-types and the like—to writing students or their teachers? At
least when the figures are very high, very low, or excessively uniform,
they may very well reflect something of interest to us. A steady pattern
of ten-to-twelve- or thirty-to-forty-word sentences rightly draws comment from all style checkers; a message that declares, ''Readers will
need a 23rd grade education to understand this writing'' is a sign of

interminable sentences and many polysyllabics. (When *Rightwriter* offered this verdict on a grant proposal of mine I knew I had achieved something.) *WWB*'s remark about sentence-openings, cited above, was prompted by a piece of student writing that regularly linked sentence to sentence with the hook-and-eye of near reference, naturally favoring early subjects: "These women . . . They . . . These cases . . . This type of behavior . . . This thought . . ." The student whose writing this was might have heeded *WWB*'s advice and, merely by varying sentence-openings, found his way to writing more complex and perhaps more intellectually robust sentences. But then his problem wasn't only with sentence *types* (*WWB*, in fact, would have assured him that he had an appropriate distribution of simple, complex, and compound sentences), but with the way he linked ideas together above the sentence level, and *WWB* is understandably cautious about commenting on long-range reference.

More important than the figures themselves is their interpretation by the applications that deliver them. By what measure does it take place? The phrase "Writing teachers stress . . ." is at least as venial a fiction as "Dentists recommend . . . ," but the source of the figure 75 percent is unclear. For other measures *WWB* does have a table of acceptable value-ranges for technical and "educational" documents, and the user can alter it. Thury's *Tools for Writers* says it judges "normality" (as in "You use *and* more than normal" [sic]) by frequency values from Kucera's and Francis's *Computational Analysis of Present-Day American English*. But in communicating their assessments, style checkers are in a real dilemma: their judgments and advice have to compromise between comment so dry and mild as to be ineffectual and stronger prescriptions that may be misleading in a single instance. With no particular distress (I was hoping for a system crash or a blown fuse), *WWB* reviewed an eight-sentence passage from Victor Turner's *Schism and Change in an African Community* heavy with weak verbs, nominalizations, and prepositions ("Implicit in the notion of reintegration is the concept of social equilibrium. The concept involves . . ."). *WWB* had no trouble with Turner's few passives (still another program, FINDBE, would have hit more of his weak verbs), but it found too many nominalizations and, applying standards for "educational" rather than technical prose, criticized the thirteenth-grade readability level of the text and grumbled a little about sentence- and word-length. *HBJWriter*'s most interesting and probably most useful checking component rendered a more persuasive verdict. The routine called "Style" can look at once for "be" verbs, prepositions, "-tion" words and a certain number of abstracts, thus delivering some of the diagnostics for Richard Lanham's "paramedic" method of revision. ("Style" thus offers some of the features of Lanham's and Michael Cohen's *HOMER—like HBJWriter,* another offspring of the UCLA writing program.) "Style" splits the screen and, displaying part of the text in the upper half, prints a kind of filtered image of the same passage below it, replacing all unquestioned words with strings of dashes and all words in target classes with other characters ("p . . ." for prepositions, "t . . . " for "-tion" words, and so forth). Thus "Implicit in the notion of reintegration" appears as

implicit in the notion of reintegration

--------   pp---   tttttt   pp tttttttttttttt

"Style's" comments were uniformly neutral and low-key, but this graphic display itself would have visually driven the point home. Had Turner been a writing student, he could not have missed seeing the collaboration of weak verbs, prepositional phrases, and Latinate nouns in his version of the High Social-Sciencese dialect.

This last instance—of a clear rendition of machine findings about a troublesome text—is unfortunately the exception rather than the rule. Prose style is something at least as complex in its regularities and deviations as the grammar with which machines are for the most part unable to deal and on which most stylistic judgments depend in one way or another. That is not to say that machines working with modest dictionaries and imaginative algorithms can't catch stylistically relevant features of texts: they do so with some regularity in machine analysis of literary texts, and students might profit from notice of basic features other than those we've surveyed: carefully defined patterns of verbal repetition, for example, or of those cohesional devices of prose that a machine could catch. The problem seems to be a little coarser. Computer programs working on or above the surface of prose are almost bound to generate far more data than are useful in the particular case and are unlikely to interpret them intelligently and emphatically enough to make their work a meaningful diagnostic aid. Those who introduced *Writer's Workbench* at Colorado backed it up with a hefty manual further explaining the machine's output and adjusting its advice to account for differing cases, and I wonder whether even those generalized explanations of partial findings were particularly helpful. *HBJWriter*'s Instructor's Manual, by Lisa Gerrard, repeatedly urges instructors to assign the various resources of the package very selectively and with concern for individual students' needs, thus involving the teacher in interpreting—even teaching—the machine before as well as after use.

What all these considerations suggest is that style-checkers such as the ones we've been considering are unlikely to work in the way that some teachers and promoters have hoped they would: as prophylactic or preparatory devices that students regularly use on their own essays before handing them in—presumably in order to save overworked instructors some trouble. Arguably, that's the wrong use to make of them for pedagogic reasons as well, for the message they send—invariably blunted in transmission—is deeply misleading: first clean up your "style" by yourself with the machine; then the instructor will deal with what you have to say. Perhaps the right way to use style-checkers is to bring them into the classroom as sources of perspective on prose features that might otherwise be only casually mentioned on the way to "deeper" ones. I could find a place for a checker in a writing course, but only to dramatize the real depth of language, to teach the limits not of computers but of brute surface scrutiny of writing, and to suggest how features like sentence length and structure, weak verbs, and frequent expletives and "ands" may (and may not) point to other more organically significant elements of prose.

More or less "integrated" packages like several we have mentioned may send larger and equally questionable messages, too, because they offer models of the writing process that transcend the mere sum of the tasks they perform. It would be unfair to accuse *HBJWriter* or *Writer's Helper* of pretending to offer a complete art of composition to writing students, but they surely suggest dubious paradigms of what it means to write. Each claims a certain unity—*HBJWriter* more emphatically than *Writer's Helper* because it includes a full word processor and because its manual appeals more insistently to "process" theories of writing. And each, in its way "dismantles" the process: *HBJWriter* by its division of components into "Prewriting Aids," the word processor, and "Revising and Reviewing Aids," and *Writer's Helper* by bracketing of the central act of composition with programs that help to "Find and Organize a Subject" and "Evaluate a Writing Project." To be sure, each manual stresses the strictly elective nature of the programs in the package, but in each case the disclaimer seems overridden by some claim to unity and sufficiency made by the application as a whole or by the label under which it travels. And yet again—the heterogeneity of contents in both cases and the space in which they are housed seem to conflict with any really holistic aims. Writers simply do more and less than prewrite, write, and review text, as the Flower-Hayes model reminds us (see page 343): they may "revise" before writing a word, and they may review or plan at any point in composition. They may, moreover, do these things in a richer and less internally partitioned "space" than exists in these packages. In *HBJWriter,* the writer has to *leave* the word processor and enter the checking routines; the routines can't be called into the word processor where the main work of composition takes place. Text has to be moved *out of* the whole of *Writer's Helper* in order to be significantly rewritten.

C. The Advent of "Hypertext": Spacious Software

For integrating "writing tools" with the writer's needs, there are, of course, other means, some of which are indeed indigenous to the more powerful word processors we looked at in previous sections. It is striking that once the prompting and analytic routines are stripped from *HBJWriter,* those that remain are basically word processing functions, some with special constraints ("Invisible Writing" closes down the screen display for a limited period, while "Freewriting" cancels editorial functions and times the flow of prose) and some with an added capability ("Commenting on a Paper" inserts a reader's remarks directly into a version of the text, allowing the writer or other commentators to read them). *HBJWriter's* most comprehensively useful *power* is its ability to display two texts in windows sharing the main screen, allowing users to work from a prewritten sketch or an outline or to address themselves to teachers' or peers' comments while they revise. But most word processors have split-screen capabilities, and those create a certain depth, a third dimension, to the space of the display—perhaps a crimp or loop in a single document, perhaps a kind of window on files in storage (when second and subsequent documents are shown). The fabled "user interface" of Apple's Macintosh—which different programs for the Mac may exploit more or less fully—embodies some of this depth in an imaginary desktop on which windowed documents overlie without replacing one another and to which various "accessories" (a clock, a calculator, a notebook) can be called, but the effect can be duplicated by diligent programming on computers with far fewer intrinsic functions.

The effect of depth or of the availability of alternative spaces in the same "space," so to speak— suggestive of Diane Balestri's "softcopy" construct—may help to compensate for the "funnel vision" and the linearity of the text that have been mentioned as possible word processor liabilities. Within that depth, texts can be linked to or mapped on each other for rather specific purposes. Take the instructor's task of reading and commenting on student work.[6] Any teacher can use any capable word processor for the job, compensating for the lack of margins by poking in symbols keyed to separate files of remarks or captions and explanations. Or he can adapt to teaching purposes a group-authoring and -commenting program like Brøderbund's *ForComment* for the IBM-PC, which enables reviewers and editors to append signed comments and revisions to selected portions of an original text and permits the original writer to collate and scrutinize them. Teachers, of course, are interested not only in writing comments but in feeling some confidence that students will read and even act on them, and *PROSE* (Prompted Revision of Student Essays) by Stuart Davis, Nancy Kaplan, and Joseph Martin, makes use of the Macintosh's windowing powers in companion programs for teacher and student, each including a word processor with modest formatting abilities. One program allows instructors to comment extensively on student writing with spontaneous remarks and canned error prompts, coded in the text and invisible until opened; the other leads students through their essays message by message, cueing revisions or corrections where they are called for, offering broader suggestions for later revision work, and supplying explanations and exercises for the familiar errors.

PROSE creates a temporary and very specialized instance of what Andries Van Dam of Brown University has called "hypertext," a "new manuscript form that consists of a computer based collection of related documents together with all their cross-references, footnotes, annotations, and other associations" (quoted in Catano, "Poetry and Computers" 269). "New" indeed, because as soon as texts can be linked in an electronic medium compendious enough to contain them and their links, several basic changes occur in the ordering of writings characteristic of print media and in their relation to the user. Texts become, as it were, nodes in a tree, mesh, or network that brings them into *immediate* contact at those points where cross-references and notes in books join them only virtually, and the possibilities for encyclopedic (self-)commentary, for digression, and for articulating one text upon another begin to make works like *The Anatomy of Melancholy* or Jacques Derrida's *Glas* look incunabular. Through sets of electronic texts authors can create "paths" which will themselves be new texts, and readers can either follow those paths or make new ones, adding commentary or documents to growing webs of information that still other readers can share and explore. Finally, with the growing power of systems and machines to support text, graphics, video displays, and audio material, *hypertext* can become *hypermedia,* reaching beyond print culture to the sensory carnivalesque.

Such, at least, is a vision that informs Brown University's ongoing development of electronic document and media systems (see Yankelovich, Meyerowitz, and van Dam). It shares one aim with textbase and database managers already on the scene in large numbers—the aim of *intensively* exploiting machines' text-storage and -retrieval abilities. Those database managers friendly to text (like FYI, Inc.'s *Superfile*) and those specializing in multidimensional outlines (generically, "idea processors" like Living Videotext's *ThinkTank)* already allow some of the multiplicity of access to writing and the discriminant communication favored by the "hypertextual" model, and it is scarcely surprising that there should appear microcomputer applications that adapt some database advantages and some resources of electronic document systems to the use of student writers.

The Prentice-Hall College Writer (formerly *Writewell),* by Ilene Kantrov and others at the Education Development Center, is a case in point. *PHCWriter* appeals to the same "process" ideals that seem to be shibboleths for all writing software developers, but it refuses to dedicate single routines to "stage" functions, to manufacture organizing forms for the student, or for that matter to check for "vague words." It is above all an elegantly simple word processor with a second screen in which the user can create and call up (*into* the word processor) documents of certain defined types: references, comments, and notes. Writers can compile reference-notes or a sources-cited list for formal papers; readers—instructors or peers—can embed comments by code in the primary text for subsequent display; and at any point in their writing students can make notes that they can name, describe, key, and recall. The "note" capacity is as "open" as the word processor itself, imposing no record format, so a student can create one set of rough notes for plans and outlines, another for the tentative sequence of sections or topics in a paper, and a third for summaries of and quotations from source material, calling them up by simple retrieval methods when their time comes. Retrieval methods are indeed simple: *PHCWriter* does not allow users to filter or join note files (i.e., the user cannot say, in effect, "show me all the notes keyed 'witches' and 'Massachusetts' and not keyed 'Salem' "), although it does allow them to queue and reorder notes freely. Nor does it offer the word processing power of commercial systems now being licensed and sometimes modified by textbook publishers for the college market like *WordPerfect* (McGraw-Hill College Version).[7] *PHCWriter's* most important achievement is opening the space of the word processor to several distinct but analogous functions, all of them intrinsically related to writing.

Another way of opening that space is to invite the user to *give* it structure of a conspicuous but flexible kind—to provide a repertory of links, paths, and kinds of text spaces that will fit together in a fully intelligible information structure that is easily modified without loss of textual integrity or "sense of direction." The more elaborate the structures that can be made, the greater the chance of disorientation for the reader, but also for the writer. Most of the applications just mentioned take the master document (the author's or student's text, formatted in something like its hardcopy form) for their primary model, associating with it files of comments, notes, suggested revisions, and whatnot in subordinate or collateral relations. So does a self-described "hypertext" manager for the Macintosh, Owl International's *Guide*, but by allowing the user to define "buttons" on the surface of the text that give access to deeper or more remote levels of information.

Yet another kind of "hypertextual" application abandons the document as the primary model and puts the user's writing *inside* the program's graphic resources. That is, it creates highly mobile text areas whose number the user can multiply at will and whose relations with each other he can manipulate in screen-space or project into other dimensions. Applications that do this combine some functions of "idea processors" and database managers with those of word processors: they allow students to order ideas, to recall and organize information, and to write in a medium that stores and displays their words and graphically represents relations of concepts and texts. Their usefulness to writing students depends on the volume of writing they can "carry" and on the number of ways in which they let the user configure and work on texts. Robert Kozma's and John Van Roekel's *The Learning Tool* presents itself as a device for mastering coursework, not for writing papers, but it can help to organize them by creating outlines in two spaces at once: in a "master list" where cells are ranked by indentation and in a "concept map" where they appear as small windows which can be opened for limited writing and *nested* to reflect their hierarchical relationship—and in addition, linked by lines or arrows to show supplementary connections. Linking takes place on one plane; it is less fundamental to the representation of structure than nesting, which opens "sub-maps" in lower or ulterior planes and which corresponds to subordinate relations in the "master list." Thus *The Learning Tool* most naturally creates trees of hierarchical relations beginning in a root or parent cell and descending through branches to the several cells to be organized. It is suited to outlining formal reports and essays in classification or definition where pure analysis is at a premium—as well as to diagramming easily "treed" structures like, for example, those of animal taxonomy.

The thoughts of working writers, however, rarely form discrete sets, nor are their relations simple. They include, exclude, overlap, and depend on each other in complex ways; some groupings are clear and others "blurry," and most are provisional. Writers' problems of organization are often less like those of scientific classification than like those presented by the monstrous *Celestial Emporium of Benevolent Knowledge* mentioned by Jorge Luis Borges, where it is written that

> animals are divided into (a) those that belong to the Emperor, (b) embalmed ones, (c) those that are trained, (d) suckling pigs, (e) mermaids, (f) fabulous ones, (g) stray dogs, (h) those that are included in this classification, (i) those that tremble as if they were mad, (j) innumerable ones, (k) those drawn with a very fine camel's hair brush, (l) others, (m) those that have just broken a flower vase, (n) those that resemble flies from a distance. (108)

If you'll allow class labels to stand for "ideas" (and suppress the wanton paradox of item [h]), Borges's encyclopedia is a good analogue for the orderly disorder that prevails when we start to plan: some ideas stand in fairly clear logical relations to others (mermaids are fabulous; "other" animals exclude "those . . . in the present classification," which includes all of the others), and some ideas are contingently or potentially related (the Emperor may or may not own most if not all embalmed, trained, and pictorially represented animals). Other subsets can be defined in any number of ways, depending on the theme or purpose of the organization; to represent one possible pattern among others takes more resources than strictly hierarchical ''idea processors'' provide. *Storyspace* by Jay David Bolter, Michael Joyce, and John B. Smith, is an application which adds new dimensions in which ''hypertextual'' relations can be realized. Its double display and nesting abilities are roughly similar to *The Learning Tool*'s (although *Storyspace* ''lists'' its cells in a true tree diagram), but it includes some powerful devices for adding further schemes of order to the hierarchy. For one thing, the user can describe cells with keywords, and the program can search and filter the cells (by keyword or title) on more than one key, thus arriving—in our example—at a set of animals that are tame but not drawn or imperial. For another, *Storyspace* uses arrows to link cells *through* as well as *upon* any number of levels; thus a relation might be set up—supplementary to the main one—among fabulous animals, mermaids, the seemingly mad tremblers, those drawn with a brush, and those that look like flies from afar. Call this the set of ''imaginatively conceived'' animals—a group corresponding, in the writer's world, to an idea worth exploring or developing. *Storyspace*'s linking power becomes really effective through the program's ability to walk through a ''path'' made by a whole sequence of links, regardless of the level or location of the cells they join. And the application allows for ''readings'' of texts in adjacent cells, either through free movements up, down, left, and right through *Storyspace*'s space or through a path the student or the instructor can create with branches at each point controlled by yes-no or matching-word questions.

If the Borges example seems frivolous (and even so it might make a good exercise teaching both the necessity and the limits of subordination), there are more obviously practical uses to be made of *Storyspace* and perhaps *The Learning Tool*. Right now I am putting together an assignment for a paper on Nabokov's *Pale Fire:* I'm asking students to build up a reservoir of thematically related quotations, images, puns, and brief episodes before they frame the distinct central question their papers will address. With *Storyspace* that operation would be swift and suggestive: clusters of related citations would grow organically and could be visibly reconfigured; commentary on them could fill linked or neighboring cells; brief topical keying of quotations and commentary would allow writers to filter and select sets of cells and examine them for relevance to each other and to an emerging central concern; and the more canny students might try to link up cells in a variety of "read" sequences to try out discursive orders for the paper. Elective movements from text to text or to commentary and the option of adding to commentary (in which the whole class might participate) would turn the accumulating material into a true "hypertext base" such as students have created on Van Dam's mainframe system FRESS (File Retrieval and Editing System) at Brown. It would be awkward to try to *write* the paper in finished form with *Storyspace,* for it lacks formatting options, but it can print out the contents of all cells or pass them back to MacWrite for final composition. The experience of manipulating text this way should lead to remarkably rich final essays.

And that is because an application like this one dramatizes an elusive but important fact about good prose: it walks and chews gum at the same time. Because subordination is so large a part of thinking and because our students so frequently lack that skill, writing teachers naturally emphasize hierarchical order: the order of topic and subtopic, generalization and example, definition and the singular instance. That is what we stress—but that is far from all we want, and what we often get is the five paragraph argumentative essay. In the writing we want to see, summary often walks hand in hand with argumentation, and exposition with "example"; a *developing* purpose or central idea accompanies the "topics" through which it grows; and the intelligence or experience we look for in the writer shows through in a certain tacit awareness of what he is doing. And that is why the Nabokov assignment seems to me only a special case of a more general principle: All good prose is "hypertextual" if not hypertext, a network and not a linear chain of related textual materials; a grid of relations that writer and reader follow in several dimensions; and a *commentary* on its subject as well, perhaps, as on itself. If computers can help us learn, study, and teach this feature of writing, they will transform the writing process and its products in more than a purely mechanical way.

NOTES

1. This section of *Teaching Prose* owes much to Nancy Kaplan and Joseph Martin of Cornell, who have offered advice and shared experience with me in

this and other projects. I am also grateful to Stuart Moulthrop of Yale and Diane Balestri of Princeton for permission to quote from unpublished papers.

2. For computer software—genus of those programs that make the machines run—I use "applications," "programs," and "systems" almost indifferently, and when the meaning is clear I don't hesitate to use "machine" to refer to the whole apparatus wielded by the user, hardware and software together.

3. Computer facilities are increasingly available to college faculty and students not only because of vast advances in semiconductor technology but because colleges have discovered persuasive reasons, not all of them pedagogic, for promoting computer use. Here financial disparities make themselves felt acutely. Some must computerize, if they can, to remain competitive in the recruiting market; many are helped by extremely generous development grants and sales concessions from manufacturers who have every reason to accustom future college graduates to buying and using machines. And many, of course, are not— and are "computer-poor" in consequence. Stephen Gilbert and Kenneth Green (33, 43) have estimated that around 300 institutions are parties to purchase agreements that allow students and faculty to buy computers at substantial discounts; these and other elite private and large public institutions may also benefit from bulk donations of equipment and support for systems and software development. Regional public colleges, together with disadvantaged and less-selective private institutions, are less fortunate. A recent Higher Education Utilization Study turned up 1500 of these with fewer than 50 microcomputers in use on campus.

Of course it is the microcomputer revolution of the early 1980s that has made the difference, creating a product to buy and sell and taking the strain of demand off heavily-used mainframes. And it has made the difference to student writers as well, who once were grudgingly admitted to the mainframes or all but debarred by strict time limits or even honor code penalties. Gilbert and Green identify word processing as the centrally important application of microcomputers for college administrators because, by their cost-benefit analysis, *"word processing alone* will soon justify computing capability for every student, faculty member, and most administrators,"* carrying, as it were, the hardware costs for all other uses of the same equipment (36–40).

4. Charles R. Smith and Kathleen Kiefer, assisted by Bell personnel, tested a cutdown version of the *WWB* programs in 1981–1982 at Colorado State University and have since expanded the project to include the entire composition program. They allotted students enough computer time to type and check their essays and later to revise them before submission. The results they have published reveal students' and instructors' enthusiasm for the programs and greater improvement by users than by control subjects—on editorial tests, not holistically scored compositions. The most that Smith and Kiefer's experience seems to show is that style checkers—whether or not they identify any features that

writing teachers consider important for their own sake—can inspire students to look again at a text and make more frequent attempts to revise it. An amusing and wholly unethical test of the application would involve putting the control group, too, at terminals, bombarding their prose with randomized mass evaluations (lengths, frequencies), and then administering those editorial tests. See Lawrence T. Frase, Kathleen Kiefer, et al, "Theory and Practice in Computer-Aided Instruction," and Kiefer and Smith, "Textual Analysis with Computers."

5. The next question, of course, is this: with such grammatical knowledge at its disposal, isn't *WWB* well on the way to being a real error-checker, capable of spotting and pointing out fragments, run-ons, agreement-errors, and so forth? It isn't, and not only because it won't commit itself to many particular syntactic identifications, but because it relies on the assumption that the text it works on is well-formed over short ranges; it doesn't try to struggle with the grammaticality of whole sentences. Significantly, the program GRAMMAR that runs in another part of the usual *WWB* package offers to spot just two local errors: split infinitives and misused indefinite articles.

A program that makes reasonably reliable local judgments on grammatical correctness must include not only a real parser but "backstop" routines to cope with and explain the *failure* of a parse. The most widely heralded such application is *Critique,* formerly *EPISTLE,* a text-analyst that has been in development and testing at IBM's Watson Research Center for at least six years. *Critique* is designed to identify certain fundamental errors like subject-verb and noun-modifier disagreement, faulty pronoun case, wrong verb forms, fragments, faulty parallelism, and some comma errors and to flag particular stylistic flaws at the word-, sentence-, and paragraph levels. These formidable tasks demand a core grammar of over 300 syntax rules, as well as peripheral procedures to handle ambiguity and to assign probable structures to ill-formed sentences. As of mid-1986 it is not generally available. For the design, see George Heidorn et al., "The EPISTLE Text-Critiquing System," and Karen Jensen et al., "Parse Fitting and Prose Fixing: Getting a Hold on Ill-Formedness."

6. There's been no dearth of labor-savers in this line, including some—like William Marling's *Writer / Grader / Reader* package (Case Western Reserve)—which allow teachers to enter error symbols and which keep records of those errors to measure students' "progress" from essay to essay. Other developers have experimented with boilerplating comments, some elaborately "personalized," for responding to whole essays. A point can be reached where weak pedagogy becomes well-intentioned fraud.

7. A special college version of Textra (Ann Arbor Software), called *Norton Textra Writer* (W.W. Norton) has been announced for publication in early 1988.

WORKS CITED

Entries marked with an asterisk are described in Chapter 8, "A Bibliographical Guide to the Profession."

Balestri, Diane. "Pedagogy over Technology." Macademia conference. Princeton, N.J., 30 June 1986.

Bean, John C. "Computerized Writing as an Aid to Revision." *CCC* 34 (1983): 146–48.

Borges, Jorge Luis. "The Analytical Lauguage of John Wilkins." *Other Inquisitions 1937–1952*. Translated by Ruth L. C. Simms. New York: Washington Square Press, 1965.

Bridwell, Lillian S., Paula Reed Nancarrow, and Donald Ross. "The Writing Process and the Writing Machine." *New Directions in Composition Research*. Edited by Richard Beach and Lillian Bridwell. 381–98. New York: Guilford, 1984.

———, Parker Johnson, and Steven Brehe. "Composing and Computers: Case Studies of Experienced Writers." Unpublished paper, 1984.

——— and Donald Ross. "Integrating Computers into a Writing Curriculum; or, Buying, Begging, and Building." Wresch, *The Computer*. 107–19.

———, G. Sirc, and R. Brooke. "Revising and Composing: Case Studies of Student Writers." *Acquisition of Written Language*. Edited by Sarah W. Freedman. 172–94. Norwood, N.J.: Ablex, 1985.

Burns, Hugh L. "The Challenge for Computer-Assisted Rhetoric." *Computers and the Humanities* 18 (1984): 173–81.

———. "Recollections of First-Generation Computer-Assisted Prewriting." Wresch, *The Computer*. 15–33.

Burns, Hugh L., and George H. Culp. "Stimulating Invention in English Composition through Computer-Assisted Instruction." *Educational Technology*. August 1980: 5–10.

Catano, James V. "Computer-Based Writing: Navigating the Fluid Text." *College Composition and Communication* 36 (1985): 309–16.

———. "Poetry and Computers: Experimenting with the Communal Text." *Computers and the Humanities* 13 (1979): 269–75.

Collier, Richard M. "The Word Processor and Revision Strategies." *CCC* 34 (1983): 149–55.

Daiute, Colette. "The Computer as Stylus and Audience." *CCC* 34 (1983): 134–45.

———. *Writing and Computers*. Reading, Mass.: Addison-Wesley, 1985.

Fallows, James. "Living with a Computer." *Atlantic* July 1982: 84–91.

Flower, Linda, and John Hayes. "A Cognitive Process Theory of Writing." *CCC* 32 (1981): 365–87.

———. "Identifying the Organization of Writing Processes" and "The Dynamics of Composing." *Cognitive Processes in Writing.* Edited by Lee W. Gregg and Erwin R. Steinberg. 3–30, 31–50. Hillsdale, N.J.: Earlbaum, 1980.

Fluegelman, Andrew, and Jeremy Joan Hewes. *Writing in the Computer Age.* New York: Doubleday, 1983.

Frase, Lawrence T., Kathleen Kiefer, et al. "Theory and Practice in Computer-Aided Instruction." *The Acquisition of Written Language.* Edited by S. Freedman. 195–210. Norwood, N.J.: Ablex, 1985.

Gallagher, Brian. *Microcomputers and Word Processing Programs: An Evaluation and Critique.* Research Monograph Series Report No. 9. New York: C.U.N.Y. Instructional Resource Center, 1985.

Gebhardt, Richard C. "Initial Plans and Spontaneous Composition: Toward a Comprehensive Theory of the Writing Process." *College English* 44 (1982): 621–25.

Gilbert, Stephen, and Kenneth Green. "New Computing in Higher Education." *Change* May/June 1986: 33–50.

Harris, Jeanette. "Writers and Word Processing: a Preliminary Evaluation." *CCC* 36 (1985): 323–30.

Hartman, Geoffrey. "The Humanities, Literacy, and Communication." *Easy Pieces,* 172–87. New York: Columbia Univ. Press, 1985.

Hawisher, Gail E. "The Effects of Word Processing on the Revision Strategies of College Freshmen." *Research in the Teaching of English* 21 (1987): 145–59.

Heidorn, George E., et al. "The EPISTLE Text-Critiquing System." *IBM Systems Journal* 21 (1982): 305–26.

Hitchcock, Susan T. "A Cautious View of Computers in Teaching Writing." *Research in Word Processing Newsletter* October 1985: 7–9.

Hull, Christine. "Effects of Word Processing on the Correctness of Student Writing." *Research in Word Processing Newsletter* November 1985: 1–5.

Jensen, Karen, et al. "Parse Fitting and Prose Fixing: Getting a Hold on Ill-Formedness." *American Journal of Computational Linguistics* 9 (1983): 147–60.

Kiefer, Kathleen, and Charles R. Smith. "Textual Analysis with Computers: Tests of Bell Laboratories Computer Software." *Research in the Teaching of English* 17 (1983): 201–14.

*Knoblauch, C. H., and Lil Brannon. *Rhetorical Traditions and the Teaching of Writing.* Montclair, N.J.: Boynton/Cook, 1984.

Kucera, Henry, and W. Nelson Francis. *Computational Analysis of Present-Day American English.* Providence: Brown Univ. Press, 1967.

*Lanham, Richard. *Revising Prose.* New York: Scribners, 1979.

Moulthrop, Stuart. "Computers and the Future of the Writing Curriculum." Unpublished paper, 16 June 1985.

————. "Computers and Writing: Observations and Indications." Unpublished paper, April 1986.

Ohmann, Richard. "Freshman Composition and Administered Thought." *English in America,* 133–171. New York: Oxford Univ. Press, 1976.

Prufahl, John. "Response to R. M. Collier." *CCC* 35 (1984): 91–93.

Rose, Mike. "Sophistical, Ineffective Books: The Dismantling of Process in Composition Texts." *CCC* 32 (1981): 65–74.

Schwartz, Helen. *Interactive Writing.* New York: Holt, Rinehart, and Winston, 1985.

Sommers, Nancy. "The Need for Theory in Composition Research." *CCC* 30 (1979): 46–49.

————. "Revision Strategies of Student Writers and Experienced Adult Writers." *CCC* 21 (1980); 378–88.

Southwell, Michael. "The COMP-LAB Writing Modules: Computer-Assisted Grammar Instruction." Wresch, *The Computer.* 91–104.

Witte, Stephen P. "Revising, Composing Theory, and Research Design." *The Acquisition of Written Language: Response and Revision.* Edited by Sarah Warshauer Freedman. 250–284. Norwood, N.J.: Ablex, 1985.

Wresch, William, ed. *The Computer in Composition Instruction: A Writer's Tool.* Urbana, Ill.: NCTE, 1984.

————. "Questions, Answers, and Automated Writing." Wresch, *The Computer.* 143–53.

Yankelovich, Nicole, Norman Meyerowitz, and Andries van Dam. "Reading and Writing the Electronic Book." *Computer,* October 1985: 15–29.

Zinsser, William. *Writing with a Word Processor.* New York: Harper and Row, 1983.

Computer Software Discussed

Bolter, Jay David, Michael Joyce, and John B. Smith. *Storyspace.* In testing, 1986. Apple Macintosh 512K.

Davis, Stuart, Nancy Kaplan, and Joseph Martin. *PROSE: Prompted Revision of Student Essays.* McGraw-Hill, 1988. Apple Macintosh 512K.

ForComment. Broderbund Software, Inc., 1986. IBM-PC 256K.

Friedman, Morton, et al. *HBJWriter* (formerly *WANDAH*). Harcourt Brace Jovanovich, 1986. IBM-PC 256K.

Guide. Owl International, Inc., 1986. Apple Macintosh 512K.

Kantrov, Ilene, et al. *The Prentice-Hall College Writer* (formerly *Writewell*). Prentice-Hall, 1987. IBM-PC 256K.

Kozma, Robert, and John Van Roekel. *The Learning Tool.* Computer Software. Arborworks, 1986. Apple Macintosh 512K.

Marcus, Stephen. *Disk Script,* part of *Computer Writing Resource Kit.* D. C. Heath, 1986. Apple IIe/IIc 64K. IBM-PC 128 K.

Norton Textra Writer. Ann Arbor Software/ W.W. Norton 1988. IBM-PC 256K.

Rightwriter. Decisionware, 1986. IBM-PC 128K.

Southwell, Michael, and Carolyn Kirkpatrick. *GrammarLab.* Little, Brown, 1987.

Thury, Eva. *Tools for Writers.* Academic Courseware Exchange, 1986. Apple Macintosh 128K.

WordPerfect (McGraw-Hill College Version). WordPerfect Corporation/ McGraw-Hill, 1987. IBM-PC 192K.

Wresch, William. *Writer's Helper.* CONDUIT, 1985. Apple IIe/IIc 64K. IBM-PC 192K.

Writer's Workbench. AT&T Bell Laboratories, 1980. UNIX System V. release 2.0.

APPENDIX 2

Writing in the Non-Writing Class: "I'd Love to Teach Writing, But . . ."

KATHERINE K. GOTTSCHALK

I. INTRODUCTION: BEYOND COMP 101

Most faculty members agree that undergraduates need to do considerably more writing in the years following their required composition classes. But few courses after freshman "comp" require much writing, and many require none at all. When students do write, their essays are often examined just for "content," as if that were wholly separable from style or structure. It's hardly surprising, then, that some students lose the writing skills they gained during their first year: they don't use them enough to keep them. When students do begin to write again, perhaps in an optional senior-year course, they don't pick up where they left off at the end of their freshman year; studies (and our own experience) show that they go back to the bad habits or unsophisticated methods with which they began college. Unlike bicycle riding (''once you've learned you

---

This essay was originally intended for use by faculty members who do not teach writing. Many of us who do teach writing, however, also teach "non-writing" courses, and certainly all of us need and seek relief from the constant pressure of responding to and grading essays. Appendix 2 outlines techniques for encouraging writing—techniques that don't require assigning essays but that do tighten the connection between writing and learning.

never forget how''), essay writing is an intellectual exercise that's only gradually learned; it must be constantly practiced, and perfected. Students need to write throughout their college years, in many courses, if they are to maintain their precarious writing balance.

Many faculty members who don't teach writing, or who don't normally require written work for their courses, would like to help with this problem. But how? It's one thing to write well yourself and to recognize good writing; it's quite another to help someone else produce it. We can recognize and enjoy a Grand Marnier soufflé without being able to explain to a novice cook how to make one, or even how to make an omelette. In the same way, it's easy to see that a sentence is ''awk'' or ''unclear'' but much harder to explain why and to suggest solutions. Even faculty members who are able to explain the awkward sentence often don't do so, for correcting papers takes time, and both in class and out of it little may be available to spend explicitly on writing.

But we can use many techniques which will help students improve their writing even if we lack the expertise (or inclination) to locate every misplaced comma and every dangling modifier. Writing is not simply a matter of correctness. In fact, most students learn where the commas go only after they have learned to care about their writing, something these techniques can help them to do. Very simply, students will improve their writing if they keep writing, especially if they do so in conjunction with studying. Concerned faculty members need primarily to provide this opportunity. *It is less necessary to grade papers than to create genuine writing situations.* Students write better when they need to write and when they do so constantly in order to work out problems—in order to think.

Fortunately, if we want to participate in improving the quality of student writing by giving students a chance to write in our courses, some fairly simple methods are available, methods that do not make undue demands on our own time, in or out of the classroom. We can put the burden where it belongs: on our students' shoulders rather than on our own.

II. PROVIDING MOTIVATION

If we and our students believe that their writing is "good enough," that writing is just a matter of a few skills mastered (or not) in their composition classes; if we and our students believe that writing is separate from the study of a discipline and in fact an unnecessary distraction from it; and if students believe they'll rarely need to write again once they've finished their writing courses, then students won't improve their writing and we won't be able to help them to do so. Why bother?

It's a mistake to think that writing, like the multiplication tables, can be mastered once and for all. Students shouldn't have this false impression, and we shouldn't encourage it. Moreover, writing is a valuable, even essential, tool for learning. Writing at one's desk and in the classroom can be a necessary means to learning a subject, not a distraction from it. Far from robbing time from our areas of concentration when we bring writing into the classroom, we will be immersing our students in them. Many of the techniques for including writing in the classroom, rather than shifting our own or our students' attention from the subject matter, actually improve the quality of student participation in classes and the effectiveness with which students work in and understand the discipline. After all, "writing *makes* knowledge; it provides the means to think through problems as we are forced to work out relationships methodically and to make connections."[1]

We can talk openly with our students about the role of writing in learning (see the following sections for detailed descriptions of that role), and we can inform them about the kinds of writing our fields demand of professionals. Many students firmly believe that when they've finished their composition courses, they're through with the subject. But almost any job for which college prepares them is likely to involve plenty of writing, and the more management status and income the job has, the more writing will be involved.[2] Engineering students, for example, are often among those claiming that they'll never need to write again once they're through with those unnecessary and distracting writing courses. But professional engineers "will spend an average of one-third of their working time writing . . . few firms can afford to hire nonwriting engineers."[3] We can let our students in on this highly pragmatic motivation for writing, and we can provide writing opportunities that will help them prepare for their professional futures.

III. WRITING AS PART OF READING

A. *Using Texts as Models*

A fundamental way to help students become better writers is to give them good models to study. Much of our knowledge about writing comes through imitation, conscious and (mostly) unconscious. If our students struggle through drearily written textbooks and find such deadly prose typical of a discipline, we need not be surprised to encounter little better in the papers they submit to us. All fields have at least a few reputable writers available—often more. Students ought to be encouraged to read them, with the understanding that there are indeed better and worse ways of writing in any field and that they can legitimately prefer and emulate the better.

If an essential textbook stands out as impossibly written and impossible to read, or as remarkably boring, spending a few minutes explaining why that text is so difficult or boring will help students read with greater success; they may also become aware of stylistic questions that affect their own writing. *Why* is Talcott Parsons nearly unreadable? *Why* are some textbooks so dull? *Why* are Stephen Jay Gould's magazine articles easier to read than the biology textbook? Should the textbook be written differently? Why or why not? *How* does extensive use of the passive voice often deaden and depersonalize prose? *Why* is prose laden with multisyllabic noun structures harder to read than prose that depends on verbs? What should the student imitate? (If you're interested in exploring this subject, you'll enjoy Chapter 6, ''Understanding Prose.'' And, of course, many faculty members in English and writing departments find the subject fascinating and welcome the chance to talk about it.)

B. *Imitating Models*

If an authority in a field is a particularly distinguished writer, students can be asked to model some of their own reports or other writing on the work of that person. In the sciences, for example, models for certain kinds of student writing might include Albert Einstein's popular essays, or articles such as N. David Mermin's ''Is the Moon There When Nobody

Looks? Reality and the Quantum Theory.'' Awareness of varieties of style and form will increase students' control of their own writing choices, as well as making them aware of the stylistic options available in any field—aware especially that audience and purpose always affect how we write. Students might look at the weekly scholarly publication, *Science,* where they can compare a research article written for scholarly peers to its précis, which is aimed at lay readers (article: ''. . . the seasonal behavior of CO_2 frost at the Martian poles is not symmetric''; précis: ''. . . frost remains at the South Pole of Mars during much or all of the year but disappears during summer at the North Pole'' [Paige 1160; 1138]).

C. *Reading with Care*

Whatever the contents of our syllabi, we should be sure our students know how to read carefully. A surprising number of students consider themselves to have prepared a text carefully if they have read it just once while making huge swatches of yellow highlighting. They don't know about rereading to identify key terms, search for transitions, or distinguish between major and minor points; they don't think to question the premises, assess the evidence, or explore an analysis—they don't write in the margins, don't carry on a dialogue with the text. Much of writing, however, means being aware of the dialogue a reader will carry on with our own texts, and that surely means students must learn to become better readers themselves. We should encourage our students to develop their ability as readers, and therefore as writers, by making sure that they read the texts in our syllabi carefully. (In the next section I explore some aids to careful reading.)

IV. WRITING AS PART OF STUDYING

Students may become more alert, better informed, and more inquiring, if we encourage them to incorporate writing into their studying. How can we usefully do so, other than by requiring essays, which we then have to correct?

A. Writing Out Questions on Readings, Discussions, and Lectures

Nick Sturgeon (Department of Philosophy, Cornell) requires written questions of his students:

> You are to bring to each class, except on days when papers are due, a written question either about the current reading or about topics left over from previous discussions. (A supply of three by five cards would be ideal for this task.) I will often ask someone to read a question for the class to discuss. At the end of each class I will collect all the questions. I will not grade them, but I will keep track of whether you've handed in a question, and this record will be a makeweight in determining final grades. I will also return your questions, with comments when appropriate.

Sturgeon has made some work for himself, as he promises to return the questions with comments. One need not, of course—the comments can be made in class when a few students are asked to read their questions aloud. Students aware they may be called on will usually be prepared and careful.

The advantages of the system are obvious: students learn to ask useful questions, questions that will help them find answers. Lydia Fakundiny (Department of English, Cornell) requires students to write out responses to questions that have troubled them; the questions and responses then form the bases of class discussion and even of future papers, if those are required. Answers that students memorize without understanding what the questions were or how to find those questions for themselves mean far less than answers emerging from a dialogue in which the student has shared. A student can memorize one way to build a bridge from a textbook, but she'll remember the method longer if she first discovers the questions that led to the solution: what physical situation, what community, what resources, require what kind of bridge?

Similar advantages come from having students write out questions about lectures or class discussions, whether in calculus or chemistry.

Doing so sharpens their investigative thinking, draws them into the intellectual community of the classroom—and improves their writing.

In a lecture class, for example, students can be asked to submit questions about the preceding lecture based on their review of their notes. These questions can, of course, keep the professor informed about what students do or don't understand. More important, by grappling with the phrasing of the question, the student will come to more intimate terms with the material. The problem that perplexes us often unravels when we are able to describe the knot. Students can learn to use writing for this purpose, but many do not realize the tool is available.

If some students read their questions aloud at the beginning of a discussion group or section meeting, other students may be encouraged to air their problems and become part of an intellectual community, a community with participants who seek to understand, question, and discover. Furthermore, students who have studied material carefully enough to ask questions about it are likely to listen well in class and to contribute generously to it.

This process calls for little work from faculty members. We may read the questions or not, record them or not; sporadic checks will suffice to keep the students working. Or section leaders in a lecture course can handle the question-checking. (For other ways to use questions, see Sections V. *C* and V. *D*.)

B. Keeping a Journal

Journals provide another way to encourage better studying and better writing. Keeping a journal about the reading encourages active thinking rather than passive memorizing (or skimming). Students who keep journals are less likely to wait for the professor to do the rest of the work—as some students would like to do. To be most effective both for writing and thinking, a journal should be kept in complete sentences: the syntactical relationships in complete sentences are how we make connections. Fragments and words don't help as much with the job of discovering relationships. It can also be extremely helpful (as an encouragement to intellectual engagement rather than aimless response) to provide students with "generic" questions to which they may respond (for examples, see Chapter 2 for Patricia Carden's list of exploratory questions, and Section V. *D* following).

By creating journals on the work they are doing for projects, whether in biology, engineering, or architecture, students may generate more ideas and information than they need for their final work. Dale Corson (President Emeritus, and Department of Physics, Cornell) determined as a result of a study for the Ford Foundation that engineering students keeping laboratory notebooks should "examine the adequacy of and the reliability of the data as the measurements are made" and that a necessary part of this examination is being "required to write a summary of [their] work in the laboratory notebook following completion of each experiment." Writing summaries as part of the laboratory journal of data, in other words, ensures that students think as well as record. And the writing/thinking habit they develop will serve them well in or out of college.

Effective journal-keeping systems may be more or less closely supervised. Students may occasionally read aloud from their journals, and faculty members may simply collect them periodically to record their continuing existence. In a discussion section, students can compare journal entries on a given subject or use them for class discussion. Ann Berthoff (Department of English, University of Massachusetts) requires a

> dialectical notebook [that] allows students to transcribe sentences on the righthand side and annotate them on the left. In reviewing such a double-entry notebook, you can tell very quickly . . . just how the student is progressing in learning to think critically. . . . [R]equiring a double-entry notebook is the only way [she knows] to defend yourself against plagiarism, if you want to assign formal term papers. (122)

C. Making Outlines, Précis, and Translations

In almost any subject students read *something,* but often they don't read very well. By writing about texts they are studying, students can improve both their reading and their writing, since "You cannot possibly write better than you can read" (E. D. Hirsch, quoted by Irmscher 157).

Many students don't know what they have read because they have never learned to look for structure. A student unable to summarize the course of an argument is in a poor position to understand or criticize it, for understanding a writer's argument often depends on being able to trace its development—on being able to outline it. We understand what we have taken apart and reconstructed. Single-word outlines, however, are not the only way to outline a text: a précis works just as well. Outlining merely with single words can actually be disadvantageous, as it's easier to fake logical connections, or ignore their absence, in a list of words. Those sequences of interrelated sentences force the writer/reader to discover logical connections—or their absence.

From time to time, or regularly, students can be required to appear in class with précis of what they have read. A few of these can be read out loud to begin the discussion or the lecture. Included in a précis ought to be a good thesis statement: a concise summary of the writer's major point. If students can write such a statement they are on the way to being good writers themselves. And because they will be reading carefully in order to summarize, they will become more aware of the features with which writers help readers: transitional paragraphs and words, summaries, key words, rhetorical questions, and so on. They will also understand these difficult texts far better than they would have otherwise, and misunderstandings will at once be evident.

When an assigned text contains a particularly important or particularly difficult sentence or paragraph, asking for a written ''translation'' can effectively focus attention on the passage's content, and on its stylistic and rhetorical features. Creating the translation can help the reader see why a passage is important, or troublesome, and come to terms with its difficulties or significance. The translation itself can take various forms—''Explain this passage to a high school student,'' for example. Variety of this sort creates awareness of style, that of the original passage and that of the translation (an inflated or overly academic style will improve in a translation addressed to a high school student).

My own students profit from translating the following passage, which they encounter in an essay by Edward Hallett Carr. Carr is quoting a passage from Acton's *The Cambridge Modern History* (1896), in which Acton reports on his edition of the Cambridge history:

> It is a unique opportunity of recording, in the way most useful to
> the greatest number, the fullness of the knowledge which the nine-

teenth century is about to bequeath. . . . By the judicious division of labor we should be able to do it, and to bring home to every man the last document, and the ripest conclusions of international research.

Ultimate history we cannot have in this generation; but we can dispose of conventional history, and show the point we have reached on the road from one to the other, now that all information is within reach, and every problem has become capable of solution. (759)

The passage is important for Carr's argument, but most of my students don't have the faintest idea of what it means. The style is impersonal and static, laden with nouns and prepositional phrases, ornate in its vocabulary, replete with undefined terms such as "ultimate" and "conventional" history. Students "translating" the passage come up with something like this (the losses and gains are obvious):

> In the Cambridge Modern History we can record the great amount of information that the nineteenth century has to give to the twentieth, so that many can use it. If we divide the job up among the best people, we can do it: we will make available every last document and the best conclusions of scholars around the world.
>
> We won't be able to write the final and definitive history ourselves, but now that we have available all the necessary information and can solve every problem, we can dispose of the old traditional (?) history and we can show how close we now are to writing the definitive history.

Neil Orloff (Director of the Center for Environmental Research, Cornell) suggests having students rewrite key summary sentences or passages in texts. One of his favorite essay assignments requires students to revise a sentence from a statute about air pollutants. He finds that the students, rather than remaining vague, must try to determine exactly what they mean and how to say it:

> It's easy to throw out an idea in speaking, and much more difficult to reduce it to precise statutory wording. When students try to reduce it to textual form, the words seem to lose much of their precision. In addition, the students start to see a multiplicity of possible problems and pregnant but unintended implications in their sentences. All this comes out of trying to rewrite just one sentence of the statute. (letter to K. Gottschalk, 13 March 1985)

Students in the sciences or mathematics reap similar benefits from translating difficult or important passages of their texts, even when the original text consists mostly of mathematical symbols rather than of prose. As Larry D. Kirkpatrick (Department of Physics, Montana State University) says, ". . . if you can't write it down, you don't understand it" (quoted in "Science and Math Professors" 20). Some professors in the sciences and in mathematics are discovering the value of another kind of translation work for their students. With their exams, their homework, or their in-class work, students occasionally provide written explanations of how they worked out problems. While the written work can certainly benefit the students, "Professors benefit from reading the students' writing, because it gives . . . insight into student problems that [can be addressed] in future lectures . . ." ("Science and Math" 21).

It's not always necessary to collect the outlines, précis, translations. If students know that the professor—and their peers—notice who can't come up with the work when it *is* requested, they'll usually do it.

V. WRITING IN THE CLASSROOM

A. *Taking Notes on or Summarizing Lectures and Discussions*

Far from interfering with lectures or discussions, writing can reinforce them. Notetaking can provide an excellent means of focusing on and organizing what is taking place. When from their notes students can recall and talk about the previous day's discussion or lecture, they are on the way to becoming active, not passive, members of the class.

But first students must take good notes:

> Notes should enact the dialogue implicit in a good lecture, but students rarely know how to do that; indeed, they often do not know what should be noted. A few weeks ago, I was talking with some Radcliffe undergraduates about this business of note taking. Most students, they said, sit there inertly in a course on the modern novel until they hear a date—and that they immediately take down: "Fitzgerald arrived in Paris in 1925 . . ."; 1925, Paris. What gets noted is what sounds memorable: pat definitions, jokes, formulations, titles, dates, but without context or perspective and without connections indicated.

> There is a technique which can help train the capacity to organize
> what is said—at least so that context can be recalled. That is to use
> law school notebook paper with very wide margins (or, of course,
> simply to draw such margins) or, better yet, to use the facing page for
> recapitulations, summaries, key terms, further study, and questions.
> (Berthoff 119–120)

Such problems and methods can be discussed with students; we can
even check their notebooks. More realistically, perhaps (given constraints of time and energy), we can at least ask students to contribute
to class in ways that depend on good notetaking habits: at the beginning
of a class period we can ask someone to review the topic of the last
class *on the basis of her notes.* What was the problem left unsolved?
What were the strongest and weakest arguments? Where did we intend
to begin today? Or, better yet, everyone can write a response to one
such question or a short summary of the previous class, after which one
or two students may read the results aloud. (The minimal recall when
you start this process may be depressing; students have to learn both to
take decent notes and then to have their notes handy or to jog their
memories in advance of class.)

Such work with notes has the significant benefit of making students
part of an ongoing intellectual process—not just fact-recorders at isolated events. Furthermore, hearing summaries and reviews may inspire
other students to ask about what they didn't understand or to supplement
gaps from their own notes. (You may also discover that you didn't
actually teach what you thought you had.) Notetaking, then, can become
a way of organizing and communicating. When students take good notes,
they are also practicing the kind of thinking they need to do when they
write their own papers. And they may discover and develop more of
value to talk about, in class, and in an essay.

B. Notetaking and Class Secretaries

Some students prefer not to take notes during a class discussion because
doing so may interfere with their concentration on the dialogue. A rotating assignment of class secretary, therefore, can benefit everyone. One
person records the discussion and at the end of the period reads the
summary aloud for amendment before it is photocopied for distribution

to the rest of the class. Both the secretary and the class learn how to organize information, and how to emphasize what is important and what is not. A less time-consuming plan is to assign two or three people as secretaries; they compare notes after class and create one polished version for distribution. (My thanks to Jean Blackall and Patricia Carden [Cornell, Departments of English and of Russian Literature, respectively], who collaboratively produced this idea for me. I have since learned that medical schools also use this technique; sometimes the professor reads and approves the summary—med-students *must* get their facts straight.)

C. Writing That Focuses a Question

Another suggestion for ensuring close, thoughtful attention to a lecture or discussion while encouraging careful writing comes from Elaine Maimon (Associate Dean, Brown University). In the first five minutes of class students write a response to a significant question with which the discussion or lecture will be concerned. (''What gene combinations make it possible for a person to have blue eyes?'' ''How does television violence affect children?'') In the last five minutes of class, one or two students read their answers aloud. The initial request causes students to spend the class period quietly rewriting their responses while the class discussion refines their ideas about the problem. That tinkering is, of course, precisely what good writers do when they revise. They rethink and rephrase as they see that their written words are not true or accurate enough, or clear enough, or detailed enough. Of course, further discussion can arise when students compare written responses and see how their interpretation of the classroom discourse does or does not match someone else's.

D. Investigating with Exploratory Patterns

Students often need considerable help in learning how to explore a subject. It's easy to be so involved in our fields that we forget about what basic strategies and perspectives may be alien to the newcomer.

We are involved *in* the process; students need to look *at* it. We can provide guides that will be useful both in and out of the classroom; the guides can be used for discussion or for written answers (produced either before class or in it) that the professor may or may not choose to have read aloud.

Writing to Define a Term:

Students sometimes fail to come to grips with a course (and consequently write badly for it) because they don't really understand its vocabulary, its basic concepts. Part or all of a class session can be usefully and energetically spent trying to determine the exact meaning of frequently used terms. Richard Lance (Department of Theoretical and Applied Mechanics, Cornell) team-taught an experimental Cornell Common Learning course, which is interdisciplinary and writing-intensive, with a writing professor, Steven Youra; they took the opportunity to try working with their students on definitions of terms such as "the law of large numbers" ("the larger the sample the smaller the deviation from the mean"?), "risk assessment" ("a method of evaluating the possible consequences of proposed actions"?), and "availability bias" ("the perception of the frequency of an event when it's easy to recall examples of it"?). As Youra noted, "spirited discussion about the nuances and implications of proposed definitions" took place, with the result that the students worked hard both on the exact use of language and on the exact meaning of concepts in the discipline (unpublished report). Students can come to class prepared with preliminary definitions, but the blackboard is a good place to complete the final written version of a definition.

Answering Exploratory Questions:

As Patricia Carden points out in Chapter 2, students tend "to confine their observations to a few tried and true formulas." We can help them "to broaden their responses by employing a series of systematic questions," questions we can specifically address in the classroom, and which students can later use on their own. We can develop such an exploratory series of questions by asking ourselves, "What kinds of questions do people in my field characteristically ask? How do these questions define the subject matter of the field?" For example, Peter McClelland (Department of Economics, Cornell) realizes that in economics courses students are often quite unaware of two major questions: What determines relative prices (the price of corn versus the price of soy beans), and Why are markets efficient? Yet, to study prices or markets at all effectively, they must ask these questions. Carden notes that

> [o]n any given day the instructor may ask [students] to attend to one or two of the items . . . but the presence of a range of questions in the background of the discussion tends to sharpen students' responses, even if those questions are not the central focus of inquiry. The list can subsequently be employed as a device for finding topics to write about or for assembling evidence in a number of dimensions . . . (Chapter 2, "Designing a Course," 37).

Using Metaphors and Analogies:

Writing out metaphors or analogies can help develop new perspectives on or insights into a situation or problem: considerable thinking goes on through finding likenesses and differences. Everyone knows that Kepler made wild analogies in the course of his exploration of the universe, but students may be startled to find they can benefit from them too. What is the unconscious like? A god or devil? A mechanism? A language? None of these? In what ways are early theories about the nature of light and the nature of electricity alike? Different?

Setting Up Systems for Studying:

Students are often surprisingly ignorant about what writers do when preparing to write about a subject. Many don't even know that before writing an essay, or when studying for an exam, it's helpful to compile lists by category—to organize what all the writers studied in a course have to say on a given subject or to look for correspondences and contrasts between writer and writer, event and event, and so on. Standing at the blackboard and working through some systematic approaches (preferably approaches we ourselves use, whatever they are) can provide students with a revelatory experience, and, of course, with methods to imitate. What students learn about methodically exploring a subject will be reflected in the thought and organization of their writing, and, of course, in their comprehension of a subject.

VI. REQUIRED PAPERS

A. *Assistance and Response*

When essays are assigned, for whatever practical purpose, they should be well corrected if students are to profit from the writing experience. Students will not benefit from "**A**: Nice job" or "**C**: you needed to develop your ideas more." Any writer needs the detailed and thoughtful comments of a concerned editor. Faculty members also need to react as genuine readers, not just as editors or grade-makers. Students need to be taken seriously as members of our disciplines, if only novice members. W. Wade Dorman and James M. Pruett point out that

> [y]ou . . . motivate [engineering] students to develop their writing by responding as an engineer to their work. They will spend most of their careers writing to engineers and managers, not to English teachers. Once they begin to write with their audience in mind, they will learn to give attention to all the elements that successfully shape communication. (656)

Audience sufficiently concerns Dale Corson that he makes the following suggestion for students writing formal reports about laboratory results:

> Sometimes the reports can be put in the form of communications to a hypothetical director of engineering or to an employer or to some non-technical or semi-technical person who wishes to know what the conclusions are and what the evidence is on which the conclusions are based. (11)

The advice holds for any discipline. Teaching proper comma use to students who don't take writing seriously is a waste of time, ours and theirs. Most writers have a stake in correctness only when they already have a stake in a purpose and audience.

And, of course, students should study our comments fairly soon after submitting their papers, not a month or semester later, if they are to benefit from those comments and reactions. The end-of-the-semester essay retrieved during the next semester, or possibly never, won't receive critical scrutiny from the student who already knows her course grade and has moved on to other courses and concerns.

To enjoy what we read (and to avoid getting papers copied from the fraternity and sorority files), we need to advise students about their writing work before they turn in the final copy. Students can compare these in class, and with guidance discover how people find good topics and just what kinds of topic are considered suitable within a field. (Such discoveries aren't going to damage their appreciation and understanding of the discipline, either.) They can read first paragraphs of rough drafts aloud in class; they can read each other's rough drafts; *we* can read their rough drafts and make specific suggestions to individuals in conference or general comments to the class as a whole.

While teaching one of Cornell's experimental Common Learning courses, Urie Bronfenbrenner (Department of Human Development and Family Studies) discovered that his students wrote much better papers after he created and circulated "Some Helpful Hints for Writing Assignments," which detailed his particular criteria for good papers and gave helpful, explicit suggestions for fulfilling his expectations. In other words, he stopped making his students play guessing games, and, he says, he now more enjoys reading the papers he receives: he jokingly admits to being impressed with the improved quality of student writing—an improvement that has accompanied the change in his writing-assignment instructions.

B. *Writing Collaboratively*

As about three-fourths of college graduates will do collaborative writing in their jobs (Faigley and Miller 45), providing some collaborative writing experience can prepare our students for their future writing work (while also supplying them with peer instruction in writing). Dorman and Pruett offer the following advice for a collaborative writing procedure. Although designed for an engineering class, it can apply to many fields:

> A typical class may be separated into groups of three or four to complete a writing assignment. We have had each group meet (members having prepared individual drafts ahead of time) and work together to produce a composite draft. Not only does this reduce superficial and grammatical errors, but it forces the better writers in each group to sharpen their skills by guiding the poorer writers. Each writer's participation can be monitored by having group members initial one

another's manuscripts, which are turned in with the final draft. The teacher need grade and comment on only the final draft, then glance over the individual preliminary writing to estimate individual participation. The amount each student contributes to the final draft should not be a major factor. Of greater importance is that each member enter the group meeting with a completed draft, insuring his interest in each part of the final one. Learning to produce a single draft through team effort can be the most worthwhile experience of the project.

Engineers who learn writing from their peers may retain that learning longer and have more conscious use of it than students who write individually. More important, however, they will have developed collaborative skills that make them better engineers. (658)

C. *Writing on Word Processors*

In another Cornell Common Learning course, Sander Gilman (Department of German Literature) discovered an unexpected advantage of word processors: because his students wrote their term papers directly on the word processors, revising an essay did not mean retyping it. He therefore freely requested several early drafts in which students commented on their problems and to which he responded. No student had to spend time retyping: all the rewriting could be substantive. Working on word processors puts students at a considerable advantage because they can so easily add evidence, reorganize, change their minds—freely use writing to think. Gilman found the final results excellent. Another time he plans to make comments directly on disk rather than on paper, as, like many of us, he writes faster and more comfortably at a keyboard. In addition, the margins are never too small when comments are inserted into a document on disk.

Stuart Davis, Nancy Kaplan, and Joe Martin (Department of English, and Writing Workshop, Cornell University) have developed a computer program, PROSE, that enables instructors to make comments directly on the disk. These comments appear in pop-up windows as the student revises; a built-in handbook permits the student to read a pre-programmed definition of, for example, "parallelism problem" and then do some exercises before returning to the text to revise. The system has many advantages: the student sees no comment other than the one with which he is immediately concerned; the handbook is built in; and revision follows automatically as a response to the instructor's comments. (See Section IV.*C.* of Appendix 1 for a discussion of this and other programs.)

Many students now own their own Macintoshes or IBM PCs, and many campuses provide access to word processors for students not owning them. Anyone interested in word-processing assistance can easily investigate these possibilities.

D. An Ironic Guideline

A succinct guide for faculty members who require and correct essays appeared in the *Chronicle of Higher Education,* where John Keenan offered "A Professors' Guide to Perpetuating Poor Writing Among Students" (64). His guide includes the following ironic points; I've added my own interpretations in brackets:

• Assign 20-page papers to freshmen.
[Students will cooperate by "padding and plagiarizing"; furthermore you'll have too big a load to do much useful correcting. Dale Corson observed that "[laboratory] reports of excessive length . . . are unwise in that they require large amounts of the student's time without providing him with adequate instruction" (11).]
• Keep the assignment or examination question as general as possible.
[That way you'll keep your students guessing about how people really write in your discipline.]
• Forbid first-person pronouns.
[Keep your students passive and your subject dead. And, of course, you should *never* allow your students to think of themselves as real members of the discourse.]
• Don't show them; tell them.
["Write a report; do a research paper; but don't ask me how."]
• Encourage polysyllabic prose.
[Don't help students notice different ways in which people write, especially in your field. Just make them use big words.]
• Never review a draft of a paper in progress.
[Students should find out whether they were on the right track or not

only after the job is done, when nothing can be done to improve it.]
  • Do not make comments on student papers unless absolutely necessary.
[You aren't a real reader—you're just a grade-maker.]
  • If you can avoid returning papers to students, do so.
[And if you can't, be sure they come back at least a month after submission. That way students won't even remember what they wrote, let alone learn anything from the suggestions or comments you made.]

Keenan's irony suggests an unacknowledged belief that only composition teachers take seriously the problems of teaching prose and of learning to write, and that most professors disclaim responsibility for or ignore the task. But in fact faculty members everywhere are asserting their active concern and personal commitment, especially as it becomes clear that writing must be emphasized beyond the freshman year. We must all do more. Our *students* must do more. Fortunately, the very nature of writing makes further writing activity both possible and desirable, and in the nonwriting course.

VII. SUMMARY OF SUGGESTIONS

To improve or at least maintain writing skills in non-writing courses, faculty can have their students

1. discuss important motives for continued writing, namely to learn, and perhaps to succeed in a job later on.

2. read well-written works.

3. occasionally discuss the style of what they are reading, and whether it is well or poorly written, persuasive or unpersuasive— and **why.**

4. occasionally imitate good models of prose.

5. write out questions about their reading and about the discussions taking place in the classroom.

6. keep journals about their reading and about their work in the course; write comments and summaries in laboratory journals of data.

7. make outlines, précis, and translations of the reading they do for the course; translate mathematical problems into prose.

8. take notes during lectures or class discussions, or write summaries of the lectures / discussions after the fact; the notes or summaries can be shared with other class members.

9. appoint rotating class secretaries to take notes and edit them for subsequent distribution to the rest of the class.

10. write short answers in response to a specific question that the lecture or discussion will address, and submit (or read) a final version at the end of the hour.

11. write out definitions of commonly used terms in class.

12. learn to investigate a subject by writing answers to exploratory questions characteristic of the field.

13. learn to explore a subject in writing by developing metaphors or analogies.

When papers are in fact required for whatever purpose, students can

1. receive preliminary help and adequate commentary.

2. perhaps write collaborative papers.

3. try writing on word processors so that rough drafts can more easily be submitted for commentary and then rewritten.

NOTES

1. C. H. Knoblauch and Lil Brannon (466). Although I have developed much of the material for this article through a process of gradual synthesis from many sources, Knoblauch and Brannon's article has been especially helpful, as has been Ann E. Berthoff's "Speculative Instruments: Language in the Core Curriculum."

2. *College Composition and Communication* 33 (Oct. 1982) is devoted to a presentation of this information.

3. Dorman and Pruett (656). My thanks to Professor Walter Lynn, Director of the Program on Science, Technology, and Society at Cornell, for sharing this *Engineering Education* article with me, and for many other helpful suggestions.

WORKS CITED

Entries marked with an asterisk are described in Chapter 8, "A Bibliographical Guide to the Profession."

*Berthoff, Ann E. "Speculative Instruments: Language in the Core Curriculum." *The Making of Meaning: Metaphors, Models, and Maxims for Writing Teachers.* 113–126. Montclair, N.J.: Boynton / Cook, 1981.

Carr, Edward Hallett. *What Is History?* London: Macmillan, 1961. Selection reprinted as "The Historian and His Facts" in *The Norton Reader.* 6th ed. Edited by Arthur M. Eastman. 759–74. New York: Norton, 1984.

Corson, Dale R. An unpublished study of laboratory instruction in engineering for the Ford Foundation. Cornell University, 1962

Dorman, W. Wade, and James M. Pruett. "Engineering Better Writers: Why and How Engineers Can Teach Writing." *Engineering Education* 75 (April, 1985): 656–58.

Faigley, Lester, and T. P. Miller. "What We Learn from Writing on the Job." *College English* 44 (Oct. 1982): 557–69.

*Irmscher, William. *Teaching Expository Writing.* New York: Holt, Rinehart and Winston, 1979.

Keenan, John. "A Professors' Guide to Perpetuating Poor Writing Among Students." *Chronicle of Higher Education* 28 (Sept. 1983): 64.

Knoblauch, C. H., and Lil Brannon. "Writing as Learning Through the Curriculum." *College English* 45 (1983): 465–73.

Maimon, Elaine. Workshop at a conference on "Writing, Meaning, and Higher Order Reasoning." Univ. of Chicago, November 1983.

Mermin, N. David. "Is the Moon There When Nobody Looks? Reality and the Quantum Theory." *Physics Today* 4 (April, 1985): 38–47.

Paige, David, and Andrew Ingersoll. "Annual Heat Balance of Martian Polar Caps: Viking Observations." *Science* 228 (June, 1985): 1160–68.

"Science and Math Professors Are Assigning Writing Drills to Focus Students' Thinking." *The Chronicle of Higher Education* 22 (Jan. 1986): 19–20.

Youra, Steven, and Richard Lance. From an unpublished report on the writing component of "Science, Risk and Public Policy" for the Common Learning Commission. Cornell, Spring 1986.

Index